Entertaining Crisis in the Atlantic Imperium 1770–1790

Entertaining Crisis in the Atlantic Imperium 1770–1790

DANIEL O'QUINN

The Johns Hopkins University Press
Baltimore

Printed in the United States of America on acid-free paper
2 4 6 8 9 7 5 3 1

The Johns Hopkins University Press
2715 North Charles Street
Baltimore, Maryland 21218-4363
www.press.jhu.edu

Library of Congress Cataloging-in-Publication Data

O'Quinn, Daniel, 1962–
Entertaining crisis in the Atlantic imperium, 1770–1790 /
Daniel O'Quinn.
p. cm.
Includes bibliographical references and index.
ISBN-13: 978-0-8018-9931-7 (hardcover : alk. paper)
ISBN-10: 0-8018-9931-1 (hardcover : alk. paper)
1. English drama—18th century—History and criticism. 2. Masculinity in literature. 3. Politics and literature—Great Britain—History—18th century. 4. Theater—England—London—History—18th century. 5. Theater—Political aspects—England—London. 6. Press and politics—Great Britain—History—18th century. 7. United States—History—Revolution, 1775–1783—Influence.
I. Title.
PR714.M37O68 2011
822'.50938541073—dc22 2010025292

A catalog record for this book is available from the British Library.

The Johns Hopkins University Press uses environmentally friendly book materials, including recycled text paper that is composed of at least 30 percent post-consumer waste, whenever possible. All of our book papers are acid-free, and our jackets and covers are printed on paper with recycled content.

For Jo

Contents

Acknowledgments

This book received generous support from the Standard Research Grant program sponsored by the Social Sciences and Humanities Research Council of Canada (SSHRC). This program involves an extraordinary level of peer review, so my first debt is to the anonymous committee members and readers who saw potential for this project. Their generosity allowed me to employ a set of research assistants over the six years it took me to compile the evidence presented here. Lindsey Lorimer, Jodie Salter, and above all Heather Davis-Fisch provided invaluable assistance with the newspaper archive well before the Burney collection was digitized. Heather Davis-Fisch's intense commitment to this project was remarkable, and she deserves my particular gratitude. It is my strong belief that SSHRC's commitment to student training benefited both my own work and the doctoral work of the students employed under the tenure of the award. At a time when government support for the humanities is not always appreciated, I want to indicate clearly that the symbiotic relation between faculty and graduate students fostered by the Standard Research Grant program is a model for humanities research and education. It is my sincere hope that the view of scholarship adopted by SSHRC in this program will continue into the future.

This is a book about sociability and much of its argument benefited from kind invitations to share research with communities of like-minded scholars. In 2006 I was part of the group of scholars invited to the Bloomington Eighteenth-Century Studies Workshop at the University of Indiana to explore the topic "Lines of Amity, Lines of Enmity." I presented a very early version of the final section of chapter 6 and received extraordinarily helpful commentary from my fellow participants, especially Mary Favret, Sarah Knott, Sarah Monks, Jody Greene, and Dror Wahrman. In 2007 I presented versions of chapter 3 and chapter 6 to students and faculty associated with the Centre for Eighteenth-Century Studies at the University of York. For this invitation I am grateful to Jane Moody because it led to stimulating discussions with Kevin Gilmartin, John Barrell,

James Watt, and Sarah Monks (again) on the Handel Commemoration. My work on Captain André's Mischianza was first tested on a group of extraordinary students affiliated with the centre: their generosity on this occasion was remarkable, and many of their questions led to important new directions for research. In 2008 the students in the PhD program in Theatre and Performance Studies at Northwestern University asked me to take part in their 2nd Interdisciplinary Conference. This honor meant that much of chapter 1 was subjected to the scrutiny not only of scholars such as Tracy Davis and Marvin Carlson long recognized as leaders in the discipline, but also of a whole new generation of doctoral students from programs across North America. The lessons learned at that gathering were invaluable. Closer to home, the Eighteenth-Century Reading Group at the University of Toronto kindly worked through my reading of the Handel Commemoration that makes up the first section of chapter 6. Kim Michasiw, Deidre Lynch, and Brian Corman all brought their considerable acumen to bear on the argument; I hope that I have fully addressed their questions. Lisa Freeman and Mark Canuel were kind enough to invite me to present chapter 4 to their departmental reading group at the University of Illinois at Chicago in the winter of 2010 just before the final submission of the manuscript. At the time, almost no one had seen this part of the book, and it was incredibly helpful to rehearse its argument with a mixed audience of graduate students and faculty at UIC. And finally, at an institution that does not draw a large number of students intending to specialize in eighteenth-century studies, I was fortunate to get to present the entire argument of this book in a graduate class at the University of Guelph. Leslie Allin, Siscoe Boschman, Mark Kaethler, Hannah MacGregor, Coplen Rose, and Janet Williams threw themselves into the turbulent mediascape of the late 1770s and 1780s and in so doing provided me with an extraordinary weekly laboratory for this book.

Beyond these highly social engagements, three friends spent a great deal of time alone with this book at different stages in its development. Donna Andrew read at least two full drafts with patience and her customary rigor. Over the past ten years she has been a source of constant inspiration and of almost limitless knowledge of the labyrinthine world of the eighteenth-century press. As with my previous book, Deidre Lynch took time from her busy schedule to read the manuscript when it was in need of a critical reappraisal. She is the most generous and responsible of readers, and her suggestions had a strong impact on both the shape and the tenor of the book. And, finally, Gillian Russell, whose work I so strongly admire, graciously read the entire manuscript at a very late stage. Her precise interventions helped me to fine-tune some of the arguments regarding the relationship between war, sociability, and the restylization of British masculinity in this period. To all three colleagues I wish to offer my thanks. I could not ask for a better set of interlocutors.

I also want to thank Mary Favret for her perceptive reading of the introduction and the coda; Tilar Mazzeo for her suggestions regarding an early draft of chapter 1 and for sharing her work on Burgoyne; Tracy Davis for her thoughts on chapter 1 and on the project in general; Sarah Knott for sharing her tremendous chapter on Major André before it was published in *Sensibility and the American Revolution*; Lisa Freeman for her incisive reading of chapter 4; and Theresa Kelley for her patient analysis of my reading of "Yardley Oak." Orrin Wang's enthusiasm for my work on the Handel celebrations in Calcutta and on Cowper's "Yardley Oak" bookended this project. He has always been the most supportive of fellow travelers. I was emboldened to conclude this book with a close reading of a poem in part because Sarah Zimmerman and Deborah Elise White responded to my presentation on Cowper at the Toronto NASSR in 2008 with such warmth.

Aside from these specific instances of scholarly generosity, there is a more general social and intellectual milieu that permeates this project. Although there was only one masquerade (thank you, Jane), there were frequent routs where ideas were weighed, tossed, and tasted. Sonia Hofkosh, Julie Carlson, Tracy Davis, Laura Rosenthal, Jennifer Schacker, Jane Moody, Lynn Festa, Teresa Heffernan, Sarah Monks, Emily Allen, Michelle Elleray, Beth Kowaleski-Wallace, Ian Balfour, Greg Kucich, Jeffrey Cox, Geraldine Friedman, Anne Milne, Michael Gamer, Jill Heydt-Stevenson, William Galperin, Misty Anderson, Lisa Freeman, Sarah Zimmerman, Tilar Mazzeo, David Clark, Gregor Campbell, Coby Dowdell, Dino Felluga, Julie-Anne Plax, Catherine Bush, Paul Keen, and Donna Pennee have all offered timely advice, thoughtful critique, and, perhaps most importantly, affable support over the period when this book was written.

A short version of the first section of chapter 1 was published as "Diversionary Tactics and Coercive Acts: John Burgoyne's *Fête Champêtre*," *Studies in Eighteenth-Century Culture* 40 (2010): 1-23. A preliminary version of the concluding section of chapter 5 appeared as "Mercantile Deformities: George Colman's *Inkle and Yarico* and the Racialization of Class Relations," *Theatre Journal* 54.3 (October 2002): 389-409. The final section of chapter 6 was published online as "Projection, Patriotism, Surrogation: Handel in Calcutta," in Orrin Wang's special issue of *Romantic Praxis* (Spring 2006) devoted to *Romanticism and Patriotism*. I owe thanks to all the anonymous readers for these publications for their helpful suggestions.

During the past two years, I have been grateful to Matt McAdam and Trevor Lipscombe at the Johns Hopkins University Press for treating my manuscript and my concerns with care and respect. Thanks to Brian MacDonald, Linda Forlifer, Leslie Allin, Maya Bringe, and Mary Lou Kenney for bringing the book through its final stages.

I also want to thank my friends and family in Toronto, Ottawa, and Vancouver. Starting with my own parents Leo and Celeste O'Quinn, I've been blessed with family and friends who believe in me and in what I do. Anne, Michelle, Roger, Babs, Liz, and Art have been with me for many years now, showing me how to live life to the fullest. My sons Gabe and Eli are a constant source of joy. And for making it all endlessly fun, this book is dedicated with love to my intrepid partner Jo-Ann Seamon.

Introduction

Entertainment, Mediation, and the Future of Empire

As with so much else, Samuel Johnson's multilayered definition of *entertainment* reveals something about a concept that is rarely considered in its full complexity:

> ENTERTAINMENT. *n.f.* [from *entertain.*] 1. Conversation. 2. Treatment at the table; convivial provision. 3. Hospitable reception. 4. Reception; admission. 5. The state of being in pay as soldiers or servants. 6. Payment of soldiers or servants. Now obsolete. 7. Amusement; diversion. 8. Dramatick performance; the lower comedy.[1]

Johnson's list of definitions can be divided roughly in two. The first four definitions refer to matters of sociability, to the all-important practices of hospitality, conversation, and social pleasure. These definitions of entertainment all open onto questions of affect, for it is through convivial exchange between individuals that the emotional bonds of society are woven.[2] The final two definitions offer a general and a specific instance of a different set of practices in which representation is mobilized not only to bring people together but also to take them away from the concerns of the everyday. These latter definitions offer amusement, whether it be in the bustling realm of farce or in a moment of more private contemplation, as a divagation from the present, where a certain distance is established between the subject and the world that allows for reflection and release.[3] But these two branches of the word do not exhaust its semantic possibility, and Johnson reminds his readers that a third, now vestigial, set of concerns is implied by the word *entertainment*: namely, the state of being in pay as soldiers or servants. The incursion of this other meaning, whose implicit connection to pain and subordination is seemingly at odds with the pleasures afforded by the other connotations of the word, has a particular resonance for this book because, in the chapters that follow, I trace the integral relationship between sociability, amusement, and the performance of martial subjectivity during the turbulent years when the American colonies successfully seceded from Britain's Atlantic empire.

This book examines the notion of entertainment at a moment when it would seem most difficult to achieve. As the men in pay as soldiers to the Crown were losing the war in America, a series of remarkable celebrations, social events, amusements, diversions, and dramatic performances were staged in London and Philadelphia that attempted to speak to the historical predicament of what amounted to a civil war in the Atlantic imperium. As numerous historians have noted, the most unsettling thing about the prosecution of the American war was that the combatants had fought side by side only fifteen years earlier in the Seven Years' War to end definitively French colonial designs on North America and to limit severely French and Spanish aspirations in South Asia and the Caribbean.[4] Out of that first global war emerged a new kind of imperial state, beset with problems of management, and a new kind of British subject.[5] As the problems of governing this new global empire reached a crisis in the 1770s, Britons were suddenly confronted with the perplexing situation of dealing with rebellious subjects whose investment in notions of liberty and property were almost the defining characteristics of the British polity itself.[6] As Lord North and his Ministry attempted to put down the rebellion on the far side of the Atlantic, the political and social world of the metropole showed signs of fracturing in increasingly disturbing ways. From the political turmoil associated with Wilkite calls for reform through the truly terrifying eruption of ethnic violence during the Gordon Riots, Britain was plunged into a condition of social insecurity.[7]

What does it mean to entertain and be entertained at such a historical moment? This question is the starting point for this book, and it is asked in different ways in each chapter. The six chapters of the book present a narrative of social anxiety and cultural loss stretching from 1774 to 1784. I also trace the afterlife of some of these anxieties into the late 1780s and 1790s. In that sense it is a book about British reactions to the American crisis, but rather than tracing that reaction through political pamphlets, the argument is presented in relation to a series of performances, some social and some more recognizably theatrical.[8] Some of these performances involved elite constituencies—such as the Fête Champêtre discussed in chapter 1 or the Handel Commemoration discussed in chapter 6—and some performances involved plebian constituencies—such as the celebrants of the Augustus Keppel acquittal or the mourners lining the streets at David Garrick's funeral. But most of the social and cultural events discussed are of a mixed nature, such as the Thames Regatta or the Mischianza, and involved a wide range of participants.

However, this accounting of who took part in the events in question was not the guiding principle in the construction of the book. Each event was chosen because it generated extensive reaction in both the press and the theatre. If one looks carefully at each chapter, one discerns that my real focus is on the mediation of these events, and thus I am offering a detailed discussion of how something as exclusive as the Fête Champêtre "plays" in the media themselves. This means that the "people" are involved in this argument in a complex and wide-ranging way. The theory of reception and media convergence that drives each chapter leads to important evidentiary matters. Put simply, the argument focuses on how the rhetorical effects of print media and the performative elements of sociability and theatre feed upon one another. Thus, each chapter lives and dies on its extensive and intensive readings of the daily papers and of the archive of performance. For example, the opening chapter on John Burgoyne's Fête Champêtre offers a reading, not of the letters and memoirs of people at the party but rather of the account put into circulation in the papers and then how that account was remediated at Drury Lane. A large part of that reading focuses on how precisely the non-elite subjects reading or watching a representation of the event were hailed into a relationship with the ideological project at the heart of the celebration.

The ultimate objective of the book is to demonstrate how mediation itself became a fundamental issue in British imperial culture at this moment. I show how the papers and the theatre built a mutually constitutive mechanism for reflecting on the present. This latter point is important because each chapter examines how these particular social and cultural events deal with the problem of the future beyond the present crisis. In this sense, a thorough consideration of the repetition of media events and the replication of specific representational dynamics yields new ways of reading specific performances of plays such as Richard Brinsley Sheridan's *The Critic* or Hannah Cowley's *The Belle's Stratagem*. At no point do I claim to be offering an anatomy of the mentality of the age. Nor do I claim to be offering an argument that can adequately deal with distinctions between metropolitan, colonial, and provincial media and their audiences. With the exception of brief forays to Philadelphia and Plymouth, this book is about the print and performance culture of London. Because I am attending so closely to the interaction of the daily press and nightly performance, the argument looks at the breakdown in the Atlantic imperium from a metropolitan vantage point.

The argument would necessarily unfold differently if it focused on different locales. I have started in the center because, thus far, no one has attempted to draw from this kind of quotidian and blended archive a coherent account of the fantasies deployed and the practices mobilized to reconstitute British imperial culture after the disintegration of the Atlantic empire.

On the face of it, that sounds like an audacious claim, especially in light of the voluminous scholarship on this historical period, but it turns on what I mean by a quotidian and blended archive. This book assumes that theatrical representation and the representational tactics of the newspapers are both mutually constitutive and central to the stylization of social relations in this era. The argument is built from the records of transient performances and from the labyrinthine coils of the most ephemeral elements of eighteenth-century print culture—precisely those sites of cultural and social exchange beyond the purview of the recent surge of interest in book history. By blending this transient and ephemeral archive, I am also committed to troubling the distinctions between culture and society, text and context, which stabilize many forms of historical or cultural enquiry. Unlike cultural historians of the period, I am not showing how cultural products thematized important social or political developments. And unlike cultural critics, I am not seeking to contextualize autonomous works of art. Rather, I use the methods of close reading associated with cultural and literary analysis to attend to the formal qualities of how social and cultural materials are represented in text and performance. In short, I am breaking down the distinction between text and context in order to offer a mode of analysis suited to the intense integration of culture and society in this period.

In *Staging Governance*, I argued that theatrical practice in the late eighteenth century, even when it was representing foreign manners and distant places, was autoethnographic. Here, I am pushing that argument even further by being much more specific about the technologies through which Londoners came to know and comprehend themselves. In his suggestive discussion of the history of the term *entertainment*, Colin Mercer makes a distinction between entertainment and amusement. According to Mercer, entertainment is much more involved in the policing of the social body than is amusement.[9] For my purposes here, his argument is merely suggestive because his discussion focuses primarily on nineteenth-century examples and does not elaborate on the emergence of a particular set of entertainment tactics after the important transformations in theatrical and print culture in the late 1760s.[10] That the papers and the theatres were involved with regulating the social body is not in question. Via the Licensing Act of 1737, the state had long been involved not only in the legitimation or delegitimation of performance venues but also in the direct censorship of plays.[11] Similarly, from the late seventeenth century onward, the state imposed strict limitations on what the papers could print. Newspapers were not allowed to report parliamentary debates, and thus the government, through occasional clampdowns on papers that reported debates, was able to restrict the public scrutiny of its actions. In addition, many of the daily papers, notably the *Daily Gazetteer,* which was an organ of Walpole's Ministry, were simply owned by the government and thus set the terms of public discussion. This is not to say that the papers or the theatres were unable to articulate forms of public dissent but rather that everything was managed under a form of surveillance and patronage.

One of the most complex aspects of the state's scrutiny of media was that it had significant impact on questions of form. The Licensing Act of 1737 gave Drury Lane and Covent Garden exclusive rights to perform tragedy and comedy, but this also came with the responsibility of maintaining five-act tragedy and comedy as the preeminent forms of theatrical expression.[12] As Susan Staves and others have argued, the middle years of the eighteenth century were not a banner period for the composition of new tragedies, but they were crucial years in the canonization of Shakespeare.[13] Of Garrick's efforts to consolidate Shakespeare's reputation I have much to say in chapter 4, but Garrick also oversaw the progressive legitimation of a host of new hybrid forms that drew on the entertainment strategies of pantomime, musical entertainment, and other forms of physical theatre. The innovations in set design and visual spectacle initiated by figures such as Philippe Jacques De Loutherbourg and the increasing importance of music to theatrical receipts would eventually transform the practice of tragedy and comedy at the patent theatres from within.[14] All of these developments were happening in complete dialogue with the Lord Chamberlain, and thus the legitimation of low entertainment cannot be separated from state sanction. This raises the unusual question of how to think about the presence of the state in the world of entertainment. Generally, this question is handled in terms of production: what did state censorship do to the writing of plays and specifically to the content that could be presented?[15] I am more interested in its effects on reception. I would like to suggest that all audience engagement with the entertainment presented at the patent theatres involved some negotiation with the state, and thus theatre always had the potential to be about governance. Even when it was not, though, the audience was in a position to ask how any particular performance was received by the state. That awareness is itself significant because audiences were also aware of how innovation, largely driven by commercial calculations, could push on the limits set by the Licensing Act.

A similar potential was activated by the state's control of the papers. With knowledge that certain kinds of information were not allowed to be printed, the reader was aware of the limitations placed on the experience of reading. My point here is not that these forms of government control were privative but rather that they generated productive strategies of interpretation. In other words, I am applying Foucault's notion of the repressive hypothesis to censorship in order to highlight the productive aspects of the restriction on content. The readers of eighteenth-century papers and the audiences for eighteenth-century plays were accustomed, indeed were required, to think metacritically because both media had built-in mechanisms either for interrupting simple consumption or for representing the way external forces impinged on their production. To make this more tangible, let us look at an example of a cultural production that highlights the sophistication required to navigate the world of signs cast up by the convergent media of the theatre and the papers.

The Papers on the Desk: *The Upholsterer*

Transformations in the press and in the playhouses were already under way when Arthur Murphy started his career. He is a notable figure for this study because he traveled both in the world of the theatre and in that of the papers. His work as a conservative propagandist in the Byng affair offers a convenient portrait of the political activities of the press during the Seven Years' War. In 1756, after achieving success as an actor at Covent Garden and as a playwright with *The Apprentice*, Murphy found himself writing a weekly essay sheet, *The Test.*[16] In the employ of Henry Fox, Murphy's task in *The Test*, which he carried out relentlessly, was to attack the Pitt Ministry. When news of Admiral John Byng's failure to engage fully the French fleet off of Minorca reached London, Murphy was among the propagandists who mobilized public opinion against Byng and eventually celebrated in his execution. The execution of Byng was a deeply divisive affair politically, but it had the effect of galvanizing the officer class.[17] In perpetual fear of court-martial, admirals and generals did everything in their power to avoid the perception of cowardice or indecisiveness for the remainder of the war.[18] In a sense, the Byng affair codified the terms of national shame not only for the Seven Years' War but also for the American war. As we will see in chapter 4, memory of the Byng court-martial was a crucial component of the newspaper coverage of the Keppel court-martial in 1778.

But Murphy's work as a playwright casts much of this work in a different light. Murphy's *The Upholsterer* is about the consumption of the news and actually focuses on the material he wrote about in the papers. Written in 1757 but not staged until 30 March 1758 at Drury Lane, Murphy's play is about an upholsterer named Quidnunc who is so obsessed with the news and with newspapers that he is unable to fulfill either the demands of his profession or the obligations to his family. Lost in the media world, he descends into bankruptcy and is saved by a rather improbable love plot. The story was well known to his audience from Joseph Addison's essay on the political upholsterer in *Tatler*, no. 155, but Murphy's particular adaptation emphasized the topical components of the upholsterer's mania for the news. Quidnunc is an intriguing creation because his subjectivity is perpetually distracted by political and economic news associated with the early phases of the Seven Years' War. Byng's failure at Minorca, Rear Admiral George Pocock's victory over the French fleet at Chandernagore, and other elements of foreign policy are referred to in such a way that presupposes audience awareness of these events. The play's precise allusions to the reporting of these events in the newspapers in the month or so before the performance of the play subtly hail the audience into a similar relation to the media as Quidnunc himself. For example, Quidnunc's reference to "Letters from the Vice Admiral, dated Tyger off Calcutta" is to an actual letter, printed in the *London Gazette*, from Rear Admiral Pocock on naval operations in India.[19] Quidnunc's concern over Indian affairs is amply dealt with later in the play, and again there are frequent references to the reporting on the activities of Suraj' ud Dowla and Jaffir Ally Cawn in February and March 1758.[20] Similarly, when Mrs. Termagant refers to the Newsman reporting the death of the emperor of Morocco, she is calling up the newspaper reports from December 1757 of Abdallah's death.[21] As we will see in chapters 4, 5, and 6, all of these topical references have afterlives in the American war: Byng's failure to engage the French off Minorca haunts representations of Keppel's performance in the Battle of Ushant in 1778; the anxiety over the fate of British East India troops at Chandernagore emerges again after the crushing defeat at Pollilur in 1781; and the Caribbean campaigns of the Seven Years' War are the backdrop for much of the reporting of Admiral George Rodney's activities in the West Indies. But the humor of *The Upholsterer*, and its importance I would argue, lies in how it separates Quidnunc's obsessive desire for the news of global war from the audience's knowledge of these events. This amounts to a distinction between the normal and the pathological, and Murphy's play is remarkably specific in its analysis of pathological reading practices.

The play features three characters whose relations to print media and to communicative practice itself have undermined their social standing. We have Mrs. Termagant, an early precursor of Sheridan's Mrs. Malaprop, who in her attempt to adopt the language of her betters consistently ends up saying the opposite of her intention. Her linguistic pretensions signal a series of concerns regarding the stability of rank. Her failed performance of social superiority hints at the possibility that more adept performers could well disrupt class identity, while at the same time holding up such a possibility to ridicule. Quidnunc's pamphleteer friend, Razor, played initially by Garrick, is a paranoid conspiracy theorist who sees in all events and utterances convincing proof of the overthrow of Protestant Britain by Papists. Here genuine political anxiety regarding global conflict with France is contained by its very exaggeration. Murphy is adapting directly from Addison, but it is intriguing to think through what his presentation on stage does. Razor's careening emotions are equated with politics itself, so he becomes in Murphy's hands the figure for a form of patriotism that cannot stabilize the nation. Razor's nationalism relies too much on this ascription of French alterity, and Murphy argues that it needs to be either counterbalanced or negated by a more substantive declaration of British identity.

Quidnunc is introduced hunched over a vast array of newspapers struggling to generate some kind of universal theory of political economy from the conglomeration of news before him:

> [Scene *discovers* Quidnunc *at a Table, with News Papers, Pamphlets, &c. all around him*]
>
> QUID: Six and three is nine—seven and four is eleven, and carry one—let me see, 126 Million—199 Thousand, 328—and all this with about—where, where's the amount of the Specie? Here, here—with about 15 Million in Specie, all this great circulation! good, good,—why then how are we ruined?—how are we ruined?—What says the Land-Tax at 4 Shillings in the Pound, two Million! now where's my new Assessment?—here,—here, the 5th part of Twenty, 5 in 2 I can't, but 5 in 20 (*pauses*) right, 4 times—why then upon my new Assessment there's 4 Million—how are we ruined?—[22]

This remarkable speech goes on for some time, but it bears some scrutiny not only because it repeatedly asks "How are we ruined?" at a point when such a question called attention to the spiraling debt incurred by the war but also because the papers themselves materialize key problems in Quidnunc's subjectivity. Quidnunc is attempting to conjure up a scheme for raising the national supply within the year—in other words, attempting to solve the impossible task of imminently funding the war effort—by scrutinizing the information presented in the newspapers.[23] The irony here is that, at the same time that he is carrying out this task, he has himself gone bankrupt and is receiving notification from the bailiffs. The key question is why he fails both to regulate his household economy and to formulate a scheme for the regulation of the national supply. The answer lies in the jumble of information on his desk.

That desk and the papers, as theatrical props, are everyday objects. But the papers themselves, as material documents, pose a number of intriguing problems. A typical paper from the period is a remarkable montage of information: advertisements sit adjacent to shipping news, political news is interspersed with social news, and everything is assembled to maximize the amount of print per page. What this means is that the logical links between items are not important to the production and layout of the page but become important in the paper's reception. The reader is transported, or rather is able to move from topic to topic, from nearby spaces to distant lands and, because of the delay in shipping time, from events that happened yesterday to events that happened six months ago. This means that the subject is rarely placed in a consistent relation to narrated events. Rather than readers of a continuous narrative, they are cast as arrangers of divergent threads of information. Reading the paper therefore becomes all about complex acts of dispersion and collection that vary from reader to reader and from reading event to reading event.[24] In short, Quidnunc is confronted with evidence that simultaneously collapses space and time and yet refuses to do so in any normative fashion. To resolve the problems of national or household economy from such an archive would require the capacity to absorb all information and give it shape and order in real time. The audience is already well aware that this is a foolhardy task; but it also knows that the desire to meet this impossible narrative demand is necessary both for the stabilization of the state finances and for the consolidation of the subject.

Murphy's characters are linked by a fundamental inability to assess and enact the correct usage of signs, whether this happens at the level of the word in Mrs. Termagant's case or at the larger level of narrative in the case of Quidnunc and Razor. Something is wrong with how they apprehend the world through its representation. Cultural and social exchange for these characters continually spirals out of control to the point where their social standing is threatened by their very distraction. In fact, one could argue that Quidnunc's subjectivity is so dispersed that he barely manages to cohere as a character. Rather, he amounts to little more than a series of interrupted citations from the papers he is reading. By the second act of the farce, it becomes clear that Quidnunc's distraction has led to his bankruptcy. He and his daughter can be saved only by the combined actions of her aristocratic suitor and a mysterious Caribbean planter aptly named

Rovewell, who turns out to be Quidnunc's long lost son. Essentially Quidnunc's speculative relation to the fate of the nation that he is searching for in the news is rendered moot by his son's injection of West Indian capital. In this sense, the play can lampoon Quidnunc's obsession with news of the Seven Years' War by asserting the continuing presence of Britain's economic gains in the West Indies that that war was striving to protect. In this sense, the play both activates and contains the anxieties generated by the war.

Quidnunc's pathological relation to the print media, the dispersion of his subjectivity, and his failure to fulfill his familial and economic obligations are all answerable in the realm of commercial exchange. As long as there is a Rovewell to save the family and the family business, then the pathology can be contained. But in expressing this, Murphy also reveals something about the merchant classes' demand for news of imperial war. Because their economic and social standing was so integrally linked to conflict and exchange in distant spaces, Quidnunc's desire for information cannot be simply brushed off as ridiculous. Murphy and his audience are well aware that the desires presented here are constitutive of the social fabric of a nation increasingly reliant on mercantile relations with its colonial holdings. Quidnunc's subjectivity is dispersed because in a time of imperial crisis—remember that in 1758 Pitt is only just beginning to turn things around in the prosecution of war—its economic base could well become as fragmented as the upholsterer appears to be.

Murphy is careful to have the papers on the stage as material properties and to code actual reported events from the papers into the play. This gesture draws the audience into Quidnunc's experience of dispersion and thus allows some of the anxiety generated by it to animate the farce's satire. The audience's experience of the mediation of the war thus becomes crucial to its identification with and resistance to Quidnunc's obsession. In this light, the play's ridiculous and formulaic resolution—the missing son returns to solve all the economic problems posed by the father's distraction—has a curiously pedagogical effect. The uncertainty that drives Quidnunc's desire—and by extension the audience's past desire for information on Minorca and Chandernagore—has its roots in the anxiety regarding the continuation of primitive accumulation in Britain's colonial holdings. Quidnunc's pathological relation to print media turns out to be a clear expression of a kind of historical anxiety that is recurrently suppressed by assertions of national supremacy and class solidarity, but which really relies on the domination of subject peoples in the West Indies. What Murphy allows us to see in the jumble of papers on Quidnunc's desk is an allegory for the anxiety that enveloped Britain in the early phases of the Seven Years' War, but which was temporarily put in abeyance after the annus mirabilis of 1759. The papers' tendency to disperse and jumble information, their lack of internal organization and coherence, and above all their unreliability offer a compelling figure for the dissolution of national identity in the face of the economic and political forces of imperial expansion. That he was so blunt in linking the cessation of that anxiety to the practice of plantation slavery should not go unnoticed.

The contribution of Murphy's farce to the cultural matrix of eighteenth-century Britain may seem slight, but even this rather insignificant play assumes a high degree of political sophistication from its audience and offers an extremely complex diagnosis of the social insecurities besetting Britain in the uncertain spring of 1758. That said, *The Upholsterer*'s utility for cultural analysis only increases with time, because it is revived again and again throughout the rest of the century to satirize the mediation of national and imperial crisis. Evidence suggests that subsequent performances replaced the topical references to the Seven Years' War with references to events more immediately relevant to the time of performance. When we encounter one such revival late in chapter 5, we discover that subsequent modifications of the play alter not only its representation of imperial war and commerce but also its representation of mediation itself.

Productive Distractions, or New Media

With the end of the Seven Years' War, a new set of protocols in the realm of both politics and media began to emerge. Changes in the economic structure of the empire, in the political dynamics of the nation, and in the metropolitan media became curiously entwined. By midcentury most papers were published by commercial entities, and by the 1760s the four-page format was a firmly established commodity in London's print world. All of the papers were essentially advertisers, or publications whose primary purpose was to generate advertising revenue. However, political essay sheets like Tobias Smollett's pro-Bute *Briton* and John Wilkes's antiministerial *North Briton* continued to compete for the attention of readers. Wilkes's deployment of the press as a force for political change is a well-known story.[25] The government's attempt to prosecute Wilkes and forty-eight others for the publication of number 45 of the *North Briton* failed in the courts. Subsequent attempts to legislate against the publication of seditious libels and to expel Wilkes from Parliament also backfired. But more important for our purposes is the challenge set by the antiministerial Letters of Junius. Junius's letters were published in one of the most widely circulated daily papers in the London, the *Public Advertiser.* As is well known, Junius's letter of 17 December 1769 in the *Public Advertiser* attacked the Crown directly, and the letter was instantly reprinted in the *London Museum*, the *London Evening Post*, the *Gazetteer*, and the *St. James Chronicle*. The government prosecuted all the owners but failed to gain convictions against any of the owners other than John Almon of the *London Museum*.

This victory both for the freedom of the press and for juries to decide whether an article was libelous coincided with a similar campaign for the right to publish parliamentary debates. Throughout the 1760s some daily papers defied convention and printed extracts of parliamentary debates. Each time "the printers were called to the Bar of the House of Commons where they were ordered to kneel before the Speaker before being confined to Newgate until they had each paid a fine of £100."[26] In 1771 three papers, the Wilkite *Middlesex Journal*, the *Gazetteer*, and the *London Evening Post*, printed debates and were served with summonses. The printers failed to appear, and the orders for arrest were traduced by the alderman Richard Oliver and the Lord Mayor, Brass Crosby, both supporters of Wilkes. As members of Parliament, they were called to account by the Commons and, when they refused to explain themselves, were consigned to the Tower. Lucyle Werkmeister summarizes the situation well, noting that,

> since the courts subsequently upheld the Common's action, the result was a triumph for Parliament. The printers had figured in the plot only incidentally, for Parliament's right to suppress publication of its debates had never been questioned, and the right had certainly not been yielded. But it seemed to the people that this was the only matter in dispute, that the printers were the heroes, and that, by submitting to imprisonment, Oliver and Crosby had somehow established the justice of their cause. As it turned out, there was something to be said for this interpretation, for, rather than risk another battle with the City, Parliament delayed further action until it was too late, accounts of the debates being by then the very heart of every newspaper. All it could do thereafter was to hold the press responsible for the contents of the debates.[27]

This story relates an important instance of where the law was obviated by the force of commerce itself. Wilkes and his supporters pushed on the limits of the law for political reasons, but the printers wanted to print parliamentary debates because they sold papers. Readers wanted access to parliamentary debate because of the intense interest in the furor surrounding events in America. Furthermore, it is important to recognize that the debates on offer were not transcriptions of oratory made in the House but rather versions of events drawn from the memory of reporters in the gallery or invented from the desks of enterprising hack writers.[28]

With the founding of the *Morning Chronicle* in 1769, William Woodfall started a fashion for daily papers that blended parliamentary debate, advertising, letters to the printer, and sundry economic and political news into a compact whole. Woodfall, whose ability to remember vast stretches of debate earned him the nickname "Memory Woodfall," was also the preeminent theatre critic of his generation. The collocation of detailed presentations of parliamentary debate and sophisticated theatrical reviews, or "Theatrical Intelligence," in the pages of the *Morning Chronicle* was a crucial development because it recognized that the same audience was interested in the performances of parliamentarians and thespians alike. This recognition was pushed to its inevitable conclusion by the *Morning Post*, which "differed from its predecessors in only one respect: whereas [other advertisers] had always assumed that readers wanted to be informed, the *Morning Post* assumed from the outset that they wanted to be entertained. The *Post* therefore extended the scope of its 'intelligence' to include everything which might amuse people of fashion, and it presented the material in a way which was itself amusing."[29] Following the innovative scandal mongering of the *Town and Country Magazine*, the *Post* entertained its readership by giving accounts of the social and sometimes private lives of wealthy or otherwise prominent people. In other words, what the *Post* added to the mix was a daily account of social performance. The *Post* was so commercially successful that virtually every other paper started including "anecdotes" and "personalities" to its columns as a way of selling advertising. As early as 1772, the daily papers offered a complex archive of social, political, and theatrical performance aimed at entertaining the readership.

This is not to say that readers did not buy papers for information but rather to insist that the flow of information was fundamentally influenced by its entertainment value. One of the upshots of this is that readers had to become considerably more sophisticated, because, as Werkmeister has argued, the practice of selling "puffs," suppression fees, and contradiction fees became a vital part of the newspaper business, and that by 1780 "there was hardly a 'paragraph' in the newspaper that was not paid for by someone."[30] This intense commercialization of information generated highly complex interpretive practices in which paragraphs contradicting previous reports of scandalous behavior, for instance, became almost proof that the person in question had committed the acts. In this regime of signs, silence about a prominent person's life was a sign of wealth and influence. These developments in interpretive skill are important for any consideration of social scandal, but they became increasingly important with the advent of the American war.

At the outset of the war in 1775 virtually every paper in London, with the all-important exception of the *Morning Post,* was against the war. From as early as 1772, all of the daily advertisers were on the side of Wilkes, and they followed his lead in resisting the war. Factionalization of the daily press arose, first, from the placement—for a fee, of course—of paragraphs in the various papers and, second, from the eventual lease of entire publications. From 1772 onward, the Tory Ministry of Lord North bought paragraphs in the *Morning Post.* The Wilkes faction "published their paragraphs in the five old advertisers and in the two new advertisers—the *General Advertiser* and the *London Courant.*"[31] This practice continued until the publisher of the *Post,* Henry Bate, broke ranks and started the *Morning Herald* in 1780 to support the Rockingham Whigs. Because the king was set against a Rockingham administration, he "arranged for a subsidy of the *Morning Post,* and in 1781 he also acquired the *Morning Herald* by outright lease of the entire newspaper."[32] With these events, the Rockingham Whigs entered the fray and essentially assigned Richard Brinsley Sheridan the task of managing the press for the party. In Werkmeister's words, he subsidized the *London Courant* and the *General Adverstiser* with funds from prominent Whigs, sabotaged the politics of the *Morning Post,* and thus left the king entirely dependent on the *Morning Herald* during the final humiliating phases of the war.[33] The king eventually regained sufficient control of the *Morning Post* to enable his appointment of Lord Shelburne as prime minister, but his chosen minister could not survive the acrimony that swept through the press after the Peace of Paris in September 1783.

Unlike many accounts of the American debacle, Werkmeister's summary demonstrates how the war itself was enveloped in a war of mediation. The Ministry was saddled with the unenviable task of fighting simultaneously a distant colonial war—which would eventually take on global proportions when France and Spain became allies of the Americans in 1778—and a local political conflict within a media world where it was decidedly on the defensive. The North Ministry's reliance on the *Morning Post* for the management of public opinion poses an intriguing set of problems. As noted earlier, the owners of the *Post* sold papers through a combination of scandal and factional reporting. Despite the fact that its scandal mongering tended to avoid the Ministry, its overall representation of the dissipation of the aristocracy not only undermined the objectives of the pro-Ministry paragraphs but also resonated with similar critiques in more radical venues. Unlike Walpole's *Daily Gazetteer,* the *Post* was mired in internal contradictions and thus proved to be an unstable political organ. This is why it was so easy for Rev. Henry Bate to precipitate a crisis in the state when he formed the *Morning Herald*. What he retained was the entertaining combination of scandal and factional accounts of Parliament, and thus the crucial issue in sales was not which faction a paper represented but rather the combination of news with anecdotes and personages. Commerce was being driven by a crucial internal contradiction in the entertainment value of the papers: on the one hand, readers demonstrated a desire for news of public affairs, of parliamentary debate, especially with regard to the prosecution of the war; on the other hand, readers also wanted to read about the vices and errors of the Town. What is so remarkable is that for each reverse in the former realm, one could find ample cause in the latter. The newspapers all proclaimed patriotic intent, but their sales were directly linked to the daily representation of the potential connection between symptom and cause of imperial decline. So what we have is a patriotic media whose commercial success relied on the decidedly unpatriotic propagation of anxiety and doubt regarding the elite echelons of society from which Britain drew many of its military and political leaders.

This seeming contradiction resonates with Johnson's definitions of patriotism itself. In the first (1755) and fourth (1773) editions of his dictionary, Johnson defines "patriot" as "One whose ruling passion is the love of his country." In the fourth edition, Johnson adds: "It is sometimes used for a factious disturber of the government." At one level, Johnson is merely registering the complex play of connotation in the politically unsettled times of the early 1770s. But the 1773 supplement also emphasizes that there is a crucial difference between country or nation and the state and that love of the former can be used to destabilize the latter. This crucial revision is as much an expression of the historical conflict between nation and state in British political thought as it is an expression of the potential for patriotic discourse to unravel the hard-won stability of the realm. This assemblage of divergent threads in the word itself resonates with much of J. G. A. Pocock's analysis of the American conflict.

Sheridan's role here is obviously important for this study because his assumption of manager of the press for the Rockingham Whigs represents merely a modulation in his career. As a dramatist, Sheridan had recognized early on the commercial potential of a blend of topicality, faction, and epistemophilia, even in a cultural field regulated by the Lord Chamberlain. One could argue that *The School for Scandal* offers a complex meditation on this problematic, which reaches its ultimate destination in *The Critic*. The former play is famously explicit about the role played by the commercial print media in the propagation of scandal. But it is less frequently noted that in the context of its first production, when audiences would have been waiting in daily anticipation of news from America, scandal was in a sense rushing in to fill the vacuum that sheer distance imposed on the reporting of the war. In this regard, Sheridan's great comedy, because it so insistently focuses on the delays and gaps inherent to mediation, is intimately caught up in a structure of feeling endemic to what Mary Favret has termed "wartime."[34] As we will see in chapters 2 and 4, *The School for Scandal* and *The Critic* provide crucial sites for comprehending how the American crisis and the transformation in media in this period are fundamentally intertwined.

But beyond the attention to mediation in his theatrical practice, Sheridan's progressive control of the media throughout the war is remarkable. He bought Garrick's share of Drury Lane theatre in 1776 and consolidated his management by buying the remaining shares in 1778. He was thus regulating roughly half of the entertainment on offer during the theatrical season, which notably coincided with the parliamentary calendar. With his election to Parliament in 1780, he was suddenly among the speakers being reported in the daily papers. Among his tasks from 1780 onward was to channel funds to opposition writers at various papers and to destabilize the *Morning Post*. Needless to say, his management of Drury Lane was no less politicized, although there has been little sustained attempt to explore the repertoire as a continuous political argument. But this would be perhaps aside from the point. The key recognition is that during this period of national and imperial crisis, one of the earliest avatars of media convergence was not only exerting considerable political force in the metropole but also exhibiting the potential for commercial representation to influence politics itself. And as chapter 5 demonstrates, this is why Sheridan is so much in Hannah Cowley's sights when she explores the contours of martial masculinity in the late phases of the American war.

This argument need not be confined to Sheridan: he was merely taking advantage of the much-copied representational and commercial dynamic first exemplified by the *Morning Post*'s collocation of social scandal and politics. As we will see in chapter 5, the *Morning Post* and Covent Garden operated collusively during the run of Hannah Cowley's *The Belle's Stratagem* to support the Admiralty. That said, theatrical intelligence was always a part of this mix, in the form of standing advertisements and regularly occurring reviews. Thus, the theatres relied on the papers for their commercial success. But the theatrical world was also deeply imbricated not only in the representation of politics but also in the abuse of people, which was so important to selling papers. Matthew Kinservik's recent study of the scandals that enveloped Samuel Foote and the Duchess of

Kingston offers a sustained discussion of precisely this phenomenon.[35] Aside from ridiculing various identifiable types, the theatres also supplied an easy group of targets from their own ranks, conventionally named actresses, for scandalous representation and, as Werkmeister notes, a ready source of suppression money.[36] Furthermore, as a site where fashionable performance and political representation were constantly on display, the theatre embodied the link between fashion and politics that the printers of the *Morning Post*—and, owing to commercial pressure, eventually all other dailies—set into type every day. In other words, the papers that circulated in the metropole during the 1770s took a preexisting performative collocation and gave it material form. What this meant was that the papers and the theatres not only were commercially linked but also provided cognate sites for conceptualizing their representational strategies.

The kind of daily paper that dominated the print public sphere after the emergence of the *Morning Chronicle* and the *Morning Post* needs to be understood as a new medium. And as Gitelman has argued, "Media represent and delimit representing, so that new media provide new sites for the ongoing and vernacular experience of representation as such."[37] As the 1770s unfold, the papers become increasingly sophisticated interpreters of the theatre. Likewise, the theatre demonstrates an intense awareness of how the new daily papers operate both socially and politically. This perhaps explains why this period in theatre history does not transcend its time terribly well, and why those plays which do get restaged on a regular basis—namely, Oliver Goldsmith's *She Stoops to Conquer* and Sheridan's *The Rivals* and *The School for Scandal*—frequently rely on a caricature of their social and historical context that is usually coded into costume and sets. It is extraordinarily rare for a modern production of these plays to give up the signs of period, and I would argue that this is not simply a matter of lack of artistic vision. In certain recalcitrant ways, these plays manifest a particular historical moment and lose their intelligibility and their intelligence when dislocated from topical details. To make up for the passage of time and the erosion of topical knowledge among audiences, later productions frequently activate a general fantasy of period in the stage properties.

This suggests that these plays and the theatre of the post-1770 era provide an auspicious site for a style of analysis attentive to the history of mediation itself. But how would we consider the theatre as a site of media archaeology?[38] Could we argue that the "intelligence" of theatre in this period lies not simply in its representation of social relations but rather in its complex engagement with the relationship between social performance and its mediation?[39] The fact that the media in question have been subsumed or replaced by different forms and structures may help to account for the obsolescence or, to put it more positively, the situatedness of these plays. In some of the most searching plays in the period, an awareness of that obsolescence was already encoded into the formal parameters of the drama.

Beyond its intense topicality, the theatrical experience on offer at the patent houses in the 1770s and 1780s was itself stranger than theatre historians care to admit. An evening's bill included a mainpiece and an afterpiece, the former usually more serious and generically regular than the latter. Between these plays, all manners of singing and dancing were mobilized to amuse the audience. The mainpiece was framed by a prologue and epilogue that not only represented theatrical production and reception to the audience but also surfaced, in many cases, in the papers a few days after the first performance as a sort of reminder of past performance and an incitement to further production. As Gillian Russell has recently shown, these paratextual materials are extremely important because they are evidence of the high degree of metatheatrical engagement in the theatre of this period.[40] These metatheatrical gestures are also significant because they were explicitly tied to representations of the theatre as a commercial activity. In the scene of performance, actors, often speaking out of character, would remind audience members that they were consumers and, as such, had a very specific kind of agency. One of the curious effects here is that, in according consumer agency to the audience, the theatre was also constituting the audience as a social entity capable of forming itself into a mass.

Just as Walter Benjamin revised his theory of distraction from simply a negative force in the cultural field to argue that through distraction a kind of productive mass consciousness was emerging to counter fascism,[41] I am arguing that the theatre and the newspapers of the 1770s and 1780s were deeply involved in the pedagogical revelation of the historical forces tearing apart the empire. And, like Benjamin, I want to argue that this politicization, although it can be found at the level of theme and plot—Hannah More's *Percy* is a good example—transforms these media at the level of their formal articulation. The strangely distracted state inculcated by the material form of the four-page advertiser or by the repeated interruptions of a night at Drury Lane or Covent Garden provides productive spaces in time where the reader or the audience can apprehend the social and economic contradictions that undergird these representations.[42] Without underplaying the difference between the media being discussed—photography and cinema in Benjamin; newspapers and theatre here—what interests me about Benjamin's mode of analysis is the way in which he attempts to understand the relationship between media, aesthetic reception, and social history.[43] In his hands, what Johnson would call low entertainment is a medium for productive engagement that operates outside the validated modes of aesthetic contemplation—in this case, those associated most frequently with civic virtue. Civic virtue—that fabric from which elite forms of martial and political masculinity are woven—comes under a lot of pressure as the American war progresses. Benjamin's point is that contemplation, already co-opted by power, does not exhaust the field of aesthetic production or political resistance and that, through distraction, the audience gains access to a different and potentially critical set of perceptions.

I am explicitly merging Benjamin's provocative remarks on media with elements of Foucault's methodological turn in volume 1 of *The History of Sexuality* away from considerations of repression toward the productive articulation of dispositions and effects. Transferring this methodological shift from the study of sexuality to the analysis of performance is not without its risks, but I believe it can dovetail with the shift within Benjamin's formulation of distraction and technological reproduction. What Benjamin recognizes in the breakdown of the aura is the emergence of a different way of apprehending not only the aesthetic object but also the social world. In spite of the clearly auratic performances of Shakespeare by Garrick—and later Sarah Siddons—that defined the height of theatrical experience for some audience members, eighteenth-century Londoners were entertained in ways that contravened these auratic protocols. We could even argue that Garrick's efforts to canonize Shakespeare were an effect of the dispersion of the aura and, provocatively, an unconscious response to his own awareness that, with his passing, that aura was in jeopardy. In the "Work of Art" essay, Benjamin argues essentially that the work of art has an aura if it establishes or claims a figurative distance from the spectator. The figurality of this distance is important, because it is primarily temporal. Jennings states that "auratic texts are sanctioned by their inclusion in a time-tested canon [and] for Benjamin, integration into the Western tradition is coterminous with an integration into cultic practices."[44] During the era of technological reproducibility, the distance described here is traduced in ways that dissolve the distance between apprehending subject and the social or aesthetic object. For the publics reading the papers or attending the theatres, this may have allowed for the formulation of relationships among participants and audiences that were conditioned not by that which was being consumed but by the historical forces that were registered in its formal and material elements. At one level, that could be read as a loss of the fetishistic power attributed to auratic art, but it can also be understood as a release from the regulatory regime of the aura. Or, perhaps more productively, the fact of mechanical reproducibility, felt so tangibly in the world of the press in the mid-eighteenth century, began to make mediation and its relationship to the historical forces inflecting national and imperial life apprehensible in some way. With the claims of tradition continually being interrupted and being made visible as claims, audiences and social actors had the opportunity to experience the present critically.

Squeezed, Bored, and Anxious

We can be much more specific about this process by looking momentarily at one of the most famous meditations on the pleasures of the newspaper in eighteenth-century literature: William Cowper's *The Task*. Book 4 of Cowper's deeply influential poem has been the subject of important recent discussions by Julie Ellison, Kevis Goodman, and Mary Favret.[45] Composed during the period in 1783 when Britain was negotiating peace with the Americans and entering into a constitutional crisis regarding the governance of the East India Company, Cowper's poem not only thematizes current events but actually remediates key elements of specific newspapers.[46] After the appearance of the much-anticipated postboy, "the herald of the noisy world,"[47] the speaker seems to welcome the newspapers in much the same spirit as Murphy's Quidnunc:

> But oh th'important budget! ushered in
> With such heart-shaking music, who can say
> What are its tidings? Have our troops awaked?
> Or do they still, as if with opium drugg'd,
> Snore to the murmurs of th' Atlantic wave?
> Is India free? and does she wear her plumed
> And jewelled turban with a smile of peace,
> Or do we grind her still? the grand debate,
> The popular harrangue, the tart reply,
> The logic and the wisdom and the wit
> And the loud laugh—I long to know them all;
> I burn to set th'imprison'd wranglers free,
> And give them voice and utt'rance once again. (4.23–35)

Like Murphy's Quidnunc in his opening speech in *The Upholsterer*, the speaker surveys "This folio of four pages" in search of information, but his subjectivity does not swirl out of control into a vortex of dissociation and citation. Rather, the act of remediating the news in Miltonic blank verse specifically provides the occasion for the consolidation of the auratic speaking subject. Cowper represents and delimits representation in a manner that allows us to see two things simultaneously. The medium of blank verse is an auspicious site for contemplation and argument; thus, the remediation of the news in *The Task* instantiates a distance between the spectator/speaker and the news/event akin to that described by Benjamin's definition of auratic art. That distance is thematically registered in the poem by the intermediary function of the newsboy and by the fact that the speaker is at a geographic remove from the represented events. But that distance is also figuratively registered by the repeated expressions of longing and desire for immediacy. What the remediation of the press in blank verse makes visible is the desire not only to be present for the communicative actions of the grand debate, the popular harangue, and the tart reply but also to "free" them through a further act of remediation. In the terms laid out by Jay David Bolter and Richard Grusin, Cowper is poised between the desire for immediacy and hypermediation, and that desire opens onto very specific forms of agency unavailable to someone like Quidnunc.[48]

That the speaker of *The Task* is no less a fictional construction than Quidnunc is important, because they are complementary figures. Quidnunc's distraction is a direct result of an inability to find the appropriate location from which to assess both the political situation of the empire and the status of his own finances. In contrast, the speaker's retreat grants him purchase not only on world historical events but also on the transient hubbub of theatrical and political performance in the metropole. Significantly, Cowper's speaker defines his experience of the papers by contrasting it with the experiences of theatrical and political life in London that are referenced in the daily press:

> Not such his evening, who with shining face
> Sweats in the crowded theatre, and squeezed
> And bored with elbow-points through both his sides,
> Out scolds the ranting actor on the stage.
> Nor his, who patient stands 'till his feet throb
> And his head thumps, to feed upon the breath
> Of patriots bursting with heroic rage,
> Or placemen, all tranquillity and smiles. (4.42–49)

The violence of Cowper's language stands in stark contrast to the peacefulness of the time of reading, but more importantly the speaker separates himself from the intense embodiment of the representative theatregoer's experience. In a remarkable contrast, "The sound of war / Has lost its terrors 'ere it reaches" the speaker of the poem (4.100–101), but the audience member is "bored" in both senses of the word—quite literally pinioned by the crowd. This theatregoer is buffeted by those around him, but he also competes with the actor on stage. Similarly, the patient activist is trapped at the political meeting but also feeds on the breath of patriots. These subjects are not simply witnesses to theatrical and political performance; they are themselves infused by the cultural and social forces around them to the point of becoming actors themselves.

What interests me here is that in the midst of representing how the performance of theatre and politics dissolves the distinction between subjectivity and the social, Cowper also indicates that the penetration of the outside world into the inner life of these performers happens in moments of distraction or boredom. Notice how the activist's incorporation of the patriot's rage occurs only after a period of patient waiting. This collocation of distraction and penetration is nowhere more evident than in the wonderful condensation of Cowper's pun on bored: the audience member "out scolds" the actor not only because he is squeezed and penetrated on all sides but also because the tediousness of the "rant" itself demands that he become the actor. It is these experiences that Cowper holds at bay but which are at the core of the vibrant cultural matrix explored in this book.

As Mary Favret and Kevis Goodman have demonstrated, the distantiation presented in the opening verse paragraphs of book 4 of *The Task* is a complex matter because Cowper's famous "loophole of retreat" provides an avenue through which to access the affective life of wartime. Paradoxically, it is through figural distance that Cowper's speaker is able to structure key involutions in the feeling of global war. Crucial to these arguments is the temporality of newspaper reading itself. Everything is pegged to the circulation of the papers; thus, the loophole of retreat also marks a space in time for a specific mode of reading and writing whereby the health of the speaker and, by extension, the nation is reconstituted. As Favret has argued, building on Benedict Anderson's account of newspaper circulation, the iteration of this temporal experience has profound implications for Romantic discourse.[49]

But I am also struck by the degree to which Cowper's remediation of the news replaces the decoding of spatial disjunctions on the page of the papers with a series of spatial figures that attempt to bring sense to the chaotic world of the four-page advertiser:

Here runs the mountainous and craggy ridge
That tempts ambition. On the summit, see,

The seals of office glitter in his eyes;
He climbs, he pants, he grasps them. At his heels,
Close at his heels a demagogue ascends,
And with a dextr'ous jerk soon twists him down
And wins them, but to lose them in his turn. (4.57–63)

As the public man makes his way across the press, the newspaper is eventually figured as a prospect:

Cataracts of declamation thunder here,
There forests of no-meaning spread the page
In which all comprehension wanders lost;
While fields of pleasantry amuse us there,
With merry descants on a nation's woes.
The rest appears a wilderness of strange
But gay confusion . . . (4.73–79)

With the translation of the material page into a figural landscape, the speaker identifies certain zones with the discourse of the sublime—"cataracts of declamation"—and others with the beautiful—"fields of pleasantry"—and this aestheticization carries with it key political ramifications.

It is useful to specify precisely what this prospect allows the speaker to see and what it occludes, for the speaker's figural distance from the text affords insight as well as blindness. He can see the cataracts of declamation and the satiric remarks regarding national decline, and they can be aesthetically processed as products of the sublime and the beautiful respectively. But there remain "forests of no-meaning," which turn out to be thickets of advertising whose tendrils extend to the farthest reaches of the empire and into the lowest forms of spectacle and entertainment (4.79–87). Julie Ellison has usefully traced the catalog that specifies the "wilderness of strange / But gay confusion" and finds an array of products and events culled from issues of the *Morning Chronicle* and the *General Evening Post* from September 1783.[50] What interests me is that Cowper's metaphors of "forests of no-meaning" and "wilderness of . . . confusion" refer us specifically to the opaque components of the daily press—those elements that Bolter and Grusin associate with hypermediation. Through the distancing power of metaphor Cowper can contain these dispersive elements of the papers, and thus the auratic control implied by the "loophole of retreat" is maintained by a careful containment and abjection of the promiscuous exchanges written directly into commercial print culture and associated with the hustle and bustle of London itself.

What I think this points to are two divergent relationships to cultural distraction in the latter phases of the American war. Cowper, writing from the realm of deep melancholia after a serious bout of depression, deploys the auratic utterance to heal subjectivity, but in doing so his remediation of the newspapers separates himself from the very commerce that defined his privilege.[51] Thus, Cowper's great innovation in the disclosure of the affective experience of war specifically occludes the economic and political adequation that secured his utterance. It is from this complex act of remediation that Cowper crafts what I am tempted to call the first great post-American work of art and, as Favret argues, the crucial text for the Romantic comprehension of "wartime." But Cowper's strategies do not exhaust or even epitomize the cultural reaction to the American war. Like Favret, I tend to see *The Task* as a harbinger. Her exploration of the notion of the "meantime" and of prophecy in Cowper offers one of the clearest avenues for comprehending much of Wordsworth and Coleridge's practice in the 1790s. My sense is that this is because Cowper's poem is attempting to reflect on the ruptures in his own life and in the imperial world at the close of the American war. The performance culture I am exploring in this book is located within a much less controlled situation because it cannot afford, in all senses of that word, the distance that enables Cowper's utterance and is everywhere inscribed in the formal discipline of blank verse.

Richard Brinsley Sheridan and Hannah Cowley, with arguably an even more intense attention to the play of remediation than that exhibited by Cowper, write for "the crowded theatre" and thus are by necessity involved in a much more sociable and commercial intervention. Furthermore, their practice has much more in common with the work of mourning than with melancholia. Likewise, the very task facing journalists, "the dissemination of ignorance in the form of facts which must be continually renewed so that no one notices," means that they are repeatedly shoring up a discursive system on the verge of collapse.[52] Their engagement with social and political crisis is marked by a certain imminence that opens the audience to feelings of critical insecurity. In both media, topicality is engaged in a fashion that bores and bores into their consumers. As I argue extensively in chapters 4 and 5, Sheridan and Cowley deploy distraction to negate obsolete styles of subjectification and, in so doing, embrace the commercial dynamics of the theatre itself as a force for social critique and as a way for working through loss. If *The Task* allows the reader to witness the emergence of a new kind of lyric subject and hence a model for historical contemplation, then the late comedies of Sheridan and Cowley discussed in this book establish the conditions for their audiences to accede to a new kind of critical subjectivity suited to the precarious moment of the late 1770s and early 1780s. It is for this reason that I believe that post-American British culture starts in the middle of the American war with *The Critic.*

In order to test this somewhat Foucauldian approach to Benjamin's concept of distraction, the first three chapters of this book, rather than address canonical works of theatre, look at seemingly trivial social events and related, often minor, theatrical performances. And yet nestled within each analysis of sociability lies an engagement with social and artistic tradition. Gillian Russell has already demonstrated why this analysis of sociability is necessary, and I want to build on her insight by arguing that the kind of attention we are used to paying to works of art needs to be directed at the formal qualities of social diversion, amusement, and entertainment.[53] During my analysis of Burgoyne's Fête Champêtre, the Thames Regatta, and Captain André's Mischianza, I use all the tools of close reading to scrutinize the social effects of distraction in order to develop a mode of analysis that will then be employed to deal with more supposedly auratic productions in the theatres. That word *supposedly* is important because, even in the attempts to eulogize Garrick or commemorate Handel, the commercial forces at play begin to impinge on the formal experience of these performances. The analyses of Sheridan's "Verses to the Memory of Garrick, spoken as a Monody" and *The Critic* in chapter 4, of Cowley's post-1780 comedies and George Colman's *Inkle and Yarico* in chapter 5, and of the 1784 Handel Commemoration in chapter 6 are explicitly poised on the recognition that, with the loss of the American colonies, Britain was faced with the real possibility that it could become disconnected from the tradition that consolidated not only its economy but also the auratic effects of the art used time and again to articulate the power of its dominant class. While close reading remains a vital tool, throughout this enquiry it is put in the service of uncovering the historical perceptions afforded by these performances and artifacts. Whether I am able to demonstrate that playwrights such as Sheridan and Cowley are effectively pioneering new perceptual experiences in the mediascape of eighteenth-century life or that the organizers of the Handel Commemoration were performing a rearguard action to harness the auratic power of art for the ruling classes remains to be seen. But I do want to suggest that the questions of perception, of historical consciousness, and of temporal rupture that Benjamin associates so vividly with the formal qualities of cinema and with Baudelaire's verse can be seen in nascent form in the heavily commercialized world of London's theatres and newspapers after the Seven Years' War.

None of this is to suggest that playwrights did not write about other media in the past or that the theatre was not always already the topic of commentary in print culture. However, I do want to demonstrate that the particular developments in the commercial press in the 1770s and the convergence of media during the American war were a crucial development in national and imperial subjectification. And as overstated as that perhaps sounds, I want to argue further that the printers of the papers, the managers of the theatres, and their shared audiences were well aware of this process. This much is evident from Arthur Murphy's *News from Parnassus*, a brief prelude staged to celebrate the remodeling of Covent Garden. Murphy's prelude was widely understood to be a response to Garrick's retirement in June 1776.[54] As Dunbar summarizes,

> When the theatres opened in September, the managers of both houses determined to present dramatic preludes. That presented at Drury Lane was Colman's *New Brooms*, meant to introduce the new managers, to compliment Garrick, and to amuse by witty criticism of the opera. Covent Garden presented *News from Parnassus*, written by Murphy, presumably at the request of Harris and his partners, evidently for the purpose of congratulating Garrick and of presenting a dramatic satire to rival *New Brooms*.[55]

Thus, at the outset of the war, both houses opened their seasons with satires on their place in the commercial culture of London. These two plays, *New Brooms* and *News from Parnassus*, have the rather strange status of being the first productions staged in the patent houses after the reception of the news of the Declaration of Independence. Significantly, both plays pay homage to the passing of one era in British theatre by commemorating Garrick's retirement, while recognizing the emergence of a new matrix of culture workers. In Murphy's play, the great Italian satirist Boccalini resurfaces in London and meets with a poet, a bookseller, an actor, a critic, and a pantomime poet. Each of these men gives an account of his trade. In response to Boccalini's curiosity as to how the newspapers carry "News from all parts of the kingdom," the bookseller, Vellum, describes the activity of the press by referring to the same bees that Cowper would employ in *The Task*:

> VELLUM: A printing house is like a bee-hive: some drones there are; the busy fly and buzz abroad in a morning, and return loaded at noon: but they never bring enough; we supply the rest. Troops in America! A letter from thence is writ in my garret.[56]

In Cowper, the bee metaphor is used capture the way that the newspaper "travels and expatiates . . . / sucks intelligence in every clime, / and spreads the honey of his deep research / At his return, a rich repast for me. / He travels and I too" (4.107–14). But in Murphy the bees of the press fail to collect enough information, and this dearth is supplemented by fictional paragraphs. It should come as no surprise that the fictional letter writ in Vellum's garret pertains to war in America: Murphy is dramatizing the desire for information about America and emphasizing that the commercial system of the press will supply the material to fill that vacuum.

Significantly, Murphy's representative poet Rebus worked for Vellum for five years and his career in the papers has had a deep impact on his aspirations as a dramatist. His comedy, like the news from America in Vellum's paper, is not based on observations of manners or men but rather on a cynical calculation of how to avoid censure. As he states,

> REBUS: My notion is that there should be sound doctrine throughout; in every scene good and generous sentiments; rising in a climax to some usefull moral in every act.—Now observe—my first act ends with "honour your father and mother." II Act, "love your neighbour as yourself."—III. Act, "do as you would be done by"—IV. Act, "charity covers a multitude of sins"—V. Act, "God save the king"—No audience can hiss such sentiments.[57]

Like his direct critique of the status of the news from America, Murphy's attack on false patriotism in the theatre is given teeth by the subsequent account of Rebus's plays. His comedy is a pastiche of sentimentalism, but its subject is the corruption of the law. In a remarkable turn, Rebus underscores not only the improbability of any kind of sentimental resolution of those abused by corruption but also the unlikelihood of any kind of filial generosity. With the representation of Rebus's tragedy, Murphy pushes the satire even further. Rebus has chosen to dramatize the shameful events surrounding the death of the Indian financier Nandakumar, which had left a lingering stain on the reputation of the East India Company, and thus what we have is a dramatist, however ineptly, stepping into the debate on imperial governance.[58] Like Vellum's "letters on America," however, Rebus proves to be a less than reliable source for information from the colonial world, and his tragedy ends up blending orientalist spectacle and moral nostrums against forgery, precisely the allegation Nandakumar made against the East India Company.

Murphy's satire is notable both for how it underlines the interconnectedness of the newspapers and the theatre and for how it assumes that the audience already comprehends the moral criteria by which Boccalini will judge Vellum, Rebus, and the corrupt critic Catcall. When Boccalini delivers the News from Parnassus—that is, Apollo's judgment of each of the men he meets—Murphy emphasizes that his condemnation of each character's cynical relation to both culture and society will be incorporated into their cultural productions. Boccalini declares the newspapers to be a poison to the soul; Vellum tells Boccalini to "Look into Poets Corner next Saturday for an epigram upon yourself." Boccalini gives specific—and predictable—instructions for the reform of comedy and tragedy, but intriguingly he remains open to the entertainment of pantomime. Despite the manifest corruption of culture in the play, and the clear invocation of an empire unraveling in America and India, Boccalini does not condemn the convergent media of theatre and the newspapers. Rather, he concludes by celebrating the commercialization of culture itself:

> BOCCALINI: In a word, let [Theatre] Managers consider themselves at the head of a great warehouse; procure the best assortment of goods, get proper hands to display them; open their doors, be civil to the customers, and Apollo foretells that the generosity of the public will reward their endeavours.[59]

It is an apt celebration of the commercial theatre pioneered by Garrick, and yet it is a panegyric haunted by the recognition that in other warehouses and zones of exchange this kind of ameliorative vision was far from secure. In Boston only two years earlier, rebellious colonists made the link between the politics of trade in India and the taxation of America explicit in something that would only retrospectively be termed a party.[60]

Both the metropolitan theatre and the London papers recognized that the operations of the media were themselves of interest to audiences and thus the object of commercial calculation. For example, letters to the printer, prologues and epilogues to plays, theatrical gossip, and even documents as seemingly arcane as David Garrick's will were circulated because they generated custom for both media. Remediation, the replication and circulation of mediated representation, itself started to emerge as a way of testing representation. The chief topoi of these metropolitan representations, fashionable sociability and parliamentary politics, were importantly enacted by a small and relatively exclusive community, but their performances, whether they took place at the Pantheon or in the House of Commons, were replicated both in print and on stage. And this is entertaining, in Johnson's complex definition, because it strikes to the heart of the political problematic enveloping the nation and empire. And that, of course, had to do with representation in a different sense.

Necessary Turbulence, or New Empires

J. G. A. Pocock's influential account of the political crisis in the Atlantic traces the dilemma of imperial governance back to two key problems: the lack of any coherent theory of confederation in British political thought and the troubling duality of the term *imperium*. As he states, "the primary meaning in English of 'empire' or *imperium* had been 'national sovereignty': the 'empire' of England over itself, of the crown over England in the church as well as state, the independence of the English church-state from all other modes of sovereignty."[61] Empire in this sense denoted sovereignty of the British realm over itself. This primary meaning came crashing into another meaning of empire following "the momentous if transitory establishment on an English-speaking universal empire in the North Atlantic and Alleghanian America" after the Seven Years' War.[62] This more recent meaning saw

> the extension of its sovereign's authority over a diversity of subject dominions in the Atlantic archipelago, the Caribbean and the North American continent. "Realm" and "empire" were therefore non-identical without being distinct, and the over-riding necessity of maintaining the unity of the crown and parliament dictated that the primary meaning of "empire" should be this institution's sovereignty over its "realm." Since all subjects within the realm were held to be represented by the parliament in which the crown exercised empire, it was an easy step to assuming that all subjects within the "empire" were under the authority which represented the realm, and it was to prove hard to assert otherwise without compromising the unity and sovereignty of the realm itself.[63]

The colonies were not represented in Parliament, and resolving their ambiguous status was the subject of a host of tracts and pamphlets on both sides of the Atlantic. But Pocock's crucial recognition is that as soon as the ambiguous status of the colonies was recognized, the unity of the king and Parliament, and thus the sovereignty of the realm, was put into jeopardy. This was because the autonomous colonial legislatures began to pass resolutions asserting that the empire must be seen as an enlarged confederacy of many legislatures each separately connected by the Crown.[64] This effectively separated the king from each legislature to make him the linchpin uniting all of the constituent elements, and thus the notion of King-in-Parliament was traduced.

This problem was crucial because "Englishmen could see that the American program entailed the separation of crown from parliament, threatening the unity of 'empire' which was the only guarantee against civil war and dissolution of government, those deep and still bleeding wounds in their historical memory."[65] The recent experience of the historical trauma of civil war and the hard won sense of stability after the Glorious Revolution and the quelling of the Jacobite Rebellion inflected all of the responses to the American crisis. This history proved to be decisive for Britain, because it meant that "the heart of the American problem for Britain was less the maintenance of imperial control than the preservation of essentially English institutions which the claims of empire were calling into question."[66]

The core of Pocock's argument merits this attention for two reasons: it helps to shift our thinking about empire to terms appropriate to the historical moment in question, and it isolates an important discursive phenomenon that I believe can be used heuristically beyond the archive of political theory. The problem faced by the theorists of politics that Pocock is reading, figures such as Thomas Pownall, Josiah Tucker, and Edmund Burke, is how to accommodate the two definitions of empire—that is, empire understood as sovereign monarchy over the realm and empire understood as "extensive or enormous monarchy." The problem comes down to how to bring the outside into the inside without exploding the identity of the latter. In each case, the theorist in question is confronted with three key obstacles. First, the "outside" is itself multifarious, but its constituent parts are lacking in any clear governmental relation to each other. The colonies are composed of separate, autonomous legislatures. Second, the "inside" is dualistic. King-in-Parliament is a dyadic structure, and thus any simple subsumption of the outside into the purview of the inside had the potential to separate Parliament from the king and precipitate a regression to either absolute monarchy or republicanism. And, third, most commentators agreed with Benjamin Franklin's demographic prediction that the thirteen colonies, already much larger than the British Isles, were soon going to eclipse its population. The obvious implication was that center and periphery might switch places.

These inside-outside problems are fundamental to representation itself. All representational systems maintain their coherence by maintaining a constitutive outside. The notion of *maintenance* here is a complex one, because as soon as one becomes aware of what must be ejected from a system to maintain its representational integrity, that integrity is radically undermined. Within the political theory of sovereignty presented by Pocock, it is the term *colony* that plays this strange role. It is the concept that must be ejected, yet maintained, to secure the integrity of the realm. The unification of Scotland and England, and all that that means politically, relies on the alienation of the notion of colony to locales across the sea. But the enhanced imperial sovereignty precipitated by the Seven Years' War raised the status of this alienated term in ways that drew attention to its necessary exclusion from the language of King-in-Parliament. As Pocock demonstrates, American secession allowed for the maintenance of "colony" as a constitutive outside for British sovereignty because America acceded to the condition of a state. Thus, one of the crucial adjustments in the era after the American war was a redefinition of coloniality itself such that colonial governance was carried out not by legislatures but rather by governors, "often military men, [who] directly exercised their sovereign's authority, representing him in his personal, imperial and parliamentary character."[67] This new imperial regime stabilized both the notion of King-in-Parliament and the new global economic networks that it enabled.[68]

From this awareness of the centrality of inside-outside dynamics to the political history of this era in British politics, I want to suggest that the complex play of inclusion and exclusion that animates so much of this book's archive is not an incidental matter but a deep-seated sign of history.[69] As every chapter in this book demonstrates, much of the entertainment in this period turned on complex rhetorical effects aimed at giving readers and audiences the sense of being simultaneously inside and outside of a public. The pleasures and anxieties associated with this type of representation are not the sole domain of this period, but the convergence of the theatres and the papers and the commercial explosion of the daily press meant that these emotional experiences could be activated on a hitherto unimagined scale. And it is my sense that they are being activated in much the way that Pocock suggests that political theorists attempted to resolve the predicament besetting British politics. In a variety of ways, Britons were exploring the problem of bringing the outside into the inside and ultimately decided to consolidate fantasies of sovereignty, whether that is understood in terms of politics or in the more expanded terms of culture and society. This is perhaps axiomatic in a play such as *The Nabob* (1772), which, as I have shown elsewhere, formally resolves the problem of colonial governance by refiguring the debt incurred by the metropolitan aristocracy to its colonial holdings as a financial and familial obligation that unites the aristocracy with its commercial relations.[70] Eventually plays about India would operate differently, but I would argue that the problem of bringing the outside inside permeates the convergent media of the period. In the material form of the papers, the outside world began to permeate domestic space. And theatregoers left their domiciles on a regular basis in order to come together as a public in their contemplation of the comic representation of domestic affiliation.

One way of thinking of this inside-outside dynamic is through the notion of identity. Dror Wahrman's account of "the subversion of every basic identity category" during the American war offers a compelling picture of transformation that seeks to describe the emergence of modernity as a historical bifurcation with the American Revolution as the crucial point where social and cultural turbulence becomes suddenly organized such that we can see a juncture between the ancien regime of identity and the new modern subjectivity.[71] Crucial to his argument is a wide-ranging discursive analysis of how tropes of race and gender are deployed in the pamphlet literature and novels of the period. What he finds is a remarkably unstable regime of signs. Of these destabilizing tropes and figures, Wahrman accords special significance to the deployment of gendered tropes, and his argument for social disjunction relies heavily on a chronology derived from a reading of the shift from gender play to gender panic in prologues to plays in the patent theatres. His analysis of the prologue to Hannah More's *Percy* is powerful, but in many ways it turns first on a crucial reduction of the audience's agency as readers and spectators and second on an isolation of the utterance from the scene of performance itself. As we will see in chapter 2, comprehending *Percy*'s prologue requires an analysis of the relationship between the paratext, the politics of Hannah More's tragedy, and the historical situation of the performances in question. Without belaboring the point, for his analysis of this transient text to carry the weight placed on it, one would like to have a firm sense not only of its relation to the mainpiece but also of its reception.

But more importantly, I want to take issue with Wahrman's analysis on a different level. Much of his evidence regarding the figuration of relations between colonies and metropole is more convincingly understood in terms of kinship relations than gender insubordination as such. As Wahrman states,

> The belief that this was indeed an unnatural civil war was frequently expressed through images of an unnatural family affair or domestic strife: historians long ago suggested that the language of disrupted family relations was "the very lingua franca of the [American] revolution." Not that this fact is very surprising. But its consequences are worth noting: for it was but a short step from the anxiety about a malfunctioning family to that about proper gender roles within the family, whether between hus-

> band and wife or between parent—especially mother—and child. Was Great Britain a caring or an unnatural—and unfeminine—mother to the colonies? Was King George an unnatural father? This was a question, as Jay Fliegelman has brilliantly shown, that reverberated with considerable consequences throughout the American crisis. . . . Such invocations of well-functioning family relationships were inevitably also references to proper gender roles. . . . Inadequate gender identities fused together the harmful consequences of civil war both in disrupting family relationships and in disrupting identity categories; as a critique of the war they therefore packed a double punch.[72]

I agree with Wahrman and Fliegelman on the ubiquity of this deployment of the family.[73] But the sudden assertion of the "inevitable" link between the performance of proper gender roles and the maintenance of sound familial relations relies on a specific deployment of sexuality that may impede analysis of these materials.[74] What family is being talked about here? Everything about Wahrman's analysis suggests that the normative tropological family in question has reproduction as its defining characteristic. But this effectively eliminates models of the family based on notions of alliance.[75] I am invoking Foucault's distinction between deployments of alliance and deployments of sexuality not to argue for the particular chronological point when one model was replaced by the other, but rather to indicate that by understanding the family in terms of reproduction Wahrman has effectively guaranteed the outcome of his argument. If we back out from this teleological set of assumptions, then we are left with a more complicated situation, one where familial tropes may invoke relations of aristocratic alliance or those of reproductive sexuality increasingly affiliated with the middling orders. In other words, I am imagining a world where both notions of familial relation retain their significance, because it is clear from the widespread concern about aristocratic alliance well past the American war that it is socially and historically still active at the same time that the middle ranks are deploying sexuality to such far-reaching effects. And this returns us to the complicated problem of kinship, which seems to trouble all discussions of the American crisis.

Critical Futures

What happens if we think through the problems of kinship in their most basic form—that is, as a structuralist? If we follow Levi-Strauss and argue that all kinship systems rely on the exclusion of incest, then the argument comes back to questions of systematicity and the need for a constitutive outside. If, as I have suggested, *colony* operates as the constitutive outside for the realm of King-in-Parliament, then how is this term tropologically excluded from kinship discourse? Of all the examples pulled by Wahrman of the subversion of identity, those figurations that sexualize the relationship between England and America, such as John Cartwright's "A Letter to Edmund Burke, Esq; Controverting the Principles of American Government," also have to separate America from a kinship relation with England.[76] If, following Johnson, we understand patriotism as a species of love, then it is worth considering what has to be done to prevent normative parent-child or sibling tropes from infelicitous sexualization. Patriotism itself would need to be channeled away from erotic connotations of love toward parental care or sibling bonds. Fliegelman and Wahrman have shown the ubiquity of these latter figures, but it is important to recognize that, because we are in the realm of figures, we can equally understand the American crisis as a conflict between competing suitors for the hand of Liberty. For the colonists, Wilkite radicals, Shelburnites, Rockingham Whigs, and their supporters—all of whom claimed British identities—the ruling elite as represented by Lord North's Ministry had become an unsuitable match for very particular idealizations of the constitutional past. The intense patriotism that fueled, in different ways, the Continental army, the pro-Wilkes mob, and the oratory of Charles James Fox laid claim to specific representations of the past. North's Tory Ministry was not a terribly compelling suitor, because it already felt that it was a husband. Its commitment was not to an idealization of Liberty—that was primarily a Whig fantasy—but rather to ownership pure and simple. The colonies belonged to the Crown, the marriage had already taken place, and thus the conflict had much the same dynamic of the wounded husband trying to rein in his errant wife. Whigs and radicals in Parliament never tired of pointing out that the Ministry was undeserving of the colonies' love and dedication either because it treated them with too much harshness or because it was itself unworthy of respect because it had undermined its own national heritage. All of these arguments rely both on notions of corrupted civic virtue and on the all-important attribution of child status to Liberty.

But as the war unfolded and the Americans demonstrated their capacity for independence, a key problem emerged.[77] If Britain were to lose the war—and after Saratoga this looked extremely likely—the Whigs, no less than the Tories, would be alienated from the object of their desire. Liberty, as embodied by the colonist's rebellion, was thriving elsewhere and did not need to marry. In a sense, Tories were in a better position to deal with the loss because their patriotism was grounded in the land itself and in the mythical body of the king. Whigs and reformers, with their vision of a mobile liberty and of limited monarchy, were faced with a rejection that separated them momentarily from their past. Suddenly, all they had was Britain and a king who did not care for them. In the turbulent period between the fall of Saratoga in September 1777 and the emergence of the Pitt Ministry in 1784, the performance of patriotism was vexed because its relation to the mythic national past was destabilized. It is for this reason that the performances and representations I look at in chapters 3 through 6 are so vitally concerned with the future. And it is this complex engagement with what was to come, what could not be known, that is ultimately the core of this book. I explore some of the strategies and tactics deployed to figure forth a post-American British imperium. To reengage the romance trope, I want to know what Britons did to make themselves attractive after the divorce, so to speak. And it is crucial to recognize that in the pages of the newspapers and on the boards of the theatre, the audiences I discuss in this book were searching for new subjectivities and new social contracts suitable for the time to come.[78]

Wahrman's analysis of the American Revolution as a point where the ancien regime of identity fractures and opens onto a new set of social and cultural relations builds its argument from an archive different from Pocock's and handles the question of discourse differently, but at least part of his argument needs to be addressed here. In a useful survey of pamphlet literature and political journalism, Wahrman demonstrates that writers of all factions attempted to explain the American crisis in terms of past social and political upheavals. It is hardly surprising to see the present being read as a rehearsal of the English Civil War or in terms of the recently quashed Jacobite Rebellion. What is important, and Pocock makes a similar point, is that not only did historicist analysis of the problem fail to demonstrate the necessary internal coherence to become persuasive, but also this lack of coherence meant that claims of patriotism—and all factions claimed to be operating out of a love of country—increasingly were grounded on often contradictory rhetorical tropes and figures. This is where Wahrman's analysis of gender becomes both illuminating and distracting. By suggesting that something changes in gender itself, Wahrman is able to link the American crisis to a problem within the public. But as noted, that argument hinges on a key redefinition of tropes pertaining to kinships into those of "gender roles." This effectively moves us from questions of social and familial relations to questions of identity. I am reluctant to move so quickly here, because, in spite of the heuristic value of Wahrman's thesis, it relocates the entire political problematic to the domain of the subject. And various important thematics, such as the fate of civic virtue in the performance of masculinity, are occluded. Pocock's analysis of this problematic demonstrates why this fracturing of historical narratives' explanatory power took place and how American secession moved the entire discursive assemblage away from a historical problematic to a future-oriented resolution not only in governmentality but also in subjectification. This keeps the question of the political open and yet does not foreclose on identity effects. I would argue that Wahrman's argument is powerful because we know what happened next. In the field of cultural criticism this new era goes by the name of Romanticism. One of the things I want to do here is attempt to look at the social and cultural forces of this period in a way that does not see the emergence of the modern self as an inevitable outcome of these historical formations. In other words, I want to give a sense of a moment when it was unclear what Britain and Britons would become.

This perhaps impossible desire to isolate the pre-Romantic arises out of a fundamental observation regarding the materials I discuss in the book. For all the invocation of past national, imperial, and cultural glory in the period, it is extremely difficult to chart a pattern of mourning or melancholia in the mass media archives. Tragedies get performed, nostalgic accounts of the past get printed, but it is in the realms of comedy, mixed entertainments, and the papers that the anxieties of the period are most profoundly explored.[79] Audiences did not respond particularly well to Richard Cumberland's lugubrious tragedy *The Battle of Hastings* or to Colman's resuscitation of John Fletcher's *Bonduca* in the summer of 1778. At this particularly low point in British fortunes audiences were far more drawn to the combination of farce and spectacle in Sheridan's *The Camp*.[80] This may be because this war is not simply about loss but may be more accurately apprehended as a recalibration of the right disposition among people and things.[81]

There is a harshness in that last sentence because it implies that governmentality operates counter to the protocols of rememoration, and frequently it is the material bodies of those who have died in service of the state that have to be effectively forgotten. These bodies, whether they be buried in Westminster Abbey, as David Garrick's was, or invoked in the same space during the Handel Commemoration, are critical to a process of mourning through which the loss of the American colonies will be politically and emotionally contained so that a very different social and cultural future can proceed. As we will see in the ensuing chapters, I trace a complex deployment of the future in the entertainment culture of London, and I argue, sometimes bluntly, sometimes more implicitly, that the drive forward implied by the projection of future states is itself integrally related to the dynamics of commerce. Because commerce is the defining objective of the media I am discussing, this amounts to arguing that the commodity form and the social function of these media are tightly intertwined, if not mutually constitutive. Furthermore, I am arguing that the deployment of the future in these media was part of the consolidation of post-American polity in the British Isles, and thus the plays, papers, and social events I examine are not simply representing existing patriot positions but entertaining, in the sense of considering, patriotisms not yet realized. I contend that only through understanding this restylization of both the subject and the social world can we understand, first, how the nation reinvigorated its relationship to its cultural heritage—that is, to itself—and, second, how a new model of empire would work. And I demonstrate that this was explicitly undertaken in relation to a necessarily unknown future.

Mary Favret has identified a similar dynamic in the wartime writing of early Romanticism, and again her insight emerges from a subtle reading of *The Task*'s remediation of the news. Because there is always a gap between the text of the papers and the reported event—and I would add a fundamental temporal disjunction between paragraphs within any given newspaper—the speaker in book 4 of Cowper's poem is frequently caught in what Favret calls the "meantime." It is in this hiatus that the affective experience of distant war suffuses the poem, and it is from these interruptions in the mediation of war that a certain predilection for prophecy emerges in Cowper's discourse. In one of these moments, the speaker looks through the window of his rural retreat and sees tomorrow:

> To-morrow brings a change, a total change!
> Which even now, though silently perform'd
> And slowly, and by most unfelt, the face
> Of universal nature undergoes.
> Fast falls a fleecy show'r: The downy flakes,
> Descending and with never-ceasing lapse
> Softly alighting upon all below,
> Assimilate all objects. (4: 322–29)

Favret's commentary here is illuminating:

> The never-ceasing lapses of time are perhaps welcome, convincing signs of a world-to-be-changed. But they are also signs of a world erased. . . . Here, in the never-ceasing lapses of falling snow, the future appears muted and nearly illegible: like and unlike the newspaper, it is a blank page "that

> assimilates all objects" into a vast sameness. It could be a figure of time redeemed, a new time, or, in its frozen stillness, the end of time.[82]

This sense of a pivot point in time between the erasure associated with the past and the redemption—or apocalypse—associated with the future receives its canonical elaboration in the discourse of Romantic prophecy, and, like Favret and others, I feel that it is a crucial legacy of this period of instability. But I want to draw attention to one aspect of the passage perhaps occluded by the figural link between the falling snow and the blank pages of the newspaper in Favret's argument. The press is a great engine of assimilation, but Cowper's lines explicitly state that the future disclosed in the changes wrought by the present is "silently performed / And slowly, and by most unfelt" (4.323–24). This attention to performance is, I believe, important, because it not only draws us to the way that the present subtly acts on the past and the future simultaneously but also indicates that not everyone "feels" historical change precisely because the changes from day to day, from moment to moment—the very iterative quality of the press that drives the mediation of wartime—quickly becomes the sediment of everyday life. As we will see when we come around to Cowper again in the coda to this book, performance is a crucial matter for his understanding of historical time.

Because performance happens in the transient present, in a moment that is always receding into the past and yet opening onto the future, temporality is always on the horizon of analysis. The vast majority of scholarship on performance focuses on the relationship of performance to history. This is in part because the analysis of performance is itself caught in this temporal dynamic. As a performance recedes into the past, we are at least left with its traces. The archive itself lends itself to a consideration of the past, of the passing of time, and of loss. It is not surprising therefore that mourning and trauma are such insistent thematics in the analysis of performance. However, as Judith Butler's work on performativity and Pierre Bourdieu's work on the habitus demonstrate, each performance, although always a re-presentation, also impinges on the future.[83] Social and cultural propagation, not to mention social change, rely on the capacity for repeated performances to call forth and thus condition the time to come. The problem, of course, is that any single performative moment is only part of a complex flow of social and cultural activity into the past and on to the future. It is in this sense that change, as Cowper suggests, is silently performed and by most unfelt.

Performance offers a particularly portentous site for thinking about these historical and temporal problematics because it is necessarily engaged with the passage of time itself. This book pays close attention to the way that social and theatrical performances shape both the participants' and the audiences' experience of time, especially the strange apprehension of the time to come. However, grasping that experience, or discussing that apprehension, cannot be achieved directly. Rather, it has to travel indirectly through the material archive of what remains from this turbulent period. As we will see, that material archive throws up rather strange shadows, and often small details will open up ways of perceiving that which has been obscured by history. At times, the tension between microhistory and the macrological demands of the overall arc of the argument will surface to remind us of the complex genealogical task I have set for these readings. What I hope will become apparent is that this same tension was felt by the audiences and participants I discuss, and that their negotiation of the ground between minor details of representation and world historical forces was a remarkable act.

In moments of social and cultural crisis, many potential outcomes are possible. With the hindsight of history, we are in a position to recognize the futures that did not take place. But from the critical standpoint adopted in this book, it is important to uncover this sense of potentiality at the heart of reception itself and to recognize the emotional impact of experiencing a performative invocation of the future that is not always already conditioned by the past or drawn into the discourse of prophecy. Uncovering the futurity of performative time in relation to specific historical moments is, I believe, crucial to understanding, for instance, the profundity of Sheridan's intervention in *The Critic*, or the extraordinarily considered representation of mediation in Cowley's late-war comedies, or the complex mobilization of Handel's vocal music in the immediate postwar period. It is my hope that the style of analysis I bring to bear on these theatrical productions and the way I read the mediation of social performances in the newspapers offer a way of reactivating our appreciation of historical change.

PART I

Diversions

CHAPTER ONE

The Agents of Mars and the Temples of Venus

John Burgoyne's Remediated Pleasures

Diversionary Tactics and Coercive Acts: Burgoyne's Fête Champêtre

On Thursday, 9 June 1774, General John Burgoyne, of Saratoga fame, arranged an elaborate Fête Champêtre at the Oaks, in Surrey, to celebrate the wedding of his nephew Lord Edward Stanley and Lady Elizabeth Hamilton. The guests included the foremost men and women of the kingdom, and this seemingly trivial gathering of fashionable society was the subject of extensive reporting in the papers. Lengthy descriptions of the event were published under the title of "Oak Gazette Extraordinary" in the *Public Advertiser*, in the *Morning Chronicle*, and perhaps most importantly in the *Gentleman's Magazine*. The title is important because the supplemental texts that were added to the papers as "Gazette Extraordinaries" were generally devoted to political or military news, and thus this text was signaling that something more than the pleasure of the elite was at stake on this evening. If the title implies that Burgoyne's Fête Champêtre is an event of some consequence, the final sentences of the "Oak Gazette Extraordinary" speak directly to charges of triviality that, despite the infiltration of cultural analysis into all manner of practices, continues to inhere: "Those who may think the repetition of this rural festival beneath the notice of a periodical work intended to record the principal transactions of the times, will, perhaps, be of another opinion, when they recollect that it is from the gravest authors we learn the diversions of the ancients."[1] The editors of the *Gentleman's Magazine* are making an argument more specific and more profound than that simply implied by the title. To suggest that this report is comparable to similar passages in the ancients is to argue not only that the magazine itself is recording a history comparable to that of the Roman Empire but also that this "diversion" tells us something about the current imperial situation.

The term *diversion* here is significant because, as the *Oxford English Dictionary* indicates, it constitutes the "turning away of the thoughts, attention, etc., from fatiguing or sad occupations, with the implication of pleasurable excitement; distraction, recreation, amusement, entertainment." As Steele indicated in *Tatler*, no. 89, "Diversion, which is a kind of forgetting our selves, is but a mean Way of Entertainment."[2] Steele's usage emphasizes that a diversion is an entertainment, however facile, that instantiates forgetting. Implicit in these definitions is a recognition that diversion is fundamentally connected to sadness or aggravation and, even in its enactment, is but a temporary abatement of displeasure.[3] The *Gentleman's Magazine* text subtly reinforces this point when it emphasizes the relationship between accounts of diversion and the gravity of ancient authors. In that term *gravity* lurks a historical shadow.

The "Oak Gazette Extraordinary" makes a great deal of General Burgoyne's management of the Fête Champêtre, and I would argue that the reiteration of his involvement in the event immediately before the editorial argument for its historical importance is not coincidental. It is important to remember that during the months when this celebration was being organized Burgoyne was an active parliamentarian working with Lord North—a notable participant in the *fête*—to pass the Coercive Acts. When news of the Boston Tea Party reached Britain in January 1774, the Ministry moved quickly to punish the residents of Massachusetts by passing the Boston Port Act on 31 March, the Administration of Justice Act on 20 May, the Quartering Act on 2 June 1774, and the Quebec Act on 16 June. A quick glance at the *Gentleman's Magazine* for 1774 or at any of the dailies in this period reveals that the press was overwhelmed with discussions of how best to discipline the American colonies. And these parliamentary measures, quickly renamed the Intolerable Acts by the colonists, not only instigated further insurrection and revolutionary organization among the residents of Massachusetts but also precipitated widespread resistance in the arena of colonial print culture.[4]

Burgoyne and Stanley were strident advocates for military intervention in America.[5] On 19 April 1774, in a widely reported speech, Burgoyne censured the colonies before the House of Commons in a symptomatic fashion: "I look upon America to be our child, which I think we have already spoiled by too much indulgence. . . . It is said, if you remove this duty, you will remove all grievances in America: but I am apprehensive that it is the right of taxation they contend about, and not the tax. It is the independent state of that country upon the legislature of this, which is contended for."[6] Burgoyne supported the so-called Coercive Acts and the appointment of General Thomas Gage as military governor of the Massachusetts Bay Colony. Yet he also found time to work with Robert Adam on the design of the "temporary building" at the Oaks, to build an *orangerie,* to write the lyrics for much of the music, and to draft the pantomime that would eventually be incorporated into a play at Drury Lane the following November under the title *The Maid of the Oaks.*[7] As the legislative timetable indicates, Burgoyne was working on both the passage of the Coercive Acts and the staging of the Fête Champêtre intermittently during the same period. Considering the fact that Burgoyne had only recently been involved, under the aegis of the Select Committee, in the acrimonious attempt to have Lord Clive impeached and to reform the East India Company, one could argue that the Fête Champêtre was a diversion charged with the very specific task of forgetting not only imperial crisis but also long-standing imperial mismanagement.[8]

In spite of the scholarly neglect of singular events such as this, the sheer cost of the Fête Champêtre and the extraordinarily detailed representation of the entertainment in the papers put it on par with any production at Drury Lane or Covent Garden. Sybil Rosenfeld made this point some time ago in her groundbreaking work on private theatricals, and Gillian Russell has demonstrated recently that these performances provide the opportunity for the detailed analysis of the interface between cultural dissemination and social practice.[9] Because of their lack of authorship, their intense topicality, and their formal variousness, diversionary extratheatrical performances have eluded cultural criticism and, hence, our understanding of enlightenment society. In this, they share a great deal with related performance practices, such as pasticcio and pantomime.[10] My intention here is to explore one example of these celebratory events and attempt to work through a style of cultural analysis that might reasonably account for the gravity of diversion. The Fête Champêtre offers a compelling example for analysis, in part because it is staged at such an important historical moment and in part because it demonstrates the combined power of formal hybridity and topicality not only to elicit pleasure but also to perform crucial historical work through mediated repetition.

Unpacking that complex sentence is the burden of the following paragraphs, but the first thing to recognize is that the Fête Champêtre incorporates formal elements of both pantomime and pasticcio. As the following account of the first masque indicates, the entertainment involves a complex theatricality:

On the right from the company, swains appeared in fancy dresses, amusing themselves at the game of nine-pins, whilst shepherdesses, neatly attired, were at the swing. On the left side were other swains with their bows and arrows, shooting at a bird which had perched itself upon a maypole; whilst others were shewing their agility by dancing and kicking at a *tambour de basque*, which hung, decorated with ribbands, from a bough of a tree.—In short, every rural pastime was exhibited.

In the centre of the *orangerie* sat Mrs. Barthelemon and Mr. Vernon, making wreaths of flowers, and continued in that employment till after the company had taken their seats upon the benches, placed in a circular form on the green. As soon as the ladies and gentlemen were thus arranged, two Cupids went round with a basket of the most rich flowers, and presented each lady with an elegant *bouquet*; the gentlemen had likewise a similar present.—When the Cupids had distributed the flowers, nimble shepherdesses supplied their baskets with fresh assortments.—Thus, whilst the attention of the company was taken up with admiring the agility and pretty manners of these little attendants accomodating the nobility and others with their nosegays, they were on a sudden surprized with the harmonious sound from the instrumental band, which being conveyed to the company through the orange plantation and shrubbery, created a most happy and pleasing effect—and which was still the more heightened by the company not being able to distinguish from what quarter it came.

This symphony, whose sweetness of sound had given every face a smile of approbation, being ended, Mr. Vernon got up, and with a light and rustic air called the nymphs and swains to celebrate the festivity of the day, informing them, that Stanley, as Lord of the Oaks, had given the invitation, and on that account he commanded their appearance to join the festive song and dance. After this air followed a grand chorus, which was composed in so remarkable a stile, and carried with it so much jollity, that the company could scarce be prevailed upon to keep their seats. Next followed a dance by Sylvans; then a song by Mrs. Barthelemon; afterwards a different dance by the whole assembly of *figurantes* was executed in a masterly stile, and was succeeded by a most elegant and pleasing duet by Mrs. Barthelemon and Mr. Vernon, which concluded with a dance. The next air consisted of four verses, sung by Mr. Vernon; at the end of each line was a chorus. The dance of the Sylvans continued during the whole time of the chorus, and had an excellent effect. (263–64)

The discourse here is typical of theatre reviews from the daily papers and informed readers would recognize the affiliations of the chief performers: both Mrs. Barthélemon and Mr. Vernon had notable London careers.[11] The event does not stage a harlequinade, but the daily papers refer to the elaborate Cupid and Hymen interlude that concludes the second masque as a pantomime.[12] And, as the *St. James Chronicle* is careful to point out, the dances, which constitute a significant portion of the entertainment, were "under the direction of Signor Lepy, the Opera House Ballet Master."[13] And yet, this is not simply a private theatrical in the sense of a play presented by and for a private audience outside the licensing of eighteenth-century theatre. These theatrical and operatic elements are mobilized within a much broader performance dynamic whose full implications require not only that we be attuned to a more various aesthetic field but also that we consider the larger physical spaces within which these more intimate performances occur.

Francophile Pleasures, or How to Read

Although not of the first rank, Burgoyne was an experienced impresario of aristocratic entertainment who had firsthand experience with continental art and sociability. In fact, his relationship with the architect and designer Robert Adam was first established in France and Italy in the mid-1750s. The Fête Champêtre was not Burgoyne's first collaboration with Adam: a year earlier, they worked together on an equally extravagant ball and supper to celebrate the coming-of-age of Lord Stanley.[14] But the Fête Champêtre marks a significant magnification of scale. The temporary building alluded to in the "Oak Gazette Extraordinary" was a completely realized pavilion, whose stateroom alone was over 120 feet long, that could accommodate more than 300 people.[15] Adam's building was reported to cost five thousand pounds and was apparently dismantled immediately after the event.[16] Furthermore, the Fête Champêtre also marks a palpable increase in aesthetic ambition because it is a complex engagement with an entire history of aristocratic sociability. One avenue for analysis would be to trace the motifs and architectural semiotics of Burgoyne's entertainment to the English court masques of King Charles I and Queen Henrietta Maria staged by Inigo Jones in the 1630s. Thomas Carew's masque *Coelum Britannicum* (1634) is particularly relevant because, like Burgoyne's *fête*, it also deploys the pagan British past.[17] But this chapter pursues a different line of affiliation. The title of Burgoyne's entertainment and many of its internal details evoke the actual practice of *fêtes galantes* in early eighteenth-century France and, perhaps more importantly, the complex representation of these forms of elite sociability in Watteau's *fêtes galantes* paintings.[18]

Specific elements of the first masque are highly reminiscent both of the self-conscious theatricality of these events and of Watteau's images.[19] The *St. James Chronicle* emphasizes that "its Name was truly characteristic, as every fanciful rustic Sport and Game was introduced; there were Groupes of Shepherds and Shepherdesses variously attired, who skipped about, kicking at the Tambourines which were pendant from the Trees, and an infinite number of persons habited as Peasants who attended Swings and other Amusements."[20] The swing, of course, is particularly iconic and, when combined with the kicking of the tambourines, activates, as Donald Posner has argued, an entire erotic economy.[21] Furthermore, the integration of pantomimical interludes into the overall proceedings goes directly to the genesis of these countertheatres.[22] Burgoyne, either through contact with the myriad reproductions of Watteau's imagery or through the dissemination of past aristocratic social practices, is staging a highly artificial form of entertainment, which despite its apparent frivolity is fundamentally connected to the recalibration of aristocratic identity during a period of increasing state absolutism.

The basis for this latter claim lies in the important work of Thomas Crow, Julie Anne Plax, and Sarah R. Cohen on Watteau's *fêtes galantes*. All three scholars have demonstrated that the intermixture of "peasants," commedia figures, and aristocrats in some apparently arcadian scene is not, pace Posner, simply a matter of invention but a complex response to the performance of aristocratic identity during a period when elite constituencies were both recognizing and strangely embracing their marginalization in the state. Citing numerous examples of elaborate country entertainments, which in their broad contours sound remarkably like Burgoyne's extravaganza, these scholars have resuscitated a performance culture that borrowed extensively from popular fair entertainments and commedia dell'arte but which was fundamentally invested in the articulation of aristocratic exclusivity and sociability beyond the immediate dictates of the king or his ministers. As Plax argues,

> Elite behaviour at *fêtes* was marked by a refusal to succumb to the liberating nature of a *fête*. . . . To do this required a distancing from and mediation of experiences that were raw and erotic. This mediation was accomplished through a highly ritualized and artificial mode of behaviour, one that masked sexual tactics. Under the guise of an artificial second self, the individual was free to enjoy the erotic pleasures and

dangers of a *fête* indirectly, filtered through an aestheticizing refinement and distancing.[23]

The complexity of the transmission and adoption of these behaviors cannot be underestimated, and it would be an error to simply read Burgoyne's Fête Champêtre as the importation of the *fête galante* not only because there are internal discrepancies in both form and content that make the party at The Oaks unique but also because such a replication would be counter to the very playfulness that Watteau's paintings reveal.[24] The relationship between Burgoyne's Fête Champêtre and these earlier *fêtes* is far more ironic than it would first appear, and I would suggest that it is the very ambivalence of Watteau's representations that gives Burgoyne the aesthetic room to develop a critical relation to the practices ostensibly celebrated at The Oaks on 9 June 1774.

That ambivalence is nowhere more palpable than in the play of desire in all of these scenes. The erotic economies of Watteau's *fêtes galantes* are famously difficult to read and thus subject to interpolation of all kinds. The long-standing controversy over the *Pilgrimage to Cythera* is only the most notable example.[25] But this is precisely the point, because Watteau is developing a kind of representation that calls the viewer to account. To borrow a phrase from Plax, the "disguised nonsignaling bodies" of Watteau's paintings test the very status of the viewer, because only the elect can recognize the code of artifice and when it is being adhered to and when it is not. As she states, "Watteau's figures send out contradictory signals and provide incomplete information in a way that visually articulates the underlying assumptions and outward forms of elite social practice. . . . The artist's visual economy and structuring of the scene reproduces in many ways the processes by which the elite play operates and produces larger meanings in real life."[26] At the risk of comparing great things to small, could we not argue that the "Oak Gazette Extraordinary" works in much the same way that Plax suggests Watteau's *fêtes galantes* paintings "represent" social practice? After all, the description of Burgoyne's extravaganza has no shortage of explicit references not only to these images but to the erotic practices carefully coded therein. The swing comes immediately to mind, as does the complex Hymeneal pantomime. For the reader well versed in these signs, the entire evening resolves into a scene of erotic play, but the specific erotic investments of the guests are indeterminate. We have a rather prominent homage to Venus, but does this imply that England, or at least this little part of it, is allegorically related to the island of Cythera? And does it imply, as in Watteau's treatment of this topos, that we are in retreat from the Temple of Mars, with all its implication of martial subjectivity and state power? These are ultimately unanswerable questions. At the representational remove of this newspaper account, what comes to the fore is not any particular erotic encounter but the movement of the entire company through a field of sexualized signs. In other words, the social identity of the guests lies not only in their facility as a collective to inhabit this space of indirection, disguise, and dissimulation but also in their capacity to read the carefully coded textualization of it. Significantly, the "Oak Gazette Extraordinary" emphasizes the exclusivity of this reading practice through a rhetoric of elision: passages such as "Thus ended the second part; of which, by this description, the reader will judge of the elegance and grandeur" simultaneously withhold information and declare that at least some part of the readership is fully capable of filling in the blanks.

But if the "Oak Gazette Extraordinary," like many of Watteau's paintings, puts the reader into a subject position wherein his or her social affiliation will be tested, there are also indications that, through the careful regulation of the flow of desire and social circulation, the event builds an argument about the relationship between elite sociability and the practices of the state. Put simply in the form of a question, what are we to make of Burgoyne staging an event that would allow the social elite to enact both its exclusivity and its distinction from the state, when he himself and many of the guests were so deeply involved in its affairs—all this at a time when the luxury and dissipation of the upper orders were the subject of intense political scrutiny and recrimination? Is this a celebration of exclusivity and aristocratic identity, or a demonstration of the dangers of licentiousness? Or both? I would suggest that a careful reading of how the events unfold indicates that Burgoyne is staging an argument about aristocratic sociability that has important implications for the martial identity of the nation.

Burgoyne's Fête Champêtre is divided into two distinct sections defined largely by their environs. The first masque takes place on the back lawn of the park, whose oak groves gave their name to the estate. The second phase of the evening, which is broken into two "masques," takes place inside Robert Adam's neoclassical pavilion, which is itself surrounded by the park. Before discussing the relationship between the distinct performances staged in these two spaces, it is important to recognize, as the "Oak Gazette Extraordinary" does, that aside from the invited guests there was a "concourse of people on each side of the road [leading into the park]," and that "the branches of the trees [were] bending with the weight of heads that appeared as thick as codlings on a tree in a plentiful season" (263). Later in the text, these observers are referred to explicitly as a "public": "Thus ended the first *masque*, which the public had an opportunity of seeing in some degree as well as the visitors; and the loud acclamations of joy at the conclusion, was a convincing proof of the high opinion entertained by the nobility and gentry of this rural festival" (264). Because this statement carefully maintains some ambiguity about who precisely breaks into applause at the end of the first masque, the "high opinion" in the final clause can be interpreted both as the approbation of the visitors with the entertainment and as the approbation of those excluded from the *fête* for the leisure activities of their superiors. At one level, it would appear that the public is presented here to simply forestall charges of excess by stating that those excluded approved of their exclusion. This ambiguity not only performs a double legitimation of the *fête* but also raises the question of the relationship between the partial view of the "codlings" and the necessarily mediated relation of the readers to the event.

If the codlings in the trees constitute a public, then what is its relation to the print public rhetorically figured forth from the "Oak Gazette Extraordinary?" The partiality of the codlings' view is important, because, despite readers' efforts to distance themselves from those physically excluded from the event, it captures the predicament of reading. The text, like the trees that give the codlings some vantage point on the action, allows the reader partial access to the world of elite leisure. But this is true only of the first masque: it is directly experienced by the guests, partially observed by the codlings, and indirectly presented to the readers. Regardless of who they are, this means that the readers are structurally aligned with the codlings aspiring to both "see" the *fête* and descend from the trees to engage in the games of love presented before them. This subtle rhetorical gesture instantiates the desire to get beyond the privation of reading and enter into the plenitude of performance—to leave the tree-like restriction of textuality. This may sound odd, but it is crucial to both the performative and textual tactics of the *fête*'s second half. The second portion of the evening is fully ensconced within Robert Adam's pavilion, and thus it cannot be observed by the public lining the road and perched in the trees. When the "Oak Gazette Extraordinary" goes on to describe the events inside the building, the reading public gains access denied to those with whom they were previously aligned. In other words, the reader is hailed into a privileged position that structurally—or, should we say, architecturally—excludes the codlings. This not only fulfills the desire generated in the first masque but also marks a distinction between this reading public and the local observers of the *fête*, whose approbation was so carefully staged.

Because everything about the account and the codlings metaphor itself renders the excluded local observers as some sort of dispossessed tenants or even peasants whose interpretive skills are so limited that they merely recognize the superiority of their betters, this invention of readerly privilege both provides a comfortable social space for the reader of the "Oak Gazette Extraordinary" and opens up a potentially critical relation to the represented practices. By asserting the approbation of the codlings and then conferring privilege to the reader, there is an opportunity afforded for the reader to own up to that privilege by exercising his or her aesthetic and moral judgment with more sophistication. In short, to now read the scene with all of one's aesthetic skill and critically engage with the performance, one will demonstrate whether one truly deserves to be among the elect. However, this also implies that election and distinction will be grounded on a critique of the practices arranged by Burgoyne.

Paradoxically, the *fête* provides an opportunity for both its participants and those reading about it to subtly distance themselves from the roles performed therein. But this act of distancing is itself carefully regulated, so that this distinction represents a very specific manifestation of aristocratic power. This is why the event is broken into an inside-outside structure, and why the Francophile *fête galante* is staged in plein air and the entertainments contained within the pavilion allegorically migrate to fantasies of British national supremacy. My contention is that the first masque is explicitly staged to encapsulate the forms of Francophile elite leisure that, despite the codlings approbation, were regularly used as examples of aristocratic dissipation. The second section of the evening rescues its elite guests—and the readers—from these charges by suggesting that to imagine that the pleasure afforded by these events somehow captures the truth of aristocratic bearing is simply another instance of the "partiality" of such a reading practice. Those invited into Adam's pavilion, including the readers of the "Oak Gazette Extraordinary," are thus privileged because they are able to read the libertine excess of the first masque as a pose or a performance that is staged in order to be both enjoyed and resisted. It is the capacity for this resistance among guests and readers alike that makes them able protectors of "the oak, its prosperity and advantage" (265). And this question of protection is not only a matter of nativism but also one of patrician military rule.

National Fantasy, or How to Feel

The spatial distinction between the first masque and the events in the pavilion can be understood via the contrasting erotic economies associated with each space. From the beginning of the first masque to its end, the guests are involved in what amounts to a pilgrimage to Adam's Temple of Love. In this sense, the first masque is a variation on the myriad pilgrimages to Cythera that preoccupied not only Watteau and other painters but also a host of French poets in the late seventeenth and early eighteenth centuries. While the direction of the movement of the guests here has none of the ambiguity of Watteau's famous painting, the space itself is replete with the signs of erotic engagement. We have already noted the prominence of the shepherdesses occupied with the swing, and how this signifies both the motion of sexual intercourse and, more subtly, female inconstancy.[27] And this well-worn figure is supplemented with the arguably even more strenuous metaphor of tambourine kicking; the text is careful not to specify the sex of those kicking at the suspended tambour, thus allowing the reader to imagine the view afforded by shepherdesses at this sport. From here the signs of sexual practice become both more chaste and more perverse.

By setting all this in a very quickly assembled orangery,[28] Burgoyne not only made yet another reference to the leisure practices of the French elite—the *orangerie* at the Palais de Louvre was replicated throughout the century—but also surrounded the visitors with orange blossoms that, because they were white, represent innocence at the same time that the oranges, like the gourds in Watteau, emblematize fecundity. But this backdrop of chastity only serves to highlight the availability of those around them. The cupids and shepherdesses unleashed on the guests draw them into their world of erotic inconstancy first by flirting with them and second by festooning them with flowers, such that the participants are swirled into an arabesque of promiscuous association—both at the level of bodily performance and at the level of signs. I am using the term arabesque here in the decorative sense. Thomas Crow has argued very persuasively that many of Watteau's key gestures in the *fêtes galantes* come from his experience producing arabesques that featured figures interacting with their decorative ground.[29] This has important resonances for Adam's design of the pavilion because his celebrated decorative insets eschew this kind of promiscuity. As we will see, Adam's pavilion is not a Temple of Venus but rather a Temple of Hymen, with all the erotic restraint implied by this evocation of conjugal marriage. In contrast, everything in the first masque—the sylvan dancers, the operatic performances, the poses of the figurantes—enacts the frequent allusions to music, dance, and theatre in the *fêtes galantes*. The artificiality of these erotic exchanges is emphasized by the almost magical concealment of the source of the music, and it should come as no surprise that Mr. Vernon both sings and manipulates the very flowers that mark the guests' role in the erotic simulation.

But there is one chain of signification that runs counter to this seeming enactment of Watteau but which actually engages with and alters one of Watteau's persistent thematics. I am referring to the King and Queen of the Oaks, who seem to operate alongside the dominant erotic economy of the first masque. In this context, the specification of these roles does not seem particularly important: it is merely another element of the sylvan topos that dominates this section of the performance. But it is important to recognize that they are not the king and queen of the *orangerie* and that therefore they move separate from the others. The scholarship on the *fêtes galantes* is in general agreement about their direct debt to the forms of commedia and pantomime practices in the fairs in Paris. In fact, it is the artifice of these theatrical forms that provides the model for the ambiguous subjectification both at the heart of the social performance of the *fêtes galantes* and at the core of Watteau's practice. Lord Stanley's and Lady Elizabeth Hamilton's appearance in the first masque as the King and Queen of the Oaks is comparable to stock roles, such as those performed by Harlequin and Columbine, in that, while they may involve themselves in the erotic lives of the inamorata, they are subtly aligned, not with the erotic world of orange blossoms and nosegays, but rather with the oaks that not only contain this artificial world but also support the lower orders, the codlings who watch the festivities from outside. As we have already noted, these codlings are invoked in order to declare their loyalty to their king and queen, and thus there is the subtle suggestion, simply in their specification, that the matrimonial couple is distinct from the erotic play of the guests. The symbolic link between the conjugal fidelity of the King and Queen of the Oaks, the loyal but excluded viewers, and the nation both metaphorically and metonymically invoked by the oaks themselves emerges as an important counterdiscourse that will eventually dominate the *fête*.

The King and Queen of the Oaks play a crucial role, because they are the ones who lead the company from the free-flowing erotic economy of the first masque into the neoclassical pavilion away from the view of their loyal but limited codling subjects. Lord Stanley and Lady Hamilton literally move the guests from one erotic realm to another, and this involves, as we will see, a shift in the dynamics of sociability, the emergence of the pavilion as an actor in its own right, and a radical reconfiguration of the symbolic economy of the staged performances. The oaks, which were partially occluded by the *orangerie* and thus consigned to the status of decorative backdrop, now emerge as the subject of repeated encomiums. The Francophilia that marginalized the oaks in the first masque dissolves, and the oak, with all its patriotic significations, becomes the dominant figure for both aristocratic and national distinction.

However, the way that shift takes place is vitally important. As the guests move from outside to inside, they find themselves in a highly regulated architectural space. Adam's pavilion features an octagonal vestibule that leads into a grand ballroom. Around the ballroom is a vast semicircular supper room, which gives the building its semicircular shape (fig. 1.1). But the floor plan does not correspond to the guests' experience of the space. The game of concealment, which saw the music hidden from view in the first masque, is here repeated but on the level of visual ornamentation and architectural space. Extensive draperies concealed the supper room and thus established the desire to see what was hidden behind these vast curtains of damask. As the entertainment progressed, these concealed zones were progressively and sometimes suddenly revealed. The second masque, therefore, moves from a restricted to an increasingly expansive space, from a state of constriction to one of increased mobility and exchange. In other words, the social territory, at first cramped, goes through a series of campaigns, as it were, until finally the company comes into full possession of Adam's building.

The shift into military and mercantile language here is intended to capture the most important aspect of the gradual revelation of the pavilion's architecture. Each moment of revelation is conducted by martial means, and thus this Temple of Hymen is fully permeated by the agents of Mars. The King and Queen of the Oaks deliver the guests two by two, saving them, much like animals in the ark, from the dangerous flow of desire on the back lawn, into the octagonal space of the vestibule:

> The noble visitors were first conducted through a beautiful and magnificent octagon hall, with transparent windows, painted suitable to the occasion: at the end of the great room hung six superb curtains, supposed to cover the same number of large windows; they were of crimson colour, richly ornamented with deep gold fringe. Colonades appeared on each side the room, with wreaths of flowers running up the columns; and the whole building was lined chair back high with white Persian and gold fringe; the seats around were covered with deep crimson. The company amused themselves with dancing minuets and cotillons, till half past eleven, when an explosion, similar to the going off of a large number of rockets, put the whole lively group into a consternation. This was occasioned by a signal given for the curtains, which we have before described, to fly up and exhibit to the company a large supper-room, with tables spread with the most costly dainties, all hot and tempting. (264)

According to Adam's drawing for the pavilion, the octagonal vestibule was no wider than thirty feet and the central ballroom was roughly thirty by sixty feet.

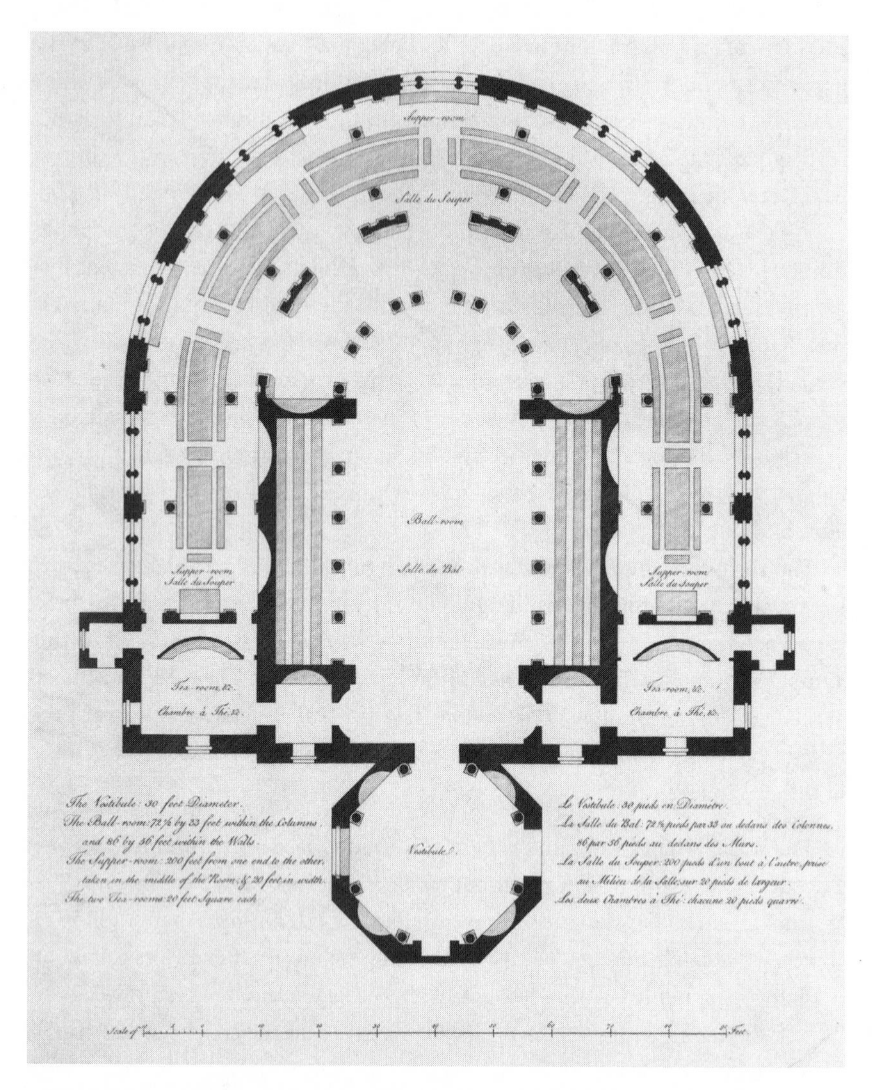

Figure 1.1. John Roberts, "Architectural plan of a pavilion erected for a Fête Champètre in the garden of the Earl of Derby at the Oaks in Surrey, with a ballroom in the centre, a supper-room surrounding and octagonal vestibule at the south entrance," engraving (1780). Reprinted in *The Works in Architecture of Robert and James Adam*, vol. 3 (1822), pl. xx. BM 1917,1208.2905. Department of Prints and Drawings © Trustees of the British Museum.

The company of roughly three hundred persons dancing in this space would be experiencing bodily intimacy of a different kind from that of the open exchange on the back lawn. After this close confinement, it is no surprise that the guests acted with consternation when the explosions signaled the rising of the curtains to reveal the supper room. They were the object of a kind of tactical maneuver aimed not only at eliciting the sublime but also at controlling their social circulation. The explosions are reminiscent of Edmund Burke's discussion of loudness and suddenness in the *Philosophical Enquiry*, but they are also textbook examples of logistical signs used to control the motion of armies. And General Burgoyne was well versed in both the aesthetic and martial effects generated here. This explosion should give us pause precisely because it is so overdetermined. As a signal for lifting the curtains, it seems somewhat extreme, but it activates a chain of martial associations that accelerate from this point onward. The explosion results in the expansion of social territory and sudden access to "the most costly dainties, all hot and tempting." It all unfolds into an apt allegory for imperial expansion: the general commands the explosion, territory is gained, and luxuries become suddenly available. In this context, the close confines of the vestibule and the ballroom, their very intimacy, constitute a kind of national space from which the guests are led to an ever more elaborate and luxurious imperium. Adam's conspicuous use of columns and classical motifs keeps the entire affair allegorically adjacent to the obvious forebears—precisely that empire referred to when the "Oak Gazette Extraordinary" refers to the gravest authors (fig. 1.2).

With this none-too-subtle invocation of empire, however, the Fête Champêtre addresses the historical significance of aristocratic leisure head on, because much of the debate surrounding the fate of the empire explicitly drew on the example of Rome to warn against excess and expansion. As much as this allegory calls up the history of Roman imperial disintegration at precisely the moment when the American colonies are in the process of dismantling Britain's Atlantic empire, it is important to recognize that Burgoyne's explosions are both tactically and logistically effective. The fear they elicit opens onto pleasure, and thus they constitute a carefully managed overcoming of social insecurity. Each spatial transition from this point onward builds on this aesthetic and tactical effect, for it unites the company and places it under the control of Burgoyne and his officers. When the curtains concealing the ballroom are drawn, "the ceremony of arranging the company next took place, and was executed by the General" (264). Burgoyne is now referred to solely by his rank, and even the King and Queen of the Oaks are under his command. The entertainment is now assigned

Figure 1.2. Robert Caldwell, after Antonio Zucchi and Robert Adam, "Inside view of the Supper-room & part of the Ball-room in a Pavilion erected for a Fête Champètre in the Garden of the Earl of Derby at the Oaks in Surry, the 9th of June, 1774," engraving (1780). BM 1917,1208.2903. Department of Prints and Drawings © Trustees of the British Museum.

to one of Burgoyne's officers. In a powerful gesture of antiquarian possession of a national prehistory, Captain Pigott comes forward as a Druid and introduces a series of songs, recitatives, and dances all "in praise of the oak, its advantage and prosperity" (265). Under military control, the oak, which was once vestigial in the performance, becomes the central sign of national and personal prosperity. Significantly, the primary agents of the erotic performance in the first masque, Mrs. Barthélémon, Mr. Vernon, and the dancers, are all recast as wood nymphs and fawns and are called into the pavilion by the Druid. This effectively reconfigures the outside erotic world of the first masque into one that is controlled by the agents of Mars. The erotic force of the songs and dances is funneled toward a fantasy of nativist national election, and thus the Cytherean script is transformed into a patriotic one.

This is nowhere more evident than in the climactic moment of the second masque, the pantomime between two Cupids that shifts the erotic narrative from scenes of inconstancy and promiscuity to one of acquisition and conjugal fidelity. Details not presented in the "Oak Gazette Extraordinary" but which surface in the papers are extremely resonant:

> A scene was also introduced exhibiting a large Groupe of Fauns and Dryads, about 30 in Number, in picturesque Habits of Tyger Skins ornamented with Oak Leaves over a fine Rose coloured Silk; these entertained the Company with a serious Dance, under the Direction of Signor Lepy, the Opera House Ballet Master. There was a Pantomime Story told by the Dance, in which Cupid and Hymen were introduced as principal characters; the little blind God was robbed of his Wings by Hymen, by way of expressing his Wish that such a Fate should ever attend his Victims.[30]

In the phantasmatic space of empire, the conjunction of oak leaves and tyger skins resolves into a fleeting expression of the Indian acquisitions that would eventually supersede the American colonies in the British imperial imaginary. But this is only a momentary allusion. The pantomime itself is arguably the evening's most important political intervention. Hymen, the god of marriage, deprives Cupid of his mobility in order to express his desire that Cupid's victims—those touched by love—would remain similarly fixed in their affections. Cupid, who is so omnipresent in the iconography of the *fêtes galantes*,[31] is here, at the Druid's request, disciplined by Hymen, such that the entire practice of love is subsumed into the institution of marriage. Patrician military rule, conjugal fidelity, and mythic figures for the longevity and endurance of the British constitution are all conjoined into a distinct fantasy of national election that is explicitly pitched as a counterperformance to the fantasy of aristocratic sociability articulated in the first masque. It is this declaration of the guests' capacity—or should we say, in light of the tactical maneuvers of the second masque, their necessity—to recognize and celebrate this conjunction that constitutes Burgoyne's articulation of an aristocratic performance suited to the historical moment. It is why this diversion is but the flip side of the coercion he was seeking to enact in the realm of policy.[32]

As we move to the end of the evening, it becomes clear that the entire event has a roughly dialectical structure. The free flow of the first masque is set in contrast to the rigorous drill-like discipline of the second masque. And Captain Pigott, in his role as the Druid, has the magical ability to effect a synthesis by transforming the outside space such that it can be united with the disciplined sociability inaugurated in the pavilion. This is hinted at when he calls the principal performers, now subtly transformed, in from the garden, but it reaches its full manifestation in the third masque. After the Hymeneal pantomime, the company is released into the ballroom where it pursues its desires first in the highly structured form of the minuet and then in the more exuberant form of the country dance (fig. 1.3). But at the very time that this is happening, the outside space is itself visually transformed:

> The Company were highly entertained with the illuminations in the gardens, which had a fine effect from the front wing of the house. Facing the temporary room was erected a large Ionic portico, supported by four large transparent columns of a bright pink colour. On a scroll on the pediment were the following words, "Sacred to propitious Venus." In the center of the pediment was a shield, with the Hamilton and Stanley arms quartered, the whole supported by a band of Cupids, who appeared to great advantage by the assistance of four pyramids of lights. (265)

The illuminations transform the outside space into another classical architectural figure, but significantly the house becomes the Temple of Venus and the pavilion, by a subtle act of subsumption, emerges as the Temple of Mars. The transit across the lawn from pavilion to house, now illuminated by pyramids of light, is no longer a self-testing journey through a dangerous space of erotic promiscuity and elite dissipation, but rather a self-consolidating exercise in fantasized election. The key word here is "propitious." By declaring the house "Sacred to propitious Venus," Burgoyne and his illuminators have entered into the realm of prophecy. And I would argue that they are suggesting that this is not simply a propitious union of husband and wife. The union effected in this synthesis of martial and marital signs generates an omen "of favourable import; regarded as indicative of the favourable disposition of God."[33] As an example of wishful thinking in its most naked form, Burgoyne's intervention invests in a fantasy of future imperial hegemony.

And yet for all this declaration of the propitiousness of the historical moment, there are figures lurking in the shadows that are not folded into the dialectical synthesis but which in fundamental ways allow for its sublation. The illumination of the garden in the third masque is clearly staged for the viewers in the pavilion, but the "Oak Gazette Extraordinary" subtly indicates that the "view" offered by the text comes from a different vantage point: "The Company were highly entertained with the illuminations in the gardens, which had a fine effect from the front wing of the house" (265). By bringing the reader momentarily to

Figure 1.3. Robert Caldwell, after Antonio Zucchi and Robert Adam, "Inside view of the Ball-room in a Pavilion erected for a Fête Champètre in the Garden of the Earl of Derby at the Oaks in Surry, the 9th of June, 1774," engraving (1780). BM 1917,1208.2904. Department of Prints and Drawings © Trustees of the British Museum.

the front wing of the house, the text does not reactivate but discretely reminds us of the former vantage point of those physically excluded from the Fête Champêtre. This reminder of the social remainder is crucial, because it emphasizes that the complex consolidation of the conjugal, national, and martial identities of the elite within the illumined confines of the garden and its pavilion is surrounded by a no-less-coercive invention of a public in the surrounding darkness. In this particular time and place, both publics, the one in the light and the one in the dark, are subject to the actual and representational discipline of the military. At the same time that Burgoyne and Captain Pigott are managing the carnivalesque potential of aristocratic celebrants, we should not be surprised to find that "A Troop of Burgoyne's Light Horse attended to prevent Disorder" in the outside world.[34] In other words, the social and aesthetic synthesis achieved in the third masque relies upon the ever-present but shadowy threat of physical force. When we remember the importance of the "consternation" generated by the explosions in the second masque, it should become clear that it is fear above all else that both makes room for and conditions Burgoyne's stylization of aristocratic sociability in the Fête Champêtre. It is confidence in military force that undergirds the celebration's certitude regarding Britain's ability to retain the American colonies.

Topicality and Repetition: *The Maid of the Oaks*

Could we not argue, though, that the readers of the "Oak Gazette Extraordinary" are relatively free of this coercion and that, in the accession to this freedom, the reading public partakes of a form of counterleisure?[35] Within the republic of letters there would appear to be a possibility, indeed a necessity, for critique. This is an important question because the mediation and dissemination of the event only becomes more complex when we follow the replication of the Fête Champêtre in the ensuing months and years.[36] Aside from myriad topical poems and satirical remarks in the papers, Burgoyne's diversion at The Oaks generated three further representations beyond the textual accounts in the newspapers and the "Oak Gazette Extraordinary": two theatrical entertainments and a set of remarkable paintings.[37] And it may well be the starting point for one of the most infamous celebratory moments in the 1770s: the Mischianza staged by Captain John André to mark General William Howe's departure from occupied Philadelphia in the spring of 1778.

The most notable of the theatrical treatments was a much-debated "Dramatic Entertainment" entitled *The Maid of the Oaks* that was written by Burgoyne himself, altered by Garrick, and staged at Drury Lane on 5 November 1774.[38] Numerous biographical sources on Burgoyne state that the play was performed at the Fête Champêtre, but I can find no evidence of this.[39] In fact, both the printed editions of the play and the smaller collection of the songs and choruses emphasize otherwise: "Considerable parts of the poetry, musick, and scenery, of the Maid of the Oaks, have been taken (by permission) from an entertainment given by a noble Lord, last summer, . . . [but] As to the piece, into which these parts are now introduced, and which bears no reference to the entertainment alluded to, it is the first attempt of the author in dramatic writing."[40] The play clearly incorporated elements of the performances from the Fête Champêtre, but these are both truncated and framed by a protocomedy clearly designed for theatrical exhibition in a licensed theatre. The play is replete with references to the performers and designers of the Drury Lane production, so what we have is a play that takes as its topic not only the earlier performance at The Oaks but also its mediation both in the papers and in the theatrical production itself.

What interests me about this situation is that an already self-referential event has been reframed for yet another consideration by the public, but now in the context of theatrical representation. The interplay between the topical knowledge of the Fête Champêtre derived from the papers—or, in a few cases, from actually being at the event—and the performance of the players becomes here a crucial element of the play's reception. "The plot," according to every review of the play, "in a great measure closes in the fourth act, and the fifth is chiefly compounded of scenery, music, and dancing introduced as a celebration of the wedding of the Maid of the Oaks, but the idea of this act is taken in many parts from a masque at the famous Fête Champêtre given by a noble Lord last summer."[41] What we have then here is a particularly rich example of the tight relationship not only between social practice and theatrical sociability but also between what I would argue are two fundamentally complementary media: the newspapers and the theatre. The subtle distinctions between the earlier representations of the event and the Drury Lane production offer a valuable site for considering the relationship between repetition and topicality in eighteenth-century theatrical experience. And I would argue that this relationship is crucial to how I want to think about theatre as a social practice in this historical moment.

Topicality, although largely untheorized, has been an issue of some concern for critics of eighteenth-century theatre because it is often simultaneously a fundamental component of a play's success in its initial productions and the very quality that compromises the ostensible aesthetic value of the play with the passage of time. This becomes a key methodological problem because most of the axiological principles that motivate literary study, and which tend to infuse cultural criticism in general, are intimately connected to notions of aesthetic autonomy that do not apply to many artistic productions in the period we are discussing. If we restrict our discussion to the theatre, one would expect that, with the monopoly afforded by the Licensing Act, the patent houses, especially in the '50s, '60s, and '70s, were in a position to categorically protect the integrity of legitimate tragedy and comedy. But, as the endless debates in the papers regarding the nefarious influence of pantomime and the roster of playbills indicate, this was precisely not the case.[42] At every juncture, one finds hybrid forms whose success depends on spectacle or topicality, asserting their palpable audience appeal in the seasons of the patent houses. And even on evenings ostensibly devoted to tragedy or five-act comedy, one is confronted with afterpieces, inserted songs, dances, and the like that compete internally with the mainpiece not only for audience attention but also for commentary in the papers. Furthermore, tried and true stock pieces were consistently, and partially, allegorized by managers and audiences alike in order to fit current and passing events.

It is not enough to simply state that these developments were driven by receipts, although that is no doubt part of the issue. The sheer expansion of commercial entertainment generated hitherto unseen social and cultural effects. Topical entertainment is part of a larger cultural development whose most obvious avatar is the newspapers. With the century's progressive expansion of daily, triweekly, and monthly venues for the discussion of social, political, and cultural affairs came new possibilities for representational pleasure. It has rarely been asked what kind of pleasure is afforded by the papers, but I would argue that the answer to this question is important to how we think about theatrical reception. A typical eighteenth-century daily prints advertising on the first page and then offers a jumble of political, social, and theatrical intelligence across the remaining three pages. Theatrical news is generally divided into three set formats: advertisements for upcoming performances; reviews and prologues and/or epilogues immediately after the first performance; and then inserted gossip about the world of the theatre, which sometimes takes the form of editorial letters. Society news often follows the same structure: key events are noted in advance, reviewed as it were, and then gossip proliferates in myriad forms.[43] What we would conventionally call "hard news" takes the form of dispatches from various parts of the globe, parliamentary reporting (after 1764), or formalized accounts of shipping, military activity, and the like.[44]

Cowper's treatment of this mélange is perhaps the most important period discussion of this representational dynamic, and much has been made of his analysis of the spatial dynamics of newspaper reading. In *The Task*, he talks of the thrill not only of transporting himself all over the globe via the papers but also of the strange frisson of finding important political news immediately adjacent to accounts of ballooning and the magician–quack scientist Katterfelto.[45] We can discern two pleasures here: that of the fantasy of unrestricted movement, and that of a carnivalesque jumbling of social hierarchies. The former seems particularly well suited to a culture involved in massive imperial expansion, and the latter captures well the emergent capacity of the middle classes to reconfigure the social field in the latter part of the century. I have argued elsewhere that these fantasies have their theatrical attendants as well, but there are other pleasures, undiscussed by Cowper, which are perhaps even more fundamental.[46]

The more that one reads the daily newspapers in this period, the more one is struck by how they play a complex epistemological game with their readers. This is most apparent in the way society news is presented. Using strategies pioneered in the *Town and Country Magazine* and then popularized by the *Morning Post*, reports of scandalous behavior, including massive losses at the gaming tables, adulterous and sodomitical affairs, dueling, and certain economic misbehaviors—in short, public representations of failures in private character—are repeatedly presented with various levels of circumlocution, euphemism, and ellipsis. This means that the reader is simultaneously put in the position of a moral judge squarely outside this realm of largely aristocratic vice and in the position of one sufficiently in the know to actually comprehend the narrative. In other words, the newspapers carefully cast the reader both inside and outside the scene of scandal and thus allow the reader to pursue his or her prurient interests, at the same time that he or she enjoys both the moral superiority and schadenfreude continually made available by the world of fashion.[47] I would argue that this feeling of being in the know, and yet somehow free of scrutiny, is one of the great inventions of the age, because it allows for a remarkable consolidation of community. To be able to piece together from ellipses and circumlocutions who did what to whom carries not only the pleasure of epistemophilia—I know the world well enough to "read" this—but also the pleasure of fictional intimacy—there is a subset of readers sufficiently in the know to understand this, and they are like me. The newspapers, with their vast market, worked out very early on how to generate a technology of intimacy that allowed individual readers to fantasize that they were part of a social circle beyond themselves, but which was nevertheless deemed exclusive. And this inculcation of faux exclusivity paradoxically relied on the mass circulation of the papers themselves.

Refinement, Remediation, Renunciation

We have to consider the possibility that a similar dynamic is at work in the audience of many eighteenth-century plays. Topical references are frequently mobilized in the theatre to generate a fantasy of either exclusive or mutual recognition. For example, according to the printed version of *The Maid of the Oaks*, the final scene in the fourth act takes place in front of a painting "taken from a Portico in the Gardens of Lord Stanley, as illuminated at his entertainment last summer." Similarly, act 5 is set in a saloon that the printed version of the play indicates is "a representation of the temporary saloon, as designed by Mr. Adam, and erected at Lord Stanley's."[48] The printed version of the play makes this explicit, but in production a significant element of the pleasure afforded by the play relies on the audience's being able to recognize these scenes. And that recognition depends not simply on—in this case—Philippe Jacques De Loutherbourg's scenic accuracy, as Allen suggests,[49] but also on the audience's memory of the reports of the Fête Champêtre six months earlier. But this rememorative act is quite complex. On opening night, before the circulation of the reviews and the publication of the play, the audience would have to make the connection to the earlier event using evidence internal to the play itself. For subsequent audiences, the reference to the earlier event would have been well enough in circulation to allow the vast majority of viewers to "recognize" the Fête Champêtre's lurking presence. So on its initial production, *The Maid of the Oaks* effectively distills its audience into a public sufficiently in the know to recognize the rehearsal of the Fête Champêtre and a counterpublic temporarily unaware of the topical reference and, thus, suddenly cast as the fluid media from which the other "exclusive" group is refined by the play. This inculcates the desire to "refine" oneself, as it were, to become the element of the mixed solution that the theatrical mechanism is pursuing. And it propagates the fantasy that such a transgression of social boundaries is possible. This means that one of the pleasures afforded by the play is that of overcoming the privation that comes with social and epistemological exclusivity. And it is this dynamic, above all, that is repeated from the "Oak Gazette Extraordinary." Remember that text performed precisely this rhetorical game with inside and outside perspectives. So, at its deepest level, the play activates a complex negotiation with notions of social and cultural inclusion.[50]

It is therefore exceedingly difficult to consider the performance as aesthetically autonomous from the social world in which it is embedded. And it is not enough to say that we need to understand the social and historical context to understand audience reception, because the distinction between representation and "context" simply does not hold. This play, and many others like it that do not fall into the generic categories of tragedy or comedy, generates pleasure by virtue of its capacity to operate on the actions and desires of its immediate and mediated audiences. This is a complex situation because the structural relationship between the play and its lightly veiled topic is always already tied to the mediascape of the daily papers and the ethnoscape of social exchange and conversation.[51] Arjun Appadurai uses these terms to account for how information flows impinge upon community formation and interaction, and what I want to argue here is that *The Maid of the Oaks* subtly explores and articulates the relationship between media and ethnicity in remarkably explicit ways.

Now it may seem odd to be importing critical terms from the study of globalization to deal with a seemingly minor play, but this production, like many others in the 1770s, is very much in dialogue with the social, economic, and cultural fallout of Britain's recent emergence as a global power after the Seven Years' War. And it is haunted by the first, and arguably the most important, threat to imperial self-definition—namely, the ongoing crisis over the governance of Britain's Atlantic empire. The key recognition here, as in the preceding analysis of the Fête Champêtre, is that aristocratic sociability, which is the topic of the play, is inexorably tied to the audience's faith in patrician governance of both the imperial state and its military avatars. If that connection seems strained, then we need to recognize that the subject is being handled not directly but through a remarkably sophisticated engagement with the public's relation to information. We should not be surprised therefore to discover that the most successful elements of the "plot" that Burgoyne and Garrick contrived to frame the topical references actually focus on the relationship between social practice and its representation in the papers. Furthermore, the paratheatrical materials—especially the prologue and the generic debate instantiated by Burgoyne's preface to the play—explicitly address the interrelationship between mediation and the desire for social refinement. As we have already noted, the Fête Champêtre was also involved in a form of refinement—its audience was refined by martial tactics to exemplify styles of normative patriotic power whose most visible elements impinged on questions of sexuality. What we need to ask is what kind of refinement is effected by this play and its remediation in the papers? Is there a theatrical equivalent to the explosions set off within Robert Adam's pavilion?

The question of refinement became a subject of explicit debate in the papers, but before we look at this we need a stronger sense of the play's implicit staging of the Fête Champêtre, along with the world of the newspapers and of aristocratic sociability in general. As all the reviewers emphasized, the plot of *The Maid of the Oaks* was neither original nor compelling, but they offered unusually detailed accounts of the "fable." As many of the papers indicated, the play resembles the kind of three-act entertainment staged by Samuel Foote at the Haymarket during this period but now inflated into five acts by the addition of extensive musical interludes and dancing. It is helpful to have Foote's *The Nabob* in mind, because it shares a great deal with this production. The play is set on The Oaks, Mr. Oldworth's estate, on the day of his elaborate celebration of the marriage of Sir Harry Groveby and his ward Maria, the eponymous Maid of the Oaks. Oldworth is clearly a thinly veiled Burgoyne, and Sir Harry and Maria correspond to Lord Stanley and Lady Elizabeth Hamilton respectively. The first act opens with the introduction of a young macaroni named Dupeley, recently arrived from the continent: "Full of all the fashionable prejudices in favour of foreign education, and above all, conceited with his knowledge of womankind, and convinced that there is not one of the sex cunning enough to impose upon him."[52] During this opening scene, Sir Harry, Dupeley, and Oldworth with his bustling servant Hurry quickly sketch in the broad contours of the day's pastoral entertainment, and the references to the Fête Champêtre are legion. It will take place at The Oaks, a pavilion and an orangerie are being hastily constructed, locals will play shepherds and shepherdesses, and by the end of the scene, Hurry even refers to the event as a "Sham-Peter" (1.1.10). With the topical reference well enough established, the scene shifts to a seemingly unnecessary burlesque of the preparations, which follows the tribulations of the architect with an Irish painter named O'Daub, whose primary function is, predictably, to drink, sing, and ridicule De Loutherbourg, who designed and executed the sets for the Drury Lane production. The reviews were generally quite harsh about this scene, but its metatheatricality is important because, like the first scene, it asks the audience not only to question the relationship of the representation to the preceding event but also to consider the artifice of representation itself.[53]

The rest of the play deals with two sexual narratives. The second act introduces us to the two principal women in the play. In an explicit contrast to O'Daub's drinking song, which closes the first act, Maria opens act 2 beneath a great oak singing a chaste song of pastoral romance. If the song has not already convinced the audience of her innocence and rectitude, the play emphasizes her modesty by contrasting her with Lady Bab Lardoon, a female gamester and scandalous member of the bon ton, played to great acclaim by Fanny Abington. As Gillian Russell states, Lady Bab is the play's finest construction.[54] Her primary function is to regale Oldworth and Maria with an account of the sexual and social dynamics of fashionable life and to carefully explicate their representation in the papers. After telling Oldworth and Maria that her visit to The Oaks is a welcome respite from a "horrid run" of gambling losses in Town, which were the subject of much public discussion, she informs Maria that she too will be the object of the papers' attentions:

LADY BAB: Oh, but you will have it [your name in the papers]—the Fête Champétre will be a delightful subject!—To be complimented one day, laugh'd at the next, and abused the third; you can't imagine how amusing it is to read one's own name at breakfast in a morning paper.

MARIA: Pray, how long may your ladyship have been accustomed to this pleasure?

LADY BAB: Lord, a great while, and in all its stages: They first begin with a modest innuendo, "*we hear a certain Lady, not a hundred miles from Hanoversquare, lost, at one sitting, some nights ago, two thousand guineas*—O tempora! O mores!"

OLDWORTH: (*laughing*) Pray, Lady Bab, is this concluding ejaculation your own, or was it the Printers?

LADY BAB: His, you may be sure; a dab of Latin adds surprizing force to a paragraph, besides shewing the learning of the author.

OLDWORTH: Well, but really I don't see such a great matter in this; why should you suppose any body applied this paragraph to you?

LADY BAB: None but my intimates did, for it was applicable to half St. George's parish; but about a week after they honoured me with initials and italicks: "It is said, Lady B. L's ill success still continues at the quinze table: it was observed, the same Lady appeared yesterday at court, in a *ribband collier*, having laid aside her *diamond* necklace, (diamond in italicks) as totally bourgeoise and unnecessary for the dress of a woman of fashion."

OLDWORTH: To be sure this *was* advancing a little in *familiarity*.

LADY BAB: At last, to my infinite amusement, out I came at full length: "*Lady Bab. Lardoon has tumbled down three nights successively; a certain colonel has done the same, and we hear that both parties keep house with sprained ancles.*" (2.1.24–26)

Lady Bab's attention to the materiality of print, to the way italics and initials activate both epistomophilia and moral remonstrance, is matched by a precise understanding of the pleasures afforded by rhetorical strategies of inclusion and exclusion. Lady Bab's discussion of journalistic prurience allows Burgoyne not only to stage a debate regarding representation and reputation but also to underline the importance of reading and artifice to both the pleasures of elite sociability and the pleasures afforded by topical theatrical representation. That she emphasizes that the Fête Champêtre, will—and, of course, already has—become a topic for such careful reading in the daily papers, signals the play's explicit engagement with the flow of information in the mediascape. Lady Bab's analysis of topical references in the papers shows that she is theoretically cognizant of the way reputation and desire rely on the artifice of representation.

The audience is hailed repeatedly into a similar analytical position, and the play stages a scene that demonstrates how such analytical tools are crucial for regulating social performance. Lady Bab's second set piece is easily the most theatrically satisfying scene in the play and shows her putting her analytical skills into practice. Upon being informed of Dupeley's transformation abroad, Lady Bab, with Oldworth's and Sir Harry's blessing, undertakes to entrap Dupeley by playing a bashful shepherdess in various states of undress. Her performance as "Philly Nettletop, of the vale" completely overwhelms Dupeley, who is convinced not only that she is a rustic innocent but that she is held in thrall by Oldworth, who has established a rural seraglio on his estate. Significantly, the entire scene is closely pegged to key elements of the first masque of the Fête Champêtre reported in the "Oak Gazette Extraordinary" and other papers. "Philly" pins a nosegay to Dupeley in a direct rehearsal of the shepherdesses, but unlike the guests of Burgoyne's *fête galante*, Dupeley fails to recognize the theatricality of the scene and thus demonstrates to both Oldworth and Sir Harry, who are hiding behind a tree, and the entire audience, that he lacks the capacity to manage the artificial games that characterize elite sociability and sexual exchange. Lady Bab's manipulation of signs, through its topicality and the mechanism of dramatic irony, casts the audience members as knowing and subtle readers of elite sociability and thus places them in the exclusive position—like that of Oldworth and Sir Harry, who are watching from the wings—of those capable of reading the moral dangers of aristocratic artifice. The shaming of Dupeley is great fun, but it is also the play's most acute satirical scene because it is part of a larger trend across a wide range of media to critique macaroni, or foppish, masculinity. Lady Bab, at the behest of Oldworth and Sir Harry, reforms Dupeley and, in doing so, also reforms herself. The Lady Bab–Dupeley plot concludes with Dupeley renouncing his "foreign"—read Francophile—ways, with Lady Bab renouncing gambling, and with the suggestion that they, like Maria and Sir Harry, will embrace matrimony. In other words, suspect forms of identity and exchange are reformed by staging the Fête Champêtre, and like a *fête galante*, the representational games test the characters' ability to read the scene of performance.

The second sexual narrative is less complex and less entertaining but, in its sheer predictability, is arguably no less important. We are introduced to Maria and Lady Bab in the same scene, and their progress is intertwined in intriguing ways. As Lady Bab educates Dupeley, Maria slowly learns who she is. Early in the play, it is hinted that Maria is not simply Oldworth's ward, and that the Fête Champêtre is being staged to enact a revelation. Maria is, of course,

Mr. Oldworth's daughter. But she is unaware of the fact because he has secreted her with a friend to raise her at a distance from the corrupting influence of fashion. Maria's hidden status as heiress is such a hackneyed device that Burgoyne was taken to task by almost all the reviews. Nevertheless, all the reviews go on at considerable length to separate Maria from Oldworth's name and thus to preserve her from inevitable corruption at the hands of fashionable fortune hunters.[55] With the eventual revelation of Oldworth's paternity, and the inevitable resolution of Groveby's disapproval of the match, Maria becomes the recipient of not only her father's but her father-in-law's fortune. Groveby, who is based on Lord Stanley's uncle Lord Strange, threatens to disinherit his nephew in part for not informing him of the marriage and in part because he immediately assumes that he has been duped by a fortune-hunting woman. When he discovers that Maria is the woman in question, he decides to both disinherit and reinherit his nephew by willing his property to Maria *and* sanctioning their marriage. Thus, Sir Harry's love is both radically "disinterested" (it involves no design on his fiancé's fortune and a seeming disconnection from his own) and doubly rewarded (he acquires two estates and Oldworth's foreign holdings, which are subtly implied to come from India) because Maria for her part is not a "designing woman."

So both Sir Harry and Maria's desire for each other is ostensibly separate from the pecuniary calculations that usually structure aristocratic engagements, and yet, through no effort of their own, they become the ideal union of domestic and imperial accumulation. The play has a number of asides that imply that Oldworth could be considered a Nabob; this helps to explain why Dupeley can be persuaded that Oldworth has a country seraglio: he has misread Oldworth as Sir Matthew Mite.[56] This brings the whole extravagance of the celebration into an existing discourse on imperial excess, but this issue, perhaps because of Foote's prior treatment of it in *The Nabob*, is rigorously contained before the end of the fourth act. After Maria's paternity is revealed, Groveby once again reconfigures his will:

GROVEBY: Ay, I must alter the disposition of my acres once more—I will have no Nabobs nor Nabobbesses in my family.

LADY BAB: The females would be the better of the two, for all that; they would not be guilty of so much rapacity to acquire a fortune, and they would spend it to better purposes.

DUPELEY: By as much as a province is better disposed of it in a jewel at the breast of a Cleopatra, than when it is melted down in the fat guts of mayors and burgesses of country corporations.

GROVEBY: I agree in your preference between the two; but an honest country gentleman, and a plain English wife, is more respectable and useful than both—so do you hear, Madam, take care to provide me with a second son, fit for that sort of family—let him be an honest fellow, and a jolly fellow, and in every respect a proper representative for Gloomstock-hall [Groveby's seat]. (4.2.62)

Like the repeated panegyrics to the Oak and the taming of Cupid by Hymen in the second masque of the Fête Champêtre, Groveby's literal investment in the offspring of Sir Harry and Maria's union reactivates a fantasy of country gentility, which is quite explicitly contrived to gloss over the fact that the economic convergence represented in the play is rigorously global in scope. In this regard, the play is fully in accordance with Thomas Oldham's solution to the threat of global capital to landed money in *The Nabob* (1772).[57] Both Foote and Burgoyne end up accepting the economic spoils of empire at the same time that they pilloried those who secured the empire in India. Furthermore, audience members would have been acutely aware that Burgoyne spent considerable time in 1772 and 1773 pursuing Lord Clive with charges of rapacity and misgovernment in India. This whole segment of the narrative amounts to not only another level of topicality, which has been carefully woven into the play, but also a retroactive exculpation of the extravagance of Burgoyne's own Fête Champêtre.[58] At a time when erstwhile "nabobs" were being taken to task because their excessive expenditure threatened the domestic economy and the established social hierarchies of Britain, *The Maid of the Oaks* attempts to argue for a contrasting style of extravagance that reinvigorates not only aristocratic rule but also the nation itself.

And this concern is not merely thematic; the question of expenditure is addressed in the very material processes of the production. It is worth noting that the mode of matrimonial accumulation celebrated in the play is explicitly set in contrast to the perpetual losses associated with Lady Bab's gaming and Dupeley's extravagance. So the celebration of conjugal normativity comes with a corresponding ejection or shaming of gender and economic insubordination. That celebration is itself a scene of unrestrained expenditure both in its initial model of the Fête Champêtre and in the theatre itself. A letter to the *Morning Chronicle* made much of Garrick's extravagance:

> I am told that the scenery only, which has been painted on purpose for the MAID OF THE OAKS, cost 1500*l*. This is a prodigious sum, yet it will not

> appear in the least extravagant to any body who sees it. The landscapes of Claud are scarcely equal to some of the views exhibited; and if nothing beyond the bare merit of the paintings was held forth to attract the town, I should not be surprised at its bringing twenty crouded audiences. Mr. Garrick's care however has not been confined to the scenery, it has extended to the minutest object that could encrease either the beauty or the magnificence of the entertainment. The number of singers and dancers who are pastorally habited on the occasion is incredible, and the engagement of SLINGSBY and HIDOU, the two greatest performers in the stile perhaps on earth, is a circumstance that deserves the highest approbation.[59]

For this letter writer, Garrick's expense was justified because he and Burgoyne were attempting to purvey a "very refined dish, which is only just come into fashion with our nobility."[60]

But this same expense was also an occasion for criticism and satire. A letter to the printer of the *London Evening Post* used the same details to suggest that there was something amiss:

> I made one at the first *route* of the "Maid of the Oaks" on Saturday night last. Notwithstanding all that has been previously said of her by *flatterers* and *admirers*, and that notwithstanding 1500 l. has been actually laid out in *bringing her up*, she, by no means answers public expectation; her conversation is little *snip snap* dialogue; her manners are *outré*, and, in every part of her deportment, she shews such an *ignorance* of *essentials*, that, on the whole, I think she may be truly denominated a *modern fine lady*, whose accomplishments consist in *music, dancing, paint, fine cloaths*, &c.—but *no mind*.[61]

By feminizing Burgoyne's play, this letter writer cleverly contrasts the production with Maria's ostensibly natural nobility and good sense and suggests that its real merits are those of Lady Bab Lardoon. The play is a product of fashion, therefore ultimately corrupt, and (like Lady Bab) most likely to start losing money. The satire has real bite because it suggests that Burgoyne and Garrick fail to see that the play's attempt to advocate for Maria's sexual normativity, which underpins the play's nationalist agenda, is undercut by the entertainment afforded not only by the spectacle, the dancing, and the music but also by Fanny Abington's erotic and comic attractions. The implication is either that the play's and, by extension, the Fête Champêtre's attempt to refine aristocratic sociability is merely a pretense for purveying more dissipation or, worse, that the play's producers are so "ignorant of essentials" that they cannot see the contradiction that undermines both their moral and patriotic objectives.[62]

The "essentials" referred to here are both the essential elements of good character, in the moral sense, and the fundamental elements of good comedy, in the aesthetic sense. In other words, the status of both the Fête Champêtre represented in the play and the play itself comes down to a generic debate that erupted in the papers, and which was addressed by Burgoyne in the printed version of the play. Five-act comedy is supposed to have a moral purpose, and the question posed by Burgoyne's preface to *The Maid of the Oaks* is whether this new kind of "Dramatic Entertainment," as it was called, could not only aspire to but supersede the ethical claims of comedy. His argument goes directly to the question of the balance between plot and exhibitions of refined elegance through music and dance "acquired" from the Fête Champêtre. After introducing the strange fiction of gaining permission from himself to replicate the elegance of the Fête Champêtre (i), Burgoyne polemically states that he wishes to join the "energy, spirit, sublimity, force of character, and of expression," which he associates with the English stage, to the "art, regularity, elegance, delicacy, touches of sentiment, adapted only to the most polished manners, [which] distinguish [French] Theatres" (ii–iii). The hybrid "species of entertainment" Burgoyne is projecting combines the performance of genteel accomplishments suited to the taste of the fashionable elite with simple, spirited expressions of British strength. As he states, "In literary warfare, we call their [French] compositions insipid; they describe ours as barbarous—both are unjust—all will agree, that to blend strength and refinement would be to attain perfection" (iii).

The theatrical hybrid Burgoyne presents here shares a great deal with the cultural hybridity of the Fête Champêtre. Remember that performance staged plein air pastoral scenes derived from Watteau in the first masque and held them in dialectical tension with the martial manipulation of signs of British national election in the second masque. The resolution of this dialectic was achieved by allegorically aligning the estate building with an Ionic temple "Sacred to propitious Venus," through the optical technology of illumination, and by subtly reconfiguring Adam's pavilion as the Temple of Mars. If we look closely at *The Maid of the Oaks*, we find a similar tension between the plot of the first four acts—which consistently disciplines, yet benefits from, the actions of characters like Dupeley and Lady Bab, whose manners are too foreign; lauds the native simplicity of Maria and Groveby and the disinterestedness of Sir Harry; and indulges in the digressions of O'Daub and Hurry, which would have been entirely at home in any of Foote's Haymarket comedies—and the elaborate dances and masques that dominate the fifth act, and which were performed by continental performers. What is curious is that the play significantly alters the way these divergent elements come together, and these alterations in how space is deployed, and in the order of spatial disclosure, should give us pause, because there is no internal resolution of the dialectic as in the Fête Champêtre. The resolution of the two strands of entertainment that combine to form Burgoyne's hybrid "Dramatic Entertainment" is hinted at by a kind of internal interweaving. Elements of the "French" entertainment are threaded through the "English" plot, and similarly, the final bits of plot business interrupt the songs and dances in the fifth act. Likewise, the spaces of the Fête Champêtre are interwoven, in reverse order, across the fourth and fifth acts.

As we come to the end of act 4, basically all of the plot complications have been resolved, the marriage procession of Maria and Sir Harry has taken place, and Lady Bab and Dupeley are left alone on the stage. Suddenly Lady Bab spots "a country cousin" dressed as Actaea approaching from offstage. Dupeley refers to her as a "barbarian," using the very term Burgoyne uses to signify Englishness in the preface. When she finally enters, Actaea offers to practice her song for Lady Bab before being called upon to sing in public. Lady Bab agrees to be her audience, but she and Dupeley steal off as soon as Actaea and her six hunters start to perform. In this context, the song suddenly becomes detached from the action: an ostensibly private performance that ends up being witnessed only by the audience. In this moment, the play's artifice is palpable because Actaea and her hunter companion play no role in the drama; they are an interruption pure and simple. The audience is left to sort out the place of this song in relation to the overall play, and there is little to do but recognize that it is a gratuitous insertion.

Here we have an interruption in the plot that explicitly moves the entertainment away from the traditional strategies of comedy toward a different kind of aesthetic experience. This is the first in a series of such distractions that move the entertainment not only toward increasingly distinct performances of dance and music but also toward increasingly specific replications of the spaces of the Fête Champêtre reported upon in the papers. It is this hailing of elements from the mediascape that I think warrants particular attention. Immediately after Actaea's song, the scene opens and discovers "The Gardens illuminated," and the text indicates that the scene painting is of the illuminated Portico from the Fête Champêtre. Actaea and her followers join the play's primary characters, but a country dance suddenly overwhelms the stage. At one level, the reference to the illuminated portico would seem to signal that the resolution of the dialectic between plot and spectacle or dance has been achieved, but Oldworth and Hurry take charge of the situation and direct the guests to the internal space of the pavilion:

> OLDWORTH: This is as it should be—a dance, or a song, or a shout of joy, meets me at every turn; but come, ladies, I shall trust you no more in the gardens; at least not my fair dancers; though the evening is fine it may be deceitful, we have prepared a place under cover for the rest of the entertainment.
>
> HURRY: Gentlemen, nobility, ladies and gentry, you are all wanted in the Temple of Venice, to—but I'll not say what, that you may be more surpriz'd; and if you are surpriz'd here, you'll be more surpriz'd there, and we shan't have done with you there neither—pray make haste or you'll get no places. (*They all croud off.*) (4.2.58)[63]

For audience members familiar with the reporting of the Fête Champêtre, Oldworth and Hurry effectively become a composite portrait of Burgoyne himself—directing the entertainment from above and below. But there are important gestures here for those capable of reading the scene. Oldworth indicates that this moment in the evening is comparable to the end of the first masque where the company left the dangerous erotic play of the plein air world and entered the more erotically safe, because regulated, space of Adam's pavilion. In other words, regardless of the fact that the marriage of Maria and Sir Harry has occurred and the garden has been illuminated, the company has not entered a space where the resolution of the tension between plot and spectacle or dance has been achieved. On the contrary, as Hurry emphasizes, surprises lie in store for both the players and the audience, who end up in a remarkably similar place as the grand ballets of the fifth act take over the representational economy. The implication is that Burgoyne is not done with his English audiences.

Like the second masque in the Fête Champêtre, the fifth act opens in a saloon, explicitly modeled by De Loutherbourg on Adam's pavilion.[64] And the events staged in this space bear a close resemblance to those of the second masque: the space contains curtained-off areas that are opened to reveal the supper room, a Druid interrupts the scene to redirect the entertainment toward an explicit celebration of British militarism, and the scene closes with a grand dance that was either the very epitome of elegance or a grand exercise in tedium.[65] The explosions that surprised the guests of the Fête Champêtre are notably absent, but they are replaced by an elaborate song by the character of Folly that interrupts a chain of pastoral songs and dances. Folly's song was not among the frequently reprinted songs, but its words explicitly relate to the critique of fashion and politics that operates both inside and outside the play:

From country elections, I gallop post haste,
For there, I am always the most busy guest;
And whether it be in the country or town,
I'm hugg'd very close, by the cit and the clown:
The courtier, the patriot, the turn-coat and all,
If I do not sweeten—breed nothing but gall.
I'm here, and there, &c. &c.

The statesman, without me, unhappy wou'd be;
No lady, so chaste, but gallants it with me;
The gravest of faces, who physick the land,
For all of their grimaces, shake me by the hand;
At the play-house, a friend to the author, I sit,
And clap in the gallery, the boxes and pit. (5.1.62)[66]

Folly's declaration of his omnipresence would appear to provide one kind of apology for Burgoyne's actions in Parliament, in the Fête Champêtre, and in this play.

But in a turn that is structurally comparable to the explosion in the Fête Champêtre, the curtains of the saloon are drawn up, the Druid enters, and Folly is banished from the feast. The message is clear: the entertainment at hand, like Burgoyne's earlier entertainment at The Oaks, has a serious objective. Then the Druid waves his wand: "The scene breaks away, and discovers the PALACE OF CELESTIAL LOVE" (5.1.63). According to the *London Magazine*, this transformation of the saloon into "one of the most beautiful scenes ever exhibited, representing a coelestial garden, terminated by a prospect of the Temple of Love, in which the statue of the Cyprian goddess appears in the attitude of the Venus of Medicis. The background is illuminated by the rays of the sun, which have a most splendid and astonishing effect."[67]

No image of De Loutherbourg's design survives, but its iconography is distinct from the image of Hymen in the supper room of Adam's pavilion. The specification of the statue's attitude links it both to one of the key examples of classicism for the eighteenth century and to the very epitome of a form of sensuality that threatens civic virtue. John Barrell's essay on the Venus de Medici is extraordinarily helpful here because he demonstrates that for

> the generation after Shaftesbury, the civic discourse appears to have found a way of embracing exactly what it was developed to denounce. The sexuality which is constituted in that discourse, and repressed in the public level of content, of narrative, returns at the private level of aesthetic form and of aesthetic response. It is because . . . the aesthetic discourse is understood as situated within a private sphere, that it is available to be appropriated by the sexuality that speaks through it. And the return of sexuality is enthusiastically welcomed, in a private celebration of sexual license, the prior and necessary condition of which is a public renunciation of sexuality. The prestige of the male ruling-class, it is claimed by the civic discourse on the fine arts, has to be earned by that act of renunciation; but the prestige of the middle-class critic and connoisseur comes to be earned in a more complicated fashion. It is won by a public *display* of renunciation, which by granting a legitimacy to an interest in the aesthetic, gives a license to exactly what it appears to have renounced.[68]

This display of renunciation is crucial to both *The Maid of the Oaks* and the Fête Champêtre, for it underpins the spatial logic of display. Here in the playhouse, De Loutherbourg has fashioned a prospect of a Temple of Venus at a distance from the scene of marriage enacted in front of his painted scenery. I would argue that the exhibition of this Temple of Venus is cognate to the illumination in the third masque of the Fête Champêtre: an ideal image of love that operates distinct from the interior hymeneal world of the pavilion. What this means is that the threatening spectacle of sensual pleasure is figured forth as the constitutive outside of the phantasmatic union of martial rule and conjugal marriage enclosed in Adam's pavilion and Garrick's theatre. It also helps us understand why the play needs Fanny Abington in the role of Lady Bab—by renouncing the woman of fashion, the play and the audience are allowed to consume her.

With the sudden projection, both psychic and material, of this Temple of Venus, the characters of the play are reintegrated back into the spectacle. It is as though the very presence of Art has the power not only to banish Folly but also to reactivate the place of reason in the consolidation of British national character.

Much as in the second masque, the Druid praises the Maid of the Oaks, and the oak figure begins to take on a life of its own. The first character to feel the effect of figuration is Groveby:

> GROVEBY: . . . this reverend old gentleman Druid has charmed me, and I hope we shall have more of his company—A contempt for old times may be fashionable, but I am pleas'd with every thing that brings them to my remembrance—I love an old oak at my heart, and can sit under its shade 'till I dream of Cressy and Agincourt; it is the emblem of British fortitude, and like the heroic spirits of the island, while it o'ertops, it protects the undergrowth—And now, old son of Mistletoe, set that sentiment to music. (5.1.64)[69]

Groveby is an important index here, because earlier in the play he recommends that Oldworth's celebration be modeled on the royal pageantry staged for Queen Elizabeth by the Duke of Leicester at Kenilworth in 1575. As the icon of British tradition, Groveby's function in the play is to repeatedly figure the entertainment in national terms. The Druid immediately complies with Groveby's request and signals for the following song for two voices:

> Grace and strength of Britain's isle,
> Mayst thou long thy glories keep,
> Make her hills with verdure smile,
> Bear her triumphs o'er the deep.
> CHORUS. Grace and Strength, &c. (5.1.65)

The combination of Groveby's memory of victories at Cressy and Agincourt and the explicit invocation of British naval victory abroad not only replicates the martial patriotism of the second masque of the Fête Champêtre but also prompts the final reform of Lady Bab and Dupeley. It is not an exaggeration to state that the ejection of Folly and the introduction of the Druid reveal the power of Art, here figured by the Temple of Venus itself—that is, by the physical space of the theatre as rendered by De Loutherbourg—to reform both the nation and its elite constituents into a cohesive social entity capable of addressing the moral and military challenges of imperial rule. In light of the preceding Fête Champêtre, we should not be surprised that the target of this reform is patrician martial masculinity and elite sexual exchange. Nor should we be surprised that the play concludes with a largely detachable ballet that stands as a further declaration of the power of elite taste to unite the company—now defined as the entire social world of the theatre—in a fantasy of political and aesthetic election. What would appear to be a demonstration of the power of autonomous art turns out to be a further sign of its deep imbrication in the social world of the audience and the political world of the nation.

Proliferating Claims on the Future

By the end of act 5, Burgoyne and Garrick had at least broached, and may have achieved, all of the ideological work of the second masque of the Fête Champêtre, but the ultimate resolution of the dialectical tension between the two strands of entertainment drawn together in this "Dramatick Entertainment" relies on a far more profound projection into the outer world of theatrical sociability and mediation. As Burgoyne states in his preface, the play is aimed at generating a new species of entertainment even if in its failure "it excites others, who may be better qualified, to pursue the same ideas" (iii). Like the Fête Champêtre's repetition of past cultural models, the play is meant not only to entertain by activating the cultural memory of the audience but also to generate further repetition and emulation.

But where that repetition takes place is important. The play's prologue, written by Garrick and widely acclaimed and reprinted in the papers, emphasizes the mutual importance of the papers and theatrical performance to the cultural dissemination that is achieved through remediation. The sense of mutuality is achieved by having Mr. King—the actor who played Groveby—speak the poem "equipped with a post-horn, and a jacket composed of the fragments of various news-papers, with Fête Champêtre labelled on the front of his cap."[70] Here was print come alive: the very figure of the interdependence of the newspapers and the theatres in the propagation of topical pleasure. And what Mr. King has to say is worth our closest attention. The poem's first two sections address the representation and remediation of the Fête Champêtre in the papers and the theatre respectively. Fame's account of the papers' mediation of the event emphasizes not only the ubiquity of its dissemination but also the tendency of even the highest forms of social practice to be replicated and eventually parodied at every level of social interaction:

> *Unlike to* ancient Fame, *all eyes, tongues, ears,*
> *See* Modern Fame, *dress'd cap-a-pee, appears*
> *In* Ledgers, Chronicles, Gazettes, *and* Gazetteers:

My soaring wings are fine Election Speeches,
And puffs of Candidates supply my breeches:[71]
My Cap is Satire, Criticism, Wit;
Is there a head that wants it in the Pit? [Offering it.
No flowing robe and trumpet me adorn;
I wear a jacket, *and I wind* a horn,
Pipe, Song, and Pastoral, for five months past,
Puff'd well by me, have been the gen'ral taste.
Now Marybone shines forth to gaping crouds!
Now Highgate glitters from her hill of clouds!
St. George's Fields, with taste and fashion struck,
Display Arcadia at the Dog and Duck!
And Drury Misses—" here in carmine pride,
"Are there Pastoras by the fountain side!"
To frouzy bow'rs they reel thro' midnight damps,
With Fauns half drunk, and Driads breaking lamps;
Both far and near did this new whimsy run,
One night it frisk'd, forsooth, at Islington:
And now, as for the public bound to cater,
Our Manager must have his Fête Champétre— (1–23)[72]

The transmission of "Arcadian" pleasures from The Oaks to Marylebone Gardens to Highgate to St. George's Fields to the Dog and Duck and finally to the world of the "Drury Lane Misses" charts a progression from zones of exclusivity to the least discriminating of venues.[73] And with that descent through the classed spaces of London comes an ancillary corruption of the sexual and national ideals articulated in Burgoyne's original event. But significantly, it is precisely the Fête Champêtre's permeation of the social landscape, to the point of even sparking a new fashion in prostitution, that prompts Garrick to bring it out of the streets and into the theatre proper.

Fame's description of the play's intent is interesting because it retains the multifariousness of this chain of replication. And, in a crucial move, the prologue aligns the production with a prior adaptation of a social celebration:

How is the weather? pretty clear and bright? [Looking about]
A storm's the devil on Champétre night!
Lest is should fall to spoil the Author's scenes,
I'll catch this gleam to tell you what he means: (24–27)

Tom King's fleeting reference to Garrick's rain-soaked Stratford Jubilee implies that *The Maid of the Oaks*'s relation to the original party is akin to the relationship between Garrick's *The Jubilee* and the failed commemoration of Shakespeare in the town of Stratford five years earlier. The choice of King here is significant because he was employed by Garrick to interrupt the celebration in the guise of a macaroni to denounce Shakespeare. Here his appearance as Fame, like his role in the Stratford Jubilee, is aimed at establishing a kind of devolution of culture against which Garrick and Burgoyne are operating.[74]

However, when Fame goes on to describe the play's particulars, he does not align its pleasures with those of elite retirement in the country:

> *He means a show, as brilliant as at Cox's—*
> *Laugh for the Pit—and may be* at *the Boxes—*
> *Touches of passion, tender, though not tragic,*
> *Strokes at the times—a kind of Lantern Magic;*
> *Song, chorus, frolic, dance, and rural play,*
> *The merry-making of a wedding day;* (28–34)

The references to Cox's Museum of mechanical exhibitions and to magic lantern shows retain the sense that the original Fête Champêtre can afford the topic for all manner of pleasures. But it is also clear that these "low" pleasures are being brought into the theatre in a way that attempts to give them moral purpose. Just as the newspapers allow their readers the dual pleasure of reading about scandal and judging the scandalous, so too will this play afford the audience all the brilliance of Cox's, and all the higher pleasures associated with "Touches of passion" and "Strokes at the times." In this light, Fame here is charting the Fête Champêtre's progress from a form of entertainment initially aimed at reforming the social and cultural elite, to a more malleable form of representation capable of entertaining even the most debased or unrefined tastes, to a new theatrical form that is attempting to reactivate the reformist agenda of the initial event while retaining its capacity to interest a mass audience. In other words, the play draws on both the initial Fête Champêtre and its less exclusive repetitions in the social world at large. And it is this duality that pushes the play into a new and, for some, a worrisome state of generic hybridity.

One could argue that the prologue itself enacts the anxiety of the social and generic hybridity instantiated by topical pleasure when Fame asks, "Whose is this piece?" It is as though ascertaining authorship will stabilize the relationship between the play and the surrounding social world. But this occasions only further questions, presented in a fashion that the audience and Lady Bab Lardoon were well acquainted with:

> *Whose is this piece?—'tis all surmise—suggestion—*
> *Is't* his?—*or* her's?—*or* your's, *Sir?—that's the question:*
> *The parent, bashful, whimsical, or poor,*
> *Left it a puling infant at the door:*
> *'Twas laid on flow'rs, and wrapt in fancied cloaks,*
> *And on the breast was written*—MAID O' TH' OAKS.
> *The actors crouded round; the girls caress'd it,*
> *"Lord! The sweet pretty babe!"—they prais'd and bless'd it,*
> *The Master peep'd—smil'd—took it in and dress'd it.* (35–43)

The sudden proliferation of indefinite pronouns and the figuration of the play as an abandoned child generates an enigma whose resolution is both the topic and the chief source of theatrical pleasure in the play. Who is who? Is that bit referring to who I think it is? And doesn't this remind you of something so and so said after reading about it in the morning paper? But this enigma is activated as a prelude to Mr. King's pro forma request for the audience's kind judgment of the play: "*As you're* kind, *rear it—if you're* curious, *praise it, / And ten to one but vanity betrays it*" (46–47). The capacity to generate curiosity is presented as the measure of this hybrid play's value, and that curiosity is not a simple interest in what a small group of aristocrats did at General Burgoyne's party last summer. The curiosity fostered here arises from the suturing of disjunctive modes of entertainment and of normally separate social fields. And it is this coming together of disparate elements in the theatre that drives interpretation and, hence, further dissemination in the social and cultural field. That commercial dissemination is figured as a species of "kindness," here understood as a kind of surrogate parentage. This parental metaphor is apt because at this stage in the repetition of the Fête Champêtre, the singular events of June 1774 are as much the property of original guests as they are of the culture at large. As we track the movement of the memory of the Fête Champêtre from individual witnesses to a broadly based and repeatedly mediated element of cultural memory, I think we can discern not only the very real pleasure afforded by this permeation of the social but also the tangible need to address the play's hybridity, not simply as an aesthetic question but as a matter of social and political concern.

As it turns out, the curiosity elicited by the play did generate a need to address the moral implications of the play's social intervention. The papers took up the challenge and generated a considerable discussion about the generic innovations of the production, and in each case the formal problems posed by the play become indistinguishable from the social dynamics of their reception. The *Morning Chronicle,* as if in explicit response, staged a debate, which ran almost a full month, between those for "refinement" and those who saw the play as an aesthetic and moral failure. The chain of letters to the printer of the paper is so carefully orchestrated that the entire debate may well be artificially propagated by the editors themselves. But that, if anything, would only make it more intriguing. The play's ostensible proponents explicitly argue that the play's elegance morally reforms the audience by bringing the socially mixed audience of the theatre into contact with levels of dance performance and visual representation normally reserved for elite consumption at the Opera House or the Academy Exhibition.[75] These arguments tend to figure the play as a "secular masque"[76] or emphasize that the play explicitly demarcates itself as something other than comedy, and therefore should not be judged as one. The play's detractors argue that the same spectacle undermines character, both on and off the stage. The generic point is akin to the argument against pantomime: that the increasing production of spectacle undermines the audience's ability to appreciate true comedy.

One could argue that both sides of this debate have merit, but what I want to stress is that the propensity to extrapolate outward to the health of the nation deserves particular attention, for precisely this desire is being resuscitated from the original Fête Champêtre and cast forward for further consideration. Here is a sample of the kind of engagement elicited in favor of the play:

> For my part, Mr. Printer, I hear your declaimers against these exhibitions . . . with the same contempt I do the crudities of unfledged City patriots, who are continually tiring us with political virtue, freedom of election, and English liberty. Let those who blame Mr. Garrick for producing these elegant spectacles, not only tell us that dramatic taste is perverted, and dramatic authors neglected, but point out to us those plays which ought to be acted, and which still lie dormant.[77]

The letter writer then goes through an extensive survey of the stock repertoire arguing that there is an ample propensity for vice in legitimate tragedy and comedy, and he rejoices that his daughters have

> an opportunity of being surprized and pleased by the finest scenery and dances, without being shocked with the wriggles of a Harlequin, or taught disobedience by the preposterous character of Columbine, whose constant plan is to cheat her father, and run away with a monster. In short, Mr. Printer, I could heartily wish, both for the credit and morals of the nation, that such pieces as the Beggar's Opera, Provoked Wife, Love for Love, &c were banished the stage, and many more such pieces as the Maid of the Oaks introduced. Not that I deny those pieces to be excellent in their kind, if morals were of no manner of consequence; as I once heard a companion of Mr. Wilkes say, that gentleman (now our present worthy Lord Mayor) would be the best company in the world, if he did not blaspheme quite so much.[78]

This is only a small portion of the letter, and even this small sample could generate considerable discussion. All I wish to draw attention to is how these remarks replicate the very strategies of the play by defending Burgoyne and Garrick's generic innovations by thoroughly embedding them not simply in the realm of dramatic criticism but within the political debates regarding what is best for the nation. For this letter writer, there is no autonomy for the world of art. The paper ultimately comes down on the side of the detractors, but I would argue that it is in the back and forth of public opinion as fictionally articulated in the papers that the resolution of the dialectical tension between divergent strands of entertainment takes place. For it is here that the full integration of social and aesthetic practice is made fleetingly manifest.

But this dialectical resolution is only fleeting. The synthesis prompts both more replication and further contradiction. And this evanescence is in part a function of the economics of entertainment itself. Perhaps the most prescient indication of the success of *The Maid of the Oaks* as a medium for social and cultural repetition can be found in a brief report in the *St. James Chronicle*:

> *Covent Garden Theatre.*—The Managers here are all asleep, but it is thought that the Noise occasioned by the Maid of the Oaks will rouse them. After letting off their two great Guns, the Barry's, and Mr. Dee's Twelve Pounder, they thought their business done, and that it was Time to take a Nap.[79]

Recognizing almost immediately that *The Maid of the Oaks*'s topicality has the potential to generate repetition and thus receipts, the paper is literally projecting the need for Drury Lane's only real competitor to enter the fray. The martial metaphor is interesting because it suggests that the internal generic conflict that drives the interest in *The Maid of the Oaks* could be subsumed into the long-standing and mutually beneficial conflict between the playhouses. Not to be outdone by the success and notoriety of *The Maid of the Oaks*, Covent Garden quickly responded with its own hybrid production entitled *The Druids*. *The Druids* combines a traditional pantomime harlequinade with clearly recognizable elements from the masques reported to have taken place at the Fête Champêtre. Referred to as a "new Pastoral Masque (with Pantomime interspersed) in two parts," the newspaper accounts of the production carefully tie key scenes to events narrated in the "Oak Gazette Extraordinary."[80] But no mention is made in any of the papers of Burgoyne or the Fête Champêtre, because the entire assemblage of figures and references is now in general circulation. Here repetition has been overtaken by a level of despecification that is crucial to the dissemination of cultural memory but detrimental to the performative thrill of topicality.

This despecification is matched by a further complication. One of the chief problems with topicality is that the unfolding of historical events has the capacity to alter meaning so radically that the initial pleasures afforded by recognition can be transformed into quite painful forms of reckoning. As we have seen, diversion generates repetition, but repetition need not retain the intention of the initial event. In the late fall of 1774, the remediation of the Fête Champêtre in both patent houses engaged the public imagination in ways similar to the reception of the initial event. Even the most critical remarks on the plays stop well short of satirizing Burgoyne and at most cite the production as evidence of the degradation of fashionable taste. As we have seen, the Fête Champêtre and *The Maid of the Oaks* regulate conjugal sexuality and martial masculinity in order to generate a fantasy of national and imperial election. In the short passage of time from 1774 to the fall of Saratoga in 1777, both elements of this phantasmatic consolidation would be quite literally in tatters. But I guess we could also say that Burgoyne was by then a changed man.

We can trace the shredding of this fantasy by looking at two large paintings by Antonio Zucchi that were produced between 1775 and 1778 for Robert Adam's elaborate renovation of Derby House. These paintings, each measuring roughly five by six feet, were prominently incorporated into the luxurious dining room and thus were permanent fixtures in what would become one of the focal points of fashionable diversion in London.[81] Lord Stanley, soon to become the 12th Earl of Derby, and his young bride, Lady Elizabeth Hamilton, as Eileen Harris states, "were full of fun and vitality, and enormously extravagant. They wanted suites of the most dazzling reception rooms in town, fashionably got up for great assemblies, gaming, balls and suppers—a house that came to life at night, and reflected and enhanced the gaiety of their lives."[82] Their continual exhibition in this space gives the Fête Champêtre and Adam's temporary pavilion a rather strange endurance that militates against the transitoriness of the original performance and building. Their almost immediate engraving and publication as part of *The Architectural Works of Robert and James Adam* meant that this visualization of the event gained an even wider circulation. Although these images are clearly part of the dissemination and celebration of Adam's own work, Zucchi's paintings of *The Supper Room* and *The Ball Room* correspond to the moments immediately after the explosion in the second masque and to the inception of the minuets in the third masque respectively.[83] (See figs. 1.2 and 1.3.) As our preceding reading of the *fête* has argued, these moments are arguably those in which the bodily dispositions of the guests are under the most assured control. In the first instance, the painting presents the guests immediately after the sublime activation of an allegory of imperial luxury. The colonnades, the statuary, and above all the inset circular lozenge depicting Venus and Cupid both structure the pictorial space and make the allegory manifest. As noted earlier, this moment is of crucial political importance because it poses a problem for reading. Is this allegorical gesture aimed at equating Roman excess with aristocratic vice and thus involved in a critique of empire? Or is it a simple confirmation of Britain's imperial power?

The answer to these questions can be broached only by looking closely at how the figures are presented and then comparing them to the later picture. *The Supper Room* is quite literally dominated by Venus and Cupid (fig. 1.2). From the lozenge in the background to the masquing guests in the foreground, the painting insinuates the flow of sexual desire. In the left foreground, an attendant in Venetian garb is leading a smartly dressed woman directly into the waiting lap of a seated gentleman. Across the table, a man dressed *a la turque* is conversing with one woman and fondling another. And in the direct foreground, two dogs—a lap dog and small hound—are engaged in some sort of frolic. In the terms set out by the larger trajectory of the Fête Champêtre, Zucchi's painting everywhere alludes to how the promiscuous exchange staged in the garden inheres well into the second masque. However, when we shift our attention to *The Ball Room*, and thus to the period following Captain Pigott's intervention and the Hymeneal pantomime, we see not only a transformation in pictorial space but also a far more restrained treatment of erotic exchange (fig. 1.3). The semicircular space of Adam's building and the regularly spaced columns allow Zucchi to separate the company into discrete parties, and to contain all of the erotic energy of the dancing within the architecture of the pavilion. The strict regimen of the minuet, which now takes over the center of the picture plane, replaces the static potentiality of the Venus and Cupid lozenge with the air of formalized gesture and carefully scripted movement. The formalized and complex movements of the minuet are a site of both controlled erotic exchange and elite performance. To be able to dance the minuet was a kind of social test.[84] The Turkish habits remain, but there are no explicitly sexual invocations as in the foreground of *The Supper Room*. Instead, the frolicking dogs in the earlier picture are replaced by a single hunting dog, which seems to preside over the proceedings, and a mother conversing with her child about the ball. In light of the preceding reading of the Fête Champêtre, it is difficult not to read the hunting dog and the mother-child pairing as Zucchi's rendering of the conjunction of martial and marital control that preoccupied the second masque. If the lone dog is a figure for Captain Pigott, or perhaps even Burgoyne himself, then the mother and child stand for the reproductive imperative implied in the masque's celebration of conjugal fidelity. As these paintings were composed and hung, Lady Hamilton would have borne three children, so it is difficult not to read this foreground figure as her representative.

Zucchi's paintings, and the related engravings, repeat and thus shore up the argument of the Fête Champêtre in part because the very transitoriness of the event means that it requires continual reiteration. With each reiteration comes a consolidation of meaning and the potential for signification to go awry. For Derby, the paintings must have been eventually permeated with irony. In light of the fact that in 1779 Lady Elizabeth Hamilton left Lord Stanley, now Lord Derby, for John Frederick Sackville, the most notorious rake of the day, these paintings must have been subject to counterreadings that would have effectively undone the complex social synthesis figured forth in the Fête Champêtre. But the corresponding dismantling of patrician military prowess would have already taken place. By the fall of 1777, Burgoyne himself would have surrendered at Saratoga and British rule in the American colonies would look anything but propitious. Most historians of the American war see the loss at Saratoga in October 1777 as the turning point in the war.[85] George Germain, the secretary of state, and the Ministry quickly closed ranks to make Burgoyne the scapegoat for the reverses in British fortune.[86] After a humiliating imprisonment in Boston, Burgoyne arrived back in London in May 1778 to answer charges against him in

Parliament.[87] At some point, in the course of his social affairs, he would have sat in Derby's dining room to contemplate the meaning of Zucchi's paintings. In this context, the paintings would have figured forth a past state of social and sexual equilibrium, whose very obsolescence would shake the foundations of Burgoyne's fantasy of patrician rule.

CHAPTER TWO

Out to America

Performance and the Politics of Mediated Space

The duality that troubles the notion of *imperium*, the nonidentity of realm and empire so forcefully articulated by J. G. A. Pocock, would seem to be an abstract matter of political theory, except that it took on material form in the both the London and the colonial papers on a daily basis. Because information traveling between colony and metropole was relayed by ship, the experience of delayed news was fundamental to both the government and the analysis of imperial affairs. In terms of the spatial design of the papers, this meant that paragraphs on yesterday's events in Parliament or on social relations in London were adjacent to paragraphs about events that had transpired in America roughly a month earlier or events that had happened in Bengal as much as three or four months in the past.[1] Readers therefore were always negotiating a temporal gap coded into the spatial dynamics of the newspaper itself. And it is important to recognize how this would have impinged on one's affective relation to the emerging conflict in America. Separated from the colonies by the Atlantic, readers of the London papers were always in a state of anticipating information from America. Like any serialization of desire, this situation not only drives consumption but also makes one aware of how mediation spaces time.

The skirmishes between Colonel Francis Smith's regulars and the hastily assembled militia at Lexington and Concord on 19 April 1775 are conventionally cited as the beginning of the American war. News of the outbreak of hostilities arrived in London more than one month later on 28 May 1775, and the reports were quickly disseminated in the papers on the following day. Roughly two months later, on 25 July, metropolitan Britons received first word of their Pyrrhic victory at Bunker Hill: British forces had captured the strategic location after three advances, but in the process they lost almost half their soldiers. Both conflicts presaged the military problems facing the British army during the ensuing war.[2] It was difficult to assess the true strength of the colonial military opposition. At one level, there was little martial infrastructure to discipline the Continental army, but at another it was clear that local militias would fight fiercely around matters of principle and local concern. It was also daunting to think through the problems of supplying an effort to reconquer the colonies. On top of these logistical and strategic problems, Lords North and Dartmouth were beset with metropolitan opposition to both their overall colonial policy and their specific strategic decisions. And finally, the Continental powers of France and Spain were watching and waiting for the moment when their entry into the war would transform a colonial conflict into a global war.

This two-month period between late May and late July was of crucial historical importance, and yet the newspapers seem, from our present perspective, distracted by apparently frivolous concerns. Thankfully, the *Morning Chronicle* printed what it called "A General Index to the Occurrences in June 1775, in Mock Heroic Verse," so that we could put everything in perspective:

The trial and condemnation of the two Perreaus
For certain, but of Mrs. Rudd's fate the Lord knows;
The counterfeit halfpence stopp'd on a sudden,
L[ord] N[orth] ready to give the crow a pudding;
With the immaculate D[artmout]h, his coadjutor,
Both sensible of the present, but not of the future
Mischiefs thro' their mal-administration,
Calculated to hurt the interest of the nation;
By measures against the Colonists coercive,
To British freedom, trade, and commerce subversive;
A raree-shew on the Thames called a Regatta,
With barges, boats, streamers, and the Lord knows what a;
The City resolved to petition the K[in]g on the Throne,
The K[in]g puzzled whether to sit thereon, or let it alone;
The Petition, &c. Carried up by the Lord Mayor, and many more;
The K[in]g, as instructed (God help him) answers as before;
The M[inistr]y in the dumps, and making long faces,
To think of the scurvy situations and cases,
At a time when the French and Spaniards are arming
With hostile intentions, truly alarming
To the people of England, K[in]g, Commons, and Lords,
May our sailors take their ships, and our Ministers their words.[3]

The poem thematizes several concerns pressing for attention in June 1775. There is the Perreau-Rudd case, North and Dartmouth's American policy, the Thames Regatta, Wilkes's inflammatory pro-American petitions to the king on behalf of the City, and potential unrest in Europe. There is no mention of Lexington and Concord, but every one of these issues is colored by anxiety regarding rebellion in the thirteen colonies.

Donna Andrew and Randall McGowan have demonstrated how and why the forgery case involving Mrs. Rudd and the Perreau brothers preoccupied the press to the point of relegating news of American matters to incidental notices. In their analysis, the Rudd case becomes anything but frivolous, because it spoke to a legion of anxieties regarding credit, social masquerade, and class prerogative.[4] This chapter looks at a similar distraction in the public sphere, the Thames Regatta, which is here figured as a mere raree show. But this spectacle monopolized much of the press coverage in the crucial months of June and July 1775, when the British lost control over New England. This chapter examines not only why the performance of aristocratic sociability became a locus for national concern and agitation but also how the mediation of this event in the print public sphere laid the groundwork for a whole host of critical cultural events and documents of the early Revolutionary period. The spatial dynamics of the regatta are themselves subject to politicization, and the mediation of space becomes a significant zone for political critique. In many ways, Sheridan's extraordinarily successful opera *The Duenna* poses many of the same questions for cultural analysis as the Thames Regatta: why would something this trivial warrant such extensive attention? The second section of this chapter moves into the period where the Ministry was actively attempting to reconquer the colonies and looks at the spatial allegory coded into *The Duenna* as a form of opposition fantasy not that far removed from the critiques published about the regatta. Finally, the chapter concludes by moving to the period when news of the British loss at Saratoga was working its way through the public sphere. The readings of the Thames Regatta and of *The Duenna* allow us to comprehend how *The School for Scandal* and Hannah More's *Percy* deploy spatial disjunctions to profit both financially and aesthetically from social contradiction.[5]

Watching the River Flow: Mediating the Thames Regatta

Rather than coming to the Thames Regatta directly, I want to look briefly at the other more obviously political couplets of the "General Index." The poem is divided into two eight-line sections of direct political discussion: the first pertains to perceived failures in the Ministry's American policies (3–10), and the second addresses the City's attempt to petition the king to recognize the legitimacy of the Americans' claims and adopt a less punitive course with regard to the colonies (13–20). These two sections are literally framed by the opening couplet on the Perreau-Rudd case (1–2) and the final couplet calling the sailors and ministers to action (21–22). The couplet on the Thames Regatta is the pivot that both frames and links the two larger sections on the American crisis (11–12), and as such it balances equal and opposite forces within the poem. This accounting of lines may seem formulaic, but the rigorously balanced structure of the poem raises important questions about space, which will impinge on the larger structure of my argument here. At one level, the lines on North and Dartmouth are about the flow of policy down the Thames, outward toward the sea, and across the ocean to Boston, Philadelphia, and New York, and the speaking voice of the poem is clearly dissatisfied with both the content and the direction of the Ministry's communication, which to this point had been unwaveringly coercive. Similarly, the lines on the City petition are also about the movement of information, but in precisely the opposite direction. During June and July 1775, John Wilkes, on behalf of the Common Council, was attempting to deliver a strongly worded petition, written by Arthur Lee, to the king, which not only condemned General Thomas Gage for starting a civil war but also argued in favor of the American claims to political liberty. Despite having received a similar petition on 10 April 1775, the king, following directions from North and other advisers, refused to receive further petitions on the throne, in order to block further pro-American interference from the City.[6] If we think about this struggle geographically, the struggle of the pro-American voices in the City against the Crown amounts to an effort to move up the Thames, from the Common Hall to Westminster, with a document that in every detail is in direct opposition to the legislation shipped downstream to the colonies by the Ministry. This movement of political documents and policy up and down the Thames, is balanced in the poem by the mocking couplet pertaining to the regatta, and thus the regatta's own negotiation of the river operates in the poem as a kind of parody of the geopolitical struggle encompassing the flow of information between Westminster, the City, and New England.

The Directions of Politics in June 1775

The space of performance is crucial to how one understands the larger historical connotations of the Thames Regatta, but the politics of space are simply unreadable without a clear sense of the social network that sponsored and organized the event. The regatta was the brainchild of Temple Simon Luttrell, a friend and supporter of Wilkes who was elected member of Parliament for Milborne Port in 1774, and Sir Thomas Lyttelton, the notorious libertine and controversial parliamentarian. Luttrell "gained some notoriety during the war against America for his attacks on the Admiralty and for campaigning against the press gang. The violence of his speeches against Lord North, however, lost him his seat" in 1780.[7] During much of 1774 and the first months of 1775, Lyttelton, from his position in the House of Lords, strongly supported the Ministry's American policy. He resisted Chatham's call for a removal of troops from Boston and stood independently in favor of further military intervention in the colonies. However, after the summer of 1775, Lyttelton returned to the Lords and quickly became the scourge of the government's policy. By October he was loudly demanding that the Ministry rescind the Coercive Acts and adopt a more conciliatory policy. So at the time of the regatta, roughly midway between these two public positions, Lyttelton's stance regarding America was changing direction.

These two men, whose public personae were deeply implicated with the public debate surrounding the American rebellion, joined forces with two other controversial figures to bring the regatta to fruition. Both Luttrell and Lyttelton were prominent members of the Scavoir Vivre Club, an association devoted to drinking, gambling, and high living, and it was through their social connections that they brought in experts in the field of sociability. Lyttelton "prevailed upon Mr. Henry Shirley, a gentleman, whose long residence in foreign Courts, excellent understanding, and other accomplishments, had gained him universal esteem, to assist in the arduous undertaking."[8] In later reports, Shirley would shoulder much of the blame for the regatta's failures, but the important element of this description from the *Gazetteer* is its emphasis on Shirley's intimate knowledge of foreign practices. As we will see, there is a strong vein of xenophobia in the reports of the regatta, which ultimately turns on the cosmopolitanism of the managers.

Luttrell, already strongly affiliated with the Scavoir Vivre Club in the press, commissioned Teresa Cornelys to manage the elaborate entertainment that concluded the event. Of all the participants in the regatta, Cornelys comes under the most direct scrutiny in part because the press had a long and profitable obsession with her activities, and in part because she was the least able to defend herself in the courts because of her reputation and her class. As Gillian Russell has recently reminded us, Cornelys was a crucial figure in the economy of entertainment in the 1760s and 1770s.[9] An extraordinarily talented promoter, her "domiciliary entertainments" held at Carlisle House in Soho constituted a new form of entertainment outside the purviews of the state licensing system. Her strategies for manipulating the press had a profound impact not only on the structure of aristocratic sociability but also on the power of the media to drive public taste. In a sense, she realized quite early on the full potential of the papers to mold the social and cultural life of fashionable society. The first members of the Ton, under the shield of a ticketing scheme managed by Cornelys for a number of prominent women patrons, were able to consort, gamble, and socialize in a manner that exerted considerable pressure on the conventional domains of entertainment in London. Her masquerades and concerts were the hottest tickets in town, and her journalistic acumen ensured that all of her activities were well before the public eye, except those which needed to remain in the dark. Garrick and other managers of the patent theatres found themselves competing with Cornelys and had to incorporate some of her strategies to retain their preeminence in the field of cultural, if not social, exchange. Her innovations were quickly picked up and developed by other impresarios, and venues such as Almack's, the Coterie, and the Pantheon flourished. However, as these new forms and sites of aristocratic sociability proliferated, so too did charges of immorality, dissipation, and corruption. Russell's superb study has tracked these scandals and argued persuasively that they were crucial to emerging arguments about the effect of luxury on the state of the nation. By the time Cornelys was taking part in the regatta, her influence was somewhat on the wane, but the mere association of the event with her name brings the entire affair into the orbit of a complex and long-running argument about the dissipation of the aristocracy. These arguments, especially at this historical moment, are inevitably linked to charges of gender insubordination, petticoat government, and compromised masculinity. These issues were central to the media response to the regatta, but Cornelys's historical affiliation with luxury was deployed in an extremely complex argument about the future of the empire.

To understand how these broader concerns are folded into the reception of the event, we need to look carefully at its structure. Like Burgoyne's Fête Champêtre, to which it was frequently compared,[10] the Thames Regatta is divided into two sections according to space. This relation to Burgoyne's fête is registered in one of the most biting satires of the regatta, "Rural Masquerade Dedicated to the Regatta'ites," which takes the events of the regatta and folds them into an elaborate and ridiculous hairpiece (fig. 2.1). These wig satires were quite popular during a period of extravagant hair styles, but this image has some disturbing elements specific to itself, not least of which is the fact that the wig is being worn by a grotesque elderly bearded woman trying keep up with the follies of fashion.

Figure 2.1. Anonymous, "Rural Masquerade Dedicated to the Regatta'ites," etching (1776). BM 5379. Department of Prints and Drawings © Trustees of the British Museum.

The wig, like the regatta itself, is divided into two parts. The first section of the regatta involved a rowing race on the river and then an elaborate procession of barges and boats, carrying notable politicians, aristocrats and ladies, upstream from Westminster Bridge to the steps at Ranelagh at the Chelsea Embankment.

This section of the regatta makes up the lower part of the wig. Boats were positioned under the bridge by color: the twelve racing boats were under the central arch and were framed first by white vessels in the next two arches and finally by red and blue boats that were stationed under the outside arches.[11] As the boats progressed, the spectators would have seen the erstwhile components of the Union Jack chaotically weave their way upstream. This section of the regatta was most directly connected to Luttrell, Shirley, and Lyttelton. Once at Ranelagh, the second phase of the event began when the guests entered a temporarily built Temple to Neptune, which continued the naval theme, but the bulk of the entertainment—dancing, musical performances, supper, and gambling—was staged within the preexisting Rotunda of Ranelagh itself. The print incorporates the Rotunda into the upper portion of the wig, but like many of the papers, it represents the masqueraders as a party of fools. The attack here is aimed quite specifically at Cornelys and her associates because it was her expertise both as party organizer and as musical impresario that was most commented on in the press. But before looking at that commentary, I want to explore the representation of the action on the river, not only because it reveals a great deal about the relationship between the regatta and the city of London, but also because it demonstrates how the political wrangling over the American colonies is coded into the mediation of the event.

Like virtually any representation of the Thames following Alexander Pope's "Windsor Forest," the transit from Westminster Bridge to Ranelagh is laden with symbolic meaning. At one level, this is quite literally a journey from Parliament to London's foremost pleasure garden, a trip no doubt taken by Lyttelton and Luttrell, both parliamentarians at this time, countless times before. But on another level, it is also a journey from the War Office to the Chelsea Royal Hospital for Invalid Soldiers, which sits immediately adjacent to Ranelagh's famous Rotunda (fig. 2.2). So the participants of the regatta were involved in a journey not only from the seat of government to the seat of social diversion but also from the place where war is managed to the place where the victims of poor strategy were destined to go. What is so fascinating about the reports of the regatta is the degree to which they keep both aspects of the event in play: it is simultaneously a movement away from the pressing exigencies of the American situation *and* a movement toward a rumination on the consequences of faulty policy and corrupted character.

Considering the duality of this movement, it is perhaps not surprising to discover that the part of the regatta that took place on the river was, to all but the most forgiving accounts, a fiasco. The *Gazetteer*, for example, was predisposed to offer a favorable account of the event on nationalist grounds, because

> there is no doubt but that a *Regatta*, properly managed, is a shew peculiarly adapted to the disposition, character, and local turn of us islanders, having all the advantages of an extensive river, and spacious shores, affording innumerable points of view, which, with the vicinity of the first city in the world, . . . unite in giving the preference to a *Regatta*, before any popular exhibition ever yet known, either among the ancients or moderns.[12]

But nevertheless, even this observer was forced to concede that the regatta did not live up to expectations, due in part to a combination of bad timing and bad weather:

Figure 2.2. Thomas Bowles, "Perspective Views / A View of the Royal Hospital at Chelsea & the Rotunda in Ranelaigh Gardens," etching/engraving (1751). BM 1880,1113.1228. Department of Prints and Drawings © Trustees of the British Museum.

> It was intended to have been given about the middle of June, then the tide would have served for the race as early as six o'clock in the evening, and the managers might have had their choice of any day when the weather should wear a favourable appearance, from the sixteenth to the twenty-second; but the public mourning for the late Queen of Denmark made it necessary to postpone the entertainment till the twenty-third, when the tide could not possibly turn till after seven o'clock in the evening, and a strong westerly wind made it hold back unexpectedly, even an hour later, so that there could have been no prospect of making up the river for Ranelagh with a procession of barges before dusk, even if the way had been clear, to start the wager boats an hour sooner than this step could possibly be effected, or even without the inconvenience of the lightermen, and others, who obstinately persisted in continually crowding the water, to the evident obstruction of the whole ceremony.[13]

Less sympathetic accounts of the Thames Regatta complained bitterly that much of the spectacle, like the late coronation, was contrived to take place in darkness.[14] And with so many boats running aground in the low tide, the papers were provided with frequent occasion for ridicule. But the *Gazetteer*'s apology for the event is more than simply a statement of regret regarding the tides and the weather. The delay in the event, which was the ultimate cause for the poor tides and the lack of flexibility on the date, is attributed to the circumstance of state mourning. And this was not any normal occasion. Princess Caroline Matilda of Wales was sister to George III and the Queen of Denmark from 1766 to 1772. Her tenure as queen was abruptly terminated when, after being arrested for adultery following a masked ball at the royal theatre at Christiansborg Castle, she was divorced and deported. Her return to England was a source of embarrassment for the king, and I would argue that the *Gazetteer* is subtly suggesting not only that her character made her undeserving of public mourning but also that the motives behind the state mourning had to do with the regatta itself.

This point is clarified later when the *Gazetteer* discusses at length the resistance to the execution of the entertainment, which was demonstrated, but not specifically declared, elsewhere in the press:

> It was natural to suppose that the same malicious spirits that were at work so industriously previous to the day of the Regatta, in a fruitless endeavour to prevent it being carried into execution, and who furnished daily supplies of wit upon drowning, balsams, cork jackets, &c. would be equally industrious, when it was over, to report it in disadvantageous terms, and that they would supply a want of real mischief by their own inventions and disingenuous surmises.[15]

This passage is largely an indictment of the press, whose pre-event coverage was replete with half-joking, half-serious suggestions that the entire affair was dangerous and that numerous participants would drown because of inept boatmanship and poor preparation. And there is no shortage of post-event coverage that ridicules the failure to provide sufficient food for supper, and the general confusion on the water. But this is all merely a set-up to suggest that the mediation of the event has been tainted by faction:

> Now, Sir, from what quarter could all this abuse and unmerited enmity spring? The scheme was at the beginning very ill received at a *certain place*, where most schemes for the public good have of late years been as ill received; the *Regatta* could expect no countenance from that quarter; it should have been on the *Tweed*, instead of the Thames, then it might perhaps have been found wise, praise-worthy, and salutary.[16]

This is typical of a vibrant anticourt rhetoric, which believed that the much-reviled Lord Bute maintained secret influence over the king and the Ministry, even in his Scottish retirement. The correspondent's anti-Scots rhetoric and his critique of the Crown, here figured by a "certain place," was driven by "an all-encompassing conspiracy theory that defined the ideology and manoeuvres of leading opposition groups well into the age of Lord North."[17] In this context, the earlier regret over the public mourning for the Danish queen, reads as a further level of critique, for it suggests that even George III's vaunted morality could be obviated to serve some greater political purpose. But what possible political purpose could the regatta serve?

One possibility for the regatta's political function is made startlingly evident as the correspondent from the *Gazetteer* continues his analysis:

> The Lord Mayor, the Aldermen, and several very respectable Gentleman of the City Companies, saw the apparent merit of the design, and the advantages that must accrue from it to thousands of poor families; they wished to turn the rage of entertainments and banqueting, which prevails so much in these our days among the polished follies of high life (since it must have its course) into a more rational channel than that of midnight jubilee and masquerading: were this, Sir, to become an annual festival, under the like encouragement and countenance which was given to the City of London in a corporate capacity to this *first attempt*, and in a manner so polite and generous, there is no doubt but that it would in a few years draw over an immense resort of opulent foreigners to refund some of the large sums expended by our travelling nobility and gentry to exotic sights of far less magnificence and public utility; . . . perhaps no exhibition on record was ever so happily calculated to serve the principal great ends of all popular games and luxurious assemblies, by keeping the rich and the dissipated at home, inviting persons of a like description from abroad, and, in a word, of gratifying the great, and serving the poor in that most essential article of wholsome and innocent employment: so that the undertaking rightly understood . . . cannot be too sufficiently commended by the public in general.[18]

Curiously enough, this passage is very much about flow, and specifically about the flow of money into and out of the City. But the flow of the text is itself important, because it starts by setting the mayor, the aldermen, and important merchants against the ostensible cabal of the king and his former Scottish prime minister. As I have already noted, the City, led by Wilkes, and its merchants were at this moment attempting to petition the king to adopt a more conciliatory approach to the American rebellion, so to what degree is the correspondent for the *Gazetteer* comparing great things to small?[19] Is the antipathy toward the regatta similar to the antipathy of the king's policy toward both the City and the colonies? Certainly the idiom in which the conflict is described would have resonated with reporting on the City petitions: much was made of the distinction between the City's political and "corporate capacity" in the king's refusal to countenance the petition on the throne.[20] When one looks carefully at the discussion of "the advantages which must accrue from [the regatta] to thousands of poor families," the argument quickly moves from one of economic interest—that is, the regatta will generate commerce within London—to one that indicts the profligate aristocracy for undermining the national interest. And this is where the directional flow reaches its figural destination.

The nobility is critiqued for moving capital out of the nation in its pursuit of pleasure, presumably on the Continent, and the regatta is praised for its potential to entice dissipated foreigners into dumping their money in London. The regatta is quite literally figured as an instrument capable of stemming the flow of money downriver out of the country and of drawing new wealth, from those inclined to part with it, upriver from across the Channel. As one paper reported, "It is supposed that the late regatta occasioned the spending of upwards of 50,000l. Consequently the community at large were benefited by the circulation."[21] What remains constant are the capacity for the "nobility and the gentry" to hemorrhage cash and the disregard in *certain places* for this perpetual loss. And it is here that the subtle political link between the American crisis and the regatta lies: basically, the *Gazetteer* is arguing that the king and his Ministry, in their attempt to manipulate reception of both events, are too preoccupied by the demonstration of their preeminence to recognize that they are not acting in the interest of the nation. The City's endorsement of the regatta, like its endorsement of the American rebels, is firmly rooted in a proto-Mandevillian analysis of historical events: because the propertied classes, in their current corrupt manifestation, are going to spend regardless of the situation, it is crucial that the money flow in rather than out.

The Floating Town, or the Present Crisis

I have attended closely to this account in the *Gazetteer*, because it participates so thoroughly in the discourses traversed by the representations of the Thames Regatta. In the form of an apology for the event, it hits on most of the crucial themes: the claims for the commercial benefits that may or may not accrue to the event, the intense fascination or scrutiny of the follies of high life, the relationship between the event itself and the state, and finally the persistent mobilization of xenophobia to clinch questionable conclusions about the cultural and social significance of the regatta. This latter issue is a prominent theme, whether texts are fulminating about "Scotch influence" or complaining about the infiltration of Italian practices into English life. A prominent insert in the *Morning Post* takes up the latter tack:

> An ancient club of gentleman rowers present their respects to the publick, and beseech their future support against the invasion of a nickname given yesterday to a rowing match, which diversion has been a common one upon the Thames without interruption every season from time immemorial, and is now on a sudden called a *Regatta*; nobody knows why, any farther than that some travelled *ninnies* of quality, and their pocket companions, the gamblers, have named it so; . . . having catched the word *Regatta* as they have before that of *Fete Champetre*, the apprentices, servants, and all others, broke loose yesterday from their duties of various kinds . . . to see the Regatta, because it was called by that *cant* Italian name. We therefore beg to have our rowing matches be named rowing matches again, as we shall then be able to enjoy them in peace and pleasure, and the English language and inhabitants of this metropolis will be maintained against the corruption of these new fangled entertainments, and the names given them by the new fangled gaming Assemblies.[22]

Because the Thames Regatta was styled on the Grand Regatta of Venice, it was susceptible to this kind of attack, frequently bolstered by an implicit complaint that the event was displacing a much more "honest" English competition on the river: Doggett's Coat and Badge Race, which was held on the first of August every summer. Raced from "The Swan" at London Bridge to "The Swan" at Chelsea, Doggett's Race awarded a bright red coat and a silver badge bearing the White Horse of Hanover and the motto "Liberty" to the victorious waterman. Its place in the public imagination was thoroughly plebian and resolutely patriotic; thus, it offered an apt contrast for satirists wishing to impugn the organizers and supporters of the regatta. This alternative race was very much a part of the theatrical response to the Thames Regatta because Samuel Foote ran Charles Dibdin's ballad farce *The Waterman, or the First of August* at the Haymarket at every possible occasion before and after the regatta.

The *Gazetteer* makes only subtle insinuations about the relationship between the regatta and the state, but other papers were much more direct in expressing their suspicions. The *London Evening Post*, in one of the earliest discussions of the regatta, declared that it was nothing less than a ministerial conspiracy to dupe the public: "The late *Littletonian*, or rather *Simpletonian* Regatta on the Thames, was a ministerial trick calculated to amuse the people, and divert the public from serious objects, and disappoint them from nobler Pursuits, the consideration of their own national security. There was not an individual who viewed this raree-shew but execrated most cordially this ill timed and most ill managed business."[23] In spite of the fact that this charge does not mention Luttrell's prominent place in the regatta's conception and management, Lyttelton's support for the Ministry before the regatta meant that this insinuation carried some political weight, which was bolstered by further allegations that he was simply angling for a patronage post.[24] What runs through all of this is a sense that corruption, already thoroughly embedded in the Ministry, is flowing through the channels of public life and, when combined with a corresponding dissipation of private character, is forming a dangerous flood tide.

Lyttelton, of course, was the flashpoint for all of this anxiety, because he was already a figure of personal and public disrepute. But it is the *Public Advertiser* that mounts the most complex and far-reaching critique both of the Ministry and of Lyttelton, and it is based on a firm sense of the regatta's theatricality: "Lord North, it is said, was the original Contriver of the Regatta, and with the same View that Sir Robert Walpole encouraged the Author of Hurlothrumbo to appear on the Stage, viz. that the Eyes of the People might be diverted from the destructive Measures which he meant to pursue."[25]

The confluence of history and theatre history is revealing, because the paper is modeling reception of the regatta on a prior instance of theatrical reception. Lyttelton is being compared to Samuel Johnson of Cheshire, the author of the opera *Hurlothrumbo*, who also played its most prominent character, Lord Flame, in its highly successful run at the Haymarket in 1729. It is an apt comparison because, like the regatta, the opera was rife with confusion and inconsistency. The suggestion that Lord North operates as Walpole did is already damning enough, but the full weight of the attack relies on familiarity with the controversy surrounding the "other Samuel Johnson." The insinuation that Lyttelton, like Johnson, is little more than a ministerial hack generates one valence of critique, but the alignment between Lyttelton and Lord Flame carries even more punch, because this character was the incarnation not only of confused politics but also of suspect masculinity. In her discussion of Johnson, Susan Aspden points out that

> the plot of *Hurlothrumbo* revolves around a rebellion at court, with all the questions of good government that such stories necessarily entail. Such a brief description hardly does the play justice, however. In its political machinations and complex love intrigues it contains elements familiar to audiences from both tragedy and opera seria, but it veers between Miltonic sublimity and schoolboy obscenity, punctuating heroic bombast with slapstick humour. And if the continually shifting register made comprehension difficult, this difficulty was compounded by the character of Lord Flame, played by Johnson himself, whose regular intrusions and manic railings—both sung and spoken—confused and frustrated plot and characters alike. . . . Descriptions of Johnson's performance emphasise the impression of unpredictable fluctuation, claiming that he performed 'sometimes in one key, sometimes in another, sometimes fiddling, sometimes dancing, and sometimes walking on high stilts,' like a performer in one of London's many freak shows.[26]

Johnson's freakish volatility is an apt figure for Lyttelton's fluctuating politics, but it is the larger connotation of suspect masculinity that is most important for subsequent discussion of the regatta. As Aspden argues, Johnson's performance style was associated with the physical abnormalities and the sexual excesses of the castrati, and thus he is also an apt figure not only for Lyttelton's libertinism but also for the overriding sense that the regatta, like *Hurlothrumbo* itself, is a sign of a debauched culture. The critiques of castrati and of Italian opera in general were tied to fears that gender insubordination was a sign of or perhaps even a cause of poor governance. In short, the *Public Advertiser*'s theatrical comparison not only reads the regatta as a symptom of a perverted social order but also suggests that the perversion of the social has the imprimatur of the state.

This discourse on sexual perversion and gender insubordination is eventually extended from Lyttelton himself to the press's representation of the Town, but as the critique becomes more general, it also becomes detached from North's Ministry. Virtually every paper prints some kind of a jest or a poem ridiculing Lyttelton, Luttrell, or other participants as macaronis. Some, such as "A Macaroni Ode, written by a Macaroni Poet on the Evening of the Regatta," amount to little more than gentle satires on effeminacy and vanity:

Little Muses come and cry,
Put your Finger in your Eye;
Join the *Macaroni* Kind,
Demn the Rain, and demn the Wind.

Winds that rumple Powder'd Hair,
Winds that fright the feather'd Fair,
Winds that blow our Hats away,
And rudely with our Ruffles play.

Winds that drown the gentle Note
Fritter'd through a gentle Throat;
Winds that Clouds around us throw,
And spoil the Glitter of our Show.

Demn the Winds that thus have stirr'd
On Friday June the twenty-third,
To plague the *Macaroni* Kind:
Demn the Rain, and *demn* the Wind.[27]

But other contributions are more pointed in their representation of the social entity progressing up the river:

> A Correspondent observes, that an *invitation to the Regatta* should have been conceived and expressed in the following terms:—*Lord Tinsel, Sir Harry Flutter, or Mr. Fribble*—presents his compliments to *Lady Fanny Cotillion*, and begs the honour of her company on Friday evening to see all that *can be seen* on the river Thames; to dance at Ranelagh, *as soon as the building erected for that purpose can be finished*; to find her way about the garden *without the aid of illuminations*, and to eat her supper, *if she can get any*.[28]

The less-than-subtle invocation of fop characters from plays such as Garrick's *Miss in her Teens* attempts to contain the threat of gender insubordination by linking it to past satires of foppery while downplaying the political implications of the *Public Advertiser's* invocation of *Hurlothrumbo*.[29] However, not all theatricalizations of the event aimed to contain its potential for figuring forth a topsy-turvy world of effeminate men and rebel politics.

The *Morning Post*'s attacks on Lord Lyttelton were especially virulent, and they demonstrate the degree to which the figuration of the event as theatre not only allowed for an intertwining critique of both the state and the aristocratic participants in the regatta but also opened onto a different and equally important allegation of vice. Its opening salvo was imbued with sarcasm regarding his private life, but it turned on a scene of theatrical reception:

> As it would have been well understood, independent of publications, that Lord L[yttelton] undertook the chief management of the Regatta from motives of patriotism, and from those refined feelings of benevolence that distinguish his character, both in public and private life; the subscribers with grateful hearts will be bold to affirm, that in case of a second exhibition more money will be collected than at the first, and that the public will receive his Lordship with louder acclamations of groans and hisses than those they so liberally bestowed on a late occasion.[30]

This sense of some abstract public hissing a bad play is given much more specificity the following day:

> It was some time ago doubted, but it now amounts to a certainty, that Lord L[yttelton] deals with the devil, as he has the power to turn day into night.—Large sums were depending on this matter at the Scavoir Vivre, and the other clubs, but such was the power of his art and judgement that he won all his bets; for at the appointed hour of seven o'clock the day (or rather the night) on which the Regatta was exhibited, began to close with such an infernal Scotch mist, with thunder, lightening and rain, that leaves not a doubt of the deepness of his skill in the art of magick; and such was his consummate power of attraction, that he carried the whole procession from Westminster-bridge to Ranelagh, in the dark, in one general chaos of confusion, with himself in the middle of them, in his favourite Wager Gondola, to the no small mortification of the numberless spectators that filled the houses and scaffolds, and lined the shores on both sides of the water.[31]

The allusion to the witches from *Macbeth* carries a heavy rhetorical burden here: it figures Lyttelton's unnaturalness; it suggests that the Thames Regatta inaugurates, as the witches' speech did, a period of political mayhem; and it allows for yet another allegation of Scottish influence. As we will see, allusions to *Macbeth* serve other purposes as well, but for the moment it is enough to recognize that all of these aberrations in the right order of things are deployed to satirize one particular vice, namely gambling. The suggestion here is that the real driving force behind the regatta is a kind of unnatural economy based on the fraudulent manipulation of wagers and bets among clubbable men and debauched women. And Lyttelton emerges as a kind Mephistophelean figure doing the devil's business by enthralling the entire Town.

Whether Lyttelton's vices are sexual or confined solely to the gaming tables is not important, because these assaults on Lyttelton's character cannot be simply ascribed to faction or to personal malevolence. Throughout this period, gaming and sexual misconduct are correlative elements of widespread criticism of the conduct of the upper ranks. For all the *Gazetteer*'s or the *Morning Chronicle*'s attempts to argue for the regatta's public good, it is important to recognize that even their apologies for the event express considerable anxiety about the private character of public individuals, especially those proximate to positions of state power. These anxieties were not new; they were part and parcel of the reporting of fashionable sociability throughout the 1760s and 1770s, particularly in its most commercialized forms. As Russell has argued, much of this anxiety was a result of the almost contradictory propagation of exclusivity and social mobility in entertainments at Carlisle House and the Pantheon.[32] These anxieties were thematized in the theatre in the early 1770s in plays such as Burgoyne's *The Maid of the Oaks* and Garrick's *Bon Ton, or, High Life Below Stairs*. Garrick's afterpiece was first staged in March 1775, and it was an obvious touchstone for newspaper accounts of the regatta, only now the scene of class mingling had expanded exponentially:

> The Ladies in general were dressed in White, and the Gentlemen in undress Frocks of all Colours; and 'tis thought the Procession was seen by at least 200,000 people. In a Word, from the mixed Multitude of Lords and Liverymen, Pinks, and Pickpockets, Dukes and Dustmen, Drabs, and Dutchesses; the whole Scene afforded an admirable Picture of High Life below Stairs, and Low Life Above.[33]

The mingling of classes and reputations was both novel and discomfiting enough to warrant extensive press coverage, and many of the themes of aristocratic dissipation and the social diffusion of vice are rehearsed with regard to the regatta.

This was particularly pointed in the case of Samuel Foote's production of Charles Dibdin's *The Waterman, or the First of August* that ran from late May until the end of the summer at the Haymarket. Advertisements for the play indicated that it was being staged "on account of the Regatta."[34] Dibdin's two-act ballad opera, or ballad farce as he calls it in his preface, was first produced the previous summer and it is perhaps best described as the kind of low entertainment that kept the Haymarket profitable in this period.[35] But in the context of June and July 1775, Dibdin's play offered a sort of counterdiscourse from which one can assess the Thames Regatta. It cobbles together a number of Dibdin's theatrical songs into a hackneyed story of two young men, the honest waterman Thomas Tug and the foppish theatregoing Robin, who are vying for the hand of Wilelmina, the daughter of Bundle the Gardener. Bundle believes in being true to his laboring origins and thus favors Thomas; Mrs. Bundle has pretensions to fashionability and thus favors Robin; but it is Thomas who wins Wilelmina's affection by winning Doggett's Coat and Badge Race. Wilelmina's first song takes the entire action of the play and locates it in one simple choice, and I would argue that the question she poses has a remarkably long life:

> Two youths for my love are contending in vain,
> For do all they can,
> Their sufferings I rally, and laugh at their pain;
> Which, which is the man
> That deserves me the most? let me ask of my heart,
> Is it Robin, who smirks, and who dresses so smart?
> Or Tom, honest Tom, who makes plainness his plan?
> Which, which is the man? (1.5.7)

The key question here, "Which is the man?" recurs with increasing urgency as the American war unfolds, only it will be asked of the leaders of the nation, and with remarkable specificity when Hannah Cowley poses the question in her complex comedy of this name. I discuss that play at some length in chapter 5, but for the moment it is important to think through the choice on offer at the Haymarket, while the rest of London is preparing for the regatta.

The two men are distinguished by their relation to their superiors. Robin and his advocate, Mrs. Bundle, are infatuated with the world of the theatre. It is at the theatre that they mix with their betters and that they have developed a desire for sentiment and, above all, class mobility. Dibdin satirizes this desire mercilessly by ridiculing Robin's affected dress and speech. His predilection for simile means that much of what he has to say to Wilelmina swirls away in a flourish of wit without substance. Tom also has little in the way of substance to offer, except his extraordinary capacity for labor. And as the opening chorus tells the audience, "Labour is the poor man's wealth" (1.1.1). He is at times referred to as a barbarian—Mrs. Bundle calls him a Vandil and a Hottentot—but this is all in aid of satirizing Robin's false civility. Tom is the epitome of the hardworking Englishman, and thus when he is confronted with the possibility of not receiving Wilelmina's hand, he first pledges to join the navy and sail on a man of war, and then decides to show his merit by winning the Doggett Race.[36] The alignments are obvious: everything drives toward the rejection of false refinement and foppish masculinity, here figured by Robin, and the validation of the honest liberty of the waterman.

But the corollary to this argument is even more important. What has to be ejected above all else are the desires generated by the excessive mixing of plebeians and patricians.[37] Dibdin's harshest satire is reserved for the termagant Mrs. Bundle, whose commitment to theatrical sociability and mixed company has corrupted her sense of class identity and her use of the English language. As act 2 unfolds, virtually every speech she has contains a misused part of speech, making her Dibdin's version of Mrs. Malaprop.[38] Late in act 2, Lady Bundle strikes out in an air that is aimed at convincing Wilelmina of the value of "accomplishments," but which instead demonstrates that those Mrs. Bundle seeks to imitate have corrupted Englishness itself:

To be modish, genteel, and the true thing, my dear,
In short, to be monstrous well-bred,
You must ogle and simper, and giggle and leer,
And talk the first nonsense that comes in your head.

In grave, fusty old-fashioned times,
'Ere ease and deportment went hence;
To be bold was the vilest of crimes,
And deceit was an heinous offence:

But the fashions are now of another guess kind,
Our modes are by no means the same;
For, bless'd with good eyes, we pretend to be blind,
And with strength to run miles, appear lame. (2.6.34)

The monstrosity of indiscriminate mixing has corrupted Mrs. Bundle's and Robin's strength of body and of mind. In contrast, Tom's most elaborate song not only celebrates his skill and strength as a waterman but also emphasizes that he is impervious to class contagion, even when he is in close proximity with its most enticing avatars:

What sights of fine folks he oft row'd in his wherry,
'Twas clean'd out so nice, and so painted with all;
He was always first oars when the fine city ladies,
In a party to Ranelagh went or Vauxhall.

And oftentimes wou'd they be giggling and leering,
But 'twas all one to Tom, their gibing and jeering,
For loving, or liking, he little did care,
For this waterman ne'er was in want of a fare. (1.5.9)

Furthermore, this argument about the mixing of ranks is carefully registered in terms of the play's scenography. We only ever hear about Robin's and Mrs. Bundle's trips to the theatre, but the resolution of the play's romantic dilemma is securely placed in "The Swan" at Chelsea, a space where Bundle, and the victorious Tom Tug, feel socially at home. Dibdin's blunt presentation of the politics of social space fully engages with the primary anxieties associated with the Thames Regatta without ever explicitly referring to the event. But audience members who attended the Haymarket productions of *The Waterman* five days before or two days after the regatta would have been well primed by newspaper reports of the event, for this careful attention to the space of sociability is a vital component of the newspaper coverage. The indirect indictment of the regatta via the production of *The Waterman* at the Haymarket was eventually made much more direct. On 14 October 1776 the afterpeice was taken up by Drury Lane and was modified so that it concluded with a Grand Representation of a Regatta.[39] The remediation of the regatta at the close of *The Waterman* was a feature of all subsequent productions at Drury Lane, and we will return to these productions at the close of this chapter.

In rehearsing the events on the river, the papers were representing that part of the regatta which was potentially available to anyone able to make their way down to shore. One paper reported that the regatta was witnessed by three million people.[40] This sense that the audience could and did include people from all ranks and backgrounds permeates the reporting of the first phase of the regatta. Many of the papers were fascinated by the intermingling of ranks and sexes and tended to figure the event as an extreme instance of other notable venues of mixed sociability, such as the theatre and the fair. What interests me about the mediation of the event is the way in which the papers both operate as the audience for the regatta and conjure up specific instances of audience response. Almost immediately after the first reports of the regatta, several letters to the printers, ostensibly written by witnesses to the spectacle, use the occasion not only to describe the event as an aesthetic experience but also to dramatize the complexity of aesthetic judgment. The most revealing of these exercises focuses on a much-harried gentleman, who tries to keep his family and servants happy by securing tickets for the regatta, but who is appalled not only by the nature of the entertainment but also by the event's monopoly on public discourse:

> Nothing, Sir, can fully describe to you the situation of my animal oeconomy for this month past, on account of the promised *Regatta*; my wife plaguing me at home, my friends teazing me abroad, all conversation turning upon this one solitary subject, even politics giving place to the *Regatta*. . . . Sleeping and waking my mind has been haunted by the *Regatta*; my nerves have been afflicted, my spirits opressed, my philosophic system disconcerted, my peace violated, and my passions tormented, with the most extravagant expectations from the *Regatta*. If I stepped into a coffee-house for a temporary relief, the *Regatta* still followed me thither. Old and young, grave citizens, with flowing wigs, and spruce Templars, with pudding curls, talked of nothing but the *Regatta*.[41]

In almost novelistic discourse, the reader is presented with an identifiable character, here named "HOMO," trying to navigate the public hysteria surrounding the regatta; he is a gentleman, of taste and education, open to entertainment, but deeply disappointed and troubled by the fare on offer.

He sarcastically rails against the "courteous advances of a very respectable member of society, who solicited me, in holiday phrases, to purchase a pennyworth of the very best hot spice gingerbread nuts to stuff in my guts, to expel wind, and employ time."[42] As the commercial advances come in from all sides, he declares that the pye-men "engaged as much of the publick attention and admiration, as any thing that was transacting on the water."[43] Put simply, the character represented by this letter is offended by the fact that he was led to expect a show that "unites the grand and the marvellous, the grace and the glitter of a multitude of fine objects; it feasts the imagination with concerts of Greek and Roman pageantries, drums, trumpets, banners, men, women, and children; trappings of the most brilliant devices, and everything that is more captivating than common."[44] But instead was presented with

> a lovely collection of wherries, cutters, barges, and bumboats, promiscuously huddled together without the minutest degree of order, decency, or beauty . . . [and] a large mob of draggle-tail'd old women crouding the shores with ardent curiosity, fifty-five thousand of his Majesty's liege subjects plaistered up to the shoulders in filth of fifty complexions, and about half a million of every denomination, age, and order, piled upon the house-tops and places provided for their reception.[45]

Despite his demonstrable disgust with the lack of order and distinction, both in the spectacle and in the audience, the gentleman's reception of the event is not simply a harangue. He states explicitly that all of this mess prompts a different kind of aesthetic pleasure:

> The first sensation of delight that operated upon my nervous system was the recollection of a favorite catch of Mr. Purcell's, called Bartholomew Fair.
>
> Here's the Whore of Babylon, the Devil, and the Pope;
> Here's the man just going to dance upon the rope;
> Tut tut tut tu goes the little penny trumpet;
> Here is Jacob Hall will jump it, jump it, &c.
>
> This you may be sure had an elegant effect upon an enthusiastic brain for the time being; but, Sir, so many extraordinary objects kept constantly crowding and shoving, and pressing upon my passions, that my whole frame was most violently electrified with rapture.[46]

This is a curious gesture because it suggests that, through the distancing strategies of satire and allusion, an event as chaotic as that represented here can afford the occasion for a kind of oppositional pleasure. The allusion to Purcell allegorizes Cornelys as the Whore of Babylon, Lyttelton as the Devil, and Luttrell as the Pope, only now the attack comes with a host of other associations regarding low entertainment. The humor of the entire piece is premised on precisely this economy of ridicule, and the readers are invited to both partake of the event and separate themselves from it. As a rhetorical gesture, it places readers both inside and outside of the space of performance and thus allows them to identify with a position of exclusive distinction—I can look on this as Pope looked upon the devolution of literary taste in *The Dunciad* —and yet still be electrified with rapture like any other member of the mob. This is an important rhetorical dynamic, because, like similar gestures already discussed in relation to the "Oak Gazette Extraordinary," it generates simultaneous fantasies of exclusivity and promiscuous inclusion. The paradoxical collocation of these two positions requires the construction of a fictional persona that enables the press to simultaneously endorse and censure the regatta.

In many cases, this fictional observer is folded into the speaking voice of the paper itself. But the vast majority of the papers sharpened the satire by carefully interweaving references to the political controversies attending the hostilities in America. Take the following description of the mustering of the barges before the wager race and the procession to Ranelagh, which was reprinted in almost all the papers:

> Before five o'clock Westminster-bridge was covered with spectators, in Carriages and on Foot, and Men even placed themselves in the Bodies of the Lamp Irons. Plans of the Regatta were sold from a Shilling to a Penny each, and Songs on the Occasion sung, in which Regatta was the rhyme for Ranelagh, and Royal Family echoed to Liberty. The tops of the houses were covered, and the sashes of many Windows taken out, and perhaps there was not one Boat disengaged, whose Owner chose to work. Before six o'clock it was a perfect fair on both Sides the Water, and bad Liquor, with short Measure, was plentifully retailed. The Bells of St. Martin were rung in the morning, and those of St. Margaret's during the afternoon.
>
> The whole river formed a splendid Scene, which was proportionally more so nearer to Westminster-bridge. A City Barge, used to take in Ballast, was, on this Occasion, filled with the finest Ballast in the World—above 100 elegant Ladies.—The Avenues to the Bridge were covered with Gambling Tables. Occasional Constables guarded every Passage to the Water-Side, and took Money for Admission, from Half a Crown to a Penny. Soon after Six, Drums, Fifes, Horns, Trumpets, &c. formed separate little Concerts under the several Arches of the Bridge. This was succeeded by firing of Cannon from a Platform before the Duke of Richmond's, who, as well as his Grace of Montague, and the Earl of Pembroke, had splendid Companies on the Occasion. At half-past seven the Lord Mayor's Barge moved, and falling down the Stream, made a Circle towards the Bridge, on which 21 Cannon were fired as a Salute; and just before it reached the Bridge, the Wager-Boats started on the Signal of a single Piece of Cannon. They were absent near 50 Minutes, and on their Return the whole procession moved, in a picturesque Irregularity, toward Ranelagh. The Thames was now a floating Town. All the Cutters, sailing Boats, &c., in short, every Thing, from the Dung Barge to the Wherry, was in Motion.[47]

The collocation of gaming, elegant women, commerce, and the names of some of the foremost men of the realm is typical of the reporting of Cornelys's entertainments, but various details, when taken together, push this account into another realm altogether. At first glance, this description seems dominated by tropes of intemperate mixing: elegant ladies are figured as ballast; the floating Town includes the Dung Barge, a general term for a boat carrying all manner of sewage and rubbish; and the most elegant wherries, church bells, and "separate concerts" come together in a cacophony of sound. This in itself is significant because it presages a confusion in ranks that can be found in more threatening forms throughout the passage. The event is described as both a "perfect fair" and a "floating Town," and thus the distinction between low and high has been rendered obsolete.[48] Ballads rhyming "Royal Family" and "Liberty," at a time when Wilkite resistance to the Crown is once again gaining momentum, are not innocuous cultural signs. No matter whether the unspoken lines reassert the Crown's relation to ancient constitutional liberty—that is, refute Wilkite critiques—or firmly endorse Wilkes's politics, the mere collocation of these words calls up past and present conflict.

Threading through this representation of boundary-breaking social mixture are signs of unrestrained commerce: ballads are being sold, cheap liquor is flowing from the avenues down to the river, and even access to the river was itself subject to an admission charge. But most importantly the passage gives a sense of almost ubiquitous gambling. The wager race at the heart of the river activities was the focus of betting, but as other papers indicated, vast sums were staked on whether the event would reach Ranelagh or on whether certain personages would participate. In this light, the entire scene is one of illegitimate commerce breaking down all manner of social distinctions.

Into this maelstrom of social insecurity, the account gives us four names of conspicuous celebrants: the lord mayor, the Duke of Richmond, George Montagu, and the Earl of Pembroke. The first three were prominent voices in the resistance to the Ministry's American policies. Of Wilkes's pro-American activities as Lord Mayor, we have already spoken. Charles Lennox, the 3rd Duke of Richmond, had been a supporter of Wilkes in the 1760s, and his biography recounts his pro-American positions:

> His opposition on American questions was comprehensive and originally reflected the Rockinghamite view that, while parliament possessed legislative supremacy over the colonies (as stated in the Declaratory Act of 1766 that Richmond had supported), it should not use its power to force the colonists to submit to parliamentary taxation. He resisted the North administration at every step, speaking frequently in the upper house and offering a variety of resolutions and protests. Like many of his fellow Whigs, he believed that curtailment of American liberty would herald oppression at home. Once hostilities began he continued his opposition, and he was relentless in criticizing the ministry's management of the war effort. He was one of the first of the Rockingham party to take the view that

the Declaratory Act needed to be repealed as a barrier to a settlement, and he was an early convert to the idea of American independence. His pertinacity made him one of the most visible members of the opposition and one of those most resented by North's supporters.[49]

George Montagu, the 4th Duke of Manchester, was an important member of the Rockingham opposition to North's American policies in the Lords. He supported Chatham in the early months of 1775 in order to prevent any breach in the opposition and predicted with great clarity that the colonies could not be conquered and that France would enter the war.[50] In other words, this description seems to suggest that the regatta was particularly patronized by the most prominent critics of the Ministry in both the City and the House of Lords. This raises the question as to whether these pro-American politicians are part and parcel of the dissolution of rank and order all around them. However, such a conclusion fails to account for the Earl of Pembroke.

Henry Herbert, the 10th Earl of Pembroke, was appointed Lord of the Bedchamber to George III in 1769 and was thus part of George III's inner circle. But he was also a notorious adulterer, whose indiscretions had been forgiven by both his wife and his otherwise prudish king. Pembroke had a disastrous affair with the actress Kitty Hunter, so in a sense he is the embodiment of precisely the dissolution of rank that pervades the passage. The fact that he is patronized by the ostensibly moral king, and is lumped together with Richmond and George Montagu, indicates that the larger argument of this representation of the regatta has less to do with partisan politics than with a universal critique of the ruling elites. This is reaffirmed later in the passage when the correspondent indicates that the kings' brothers, the Duke of Cumberland and the Duke of Gloucester, were present as spectators but did not fully participate in the event, raising the question as to whether they were simply not cognizant of the regatta's subversive connotations or whether they were aware but unable to harness their authority to draw anything but the most cursory attention.[51] Neither possibility is especially flattering to the king. What this means is that for the papers and magazines that utilized this description, the regatta was aligned with notions of a society unraveling under the pressure of its own profligacy, with antiministerial politics and pro-American sympathies, and finally with a deep-seated anxiety that the nation and its ruling elites were not up to the challenge to authority being mounted not only in Boston, Philadelphia, and New York but also in the heart of the metropole itself.

The Tattered Pavilion, or Lord North's Hair

Thus far I have attended only to the river itself and to the men whose careers and reputations were most affiliated with the flow of power on the river. In this space, there is a subtle but consistent undercurrent of political commentary, either direct or allegorical, that blends the sense of crisis surrounding American affairs with suggestions that society is in a state of irrevocable decline. But there is a substantial shift in how the Thames Regatta is represented when the procession finally alights at Ranelagh. As the entertainment enters its second phase, a different set of anxieties is activated, and these turn less on the complex relationship between social exclusivity and the dissolution of rank and order than on the failure to sustain aristocratic sociability. As noted earlier, Teresa Cornelys was given the task of throwing a grand musical entertainment, a supper, and a ball in a hastily constructed Temple of Neptune adjacent to the Rotunda at Ranelagh. The following description is typical of the coverage in that it gives a rough sense of the entertainment, but the satirical gibes are considerably more muted:

> The company landed at the stairs between nine and ten o'clock, when they joined the assembly which came by land to the *Temple of Neptune*, a temporary octagon kind of building erected about twenty yards below the Rotunda, lined with striped linen of different coloured flags of the navy, with light pillars near the centre, ornamented with streamers of the same kind loosely flowing and lustres hanging between each.—It happened, however, that this building was not swept out, or even finished, when the company assembled, which prevented the cotillion-dancing till after supper: this room discovered great taste, but we cannot reconcile the temple of Neptune's being supplied with musicians in Sylvan habits.
>
> At half after ten the Rotunda was opened for supper, which discovered three circular tables, of different elevations, elegantly set out, though not profusely covered: the rotunda was finely illuminated with party-coloured lamps, and those displayed with great taste and delicacy; the center was solely appropriated for one of the fullest and finest bands of music, vocal and instrumental, ever collected in these kingdoms; the number being 240, in which were included the first masters, led by Giardini; and the whole directed by Mr. Simpson, in a manner that did him great credit.—It was opened with a new grand piece composed for the occasion, after which various catches and glees were admirably sung by Messrs. Vernon, Rein-

> hold, &c. &c. But the illumination of the orchestra had been unfortunately overlooked which gave that part of the design a gloomy appearance.
>
> Supper being over, a part of the company retired to the temple, where they danced minuets, cotillions, &c. without any regard to precedence: while others entertained themselves in the great room.—Several temporary structures were erected in the gardens, such as bridges, palm-trees, &c &c. which were intended to discover something novel in the illumination style, but the badness of the evening prevented their being exhibited.
>
> The company consisted of about 2000, among which were the first personages of distinction: viz. their royal Highnesses the Dukes of Gloucester and Cumberland, Duke of Northumberland, Lords North, Harrington, Stanley, Tyrconnel, Lincoln, their respective ladies, &c. also Lord Lyttelton, Coleraine, Carlisle, March, Milbourn, Cholmondley, Pertersham, &c. the French, Spanish, Prussian, Russian, and Neapolitan Ambassadors, &c. &c.[52]

There is an implicit recognition throughout the press that the Thames Regatta's structure mimicked that of Burgoyne's Fête Champêtre, in that the participants were under public scrutiny during the procession from Whitehall to Ranelagh but that the rest of the evening constituted a more "private" affair.[53] The event represented here is marked by its exclusivity, and, although less exalted types were in attendance, one is given the impression that the evening was dominated by a very particular strain of the Ton. The list of personages of distinction is in this case is quite revealing, because it is composed largely of discredited royals, dissipated and extravagant young lords, and elderly ineffectual army officers or parliamentarians. Lord North stands out in this company, and I would suggest that he is being subtly diminished by his inclusion.

What this means is that the struggle between the City and the Ministry, which kept floating through the accounts of the procession, disappears from view, and the reporting turns its attention to the politics of pleasure, or rather, to the politics of pleasure lost. However, this does not mean that the American question is drowned out by reports of high living; rather it resurfaces in a different historical mode. If the confusion on the river seemed to allegorize the political disarray instantiated by events in America, then the disrepair of the Temple of Neptune and Cornelys's failure to provide sufficient entertainment at Ranelagh seemed to presage something even more disturbing. Many of the papers describe the pavilion and the Rotunda as mere ruins of a palace of pleasure or as a postlapsarian garden where the exalted guests are starving and isolated from one another in the dark. In a damning comparison to the similar failures of Garrick's Shakespeare Jubilee, the *St. James Chronicle* stated that at least the "*Personae Dramatis* . . . were kept within doors by the Rain."[54] Even the *Gazetteer* in its most apologetic mode gives a clear sense of unfulfilled pleasure:

> The violence of the wind and the rain not only hurt the shew on the water, but effectually demolished the decorations without doors at Ranelagh; the exterior part of the Rotunda was hung with near four thousand white lamps, not one of which could be kept in; and there were various obelisks, arches, paintings, illuminations, &c. all executed from the designs of the most eminent artists, and conformable to every idea of marine character, as the foundation of the whole festival, and each of which were rendered useless.—The grand pavilion which communicated with the Rotunda by arcades, was nearly finished on the preceding day, and most superbly decorated with naval trophies, pendants, ensigns, streamers, &c. but the violence of the wind, during the hurry on the 23d, not only damaged the foundation, but rent a great part of the canvas on the outside, and there was not sufficient time for the restoring it to its original state; besides which, the band of music, habited like Tritons and Nereids, which were intended for the pavilion, were kept so late on the river . . . that the managers were obliged to order one of the bands of Satyrs and Fawns to leave the garden and entertain the company under cover (from the rain) in the Temple of Neptune.[55]

It is clear that Cornelys's design for the entertainment at Ranelagh intended to use the aquatic occasion of the regatta to celebrate naval supremacy. This much is reflected in the remarkable tickets produced for the event in which Neptune, at Britannia's behest, adjudicates the race on the Thames with the Rotunda of Ranelagh discreetly nestled in the background (fig. 2.3). But it was precisely these naval and national emblems, due to either damage or lack of preparation, that had to be jettisoned or, worse still, retained in a ruined state. Readers of the papers were left to contemplate a scene that leant itself to a particularly gloomy allegorical reading. With the navy quite literally in tatters, and the representatives of the army struggling to scare up some supper among a host of macaronis and other people of dubious reputation, the celebration starkly emblematizes a postimperial future.

This emblematic reading of the event becomes more elaborate and more entrenched when we look carefully at the elements of Cornelys's preparations that generate the most criticism: the dissonant presence of satyrs and fawns in the Temple of Neptune, and, of course, the scanty supper. Cornelys's reputation as

Figure 2.3. Francesco Bartolozzi, "Ticket: Regatta-Ball at Ranelagh XXIII June MDCCLXXV," engraving (1775). BM 1897,1231.369. Department of Prints and Drawings © Trustees of the British Museum.

a hostess turned, above all, on her management of musical entertainments, and the regatta celebration demonstrates that her ability to marshal prominent musicians was undiminished. As reported, the orchestra was the largest convened before the Handel Commemoration in 1784, which we will be considering in chapter 6. No less a personage than Felice di Giardini, the great violinist and conductor who revolutionized the orchestra at the King's Theatre, was employed to oversee the music, and the evening featured famous singers, culled from the ranks of Covent Garden, such as Joseph Vernon and Frederick Charles Rheinhold. In other words, Cornelys was after a certain kind of grandeur that is reflected in the musical program itself, which is dominated by selections from Handel's *Acis and Galatea*, *Alexander's Feast*, and especially *L'Allegro, Il Penseroso et Il Moderato*, and supplemented by popular compositions, such as Brewer's

"Turn Amaryllis to thy Swain" and Este's "How Merrily we live." The opening song from *Acis and Galatea*, "Oh the Pleasures of the Plains," establishes the pastoral idiom of the evening's entertainment, and it is reinforced by repeated returns to the L'Allegro passages from Charles Jennens's 1740 adaptation of Milton's poems. The uninhibited pastoralism of the program gives us a clue as to what was really at stake in Cornelys's design for the evening at Ranelagh.

If the weather (and poor preparation) had not intervened, the company would have found itself strolling among physical emblems of naval supremacy and served by attendants dressed as Tritons and Nereids. The scene of entertainment would have been secured and permeated by a sense of oceanic control. This is stated explicitly in "An Ode for the Regatta, or Water Jubilee, performed on Friday night at Ranelagh," which was widely reprinted in the papers:

BRITANNIA! blest with soft repose,
(Whose fields in richest repose are drest,
Whose vallies spread their verdant vest)
Thus from her peaceful palace rose,
And to the Deities her pray'r addrest!
"O'er my fair isle (the glory of the main)
This day may Love triumphant reign!"
    The Goddess never prays in vain;
At Jove's supreme, propitious nod,
Forth from the chambers of the main,
Quick darts the coral-crowned God!
Glad Tritons at his presence sounding!
Notes from Albion's rocks rebounding!
His awful trident shakes the ground!
What solemn silence reigns around!
Nor surges lash the trembling shore,
Nor dare the winds tumultuous roar.
But slowly slide the conscious billows—
Softly wave the list'ning willows!
Whilst Neptune, with majestic smile,
Accosts the Goddess of our Isle!
    "To crown this chosen, happy day,
My offspring shall my will obey;
The daughter of the genial main,
The Queen of youth and rosy smiles!

(Queen of dimple-dwelling wiles)"
Comes, with all her Paphian train!
She comes! The conscious sea subsides!
Neptune curbs his hundred tides!
Smooth the silken surface lies,
Where Venus' flow'ry chariot flies!
Paphian maids around her move,
Keen-ey'd Hope, and Joy, and Love!
Close by her side, her darling son she brings,
With quiver full! He claps his wanton wings!
He takes his aim! behold each pointed dart!
With pleasing anguish pierce the destin'd heart!
Love and Music spring from heav'n!
Sovereigns of the human soul!
And by Nature wisely giv'n
Ruder passions to controul.
Beauty's empire far extends,
O'er the ocean's wide domain:
From the world's extreamest ends,
To Britannia's happy plain.
Behold! In every youthful breast
(Thames' banks have nurst the flame)
Venus, ever-welcome guest,
Courts the generous Sons of Fame!
(FULL CHORUS)
Happy Island! happy King!
Where the free-born subjects live!
Where the circling seasons bring
All that Love and Glory give.[56]

What is significant here is the relationship between Jove, Neptune, and pastoral pleasure. Commanded by Jove, Neptune guarantees stability for the pursuit of love and peace. As long as the sea is calm, pastoral pleasure can flow unabated. The peace of the isle is necessarily tied to the control of the main—hardly a novel construction, but one that recognizes that the navy's control of the oceans is a prerequisite for imperial stability. Furthermore, the entertainment's nationalist gestures, like those activated in Burgoyne's Fête Champêtre, are not only fully aligned with pastoral images of verdant valleys but also contingent upon a normative economy of desire, here figured by Venus and Cupid, which is itself secured by Britannia's prayer to Jove and Neptune. Thus, the erotic dynamics of the regatta entertainment, as projected both here and in the musical program, are folded into a sweeping fantasy of empire. But with the Tritons and Nereids lost somewhere on the river, the entire symbolic economy of the entertainment was destabilized; and suddenly the pursuit of pastoral love, and the nationalist imperatives attached to it in the song, turned in on themselves, and became signs of failure or, worse, perversion. This accounts for the proliferation of jokes regarding "Master-misses" and other macaroni types dominating the scene.[57] By the terms set out in this ode, it would appear that Britannia may have prayed in vain and that the regatta, by virtue of its failed figuration of aquatic, pastoral, and erotic stability, had the capacity to figure forth not only a state that has been abandoned by the gods but also a nation where Love and the land are stricken with barrenness.

Nowhere is this sense of barrenness more explicit than in the widespread criticism of Cornelys's supper. If the pastoral music was a dissonant presence in the ruined aquatic scene, then the scanty supper was met with particular consternation as a sign not only of poor preparation but of poverty. With Cornelys's past social successes in the background, her failure to provide food, drink, or even shelter seems to capture fears regarding the future. In a curious reversal, Cornelys's blazing masquerades and concerts at Carlisle House, which were so ruthlessly critiqued as symptoms of social decay in the late 1760s and 1770s, suddenly become signs of national health, because their very excesses are indicators of economic stability and luxury. The unwritten assumption is of course that Britain is well on the way to a commercial collapse, and that the regatta, like a canary in a coal mine, is an indicator of social and political disaster.

This disaster is once again figured in theatrical terms, and it is here that previous references to *Macbeth* gain traction:

> It is allowed on all Hands that the Supper at the Regatta was execrably bad. It is true that Mrs. Cornelys possesses the Art of feasting the Eye, but affords no proportionate Entertainment to that part of the Body which the English are particularly solicitous to please. The supper only revived the memory of those which are set before the *Nobles of Scotland* in *Macbeth*, or the *Knights* in the *Installation* represented at Drury-Lane.[58]

Like the banquet scene in *Macbeth*, the party at Ranelagh is being figured as a turning point, or as a prophecy of sorts, in which the celebration is haunted by the ghost of the murdered friend. In the context of the American troubles, this amounts to saying that the Macbeth-like Crown and its Ministry, out of unnatural ambition, have not only slain liberty but also had to murder their closest friend, the Banquo-like Americans. Macbeth's horror, and the audience's understanding that his actions will fail, suffuse the scene. In this context, the paltry supper, the tattered pavilion, the macaroni celebrants, and even the uncooperative weather become prophetic signs of world-historical importance presaging a future where liberty and true English values will be carried on by the progeny of Banquo—that is, by the Americans.

This prophetic reading of the regatta is presented in far more blunt terms elsewhere in the press. Dropping the specific theatrical allegory, yet retaining the affective structure of the scene from *Macbeth*, two papers became preoccupied with Lord North's hair. According to the *Morning Chronicle*, "Lord North appeared at Ranelagh, on Friday, with his hair about his ears, as if he had been frightened by the last American news."[59] For the jocular *St. James Chronicle*, North's hair suddenly becomes a revelatory sign:

> It was thought that the Appearance of *Lord North* at *Ranelagh* would have occasioned some Fluctuation in the Stocks. He came in with his Hair in the utmost Disorder, and appeared in a State of Terror, which at once added to the Gracefulness of his Figure, and might have led the spectators to believe that he was pursued by Messrs. *Hancock* and *Adams*, with a Legion of *Bostonian Saints* at their Heels.[60]

John Hancock and Samuel Adams, presumably riding the Horses of War and Famine, bring the full force of Revelation onto the Ministry, and the effects will be registered on the Exchange. Lord North's hair, like the jokes themselves, betrays a certain level of fear that permeates not only the coverage of the regatta but also the representation of national and imperial affairs in the turbulent month of June 1775. This sense of fear was abiding and reached its apogee after Burgoyne's disastrous surrender at Saratoga in October 1777 and the entry of France and Spain into the war in 1778.

As one can imagine, these faux prophecies regarding the regatta are just one strain of a number of dire predictions for the outcome of the dispute with the American colonies. In Parliament, opposition leaders such as Charles James Fox in the House of Commons and the Dukes of Richmond and Manchester in the Lords argued vociferously that the colonies could not be conquered. But the representation of the regatta offers a comprehensive survey of the causes, not for the conflict, but for the lack of confidence in the patrician elites charged with defending the national interests. And the regatta provides a useful key for analyzing not only the representation of the Ton's fascination with camp culture in 1778 but also the primary strategies for the political satire on aristocratic folly in plays such as Sheridan's *The Camp* and Frederick Pilon's *The Invasion*. These plays and their relationship to reporting of the sociability of the camp at Coxheath have been the subject of superb readings by Gillian Russell and Robert Jones, so I am not going to rehearse these issues here. In the ensuing chapters, I turn to other performances from 1778 and 1779 in part to explore the proliferation of diffidence in the imperial imaginary and in part to offer a retroactive justification for the microhistory of performance you have just read.

The microhistories of performance presented in chapter 1 and in my reading of the Thames Regatta share an acute awareness of how space can be deployed to build complex political arguments about sociability itself. In this light, it is not surprising that the mediation of these events is so attentive to the spatial dynamics of performance and of the potential for space to signify a whole range of social concerns. Despite their status as temporary structures, Robert Adam's pavilion—and De Loutherbourg's remediation of it—stand in stark contrast to the "Tattered Temple" of the regatta. And it is clear from the newspaper reporting that the "stability" of the former and the fragility of the latter are directly linked to an argument that was seeking to shore up the masculinist institutions represented by someone such as Burgoyne from the incursion of forms of sociability, exchange, and culture associated with Cornelys and the other organizers of the regatta. And yet it is also evident from the press that there was a fascination with entropy, with the collapse of structure, with the disintegration of the "inside" world. This fascination, I would argue, is directly linked to the social insecurity prompted by the American war and it plays a crucial role in some of the most aesthetically effective theatre of the period. As we will see in the following example, questions of the relationship between inside and outside, kinship, and above all the capacity of the family romance to figure for the state lay at the core of a remarkably trivial distraction by one of the foremost political operators of the age.

Declaring Dependence: Opposition Fantasy in *The Duenna*

In light of the American crisis, how could a play such as Sheridan's *The Duenna* so radically and insistently take the town by storm? Sheridan's collaboration with Thomas Linley was first performed in the Covent Garden Theatre on 21 November 1775 and was staged 75 times in its first season. By the end of the century, it would have been performed 254 times. Written expressly for Covent Garden, the preferred site of musical theatre, it is arguably the epitome of Johnson's definition of entertainment as diversion or lower comedy. Linda V. Troost persuasively demonstrates that the power of Sheridan's opera lies in the music's capacity to add substance to otherwise stock characters.[61] But unless one is simply willing to attribute its extraordinary success to sheer musical genius, one has to confront the strangeness of its appeal. This has proved to be a real challenge for most scholars of Sheridan's work, who find it, in the words of John Loftis, "most innocent of thought on serious subjects."[62] But when Durant defends the opera on the grounds that it addresses significant themes, such as the "superior worth of individual freedom, especially freedom of mind and will, in its struggles against arbitrary counter-authority," it is difficult not to hear political connotations that resonate with Sheridan's own Rockingham principles.[63]

But this kind of thematic defense moves too quickly away from the opera's formal concerns, on the one hand, and from its particular historical situation, on the other. *The Duenna* has the auspicious distinction of being the first and unquestionably the most successful new mainpiece mounted in the patent theatres after the outbreak of war in the skirmish at Lexington and Concord. It was in almost constant performance until 1 June 1776 and then returns to the stage 9 November of the same year. In the hiatus between theatrical seasons, news of the Declaration of Independence swept through the press. Looked at in relation to these events, *The Duenna* seems best understood as an escape from history rather than a sign of it. But if we look carefully at *The Duenna*'s structure, what we discover is a very careful management of space that figures for a complex negotiation with the political problematics posed by American secession. Louisa flees the patriarchal authority of her father's house and finds herself in the carnivalesque danger of the streets. Sheridan mutes the danger of her situation, but the instability of the outdoors world, inherited from the Spanish honor play, serves Sheridan's interest well, because it allows him to explore the corruption of the interior spaces. The inside world is dominated by Don Jerome and Don Isaac Mendoza, two ancient figures whose escalating fantasies of acquisition drive the plot. For his part, Don Jerome wants to maximize the exchange value of his daughter by coercing her to marry Mendoza. Mendoza wants to acquire his prize at the lowest possible rate. Mendoza's attempt to outwit Don Jerome and avoid a settlement for Louisa backfires and he ends up not only enabling Louisa's and Clara's marriages to their preferred suitors but also marrying the Duenna himself.

What kind of questions should we be asking of a play like this? Should we be looking for a direct thematization of history, or evidence of attempts to avoid all reference to the crisis enveloping the empire? Neither of these approaches yields much. Both ways of handling the play run aground almost immediately because in the first scene both Don Jerome and Don Isaac Mendoza are figured as warriors. In act 1, scene 1, Don Jerome chases off Antonio with a blunderbuss, but, more significantly, Don Isaac is described as "an unskillful gunner" who "usually misses his aim, and is hurt by the recoil of his own piece."[64] Eighteenth-century theatrical audiences were highly attentive to topical allegory, and there is much to support an allegorical reading of the opera—especially because such an allegory makes frequent comparisons between the family and the state. In the opening act, war is invoked as a figure for the struggle of parents and suitors to control the objects of their desire. Mendoza and Jerome see Louisa primarily as a commodity over which they fantasize sovereign authority. Both men want to maximize her exchange value—Don Jerome wants as much as he can get for her, Don Isaac wants to get as much as possible for as little outlay. In a sense, the play works to ameliorate Louisa's commodity status, not by taking her out of the realm of exchange, but by ensuring that she is transferred to an owner of her choosing. That transferral is dramatically satisfying because her sojourn outside her father's protection, in the marketplace of the external world, is fraught with insecurity and potential threat.

With the commencement of hostilities at Lexington and Concord, Britain found itself in a curious position. Rebellious colonists, rather than following the precepts of their king, had taken up arms against his forces. In a remarkable way, the rebellious colonists had opened up an outside space within the empire. This performance of rebellion has its linguistic counterpart in the Declaration of Independence. Sheridan's play, pitched between the act of rebellion and the Declaration of Independence, approaches these events obliquely in order to lay out a series of wishful scenarios—the kind of oppositional response not taken by the Ministry and thus a kind of future not taken. If we wish to flesh out this allegory, Louisa's rebellion can be understood in a similar way to events in America, not simply because she is referred to as a "Virginia nightingale" (2.1, 248), but because she retires to a hidden space on stage and reemerges not as herself but as her Duenna. Masquerading as someone external to the family, Louisa is able to move from the inside to the outside world, from the palazzo to the piazza.[65] Once outside her doors, she can then become fully herself. It is only in the outside world that she can retroactively assert her independence from both her father and her Duenna. In this case, that independence is qualified because it is merely a transference to the object of her desire. It is more properly understood as a declaration of dependence. But perhaps we should not underestimate the radicality of that choice.

The Duenna herself embodies at least one strain of the opposition to the Ministry's response to colonial rebellion. Like many opposition figures in Parliament, she is inside the patriarch's house but excluded from Don Jerome's family at the play's outset. A trusted servant, she betrays Don Jerome and is explicitly recognized as a traitor to his interests twice in the play: first, when "she"—actually Louisa—is thrown out of his house for lack of loyalty and, second, when she—dressed as Louisa—is married to Don Mendoza. Remember this is a period when opposition members were regularly lampooned for "treason." Although she is able to pass as Louisa, her complex alterity is registered to the audience by her age and her supposed ugliness. When she accuses Don Jerome of tyranny in act 1, scene 3, he unleashes a vitriolic attack on her that makes much of her "dragon's front"; but his outburst ends with a very specific comparison to the Witch of Endor from 1 Samuel 28:7 (1.3, 239). Again the specificity seems to call for allegorical reading because it refers to one of the most potent political allegories in the history of dramatic music. This is no ordinary witch, for she plays a crucial role in one of the most important political allegories of the eighteenth century, namely Handel's *Saul*. Tragic in structure, *Saul* takes the confusing narrative of succession from the Bible and charts the transformation of King Saul's jealous antipathy for David into full-blown mania in which he inadvertently kills his son. In the final act of the oratorio, Saul breaks his own religious proscription and seeks the prophecy of the Witch of Endor before going into battle on Mount Gilboa with the Amalekites. She raises Samuel from the dead, and he reminds Saul of an earlier prophecy that declared that he would be destroyed by the Amalekites for his disobedience. Saul goes into battle and is killed by an Amalekite, whom David slays in turn. The oratorio ends with a remarkable funeral for both slain father and son that points to the emergence of David as the new king who will unite the tribes of Israel. As Ruth Smith and others have argued, the slaying of Saul by the Amalekite had always been read politically. In initial productions, the allegory was to the execution of James II.[66]

Here I would argue that the Duenna shares much with the Witch of Endor: she is a prophet who discloses the disintegration of one regime and ensures the emergence of another. Only here the new regime is basically a Whig fantasy of an Atlantic imperium ruled by a new Ministry and built of an alliance of states, rather than an empire ruled by a despotic king. The Duenna's specific charge of tyranny is part of a tactic to get her thrown out of Don Jerome's house and thus allow for the substitution of Louisa for the Duenna. Thus, she is able both to predict the dissolution of Don Jerome's control over Louisa and to effect her marriage to Antonio because her actions cause these events. She has been described by critics as a grotesque, and her physical repulsiveness is crucial to much of the play's humor, especially in the scenes where Don Mendoza pays her suit.[67]

These scenes are intriguing because two figures marked by their physical alterity are deployed to ensure that Louisa's passage from inside Don Jerome's house to the outside world and then to the arms of her husband is fully achieved. These two outsiders are brought together to liberate Louisa from parental tyranny. But it is important to note that Don Mendoza and the Duenna are opposite versions of the same prophetic figure and that their "entertainment value" turns on their relation to the future. Mendoza acts and the future turns out to be just the opposite of what he arrogantly predicted. The Duenna acts and her intentions are always fulfilled. The crucial recognition is that the combined efforts of Mendoza and the Duenna—the warrior suitor and the witch who can see how history will unfold—not only liberate Louisa but also ensure that the errant father is replaced by the new patriarch. Antonio and Louisa emerge as the new David and Michal, and a reconciliation is effected that guarantees the continuation, with a difference, of the nation. It is very tempting to read allegorically Don Jerome as a composite figure for Lord North and the king and Mendoza as a figure for the hapless military led by the already compromised George Sackville. In such an allegory, the Duenna emerges as the oppositional public already fully aware of the necessity of Louisa/America's transit from her father's house. In this allegory, the opposition—and notably Sheridan—finds itself in the position of the grotesque: a hybrid position from which both to observe and to assist in the dismantling of the father's tyranny. The key dramatic question is which grotesque relation to the future will be legitimated in the end. This is why the play refers to the reconciliation of the love plots as treason (234). Marriage to Antonio inaugurates a new patriarchal regime, and the audience is put in the position of watching and, in its desire for comic closure, abetting Louisa's rebellion. Because the play achieves this closure, Sheridan and the opposition find that their relation to the future is akin to that of the Duenna. She emerges more prosperous than before, but she is not separated from her "soldier" husband; rather Mendoza will clearly be subject to her petticoat government.

As the play moves from one patriarchal regime to another, literally reinaugurating patriarchal authority, the caricature of Mendoza remains an unrelenting constant in the structure of the play. His Jewishness was played for maximum effect by John Quick, but Sheridan's critique of Mendoza goes beyond typical eighteenth-century anti-Semitism by attacking Mendoza's delusion that he can outwit and outstrategize all those around him. *The Duenna*'s key satirical move turns on the fact that all of Mendoza's actions bring about the opposite of their intent. By marrying "Louisa," he ensures that she can marry her true beloved. It is helpful to see his actions as failed performatives, because in each case, but most obviously in the marriage, his actions formalize a discontinuity within Don Jerome's family that ultimately makes a mockery of his own marriage. If we understand Don Jerome and Mendoza as co-conspirators in the containment of Louisa's rebellion, then their failure needs to be considered first, as an effect of their own performance and, second, as a remarkable victory for Louisa and the Duenna's strategy.

Basically, Louisa and the Duenna enact a conspiracy of their own that not only declares their independence from the men who attempt to control them but also enacts a new kind of shared sexual sovereignty. At a certain level of allegorical signification, we could argue that, by masquerading as each other, they enact the emergence of a new kind of subject from a state of paternal and potential marital tyranny. At this level, they look similar to the "people," who, in declaring themselves independent, became sovereign. In other words, the allegory has the potential to get out of hand and figure for a complete revolution, not simply a shift from one Ministry to another. *The Duenna* plays out a simple fantasy wherein the American crisis is countenanced in its most benign form, because, of course, the disruptive potential of this allegory is contained by the fact that Louisa's marriage is in the end sanctioned by her father. She is brought back inside the family—and the play returns indoors—but in a significantly changed form. She is no longer a daughter-commodity, but now the property of another—that is, a wife-commodity. Whatever we might want to say about her performance of agency in the lead-up to her marriage, the play ends with a sort of diplomatic relation between her father's house and the house of her husband. Here is a post-American fantasy remarkably similar to that which would eventually come to pass. What Sheridan saves his audience from is the horrible period of all-out warfare, carnage, and loss that would precipitate Britain's eventual recognition of a new state on the far side of the Atlantic. And he offers instead a remarkable closing scene where the formerly decisive distinction between inside and outside, palazzo and piazza, dissolves into a wedding celebration where masqueraders traverse the threshold of Don Jerome's house.

The propagation of the opposition fantasy is effected by Louisa and the Duenna's ability to gull the play's tyrants, but that does require a sacrifice of sorts. The Duenna must marry Mendoza, and we need to consider the complexity of this union. What kind of a marriage is this? At one level, the marriage is financially lucrative for the Duenna, but it is somewhat jarring that the Duenna's intelligence and independence will be yoked to one as superficial and arrogant as Mendoza. I would argue that their age is a critical issue for understanding their ultimate significance. If we are reading allegorically, the Duenna steps in to preserve Louisa from the greed of both her father and his chosen Jewish suitor. In marrying Mendoza, she avails herself of his fortune, and thus what remains constant is her desire to maximize her social and economic advantage.

As one not provided for in Don Jerome's world and eventually thrown out of it, she builds an alliance that both secures her own standing and enables Louisa's liberation from and eventual reconciliation with her father. A necessary hinge in the plot, she is rendered old and unattractive as a way of registering that which the play is so careful to suppress: namely, that the transition afforded by the conspiracy of Louisa and the Duenna comes at great risk. The Duenna is grotesque because all of the violence and all of the fear unleashed by the rebellion of the American colonists in 1775 is tightly wound inside her. She is a sign of the disruption necessary to take Louisa and the colonies from one state to another. That Sheridan could understand her as a comic figure, as one able to act as the constitutive outside required for his audience to be productively distracted by their historical predicament, was wishful thinking. And it ensured that the play would survive as more than a simple diversion. After news of the Declaration of Independence reached London and *The Duenna* surged in popularity, the audience found itself able to imagine an end to the conflict that did not spell the end of its own way of life. In short, it could imagine a future that was not simply prescribed by the Ministry. That the audience could do so at such an early point in the conflict and via such indirect means cannot be proved, but I would like the reader to consider the possibility that such allegorical work was possible at this time of intense media saturation.

Whether or not the above allegorical reading of *The Duenna* is persuasive—and I would hope that it seems strained to readers familiar with the play—the reviews in the newspapers make no mention of it. Direct evidence that anyone experienced the opera in this way just does not exist. More could be done through an internal reading of the script to shore up the reading, but it is worth considering what did catch the papers' attention. As one might expect for such a popular production, the reviews are laudatory. But if one looks across the papers, virtually all of the papers register some discomfort with the relationship between the music and the spoken script. In some cases, this takes the form of a lament that Sheridan was contaminating the moral objectives of comedy by playing to the audience's low desire for musical entertainment. This discomfort with the hybridization of genre and with the threat to theatrical legitimacy was not uncommon, and in the hands of a correspondent to the *Morning Chronicle* named "Adelphos," it takes the form of a backhanded compliment in which Sheridan is chastised, first, for "driving the comic muse off the stage" by indulging her "childish music sister" and then, second, for wasting his obvious talent when he could be crafting a great tragedy or comedy.[68] Adelphos goes so far as to suggest that the "musical appendage" should amputated and the play run as a comedy. The *London Packet* concurred: "*The Duenna* is more like a comedy than any piece exhibited in either theatre since Mess. Garrick and Colman clubbed their wits to produce that excellent play THE CLANDESTINE MARRIAGE."[69] So here we have an opera, which everyone recognizes as the finest production of its kind since John Gay's *The Beggar's Opera,* actually being referred to as an engine for the reformation of comedy. William Woodfall in the *Morning Chronicle* states this most succinctly by starting his opening-night review with the declaration that *The Duenna* "might very aptly . . . be stiled a COMEDY interspersed with an OPERA."[70]

What interests me about this generic concern is the degree to which it supplants any discussion of the production's narrative or its meaning. Critics declare that it is funny or that it is pleasing. The king and queen demand back-to-back command performances.[71] But the press is most interested in the precise ways in which the songs and the script are knitted together. In the *Morning Chronicle* this is referred to first as an act of "interspersion," but later Adelphos argues, "The spirited dialogue of that piece is interrupted by the songs."[72] This sense of interruption takes on a life of its own when various reviewers recognize that the role of Carlos, played by the great singer Michael Leoni, has no function other than to provide the occasion for a demonstration of his virtuosity at the end of act 1.[73] The press is also quite intrigued by how the songs work as entertainment in and of themselves. Thomas Linley provided much of the music and some of the words for the songs, but the press was interested in two things: first, that the opera was composed of an amalgamation of new and old airs and, second, that some "airs were rather ill-adapted to the words they accompanied. Those that were composed did not please so much, and not for want of innate merit, but on account of their being more serious than the subject seemed to require."[74] Because many of the tunes were compiled from famous Scotch and Irish airs, well known to audience members, much of the amusement afforded by the opera lay in the way that Sheridan's words invoked, parodied, or commented on their precursors. This sense of the difference between the precursor song and present performance set up a dynamic historical gap within the music itself that was picked up by all the reviewers. Whether they were commenting on the difference between the style of performance between the songs in opera and their traditional counterparts, or the poor fit between words and melodies, or the jarring solemnity of much of the music composed for seemingly light situations, the press is indicating that the music is not only interrupting the "Comedy" but also eliciting a sense of disjunction throughout.[75] The *Morning Post* went so far as to suggest that the music did not do justice to the words.[76] And yet, for all of the unanimity on this point, the reviewers repeatedly attest to the pleasures afforded by the songs and the singers.

We know from the accounts of the composition of *The Duenna*, that the interspersion of opera into Sheridan's comedy was an extraordinarily difficult task.[77] We could argue that these remarks about the music are simply a sign of the harsh conditions of production Linley had to work under: Sheridan knew little about music and was basically improvising the libretto right to the last moment.[78] But I would prefer to understand them as signs of certain unrest coded directly into the formal structure of the opera. These interruptions and disjunctive performance moments were pleasurable in and of themselves, but they also interfered with the progress of the "spirited dialogue" of Sheridan's comedy. In an almost Brechtian fashion, both the interruption and the montage of airs prevent the play from unfolding as a legitimate comedy. The "opera" works as a kind of critical interference that is crucial to the production's popularity. When we recognize that the comedy has the potential to act as an allegory either for the successful secession of the thirteen colonies from the increasingly untenable Atlantic imperium, or for the transferral of power from North's Ministry to the Rockingham opposition, then the musical interruptions have the effect of keeping the disclosure of that allegory from overwhelming the audience. In effect, the allegory is attenuated so that the audience can gain some purchase on the emotions it has the potential to unleash.

If I am correct about this, the formal effects of interruption and bricolage that lay at the heart of Linley's and Sheridan's compositional strategies carry the affective burden of the allegory revealed through close reading of Sheridan's script. At the level of evidence, the remarks on music stand in lieu of commentary on the allegorical or thematic possibilities of the play. What is crucial is that Linley and Sheridan devised a method for staging disjunction that registered with the audience, but which did not escalate into a full-blown thematic or allegorical treatment of the historical situation. In other words, they devised a procedure whereby the audience could retain a certain subjective purchase on its historical position at a moment when imperial subjectivity was anything but stable. In a moment where the uncertain future of the Atlantic imperium had the potential to unravel the social fabric of the British nation and generate hitherto unseen disruptions in national subjectivity, this seemingly trivial entertainment offered a place where these historical conditions could be perceived, if need be, on a nightly basis until they could be fruitfully resolved. This is what I think is at stake in Benjamin's productive notion of distraction, for it is through these indirect but productive strategies that a new social body could emerge. Benjamin referred to this as a mass in order to deflect the problematic away from the identity effects traditionally associated with aesthetic contemplation. A similar deflection is helpful for this book's argument, especially when we look at Sheridan's remarkable treatment of Garrick's auratic performances in chapter 4, at Hannah Cowley's and George Colman's experiments with theatrical remediation in chapter 5, and at the suturing of Handel's Israelite oratorios in chapter 6. And as we will see in chapter 3, these kinds of disjunctive strategies can also be found in Captain John André's remediation of the Thames Regatta in Philadelphia in the spring of 1778.

How Far Away Is the Past?

As is well known, Sheridan's *School for Scandal*, which had taken the town by storm in the spring of 1777, dominated the theatrical calendar for the remaining years of the war.[79] It was presented forty-five times in the 1777–78 season and thirty-one times in 1778–79. Gillian Russell has recently provided an in-depth account of its critique of the mode of fashionable sociability pioneered by figures such as Teresa Cornelys, and, as such, it plays an important role in the cultural struggle over the dissipation of the upper orders.[80] Implicit in her argument is a recognition that this struggle is not simply about gender roles or hypocrisy, but rather that the incursion of women into the public sphere and the ensuing commercialization of fashionable sociability prompted widespread anxiety about the stability of the ruling elites. The charges of gender insubordination, of indiscriminate mixing of ranks, and of failed leadership surface frequently in the discourse surrounding the war, thus Sheridan's engagement with these issues is always already involved in the debates surrounding the American colonies.

In this light, it is intriguing that the play's explicit engagement with questions of empire is thoroughly oriented toward the East. As I have argued elsewhere, Sheridan offers a counter to Foote's highly successful excoriation of the East India Company in *The Nabob* that is remarkable for its realignment of the class dynamics of nabobry.[81] Although Sheridan's play is literally secured by East Indian capital, its representative of the East India Company is not a merchant or a man from the middle ranks. One of the most important elements of the portrait scene is that Charles is knocking down portraits that, in their specific details and in their totality, represent the landed gentry of England.[82] Thus, Sir Oliver witnesses the disposal not only of the aristocratic past but also of a chain of patriotic associations with the Duke of Marlborough and Britain's first empire. This fascinating scene quite literally presented the audience with an enactment of cultural and social disintegration that was not only perfectly apposite with Sheridan's attack on domiciliary sociability but also easily recognizable as part of the critique of the patrician elites running the war effort. Two questions are posed quite directly: How distant is the present moment from the glorious past of the Duke of Marlborough's martial fame? And can the connection to these ancestors be reclaimed in anything other than a nostalgic mode? Remember Charles demands that Sir Oliver exercise great care for the pictures because they are accustomed to veneration. Thus, transferring the pictures from Charles to Sir Oliver ironically amounts to putting Britain's cultural and social patrimony into safe storage in a time of emergency.

But even as it was activating this anxious relation to the first British empire, the play also promulgated a misrecognition of Britain's adventures in India: here the nabob is an aristocrat, not a merchant, whose capital is secure even when India no less than America was a site of intense contestation in this period. This is important because it mirrors the play's remarkably equivocal final scenes: all the signs of social disintegration routinely aligned with critiques of the aristocracy and the Ministry continue unabated at the end of the play, and the reclamation of truth and good English character is projected into the future. That these are so directly associated with the difference between the crisis in the Atlantic empire and the yet-to-be-realized fantasy of a burgeoning economy in the Asian subcontinent means that the play's two "outside" spaces exert remarkable pressure on the play's moral economy. As a play rigorously set in the interior spaces of fashionable London, it is as though Sheridan is arguing that these distant outside realms permeate British society to such a degree that proximate relations are themselves disrupted. In Pocock's terms, the empire has reconfigured the realm to such an extent that British identity is itself being turned inside out. What is fascinating is that the play locates all of these anxieties in the mediation of character, event, and situation. This is a play where ascertaining the truth requires a vigilant negotiation with how representation operates to separate intention and action, character and reputation, value and currency.[83] In the world of *The School for Scandal* it is impossible to measure the ethical relations between characters without thinking through how the distance between individuals is mediated, deformed, and interrupted by the commercial economies of sociability at home and empire abroad.

What Sheridan brings to the theatre in this period is a kind of social diagnostic that turns not only on an explicit derogation of suspect forms of sociability but also on a series of unresolved formal and thematic disjunctions that keep the anxiety that runs through his representation of the present from being resolved.[84] In other words, I would venture that the play's success lies in part in its capacity to productively engage with the social insecurity of the audience. What the mediation of the Thames Regatta brings to the forefront is the way that the press was able to generate a complex web of associations that do not directly impinge on government policy but which impugn the broader social world of London at this historical juncture. The press attacks not simply those involved in the event but also those who came down to the banks to watch it. Because this latter group included the speaking personae of the commentators in the press, the desire to witness fashion in all its glory or dissipation became a crucial part of the critique. It is not simply the scandal that is being explored by the press but also the fascination with scandal itself.

As the coverage of the Thames Regatta demonstrates, the press was interested in the way that fashion seemed to engage both its adherents and its observers into one large social symptom. I would argue that a similar gesture is crucial to *The School for Scandal* because so much of Sheridan's attention is placed on having the audience watch differential responses to moral and social corruption.[85] This is most obvious in the masquerade of Sir Oliver Surface: whether he is performing as Mr. Premium with Charles or Mr. Stanley with Joseph, he acts as an intermediary between the audience and the moral decay of his nephews. Watching Sir Peter Teazle react to the calumny of the scandalmongers in act 2, scene 2 operates in a similar fashion, but it also offers an important counterexample. Because he is less normative than Sir Oliver, the audience's judgment of his responses is far more complex and equivocal. This problematic perhaps reaches its most intense form with Lady Teazle in the screen scene, because the audience is forced to look at the ethical dilemma posed by the scene from both inside and outside her subject position. The play's equivocal treatment of her after the revelation carries the clear implication that scandal will not go away: it inheres in conversation, in print, and in the very theatre in which the audience sits. In this sense the comedy is a spectacle of reception and thus is not at all distant from Sheridan's and De Loutherbourg's more obvious experiments with theatrical spectacle in *The Camp*, "Verses on the Death of David Garrick, Spoken as a Monody," or *The Critic*.[86]

But, as my reading of *The Duenna* suggests, Sheridan was extremely cognizant of the way that the thresholds between spaces on stage could allow the opportunity for not only great comedy but also the potential for activating the deep-seated anxieties about the relationship between political inclusion and exclusion. The screen scene, for instance, is justly famous for its comic effect, but what really happens when the screen comes down? The barrier between two scenes of colloquy dissolves, and a radical leveling of the social landscape takes place. This device is hardly novel, but in light of the way that Sheridan dissolved the threshold between inside and outside in the marriage celebration of act 3, scene 7 of *The Duenna*, it represents not an opposition fantasy of imperial reconciliation according to Whig principles, but rather a recognition that resolving the social insecurity of the play and the empire is not going to occur so easily. In short, if *The Duenna* can be read as a form of wishful thinking on the part of the opposition, then *The School for Scandal* indicates that that reconciliation is a fantasy. It is from that recognition that Sheridan instantiates the critique of British society required for imagining a post-American world. In this regard, I argue in chapter 4 that *The Critic* is the final stage of a critical arc that emanates from *The Duenna*'s fantasy of reconciliation and proceeds through *The School for Scandal*'s diagnostic exemplification and then concludes with an extraordinary turning of the space of the theatre on itself.

One of the corollaries of this argument is that the paying customer of Drury Lane during the great run of Sheridan's comedy was at some level seeking to engage with this diagnostic. With the crisis of the American war raging, social critique was not only desired but commercially successful. This is an important point because the runaway success of *The School for Scandal* at Drury Lane prompted a very specific and intriguing response from Covent Garden. Once Sheridan's play hit the boards in May 1777, Covent Garden struggled to find a competing show. After the summer layoff, the managers of Drury Lane did not bring *The School for Scandal* back to the stage until 22 October. It was paired with *The Quaker* for much of the season and continued to generate extraordinary receipts. Covent Garden fell back on the stock repertoire for much of the fall until its new comic opera *Love Finds the Way* by Thomas Hull was presented on 18 November. The play was mounted twelve times but did not survive the season. Hull's adaptation of Murphy's *School for Guardians* was mercilessly ridiculed by both the papers and the opening-night audience.[87] On its second night, a slightly improved version ran against *The School for Scandal*, and the managers at Drury Lane decided to supplement Sheridan's comedy with Dibdin's *The Waterman* complete with a reenactment of the Thames Regatta tacked on the end that was most likely designed by De Loutherbourg. The Haymarket performances of *The Waterman* were intermittent in the period after its composition and confined to the spring and summer, but at Drury Lane the augmented show was frequently mounted to much acclaim, and I would argue that the reenactment of the regatta was vital to its success.[88] But on the evening of 19 November, the Thames Regatta was remediated yet again to maintain the dominance of Sheridan's critique of fashionable society. The regatta's reenactment at this late date reminded the audience not only of the chaotic failures of the event, and especially its disastrous celebration of naval power at Ranelagh, but also of the fact that this distraction coincided with the onset of the war. It is as though the afterpiece traces many of the problems explored in *The School for Scandal* to a specific moment and style of social performance. In this pairing of main- and afterpiece, it is possible to discern a consistent critique of suspect forms of fashionable sociability that is rooted in the dis-ease over indiscriminate mixing of ranks and sexes that was manifest in the lead-up to the war with America.

It was not until 10 December, with the opening of Hannah More's *Percy*, that Covent Garden found a suitable competitor for *The School for Scandal*. The plays were offered head to head on 12 December and generated comparable receipts; when the plays were next paired, this time with the same afterpiece—*Comus*—on 17 December, Sheridan's play had already reasserted its commercial dominance in spite of the fact that this was its thirty-sixth night. As anyone who has read *Percy* can attest, it is a considerably less entertaining play than *The School for Scandal*; but it was a major critical success that propelled Hannah More into the forefront of literary London. Set in the Middle Ages, the play's eponymous English hero returns from defeating the Saracens in the Crusades to find that his beloved, Elwina, has married his Scottish rival Douglas. Elwina still loves Percy but was forced to marry Douglas out of duty to her father. Despite her loveless marriage, Elwina is a paragon of virtue and resists her desire for Percy. However, her husband is a study in jealous rage and suspicion. Douglas kills Percy in a duel, but Elwina believes that it is her husband who has died. In the event of his death, Douglas has prepared a poison to ensure that Percy will never have his wife. Elwina, in a suicidal expression of chastity, takes the poison, but in a key reversal, the audience discovers Douglas has killed Percy. Douglas for his part discovers that his suspicions have been ill founded, and thus he has killed Percy and precipitated the death of his blameless wife. He too kills himself in remorse, and Elwina's father Raby closes the play by declaring that the tragedy was instantiated by his earlier coercion of his daughter to marry Douglas.

On the face of it, *Percy* would appear to be the opposite of *The School for Scandal,* but it is remarkable the degree to which it engages with many of Sheridan's primary concerns. First, More's deployment of virtue engages with the social mores of Georgian London. The play was critically hailed because it presented the discourse of chivalry in a manner that allowed More to explore the effects of domestic tyranny.[89] Both the *Morning Chronicle* and the *Gazetteer* opened their reviews by indicating that the play does not explore specific historical events even as they are mediated in the play's source texts, the ballad of Chevy Chase and the Belloy's tragedy *Gabrielle de Vergy.*[90] More's target in the tragedy is the abuse of domestic power. In an act of spite, Elwina's father forces her marriage to Douglas because of a trifling affront from Percy's servants during a hunt. For his part, Douglas strives for total domination of the marriage state to the point where his judgment is so clouded that he cannot even communicate with his wife. Both father and husband ignore the words and desires of Elwina, and this fundamental lack of respect ends in disaster. In that regard, *Percy*'s critique of the power dynamics of the patriarchal household is devastating, but the play also engages in a specific critique of global politics as well that bears comparison with *The School for Scandal*'s engagement with the East.

More's tragedy reveres the martial past of these crusading knights, yet argues explicitly that their bellicosity must be tempered. When, in the second act, Percy's messenger Sir Hubert declares, "The king is safe, and Palestine subdued," Elwina goes so far as to argue that the Crusades are misguided policy masquerading as religion and thus thoroughly offends her father.[91] More's tragedy thus simultaneously praises female virtue and critiques excessive violence when it presents itself as duty, whether that be understood in familial or political terms. In other words, when her father and husband pursue their hatred of Percy in the name of filial piety or marital fidelity, More is implying that they are no different from the Crusaders who pursued avarice in the name of religion. The potential allegorical link between America and Palestine is explosive, and the play backs away from it to concentrate most insistently on its domestic components.

In spite of this restraint, however, the play is extremely attentive to questions of mediation that open onto one of the most important emotional experiences of life during wartime. All of the violence in the play, as one might expect, happens offstage, but Elwina's knowledge of the outside world and of Percy's actions in particular, whether they be in Palestine or during the duel in act 5, are mediated through her servants or lesser characters. Although their motivations are radically different, Elwina's servant Birtha is the tragic version of Lady Sneerwell's Snake: she moves between the enclosed world of her employer's realm and the dangerous exterior where reputations and bodies are in peril. In fact, it is the delay—and the potential for misconstrual—inherent to the reporting of the duel between Douglas and Percy that opens the space for Elwina's suicide. Elwina's desire for information, her anticipation of news regarding the conflict between Douglas and Percy, would have tapped into an affective pattern familiar to readers of the press anticipating news from America. And this activation of the anxiety of anticipation is as fundamental to More's practice in tragedy as the careful handling of the anxiety about the mediation of reputation is to Sheridan's practice in comedy.

If we begin to see how More is capitalizing on the anxiety inherent to the temporal delay in mediation itself, then it also becomes clear that the Gothic past is being mobilized in much the same way that Nietzsche envisaged critical history: as that which undermines both the self-deluding claims of monumental history and the quietism of antiquarianism.[92] Elwina's critique of the Crusades can operate as an attack on both the Ministry's policy in America and the policies of the East India Company, which had so troubled Parliament in the early 1770s. No less than Sheridan, More is engaging the theatre to intervene in the social and political crisis enveloping the nation. And her target, like Sheridan's, is hypocrisy: especially the hypocrisy of the avatars of power in both the domestic and the political realms. As we will see in the next chapter, a similar deployment of the Gothic past occurs when John André stages *Douglas* in Philadelphia, a play that in many ways operates as a precursor for More's tragedy.

But how do we understand the paratexts that framed More's allegory? Garrick in a rather unusual move composed the prologue and epilogue for the Covent Garden show. And they are themselves notable in that the prologue, normally spoken by a man, was written for performance by Mrs. Bulkley, and the epilogue, normally spoken by a woman was performed by Mr. Lee Lewes. Dror Wahrman's extended analysis of the prologue and epilogue rightly sees them as an exercise in gender play.[93] The prologue addresses the fact of More's female authorship by going through a catalog of masculine roles now being performed more admirably by women. Likewise, the epilogue gives Mr. Lee Lewes the opportunity to send up the effeminacy not only of men of fashion but also of soldiers and statesmen. The framing materials for More's tragedy figure forth a historical condition where a critical reversal has taken place: women for men, men for women. And crucially, it is More's play that stands as evidence of this reversal. The performance of *Percy* that follows Garrick's remarks on Amazonian playwrights in the prologue is evidence that the world is turned upside down.

What this means is that regardless of the effectivity of More's allegory, the play's enactment testifies to the corruption of present society.

What needs to be recognized is that this is one of the arguments of the play itself, because by situating her model of normative familial and governmental relations in the Gothic past, More is suggesting that this normativity is no longer present. As the theatregoer is incited to mourn not only for Percy—the obvious avatar of true patriotism—but also for the original marriage contract between him and Elwina, More has mobilized all the devices of sentimental tragedy to elicit tears for a fantasy of just domestic governance based on virtue and true piety. In this context, the entire performance becomes a symptom or a diagnostic in much the same way as *The School for Scandal,* only here the critique is amplified not by a set of internal thematic and formal disjunctions but by an overall rupture between the play and the framing paratexts. The spatial distinction between inside and outside that is so crucial to the scenography of Sheridan's plays is here mapped onto the distinction between play and paratext. So strangely, the patriotic script of *Percy* is deployed to recognize the unviability of patriotic subjectivity in a culture where virtue and sympathy have been hollowed out by the refinements of fashionable sociability.

This forces a rather different reading of the prologue and epilogue and indeed of the play itself than that put in motion by Wahrman. Here so-called "gender play" is deployed to make the audience aware that norms of social and civic behavior are dropping off the horizon of history, and thus exist only in fantasies of past greatness. When Mr. Lee Lewes declares that he will "drive these ballad-heroes from the stage," he is also indicating that what remains—namely himself and other men of fashion—are fundamentally separated from the manly arts of hunting and warfare. As he states:

> What! Shall a scribbling, senseless woman dare
> To your refinements offer such *coarse* fare?
> Is Douglas, or is Percy fir'd with passion?
> Ready for love or glory, death to dash on,
> Fit company for modern still-life men of fashion?
> Such madness will our hearts but slightly graze,
> We've no such frantic nobles now a-days.[94]

Garrick had used this device before when he had Thomas King, playing an aristocratic fop, interrupt Garrick's performance of the "Ode" at the Shakespeare Jubilee to complain that such rough fare as Shakespeare was incompatible with good breeding.[95] Only on that earlier occasion the "Ode" itself was staged to discredit the interruption. Here the epilogue concludes with a rather harsher indictment of its speaker:

We wear no armour now—but on our shoes.
Let not with barbarism true taste be blended,
Old vulgar virtues cannot be defended,
Let the dead rest—we living can't be mended.[96]

Alienated from virtue, Mr. Lee Lewes points to the very problematic that pamphleteers and analysts of the American war were attempting to negotiate: how to govern the imperium when the language of republican virtue had migrated to the side of the colonists. Here the combined force of Garrick's epilogue and More's tragedy suggest that corruption has come too far to be corrected. It is that predicament, with its attendant anxieties that constitute the core of the entertainment on offer not only at Covent Garden on that evening but also when Drury Lane staged *The School for Scandal*, for in both instances the audience is called upon to assert its difference from the representation of the present. In other words, the two nights where these plays ran against each other need to be understood as synchronous expressions of an overall imminent critique of British society. Sheridan's critique is arguably a totalizing one because even the play's positive characters are less than compelling. With the character of Percy, More's play seems to raise the possibility of resuscitating past models of virtue, but that potential renovation is put under serious pressure by the epilogue. Garrick's frame for More's play salvages it from nostalgia and orients it toward a critique of the present.[97] Gender insubordination was a crucial tactical tool or rhetorical device for signaling this reorientation. And it is remarkable that, at this moment in history, this was precisely what audiences for the commercial theatre desired.

By January 1778, the news of the British loss of the Battle of Saratoga had rocked the Ministry, and the entire strategic plan for reconquering America was being hastily rejected. The social insecurity latent in the reports of the Thames Regatta and realized in the dramatic innovations of *The School for Scandal* and *Percy* became palpable elements of the public's response to the Ministry's prosecution of the war. The patent theatres attempted to mobilize British history to bolster the war effort in plays such as John Home's *Alfred* and Richard Cumberland's *The Battle of Hastings*.[98] *Alfred* was a critical and commercial disaster, and although Cumberland's play was initially "received with uncommon applause . . . and [Palmer's] heroic exclamation—'all private feuds should cease when England's glory is at stake' was so sensibly felt by the audience that a repetition was called for, but judiciously refused, as out of character in a tragedy," it was also widely recognized that the play was an aesthetic failure.[99] At the height of the success of *The Battle of Hastings* in January and February 1778, *The School for Scandal* and *Percy* still generated greater or comparable receipts, thus suggesting that audiences were drawn to the complex critique of contemporary society promulgated in the work of Sheridan and More. By March, Cumberland's lugubrious patriotism had lost its appeal. As we will see in chapter 4, Sheridan would put the shortcomings of traditional patriotic discourse, and specifically *The Battle of Hastings*, to good end in his last great play, *The Critic*. But for the moment, it is important to recognize that the groundwork was being laid for a thorough restylization of the social order *before* events in America would confirm Whig views that the colonies were unconquerable.

PART II

Regime Change

CHAPTER THREE

To Rise in Greater Splendor

John André's Errant Knights

> Americans and feathers and masquerades will drive us into libraries . . .
>
> Horace Walpole, 1775

Late in 1778, John Burgoyne, like many avid readers of the papers, would have been closely following not only the stern recriminations regarding his own failure at Saratoga but also the vicious debate surrounding William Howe's command of the British forces in New York and Pennsylvania. The level of acrimony over Howe's command in late 1777 and early 1778 had been intense, and, if anything, the ensuing attempts by the Howe brothers and Burgoyne to justify their conduct in America only deepened the sense of conflict over British colonial affairs.[1] Despite his prominence, Sir William Howe is a somewhat enigmatic figure in the history of the American war. Like Burgoyne, Howe had a distinguished military career before the 1770s, especially during the Seven Years' War. Recognized for his bravery on the Plains of Abraham, he played important roles in the British victory over the French at Quebec and Montreal, not to mention distinguished service in the Caribbean. Although a less prominent parliamentarian than Burgoyne, he was an independent member for Nottingham from 1758 to 1780. But unlike John Burgoyne, William Howe did not support the Coercive Acts:

> He had a deep affection for American colonists, especially the people of Massachusetts who had been his comrades during the Seven Years' War and who had honoured his brother, George Augustus, with a memorial in

> Westminster Abbey. He had also been publicly critical of British efforts to punish the people of Massachusetts for having resisted imperial taxes. Yet in January 1775 he let friends in the government know that he would accept appointment as second in command of the British army at Boston. He offered to go to America in hopes of succeeding General Thomas Gage as commander-in-chief and of promoting a reconciliation between mother country and colonies.[2]

Howe entered the war to conduct peace, and, in the summation of his biographer, his inability to decisively suppress colonial rebellion over the ensuing three years was a result of serial attempts to diplomatically resolve the crisis.[3]

Significantly, what Howe got up to when not actually engaging with the enemy became a topic of some concern to Britons and rebel colonists alike. While in New York in the winter of 1776 and 1777, officers under Howe's command established a successful season of theatrical entertainments in New York. With much of the organizational structure intact, the same officers commenced an ambitious roster of plays shortly after occupying Philadelphia. The season opened on 19 January 1778 with a production of Susannah Centlivre's *The Wonder, or A Woman Keeps a Secret* at the Southwark Street Theatre and "proceeded to present a play every Monday evening."[4] The season included five productions of *The Wonder,* Arthur Murphy's *No One's Enemy But His Own,* two productions each of Samuel Foote's *The Minor* and *The Liar,* two each of George Farquhar's *The Constant Couple* and *The Inconstant,* two productions of Shakespeare's *Henry IV, Part I,* and numerous afterpieces. The lion's share of these plays was produced after Howe tendered his resignation as commander in chief. As he waited for a reply from Germain, he refused to carry out any further offensive operations.

Howe and his officers were generally held in contempt for the reckless pursuit of luxurious entertainment and diversion during the occupation. And the theatre was a site of both recrimination and self-recognition. According to Jared Brown,

> Captain Johann Heinrichs, a Hessian mercenary with the British army, captured the spirit of that winter when he wrote in his letter book, "Assemblies, Concerts, Comedies, Clubs, and the like make us forget that there is any war, save that it is a capital joke."
>
> Benjamin Franklin also noted Howe's inability to put military matters ahead of social ones. When he was informed that Howe had captured Philadelphia, he is said to have responded, "No, Philadelphia, has captured Howe."[5]

This critique of the sociability of the British officers in Philadelphia was mobilized both by figures such as Franklin, obviously critical of the British cause, and by someone like Heinrichs, who was putatively on the side of Howe and his officers. Despite this widespread critique of luxury, many of the loyalist families of Philadelphia threw themselves into the whirlwind of social activity associated with the military theatre.

After his recall, Howe, like Burgoyne, struggled to defend himself before the public and before Parliament, and at least part of his difficulty can be ascribed to a divided sense of purpose. He stated in his letter of defense that,

> although some persons condemn me for having endeavoured to conciliate his majesty's rebellious subjects, by taking every means to prevent the destruction of the country, instead of irritating them by a contrary mode of proceeding, yet am I, from many reasons, satisfied in my own mind that I acted in that particular for the benefit of the king's service. Ministers themselves, I am persuaded, did at one time entertain a similar doctrine, and from a circumstance not now necessary to dwell upon, it is certain that I should have had little reason to hope for support from them, if I had been disposed to acts of great severity. Had it been afterwards judged good policy to turn the plan of the war into an indiscriminate devastation of that country, and had I been thought the proper instrument for executing such a plan, ministers, I presume, would have openly stood forth, and sent clear, explicit orders. Ambiguous messages, hints, whispers across the Atlantick, to be avowed or disavowed at pleasure, would have been paltry safeguards for the honour and conduct of a commander in chief.[6]

Howe's repeated concern for avoiding the "devastation of the country" can be ascribed equally to ostensible sympathies for the colonists, and to the more pragmatic recognition that "indiscriminate devastation" was not in Britain's economic interests. Whatever the motive, the complexity of Howe's position could be perceived as tentativeness, and that perception, regardless of the degree to which it was matched by much of the thinking on war in America, was politically destructive. As Gruber states,

> Howe was an accomplished soldier. In more than half a century of service he proved himself a knowledgeable and meticulous officer and a skillful commander. Yet because he did not end the American rebellion when it seemed most vulnerable he was widely criticized. . . . It is now clear that

> he was not the victim of instructions that required him to combine force and persuasion, of cautiously conventional strategic thinking, of his own lethargy, or even of a rebellion too well established to be ended by force. Rather, he failed because he persisted in trying to make peace when empowered to make war. His efforts were especially destructive of the British government's plans for ending the rebellion because he had the skill and reputation to place him beyond the government's direction or recall until an army had been lost and the Anglo-American War had become a world war.[7]

Howe's critics had little time for this kind of geopolitical complexity and opted instead to make him the epitome of misrule.

The terms on which that attack were mounted are particularly interesting, not only because they turn on questions of character but also because they were accepted by and were useful to both hard-line British critics of the Ministry and equally committed patriots rebelling against British rule. Some British critics of Howe concurred with a blistering issue of *The Crisis*, in which Thomas Paine stated provocatively, "That a man, whose soul is absorbed in the low traffic of vulgar vice, is incapable of moving in any superior region, is clearly shown in you by the event of every campaign."[8] This rare moment where patriots on both sides of conflict come together turns on their reception of a now infamous entertainment called the Mischianza, which was reported in the *Gentleman's Magazine* in August 1778. This chapter contends that a full consideration of that celebration's relation to precursor events and its complex mediation in both London and the colonies allows one to discern not only a number of important dynamics in the representation of British imperial relations in the midst of the American conflict but also a range of issues pertaining to the stylization and performance of masculinity at this historical juncture. As we will see, the formal complexity of the Mischianza does not lend itself to straightforward interpretation or authoritative statements about its meaning. In what follows, I want to give a sense of how its own hybridity reflected an emerging diffidence about the progress of war in the American colonies, and how that diffidence was first registered and then contained. I then offer a speculative reading of the final theatrical effort of the British officers in occupied Philadelphia: a production of John Home's *Douglas* staged in the Southwark Theatre on 19 May 1778, the day after the Mischianza on the day of Howe's departure for Portsmouth.

"I shine in setting": Captain André's Mischianza

In response to the escalating criticism of Howe's command in the fall of 1777 and winter of 1778 in both Britain and America, Captain John André staged the Mischianza on the eve of the disgraced general's departure from occupied Philadelphia in the spring of 1778. Held on 18 May 1778, the event was essentially a succession ceremony, with command of the British forces in America transferring from Howe to General Henry Clinton. The question of succession will become quite significant later in this chapter, but for the moment it is important to recognize that within metropolitan print culture Howe was returning to Britain to face allegations of incompetence. In the face of specific criticism of Howe's leadership, André's lengthy letter to the *Gentleman's Magazine* describing the Mischianza was aimed explicitly at generating a counterdiscourse, whose objective was to emphasize the confidence of Howe's officers in his command:

> For the first time in my life I write to you with unwillingness. The ship that carries home Sir William Howe will convey this letter to you; and not even the pleasure of conversing with my friend can secure me from the general dejection I see around me, or remove the share I must take in the universal regret and disappointment which his approaching departure hath spread throughout the whole army. We see him taken from us at a time when we most stand in need of so skillful and popular a commander; when the experience of three years, and the knowledge he hath acquired of the country and people, have added to the confidence we always placed in his conduct and abilities. You know he was ever a favorite with the military; but the affection and attachment which all ranks of officers in this army bear him, can only be known by those who have at this time seen them in their effects. I do not believe there is upon record an instance of a Commander in Chief having so universally endeared himself to those under his command; or of one who received such signal and flattering proofs of their love. That our sentiments might be the more universally and unequivocally known, it was resolved amongst us, that we should give him as splendid an entertainment as the shortness of the time, and our present situation, would allow us. For the expenses, the whole army would have most chearfully contributed; but it was requisite to draw the line somewhere, and twenty-two field officers joined in a subscription adequate to the plan they meant to adopt.[9]

André's expression of officer corps' confidence in Howe's leadership is figured as a species of love, and at one level the Mischianza metaphorically stands for the officers' affection and loyalty. But the love demonstrated here is also manifestly political in intent: the event is staged so "that our sentiments might be the more universally and unequivocally known." In a very real way, the Mischianza happens in order for it to be recounted in the London papers and in prominent monthlies such as the *Gentleman's Magazine*.[10] All this would be simply politics as usual, except that the way that martial subjectivity and love come together in the Mischianza is so radically overdetermined.

The Mischianza has been frequently proffered as a particularly embarrassing moment of patrician British officers either misrecognizing their historical situation or explicitly hiding from the signs that all was not well. The crippling loss at Saratoga was only seven months in the past, the British army had suffered recent defeats at Trenton and Princeton, and, despite holding Philadelphia, Howe's forces had not fared well in engagements with Washington's forces in Pennsylvania.[11] With the benefit of hindsight, it is difficult not to read the Mischianza's excesses as an embarrassing spectacle. The event combined a complex regatta on the Delaware River with a faux-medieval tournament at Knight's-Wharf at the northern extremity of Philadelphia. During the tournament, prominent officers under Howe's command, masqueraded as either Knights of the Blended Rose or Knights of the Burning Mountain and contended for the hearts of fashionable Philadelphia women, who were costumed by André in what he fantasized was Turkish dress, and who were attended by African Americans dressed up as harem eunuchs. The festivities then progressed to an elaborate dinner and ball, which bears comparison to Burgoyne's *fête*, and concluded with illuminations and fireworks. Linda Colley's appraisal of the event reads the event as a symptom:

> Superficially, the event was just one more manifestation of that taste for gothic romance and orientalism that was so prevalent in European polite culture at this time. Yet more was at stake here than just a stylish entertainment. Chivalry's essential function, Maurice Keen has written, is always to hold up an idealised image of armed conflict in defiance of the harsh realities of actual warfare. By definition, chivalry also reaffirms the paramount importance of custom, hierarchy and inherited rank. General Howe's tournament occurred just seven months after the crushing British defeat at Saratoga and was organized, we know, by a set of idealistic young army officers from comfortably landed backgrounds. As such, it can be

> seen as a window on the minds and manners of an élite under stress. After three years of indecisive war in raw, uncongenial territory, and in the face of doubt, disappointment and vague premonitions of defeat, the cream of the British officer corps sought a brief escape in an ordered and glamorous past. Sword-in-hand and on horse-back, they reconstructed the war with the American colonists as they would ideally have liked it to be: a splendid crusade fought according to the rules by men of birth, and fought successfully.[12]

I have repeated Colley's analysis here at length because in the effort to configure the Mischianza as a symptom of patrician martial psychology attempting to frantically shore up its crumbling foundations, it fails to read either the event itself or its representation in metropolitan print culture. And along the way it makes some rather symptomatic errors of its own, which have a significant bearing on how we think about Howe and André's conflicted performance of martial subjectivity.

Pressure needs to be put on the suggestion that the tournament and the faux hand-to-hand combat staged for the ladies of Philadelphia were somehow a phantasmatic reconstruction of the conflict between Britain and the Continental army. This would suggest that the Knights of the Blended Rose and the Knights of the Burning Mountain somehow allegorically represented opposing sides. The evidence is quite to the contrary: officers appear to have been assigned to either side, and the conflict itself is no more resolved than the American war was at this time. The "conflict" is called off in the ladies' name before any decisive conclusion, and the company retires for dinner. This sense of attenuation, rather than closure, is also evident in the tickets to the event (fig. 3.1). The central image of a setting sun is inscribed with the words *Luceo discedens aucto, splendore resurgam*, or "I shine in setting; I shall rise in greater splendor." This figures Howe's departure as a lapse into darkness, which promises an even brighter future. And yet for all its optimism, such an image retains a sense of stasis, not decisive success, most notably because it projects victory into a mythic future. In the simplest sense, the tickets suggest that the event is staged to mark a hiatus in British fortunes due to a temporary lack of confidence in Howe's leadership among the Ministry. At least part of the objective is to argue that this exhibition of diffidence on the part of the Ministry is a failure in policy, and thus the event is far more critical than Colley suggests.

We also need to look closely at the generic claims regarding chivalric romance. As James Watt has ably demonstrated, both Gothic romance and historical

Figure 3.1. Meschianza Ticket, designed by John André (1778). Courtesy of the Thomas Fisher Rare Book Library, University of Toronto.

accounts of chivalry were anything but unified fields, and the relationship between these genres and the world of politics in the 1770s was extremely complex. Watt distinguishes between the strategies of bricolage mobilized by Walpole in the formal structure of both his estate at Strawberry Hill and his novel *The Castle of Otranto* and the allegorical strategies of the kind of loyalist romance that emerged after the American war.[13] The Mischianza is staged between these two deployments of chivalry, and it cannot be read solely in terms of one discourse and not the other. As its very name indicates, it is a blended entertainment; Brown notes that "the word is derived from two Italian words: *mescere*, to mix, and *mischiare*, to mingle."[14] This formal quality draws it into the orbit of Walpole's self-conscious mixing of old and new, high and low in his Gothic productions of the 1760s. As Watt states,

> Rather than being a proto-historical novel preoccupied with the accurate description of medieval customs and manners, *Otranto* like Strawberry Hill seems to have been based upon a recourse to the past which was mainly concerned about, on the one hand, subsuming eccentricity for a modern, leisured audience, and, on the other, confounding those readers without the necessary discrimination to accommodate such novelty. *Otranto*, like Strawberry Hill, offered (at least) a "doubled" meaning, but the nuances of the higher or private perspective were at first available, it seems, only to a select group who were initiated into a knowledge of what Walpole was doing.[15]

As in Burgoyne's earlier staging of the *fêtes galantes*, the proliferation of meaning at the heart of the Mischianza, combined with its self-conscious frivolity, asks the reader to recognize that chivalry is being mobilized as a form of parodic aristocratic display aimed at mocking the very military tropes Colley argues it is ostensibly allegorizing. The Mischianza's tournament is less of a historical reenactment, as Simon During has recently suggested, than an occasion to test the reading skills of the audience.[16] Those among Howe's critics who read the tournament "straight," such as Paine and the anonymous author of the *Strictures on the Philadelphia Mischianza*, only displayed that they did not understand, or chose to demonize, the event's relation to aristocratic performance, and the importance of frivolous diversion to patrician subjectivity.

That said, the event also shares some strategies with loyalist romance, especially its hypostatization of military signs immediately following the tournament. As Watt argues, "During the period that encompassed the loss of the American colonies and the protracted conflict with France, the drive to refashion the self-image of Britain led to the 'historical' category of Gothic being purged of its associations with either democracy or frivolity and defined increasingly in terms of a proud military heritage."[17] Throughout the final years of the American war right through to the early nineteenth century, narratives of ancestral heroes such as Edward III, Alfred the Great, and the Henries began to proliferate in all media.[18] This is significant to the story of the Mischianza because Edward III is an explicit reference point for André's celebration of militarism, and he is indebted to Richard Hurd's analysis of the function of jousting for the code of chivalry. What is so complicated about the Mischianza is that Walpolean frivolity is itself mingled with military allegory; in fact, they abut one another in the central episodes of the entertainment. My subsequent reading of the celebration demonstrates not only how these competing discourses are deployed but also how their very incommensurability is suited to the historical predicament faced by André, Howe, and, by extension, Britain at this point in the American war.

Colley's assumptions about the participants also need to be more carefully scrutinized. The major organizers of the event were not men of "comfortably landed backgrounds." André, the man most directly involved in the planning and execution of the Mischianza, came from a family of Genoese immigrants working as accountants in the City, and at least part of his role here is, like that of Alexander Hamilton on the American side, who would write so eloquently about André's execution for espionage two years later, that of a young man on the make, seeking to better his social standing through his loyal service to his superiors.[19] In other words, there is a significant element of sycophancy in this entire proceeding, which is part of the competitive structure of military life. I agree with Colley's suggestion that this entertainment was a diversion, but it was part of an extended program of entertainment and thus needs to be considered in relation both to other theatricals in Philadelphia and to similar entertainments in England.

As with the diversion staged by Burgoyne at The Oaks, there was more at play here than a combination of displacement and forgetting. All diversions carry an implicit sadness, and the Mischianza is no exception. In this instance, the sadness is directly stated in André's preamble to his description of the celebration. The Mischianza, like Burgoyne's entertainment, is structured around a complex argument about the place of elite masculinity in what many of the participants understood to be a civil conflict, a conflict among brothers. The Mischianza gives us a sense of what happens when martial subjects use love to make war, but in this case the war was waged not against the enemy but rather against the state itself, which sought to hold Howe responsible for a set of irresolvable contradictions in imperial rule. And the locus of the battle was squarely in the realm of the newspapers.

The Mischianza was an event staged to be written about. And like other accounts of elite entertainment in the 1770s, Captain André's representation of the Mischianza is deeply aware not only of the intensely intertextual world of the newspapers but also of the keenly contested status of diversionary entertainments in metropolitan life. As Gillian Russell has argued, the diversification of private domiciliary entertainment by prominent and often notorious women had considerable impact both on the structure of sociability and on the trajectory of commercial entertainment in the 1760s and 1770s.[20] Innovators like Teresa Cornelys, whose entertainments at Carlisle House exerted significant pressure on conventional sites of "manly" national entertainment such as the theatre, prompted a range of responses both in the press and in other cultural venues. The success of Cornelys's musical entertainments, and of the proliferation of sites of elite sociability such as Almack's, the Coterie, and above all the Pantheon, had a profound impact on the social dynamics of theatrical life and eventually impinged on the formal parameters of dramatic representation. As we have already seen in relation to Burgoyne's Fête Champêtre, and Garrick's production of Burgoyne's *The Maid of the Oaks*, one of the most important responses to women's ever more prominent presence in public entertainment, was a co-optation of strategies developed by Cornelys and other purveyors of nonlicensed entertainment. Burgoyne's Fête Champêtre can be understood as a masculinist rehearsal of the kind of masques staged at Carlisle House and the Pantheon, and its reformist agenda needs to be read in the context of this cultural war against aristocratic dissipation and the feminization of public life. Similarly, the formal experiments of *The Maid of the Oaks* are a direct response to the very popularity, and commercial success, of the kind of freewheeling entertainments offered in these ostensibly private sites.

This cultural conflict is relevant here because the Mischianza exhibits specific elements of two prior entertainments. If we look carefully at the formal structure of the Mischianza, we can discern three separate sections that are separated by important transitional phases. The event starts with a regatta, which was based on the Thames Regatta of 23 June 1775.[21] After a somewhat messy disembarkation, the company then proceeded to a space marked by two pavilions for the aforementioned quasi-medieval tournament. This tournament appears to have no obvious precursor and thus is the Mischianza's most innovative element. Its fusion of chivalric and orientalist tropes accords it a level of specificity that bears careful analysis. After the tournament, the company undertakes a complex procession, which also quotes from the regatta, and retires to a temporary building for dancing, fireworks, supper, and a series of toasts, which clearly cite the second masque of Burgoyne's Fête Champêtre.[22] In other words, the Mischianza, as its name suggests, is a rigorously blended entertainment. All of the papers reporting on the event explicitly make the connection to the Thames Regatta and the Fête Champêtre.[23] André's celebration takes elements of two very famous parties, which already had an implicitly oppositional relation to one another, and reorients them to produce a new aesthetic and social experience. And this formal accommodation is not only subtle but also quite aware of the arguments surrounding gender, aristocratic dissipation, and the public sphere, which were very much a part of the precursor performances. The Mischianza satirizes both events and, in so doing, opens up a middle way for the performance of martial masculinity that navigates between the Scylla of petticoat government associated with the organizers of the regatta and the Charybdis of misplaced bellicosity that Howe associated with Burgoyne.

As I have already argued, one can detect in the reporting of the Thames Regatta an uneasiness with the foreignness of the Venetian model for the event, with the staging of elite entertainment for a necessarily mass audience (the plans and ballads being sold at the event come under particular pressure), with the proliferation of gambling, with the prominent place of women in this "floating town," and, above all, with the role played by impresarios such as Teresa Cornelys in the organization of the event. But it is precisely these suspect elements—gaming, commerce, and the spectacle of elite women in the public sphere—that are so important to Howe's officers' replication of the river entertainment in the Mischianza. The organizers of the Mischianza retain the level of spectacle of the precursor event, but André's account eschews the critical tone of the press's account of the Thames Regatta and rigorously highlights the naval elements of the display, while downplaying any sense of the nonparticipant spectators' involvement in the event:

> A grand regatta began the entertainment. It consisted of three divisions. In the first was the Ferret galley, having on board several General-Officers, and the number of Ladies. In the center was the Hussar galley, with Sir William and Lord Howe, Sir Henry Clinton, the Officers of their suite, and some Ladies. The Cornwallis galley brought up the rear, having on board General Knyphausen and his suite, three British Generals, and a party of Ladies. On each quarter of these gallies, and forming their division, where five flat boats, lined with green cloth, and filled with Ladies and Gentlemen. In front of the whole were three flat boats, with a band of music in each—Six barges rode about each flank, to keep off the swarm of boats that covered the river from side to side. The gallies were dressed out in a variety of colours and streamers, and in each flat boat was displayed the flag of its own division. In the stream opposite the center of the city, the Fanny armed

> ship, magnificently decorated, was placed at anchor, and at some distance a-head lay his Majesty's ship Roebuck, with the Admiral's flag hoisted at the foretop-mast-head. The transport ships, extending in a line the whole length of the town, appeared with colours flying, and crouded with spectators, as were also the openings of the several wharfs, on shore, exhibiting the most picturesque and enlivening scene the eye could desire. The rendezvous was at Knight's-Wharf, at the northern extremity of the city. By half after four the whole company were embarked, and a signal being made by the Vigilant's manning ship, the three divisions rowed slowly down, preserving their proper intervals, and keeping time to the music that led the fleet. Arrived between the Fanny and the Market Wharf, the signal was made from one of the boats a-head, and the whole lay upon their oars, while the music played, *God save the King*, and three cheers given from the vessels were returned from the multitude on shore. By this time the flood-tide became too rapid for the gallies to advance; they were therefore quitted, and the Company disposed of in the different barges. This alteration broke in upon the order of procession, but was necessary to give sufficient time for displaying the entertainments that were prepared on shore.[24]

This has the effect of temporarily erasing the importance of both gambling and commerce to this kind of entertainment. Gambling, and particularly women's gaming, returns later in the Mischianza, but here these unsettling elements of domiciliary entertainment regularly associated with Teresa Cornelys are thoroughly subordinated to military and national display. Ships of the British navy become prominent props, and the officers themselves—both General and Admiral Howe, General Clinton, and others—replace suspect men of fashion such as the Duke of Cumberland in this version of the floating town. Rather than sellers marketing satirical ballads "rhyming Royal family with liberty,"[25] we are presented with a fully staged rendition of "God save the King" and a completely scripted, because military, response. In short, Howe's officers have co-opted the regatta, in which national purpose and elite sociability were represented as perhaps not quite in sync, to present a seamless revision where patrician military rule and women's subjection mutually consolidate one another. Gone are the gaming, the corrupted members of the Ton, and the promiscuous masses. And gone is Cornelys herself, for there is no question of women organizing or leading this event; the young belles of Philadelphia are simply and truly ballast, to use a word from the earlier reporting of the Thames Regatta, helping to keep this gendered fantasy of public display afloat.

But this is not all that is being excised or contained here. As I argued in chapter 2, the Thames Regatta was insistently linked to pro-American voices both in the City and in the parliamentary opposition. And its manifest failures, the scant supper, the tattered pavilion, and the general confusion on the water became prophetic signs of the Ministry's inability to successfully avert or put down the rebellion in America. The Mischianza restages this event in a fashion that not only elides the insistence of pro-American voices in Britain but also reconstitutes the broken props of naval supremacy and ministerial competence. In this sense, Howe's officers' reenactment of the Thames Regatta on the Delaware shares a great deal with Burgoyne's Fête Champêtre. It not only cites a notable instance of sexually and commercially suspect sociability in order to argue for reforms that impinge on the performance of masculine martial homosociality but also repairs the broken signifiers of martial and imperial rule that had made themselves available to oppositional readings of elite governance.

What is intriguing, however, is the degree to which André has to direct the reader's attention away from the audience—that is, from the shoreline—to maintain his reformist agenda. For readers cognizant of how Cornelys's entertainments were represented, and in particular how the Thames Regatta was framed by the promiscuous commerce of urban life, the nonrepresentation of the Philadelphian audience becomes paramount. Unlike the "Oak Gazette Extraordinary," which staged the presence of the "codlings" in order to develop a complex rhetoric of inclusion and exclusion, André's letter curtails dissent by not representing the citizens of Philadelphia, except those young women who have been hand chosen to figure so prominently in the tournament. This is no doubt because the shoreline in this case was a space not simply of class otherness but rather of colonial subjection and political contestation. What André has excluded here is the fact of occupation, conflict, and resistance, which everywhere surrounds this celebration. That exclusion is fundamental to the Mischianza's reformist agenda in the realm of sociability. But this act of rhetorical exclusion has the unintended effect of failing to provide a place for the reader in the scene, which ends up locating the reader in the same space as the occupied Philadelphians. This rhetorical error allows readers unsympathetic to Howe's commission to hold the Mischianza up as an embarrassing spectacle that vindicates much of the American colonists' resentment of British rule. But if this rhetorical error opens André to charges of flattery and corruption, and Howe to charges of willfully misrepresenting his military actions, it also provides a certain level of stability from which to engage more fully with Burgoyne's previous attempt to co-opt Cornelys's innovations in the social life of the elite.

For all it shares with Burgoyne's Fête Champêtre, the Mischianza also offers a critique of that performance as well, and its target is Burgoyne's hypostatization of bellicose masculinity. The Mischianza replaces the second half of the Thames Regatta—the events at Ranelagh—with the tournament and the modified version of the second masque of the Fête Champêtre. Or, alternatively, one could argue that the Mischianza replaces the first masque of the Fête Champêtre—the Watteau-like masque of shepherds and shepherdesses—with the regatta and the tournament. Whichever way you choose to read it, the most problematic elements of the precursor performances are either suppressed, satirized, or contained. For example, in my prior reading of the Fête Champêtre, I argued that the Watteauesque *fête galante* of the first masque is staged as an exemplification of a style of sociability that the second masque rigorously critiques. It operates as that which the rest of the performance argues against. In the case of the Mischianza, I would suggest that the first movement, the regatta on the Delaware, cites a similar instance of suspect sociability much as Burgoyne cites Watteau. But the Mischianza diverges slightly from Burgoyne's practice, because in citing the Thames Regatta it also reforms it: first, by containing all instances of gender and class impropriety and, second, by occluding the response of the nonparticipants. This latter strategy is in some sense dictated by the fact that the fantasy of subjection that underwrote the representation of the nonparticipant observers, or the codlings, in the "Oak Gazette Extraordinary" was simply not tenable in occupied Philadelphia. In addition, there is a further formal divergence that comes with introducing the tournament between the regatta and final celebration in the temporary building. How the placement of the tournament operates in this complex agenda of critique is somewhat cryptic until one looks carefully at how André and his associates rehearse the Fête Champêtre's second masque.

That rehearsal is remarkably true to the narrative trajectory and the spatial strategies of Burgoyne's earlier diversion. The company moves from the garden into a hall "painted in imitation of Sienna marble, enclosing festoons of white marble: the surbase, and all below, was black," which opened onto adjoining apartments, one of which would eventually house the faro tables. From this antechamber, the guests were

> conducted up to a ball-room, decorated into a light elegant stile of painting. The ground was a pale blue, pannelled with a small gold bead, and in the interior filled with dropping festoons of flowers in their natural colours. Below the surbase the ground was of rose-pink, with drapery festooned

in blue. These decorations were heightened by 85 mirrours, decked with rose-pink silk ribbands, and artificial flowers; and in the intermediate spaces were 34 branches with wax-lights, ornamented in a similar manner.

On the same floor were four drawing-rooms, with side-boards of refreshments, decorated and lighted in the same stile and taste as the ball-room. The ball was opened by the Knights and their Ladies; and the dances continued till ten o'clock, when the windows were thrown open, and a magnificent bouquet of rockets began the fire-works. These were planned by Capt. Montresor, the chief engineer, and consisted of twenty different exhibitions, displayed under his direction with the happiest success, and in the highest stile of beauty. Towards the conclusion, the interior part of the triumphal arch was illuminated amidst an uninterrupted flight of rockets and bursting of baloons. The military trophies on each side assumed a variety of transparent colours. The shell and flaming heart on the wings sent forth Chinese fountains, succeeded by fire-pots. Fame appeared at top, spangled with stars, and from her trumpet blowing the following device in letters of light, *Tes Lauriers sont immortels.* —A *sauteur* of Rockets, bursting from the pediment, concluded the *feu d'artifice.*

At twelve supper was announced, and large folding doors, hitherto artfully concealed, being suddenly thrown open, discovered a magnificent saloon of 210 feet by 40, and 22 in height, with three alcoves on each side, which served for side-boards. The cieling [*sic*] was the segment of a circle, and the sides were painted of a light straw-colour, with vine leaves and festooned-flowers, some in a bright, some in a darkish green. Fifty-six large pier-glasses, ornamented with green silk artificial flowers and ribbands; 100 branches with three lights in each, trimmed in the same manner as the mirrours; 18 lustres each, with 24 lights, suspended from the cieling, and ornamented as the branches; 300 wax-tapers, disposed along the supper tables; 430 covers, 1200 dishes; 24 black slaves, in oriental dresses, with silver collars and bracelets, ranged in two lines, and bending to the ground as the General and Admiral approached the saloon: all these, forming together the most brilliant assemblage of gay objects, and appearing at once as we entered by an easy descent, exhibited a *coup d'oeil* beyond description magnificent.[26]

André's description here is remarkably attentive to architectural detail, because, in both scale and design, the building is a copy of Adam's pavilion for the Fête Champêtre. Adam's classical motifs, which figured so prominently in the decorative plasterwork, appear to have been replaced by mirrors, but that simply cuts to the chase of Adam's allegorical arabesques. The classical figures in his pavilion figured forth imperial rule and implicitly linked Britain and Rome. In this case, perhaps because of time constraints, the guests simply looked at themselves and dispensed with the pretense of allegory altogether. It is a fascinating move because it simultaneously signals confidence—we need only look to ourselves—and diffidence. Perhaps the Roman comparison carries with it too many counterreadings.

Furthermore, the progressive expansion of the entertainment space after the fireworks precisely replicates the order of events in Burgoyne's celebration. And the regulation of desire is similarly achieved through explicitly martial tactics: fireworks led by the corps of engineers and toasts by the preeminent officers. But again, the divergent features are intriguing. Unlike in the Fête Champêtre, where the explosions terrified the guests and signaled the expansion of space, the Mischianza expanded the firework display and shifted the terms of reference from the sublime to the beautiful. This allowed for a significant escalation in content. Suddenly the fireworks carried discernible meanings, rather than forcing the observers to contemplate the loss of meaning. The illumination of Fame and the phrase "*Tes Lauriers sont immortels*" are clearly intended to refer to Howe's leadership, but André's description, perhaps in spite of itself, indicates that these pyrotechnic displays did not instill awe but rather incited the guests to further pleasure. One could argue, therefore, that, unlike Burgoyne's critical manipulation of social desire in the Fête Champêtre, the Mischianza's rehearsal of Burgoyne's tactics consolidate the officer corps through the consumption of feminized and feminine pleasure. This means that unlike Burgoyne's martial regulation of the Temple of Venus, André and his associates have succumbed, even in their martial practice and homosocial affiliation, to the idealized women in their midst. The fact that these same women, as colonial subjects, are also ostensibly under British rule gives this almost parodic rehearsal of the Fête Champêtre a complex political valence, which needs further elucidation. What appears to be a counterintuitive self-satire is explicitly adopted by André later in his account of the event.

The most revealing part of the Mischianza is captured in an element of the performance that was apparently not presented but nevertheless given prominent place in André's account. This is the address to the company, penned by André and intended for the Herald of the Blended Rose. This Herald, as André emphasizes earlier in his letter, wore a tunic bearing the emblem of two crossed roses and the motto "We droop when separated."[27] The motto is a remarkable compression of the sexual politics of the event because it suggests quite bluntly that potency is not a matter of individual masculine performance but rather one of group cohesion. In the context of Howe's recall, the implication is that by removing Howe from command, the Ministry has compromised the masculinity of all whom he commanded. This is homosociality figured forth as a fantasy of national sexual power. This has rather unexpected implications for the tournament itself, but in the context of the final portion of the entertainment it marks a rather significant shift from Burgoyne's program of martial and marital reform. This is because the Herald of the Blended Rose plays the role Burgoyne scripted for the Druid. Like the Druid, he interrupts the supper and hails the company into an expression of national solidarity:

> Towards the end of supper, the Herald of the Blended Rose, in his habit of ceremony, attended by his trumpets, entered the saloon, and proclaimed to the King's health, the Queen, and Royal Family, the Army and Navy, with their respective Commanders, the Knights and their Ladies, the Ladies in general; each of these toasts, was followed by a flourish of music. After supper we returned to the ball-room, and continued to dance till four o'clock.[28]

However, unlike the Druid in the Fête Champêtre, he directs his encomiums not at the figural King and Queen of the Oaks but rather at the literal King and Queen of England. In the former occasion, the figurality of the address allowed for a fairly straightforward equation of the space of The Oaks and the nation. In this context, the literal invocation of the King and Queen raises a question concerning the space in which this event takes place. All of a sudden, the fact of occupation and rebellion comes flooding into the event. To complicate matters further, the Druid's praise of the conjugal fidelity of the King and Queen of the Oaks and the Hymeneal pantomime that concluded the second masque of the Fête Champêtre are here aligned with George III and Queen Charlotte. The idealization of royal conjugality is not a problem, but if there is any instability either in the spatial metonymies that align the Oaks event with the Mischianza or in the perceived cohesion of the martial elite here celebrating itself in the face of widespread criticism, then the entire figural assemblage has the potential to unravel into a satire of itself.

This is why André's address is such a vexed document, because, unlike in Burgoyne's second masque, the agents of Mars do not contain and regulate the forces of Venus but, rather, succumb to them:

MARS, conquest-plum'd, the Cyprian Queen disarms;
And Victors, vanquish'd, yield to Beauty's Charms.

After banging the wreath on the front of the pavilion, he was to have proceeded thus:

HERE then the laurel, here the palm we yield.
And all the trophies of the tilted field;
Here Whites and Blacks, with blended homage, pay
To each Device the honours of the day.
Hard were the task, and impious to decide
Where all are fairest, which the fairer side.
Enough for us, if by such sports we strove
To grace this feast of military love,
And, joining in the wish of every heart,
Honour'd the friend and leader ere we part.[29]

In this opening stanza, the Herald indicates that the Knights, whose status as victorious figures is somewhat strained in that the tournament is itself inconclusive, are subject to the Cyprian Queen.[30] Venus's representatives here are colonial women, and however loyal or disloyal they may be, their power over the British officers has the potential to be deeply disruptive.[31] At the very least, the stanza suggests that martial aptitude is subservient to desire. At the worst, it suggests that these men are already in the thrall of the women of Philadelphia. This latter possibility is crucial because it helps to explain why André costumed the women in turbans: like many fantasies of eastern sexuality, it turns on the feminization of the sultan by his profligate desires. No commentator as far as I know has dealt with the strange collocation of chivalric and orientalist motifs in the Mischianza, and I would argue that this combination of signs is more than simply a result of enthusiasm for gothic and oriental tales, as Colley suggests, but rather a specific formal and political decision that marks the very specificity of André's intervention in the political situation of Howe's recall. André's allusion to subject orientalized women ruling over the forces occupying Philadelphia reconstructs military failure as a function of the kind of sexual excess associated with weak despotic rule. And that weak despotism, symptomatic of corrupt ruling subjectivity, is firmly located not only in the officer class of Howe's army but also in the highest echelons of the state. How one reads this representation of Howe determines, in André's eyes, one's capacity to correctly read the scene and, by extension, one's capacity to judge the progress of the war.

What I am suggesting here is that André's undelivered address and the Mischianza's parodic rehearsal of the Fête Champêtre are part of a broader strategy of satire aimed at entrapping Howe's critics. We know from André's biographer Winthrop Sargent that this kind of satirical critique of Howe's leadership by his own officers had occurred before, and it utilized a cognate set of tropes. As he states, in the opening campaign of 1778

> Sir William was looking about for an opening to cover his retirement with an active lustre; stimulated, perhaps, thereto by the friendly satire of his subordinates, one of whom (afterwards General Meadows, then the lieutenant-colonel of the 55th, Howe's own regiment) bluntly reproached his commander's slothful devotion to pleasure, and asked him if he did not think it was now time to get out of his bed and to get on his horse.[32]

This is Howe as the dissolute sultan, too mired in pleasure to attend to the affairs of state, and I would argue that the entire company is figured forth in this way in order to stage a counternarrative capable of recuperating Howe's entire command.

Immediately after his declaration of the disarmament of the agents of Mars by Beauty's charms, André's address shifts gears and calls forth a specific scene where victory was snatched from almost certain defeat, namely the Battle of Poictiers of 1356, where Edward the Prince of Wales, despite being massively outnumbered and almost surrounded by the French King John, routed the French forces:

> When great in arms our brave forefathers rose,
> And loos'd the British Lion on his foes;
> When the fall'n Gauls, then perjur'd too and base,
> The faithless fathers of a faithless race,
> First to attack, tho' still the first to yield,
> Shrunk from their rage on Poictiers' laurel'd field;
> Oft, while grim War suspended his alarms,
> The gallant bands with mimic deeds of arms,
> Thus to some favourite chief the feast decree,
> And deck'd the tilting Knight, th'encountering steed.
> In manly sports that serv'd but to inspire
> Contempt of death, and feed the martial fire.
> The lists beheld them celebrate *his* name
> Who led their steps to victory and fame.

Thro' ev'ry rank the grateful ardor ran;
All fear'd the chieftain, but all lov'd the man;
And, fired with the soul of this bright day,
Pay'd to a *Salisbury* what to *Howe* we pay.[33]

The parallels between Edward at Poictiers and Howe at Philadelphia are hopeful to say the least, especially after Howe's failure to engage with Lafayette in the months before the Mischianza, but they offer a framework within which to read the deployment of medieval and chivalric tropes in the Mischianza. Edward's victory at Poictiers emerged from apparent defeat—he was retreating when he was hemmed in by the French—and it was followed by a storied act of chivalry: he waited on the vanquished king at table. In the context of Howe's recall and France's entry into the war, the clear suggestion is not only that Howe possessed strategic acumen similar to Edward's but also that it would be a historical error to abandon him after temporary signs of reversal. As James Watt has argued, Edward III is frequently deployed in later loyalist gothic romance not only to critique (frequently Gallic) corruption but also to celebrate a time when "true subordination of ranks and degrees was observed."[34] In other words, this refiguration of Howe as Edward III is aimed at critiquing both the martial masculinity of those critical of his command and the degeneracy of the state itself. And that charge of degeneracy is subtly tied to how one reads jousting.

In the preceding passage, the account of the tournaments staged "while grim War suspended his alarms" amounts to a justification of the Mischianza itself. This brief gesture toward the political logic behind jousting partakes of Richard Hurd's account of the historical origin of tournaments within the governmental strategies of feudalism in the second *Letter on Chivalry and Romance*.[35] According to Hurd, because

> there being little or no security to be had amidst so many restless spirits and clashing views of a neighbouring numerous and independent nobility, the military discipline of their followers, even in the intervals of peace, were not to be relaxed, and their ardour suffered to grow cool by a total disuse of martial exercises. And hence the proper origin of JOUSTS and TOURNAMENTS; those images of war, which were kept up in the castles of the barons, and by an useful policy, converted into the amusement of the knights, when their arms were employed on no serious occasion.[36]

The explicit linkage between amusement and governmental policy is crucial, because it suggests that if the "knights" appear frivolous, it is because their rulers amount to little more than "petty tyrants" who fail to recognize the advantages of the security Howe was attempting to secure through diplomacy. It is from here that André explicitly attacks Howe's critics:

> Shame to the envious slave that dares bemoan
> Their sons degenerate, or their spirit flown—
> Let maddening Faction drive this guilty land
> With her worst foes to form th'unnatural band;
> In yon brave croud old British courage glows
> Unconquer'd, growing as the danger grows.
> With hearts as bold as e'er their fathers bore,
> Their country they'll avenge, her fame restore.
> Rouz'd to the charge, methinks I hear them cry,
> Revenge and glory sparkling from each eye,
> "Chain'd to our arms while Howe the battle led,
> Still round these files her wings shall Conquest spread.
> Lov'd tho' he goes, the spirit still remains
> That with him bore us o'er these trembling plains.
> On Hudson's banks the sure presage we read
> Of other triumphs to our arms decreed;[37]
> Nor fear but equal honours shall repay
> Each hardy deed where Clinton points the way."[38]

By casting shame on those who critique Howe or his officers as degenerate, André argues that those critical of Howe's record have been too hasty in their judgment. And in their haste they have mistaken Howe's advocacy of diplomacy and his sponsorship of theatrical sociability—both in the theatre and in the Mischianza—as signs of degeneracy, when in fact the true degenerates are not only the "unnatural" combination of American Faction and French faithlessness but also the bellicose "petty tyrants" in Britain who see violent suppression of the colonies as the only effective imperial policy.

This preemptive failure in reading, here ascribed to Howe's critics, is significant because it folds into one of the primary rhetorical strategies already discussed in relation to Burgoyne's Fête Champêtre. As noted earlier, the "Oak Gazette Extraordinary" tests its readers' ability to read the complex signs of sociability, specifically the way prior acts of social exchange are staged and resisted. André's address states explicitly that there is a constituency that cannot distinguish the Mischianza's staging of notable scenes of aristocratic dissipation, and of the subjection of martial masculinity to feminine colonial influence, from the degeneration of British notions of liberty into the rebellious ideals of American autonomy and independence. That latter degeneration is signaled by the "unnatural" alliance with France, and the implication, I believe, is that those who have mistakenly recalled Howe have also failed to recognize the upstart colonists as a foreign threat whose enmity is akin to France's historical threat to English sovereignty. Failure to read the Mischianza's internal satire—its orientalist component—as a form of self-critique is a sign of a much more dangerous failure to discern the "real" historical situation. In other words, how one reads the central tournament, where the tropes of chivalry and oriental subjection are laced together, becomes a question of how one reads the political scene that surrounds its patently absurd rehearsal of "manly sports" and "Beauty's charms."

As noted earlier, the tournament and its ensuing procession occur between what we can now explicitly recognize as parodies of two famous examples of aristocratic sociability. The Mischianza's parody of the Thames Regatta disengages it not only from the mutually constitutive practices of gambling and adultery but also from the suspect assertion of women in the public sphere. And the parody of the Fête Champêtre undercuts that performance's rather simplistic equation of national strength with nativist tropes of patrician martial rule and conjugal fidelity. Put reductively, the Mischianza attacks two extremes of gender performance, petticoat government on the one hand and misplaced bellicosity on the other. Both imply a devolution in masculinity. What links both parodies is the importance of normative femininity to figures of national and martial strength, and yet the very sign of normativity—marriage—which was so important both to the critique of Cornelys's entertainments and to Burgoyne's revision of Cornelys-style social masquerade, is nowhere to be found. Instead André and his associates chose to explore rather different fantasies of feminine propriety and gendered power in the central episode of the Mischianza. What is so strange is that the very issues satirized in the opening and closing sections of the Mischianza—petticoat government and hypermasculine bellicosity—are staged in the tournament itself.

After alighting from the ships and barges on the Delaware, the participants in the Mischianza proceeded toward the previously described building,

> bounding the view through a vista formed by two triumphal arches, erected at proper intervals in a line with the landing-place. Two pavilions, with rows of benches, rising one above the other, and serving as the advanced wings of the first triumphal arch, received the Ladies, while the Gentlemen ranged themselves in convenient order on each side. On the front seat

of each pavilion were placed seven of the principal young Ladies of the country, dressed in Turkish habits, and wearing in their turbans the favors with which they meant to reward the several Knights who were to contend in their honour. These arrangements were scarce made when the sound of trumpets was heard at a distance; and a band of Knights, dressed in ancient habits of white and red silk, and mounted on gray horses, richly caparisoned in trappings of the same colours, entered the lists, attended by their Esquires on foot, in suitable apparel, in the following order: — Four trumpeters, properly habited, their trumpets decorated with small pendent banners —A herald in his robes of ceremony, on his tunic was the device of his band, two roses intertwined, with the Motto, *We droop when separated.*

Lord Cathcart, superbly mounted on a managed horse, appeared as chief of these Knights; two young black slaves, with sashes and drawers of blue and white silk, wearing large silver clasps round their necks and arms, their breasts and shoulders bare, held his stirrups. On his right hand walked Capt. Hazard, and on his left Capt. Brownlow, his two Esquires, one bearing his lance, the other his shield.[39]

In this carefully arranged field of chivalric signs, one cannot help but notice the strange interpenetration of Christian and Turkish figures. If the officers are intent on staging some kind of chivalric romance, then why dress the women in Turkish habits? And why supplement the conventional knights' squires with slaves, here refigured as the sultan's minions? One could argue that the conjunction of these codes is simply aimed at maximizing the erotic economy. After all, injecting a harem fantasy into the gyniolatry of chivalric romance carries with it a double idealization, while retaining a sense of sexual subjection and hence accessibility. In other words, the fusion of these two codes simultaneously allows women to be worshiped and subjected. One could argue further, that these are simply two sides of the same misogynist fantasy, which is rather bluntly summarized in the homosocial motto inscribed on the Herald of the Blended Rose's tunic: We droop when separated.

But this fusion of codes also allows for the martial and erotic topoi addressed in the opening and closing sections of the Mischianza to be handled simultaneously. The highly charged social and political divisions that separate the men and women in this event bring the question of war and colonial rule directly into the scene. All of the women in Turkish habit are from elite loyalist Philadelphia families. But nevertheless, even the most loyal of these women remain fully identified with colonial America in André's letter. Therefore, the displays of valor staged at the Mischianza amount to the performance of martial metropolitan men for the favors of elite, marriageable, colonial women. Within conventional romance scripts, the competition for women's favors through "mimic deeds of arms" substitutes sexual approbation for national or military glory. And the approbation sought among the homosocial community of the officer corps is understood to be from women who are "on the same side." At this level, placing these select women of Philadelphia in the scene of adjudication brings them over to the British side and alienates them from the Revolutionary cause. In this light, the faux conflict staged by the officers in the tournament already presupposes American autonomy and goes on to replace the Americans with themselves. It is as though they are saying: we own your women, we own your slaves, but not as you do. We own them rather according to fantasies of absolute dominion, according to specifically non-Whiggish understandings of sovereignty. And thus the imperial fantasy promulgated here relies on the figuration of the colonial population, not as a community of brothers related to their British kin, but rather as a radically other constituency of feminized objects. And that objectification partakes of all of the preexisting tools of religious xenophobia and misogynist fantasy.

Above all, it is the Turkish costume designed and perhaps fabricated by André[40] that marks the colonial women as different from the Knights of the Blended Rose and the Burning Mountain and forces the reader to consider where their difference lies (fig. 3.2).[41] Are the readers supposed to imagine that they have been rescued from the harem by the Crusader Knights? This would suggest that the occupation of Philadelphia, and the larger American conflict, is comparable to a crusade against republican despotism, against the perversion of British political ideals by American patriots. But this would presuppose consensus about the relationship between ancient constitutionalism and bellicose patriotism, which, as Brewer and others have argued, just was not tenable as the rhetoric of patriotism bifurcated in the 1770s.[42]

For many Britons, including Walpole, the American crisis was "the revenge of Old English political virtue upon modern English corruption."[43] Furthermore, reading the scene as one of rescue and liberation from despotic American political innovation does not fully account for the way the performance of martial valor is cut short in the name of the subject women:

> After they [the black Knights of the Burning Mountain] had rode round the lists, and made their obeisance to the Ladies, they drew up fronting the

Figure 3.2. Costume design for women participants in the Mischianza, designed by John André (1778). Courtesy of the Thomas Fisher Rare Book Library, University of Toronto.

White Knights; and the Chief of these having thrown down his gauntlet, the Chief of the Black Knights directed his Esquire to take it up. The Knights then received their lances from their Esquires, fixed their shields on their left arms, and making a general salute to each other, by a very graceful movement of their lances, turned round to take their career, and,

> encountering in full gallop, shivered their spears. In the second and third encounter they discharged their pistols. In the fourth they fought with their swords. At length the two Chiefs, spurring forward into the Centre, engaged furiously in single combat, till the Marshal of the Field (Major Gwyne) rushed in between the Chiefs, and declared that the Fair Damsels of the Blended Rose and Burning Mountain were perfectly satisfied with the proofs of love, and the signal feats of valor, given by their respective Knights; and commanded them, as they prized the future favors of their Mistresses, that they would instantly desist from further combat. Obedience being paid by the Chiefs to this order, they joined their respective bands. The White Knights and their attendants filed off to the left, the Black Knights to the right; and, after passing each other at the lower side of the quadrangle, moved up alternately, till they approached the pavilions of the Ladies, when they gave a general salute.[44]

André emphasizes that the faux jousting is stopped in the ladies' name by Major Gwyne, the marshal of the field, and thus we are presented with the spectacle of the officers not only fighting among themselves for the favors of the women but also speaking for the women in such a way that simply assumes their approval. This has the effect of containing both the threat of rejection or failure, which attends any conferral of sexual favor, and the threat of rejection or rebellion that attends the performance of imperial and colonial relations. In other words, the dangers of sexual exchange are as carefully managed as the dangers of colonial rule. And that management turns on the erasure and refiguration of colonial women as the commodity that underwrites the ascendancy of Howe's officer class.

This is a startling shift from the politics of conjugality discussed earlier in relation to Burgoyne's Fête Champêtre in that women enter the scene only as the occasion for declarations of homosocial cohesion. The suggestion that the national task can be supported by exemplary aristocratic sociability, signaled explicitly through the idealization of aristocratic marriage in Burgoyne's celebration, is simply rendered obsolete by a reinvestment in signs of martial hierarchy and extramarital heterosexual appropriation. The latter is given ample rehearsal in the remarkably inconsequential list of devices and mottos that ornament the tunics of the knights. Images of two cocks fighting (André's device), of burning hearts, and of Cupid attacking all manner of hearts are aligned with stock phrases of fidelity, which remain nevertheless rigorously separated from any sense of familial or marital commitment. Any hint of affiliation would undercut the fantasy of separation between colony and metropole that is so important not only to the tournament's performance but also to the satirical deployment of women in the parody of Burgoyne's Fête Champêtre.

The deployment of colonial women in the chivalric/orientalist scene of the tournament carefully stabilizes two mutually constitutive fantasies: one sexual and one imperial. Women are placed in a position of supposed otherness, only so that their grateful approbation of martial performance can appear to come from somewhere other than the men themselves. Likewise, these same women, as representatives of occupied Philadelphia, are placed in a position of alterity, in order to demonstrate that they have been liberated from their erstwhile Revolutionary captors and now wish to express their grateful "return" to their rightful masters. The circularity of the two fantasies provides both its primary strength and its fundamental weakness. In this tight circuit of hegemonic control, there is little for the women to do but play along. They are spoken for. But it is precisely this silence that necessitates the satirical gestures of André's address, because there is little separating the British officers' appropriation of these women and their figural "enslavement" by the "sultans" of revolution. The latter enslavement is a figure generated by the performance itself to characterize the political distinction between British officers fighting for their king and colonists fighting for their independence. But the former appropriation of the women of Philadelphia in performance is made manifest, or literalized, by the actions of the officers. In performance, the projection of eastern despotism onto the Americans is far less stable than the enactment of despotism by the men in the tournament.

Thus, André's address attempts to turn the literal subjection of the women in the performance, and by extension the subjection of the colonies to the king, into a figure. This explicit adoption of figurality is a complex rhetorical move because it demands that the reader recognize that the appropriation of colonial women's consent is part of a representational game in which the British play at the kind of absolutism that was not only ascribed to them by the Revolutionary colonists but also projected onto the Revolutionary colonists by the performance of the tournament itself. This sets up a rather strange situation where André satirizes the very power dynamics of the event in order to show the reader that the participants are knowingly staging hegemony. For this reason, Howe and the officers can be represented as despots who allow themselves to be "ruled" by the women they ultimately control. And by granting figural rule to the women, actual power can be retained by Howe and the Crown, and all manner of despotic figures can be projected onto the enemy. By performing the sexual weakness associated with fantasies of eastern despotism, Howe's officers can forestall charges of real despotism. What this means is that the orientalist fantasies that suffuse the event are precisely the diversionary tactic required to allow for the political consolidation of the officers' mission in America.

And of no less importance is that the rhetorical gambit tests the reader's ability to recognize the figural strategies that allow André and his associates to simultaneously critique Cornelys's Thames Regatta and Burgoyne's Fête Champêtre. What André's representation of the Mischianza requires the reader to do is to isolate the sexual fantasies associated with both prior events and work through the way Howe's officers not only critique both prior events but also test out a divergent model for the consolidation of martial masculinity. Cornelys's regatta, like its patron, was associated with aristocratic adultery and suspect forms of commerce. The Fête Champêtre, like Burgoyne himself, was associated with the fusion of patrician bellicosity and normative models of heterosexual exchange. By 1778, both sets of associations were in equal disrepute. Cornelys and the kind of aristocratic sociability she propagated had long been the target of nationalist arguments about the degeneration of the ruling elite. Burgoyne's model of patrician rule had proved inadequate at Saratoga. As we have seen, the Mischianza rehearses both prior events but rigorously ejects the suspect element of Cornelys's Thames Regatta from the Delaware Regatta and subtly inverts the martial figures of the second masque of Fête Champêtre so that "Beauty's Charms" disarm the agents of Mars, and the explosions of the fireworks exhibit beauty rather than putting "the whole lively group into a consternation." In other words, the Mischianza displays the promiscuity and the bellicosity of the prior events at the same time that it renounces them. As we have seen, André's letter simply puts the question of promiscuous association in abeyance by scrupulously eliding the event's reception among the nonparticipants. This has the salutary effect of forestalling criticism of the officers' character and of the style of display itself. But how the event handles bellicosity is perhaps of more import, because Howe himself was critical not only of the Coercive Acts but also of the war in general. Unlike Burgoyne, he was not interested in punishing Massachusetts, and he would have preferred a resolution to the war that gave colonists the feeling of autonomy, while retaining monarchical control over the empire. In other words, he would have preferred an arrangement roughly analogous to that articulated in the tournament, where the colonists were given some measure of figural autonomy as long as their actions and utterances were scripted for them by the Ministry. But in this kind of hegemonic solution to the American crisis, what was the military to do?

The specific deployment of sexuality throughout the Mischianza consistently stages the subjection of Mars to Venus. However, I would argue that this playing at subjection in the tournament and the final ball is made possible by a scene of compensatory projection. I am referring to the remarkable procession that leads the company from the space of the tournament to the temporary building that housed the ball and the supper. Between these two spaces of erotic display and self-satire lay a space devoted entirely to the veneration of the military and, hence, to the veneration of themselves. After the tournament, the entire company was asked to demonstrate its allegiance to both General William Howe and Lord Howe, to both the army and the navy:

> A passage being now opened between the two pavilions, the Knights, preceded by their Squires and the bands of music, rode through the first triumphal arch, and arranged themselves to the right and left. This arch was erected in honour of Lord Howe. It presented two fronts, in the Tuscan order; the pediment was adorned with various naval trophies, and at top was the figure of Neptune, with the Trident in his right hand. In a nich, on each side, stood a Sailor, with a drawn cutlass. Three Plumes of Feathers were placed on the summit of each wing, and in the entablature was this inscription: *Laus illi debetur, et a me gratia major.* The interval between the two arches was an avenue 300 feet long, and 34 broad. It was lined on each side with a file of troops; and the colours of all the army, planted at proper distances, had a beautiful effect in diversifying the scene. Between these colours the Knights and Squires took their stations. The Bands continued to play several pieces of martial music. The Company moved forward in procession, with the Ladies in the Turkish habits in front; as these passed, they were saluted by their Knights, who then dismounted and joined them: and in this order we were all conducted into a garden that fronted the house, through the second triumphal arch, dedicated to the General. This arch was also built in the Tuscan order. On the interior part of the pediment was painted a Plume of Feathers, and various military trophies. At top stood the figure of Fame, and in the entablature this device, — *I, bone, quo virtus, tua te vocet; I pede fausto.* On the right-hand pillar was placed a bomb-shell, and on the left a flaming heart.[45]

The triumphal arches, plumes of victory, the Latin tags, and other martial signifiers operate as the necessary reassertion of homosocial power between the two moments in the party when the colonial women are given Pyrrhic power over the officers. In this zone of mutual admiration, the silence of women takes on a different significance, because they are not looking at themselves but at their rulers. If this moment amounts to little more than an elaborate mirror game for the officers, akin to the proliferation of mirrors in the ballroom, then it is a blunt assertion of difference and commodification for the women.

It was these expressly martial elements of the Mischianza that elicited the most strident resistance in metropolitan audiences critical of Howe's inaction and in colonial audiences critical of British arrogance. And these critiques took up the question of narcissism and hegemony respectively. As the British author of *Strictures on the Philadelphia Mischianza or Triumph upon leaving America Unconquered* succinctly states,

> Upon what pretence . . . could this gentleman suffer himself to be crowned with laurels which he never won? Or encourage the *dedicating* a triumphal arch with plumes and military trophies to his honour, without his having once had the honour of a conquest?
>
> A General with so extensive and uncontrolled a command, cannot want flatterers enough among his numerous dependents, who may have been promoted by his favour, or possibly enriched by his connivance.
>
> But when so very extraordinary a method has been taken to persuade us of the high estimation in which he is held for his military abilities [even on the admission tickets, the General's crest was encircled with military trophies], it is a piece of justice due to the public, to produce the opinion of which the rest of the Americans entertain of him—so very different from that which is here given by his flatterers and dependents.[46]

The attack here explicitly mobilizes the combined rhetoric of weak despotism and aristocratic narcissism against Howe. The emphasis on flattery and sycophancy is a variant on the charge that Howe has, like the feminized sultan, succumbed to lassitude and the pleasures that surround him. Only such a corrupt official would allow himself to be represented in this way. This was precisely Thomas Paine's evaluation of Howe's command in *The Crisis*, and Paine's attack is cited at length in the *Strictures* and in a series of other precursor pamphlets. As noted earlier, Paine's attack closely aligns charges of vice with imputations of cowardice:

> That a man, whose soul is absorbed in the low traffic of vulgar vice, is incapable of moving in any superior region, is clearly shown in you by the event of every campaign. . . . Let me ask, Sir, what great exploits have you performed? Through all the variety of changes and opportunities, which this

> war hath produced, I know of no one action of yours that can be stiled masterly. You have moved in and out, backward and forward, round and round, as if your valour consisted in a military jig. The history and figure of your movements would be truly ridiculous, could they be justly delineated. They resemble the labours of a puppy pursuing his tail; the end is still at the same distance, and all the turnings round must be done over again.[47]

As this opinion is repeated in British pamphlets, it is bolstered by citations from André's account of the Mischianza, such that the celebration becomes a confirmation of Paine's critique. Here is one such example:

> Such are the sentiments which the Americans entertain of this gentleman, and so great the contempt they express of him.
>
> What would have been said of the Duke of Marlborough's vanity, if, after forty thousand enemies killed and taken at the battle of Blenheim, he had encouraged his officers and dependents to dedicate to him a triumphal arch, and had employed even the enemies standards taken in battle, in forming an avenue for himself and fellow conquerors to have walked through.
>
> What then are we to think of a beaten General's debasing the King's ensigns (for he had none of his enemies) by planting all the colours of the army in a grand avenue three hundred feet in length, lined with the King's troops, between two triumphal arches, for himself and his brother to march along in pompous procession, followed by a numerous train of attendants, with seven silken knights of the blended rose, and seven more of the burning mountain, and their fourteen Turkey dressed damsels, to an area 150 yards square, lined also with the King's troops, for the exhibition of a tilt and tournament, or mock fight of old chivalry, in honour of this triumphant hero; and all this sea and land ovation made; not in consequence of an uninterrupted succession of victories, like those of the Duke of Marlborough; not after the conquest of Canada by a Wolfe, a Townshend, and an Amherst; or after the much more valuable conquest of all the French provinces and possessions in India, under the *wise* and *active* General Coote; but after thirteen provinces wretchedly lost, and a three years series of ruinous disgraces and defeats.[48]

Putting Howe's actions and the Mischianza in relation to the heroic past is devastating, but the most telling element of this critique is the suggestion that Britons and Americans can accede to the same opinion about this scene of self-veneration. And it was precisely this collapse, this union of British and American opinion regarding Howe's command, that the Mischianza's deployment of sexuality was intended to obviate.

Despite the vigor of these attacks on Howe and the Mischianza, I would argue that the most eloquent response to the Mischianza's laborious attempt to find a way through this thicket of martial and sexual signs comes from one of the attending women silenced by André's letter. Captain Watson was the Chief of the Knights of the Burning Mountain, and he fought in honor of Miss Rebecca Franks, daughter of New York loyalist David Franks. During the toasts that interrupted the dancing, General Clinton, who had only just arrived to replace General Howe, called for the band to play "Britons strike home!" Known for her wit, Rebecca Franks corrected Clinton by simply asking for clarification: "Britons *go* home, you mean."[49] The play of citation and repetition here is apt, considering the degree to which the entire event cites and repeats both prior events and itself. Clinton's request for one of the chestnuts of naval patriotism aims to place current events in a long history of victory and national celebration. Rebecca Franks's simple repetition, with a difference, of Clinton's request subtly uses a synonym to reverse the meaning of the entire performance, and hence it injects a whole new level of satire. The gesture is not at all distant from the repetition of the central concepts of British political theory to argue against colonial rule, only here we have a loyalist parodying Revolutionary positions. Furthermore, in its performance this simple clarification undoes the circularity of the sexual tropes and punctures the scene of narcissism by suddenly giving free rein to the voice of the colonial woman, which had hitherto been so rigorously contained. And Rebecca Franks's imitation speaks specifically to the larger question of imitation here. In the mirrored space of the ballroom, as in the auto-reflective space between the triumphal arches, the question of mimetic truth is simply assumed by the officers, and only ever challenged by someone outside, yet projected into, the scene. Rebecca Franks's resistance is performative, wittily staged within a scene that blurs the distinction between private and public, not to mention the distinction between colony and empire, and which affords her a certain latitude for raillery, because she has been already deemed subordinate by virtue of her gender. So the author of the *Strictures* and Rebecca Franks share common ground—they are both ratifying Howe's recall—because their social and spatial location as readers of the performance gives them purchase on the representation. André's complex rhetorical gambit fails because words, whether printed in the metropolitan press or spoken inside the ballroom, cannot fully choose their audience.[50]

To Rise in Splendor: *Douglas* in Philadelphia

It is doubtful that many of the Mischianza's hungover celebrants rose in greater splendor on 19 May 1778, but at least some of them were confronted with the task of performing John Home's tragedy *Douglas* that evening. The choice of Home's tragedy for the final British theatrical production in occupied Philadelphia seems out of character with the rest of the repertoire—it is the only tragedy presented by the officers at the Southwark Theatre—but I believe that this particular performance makes the argument of the Mischianza even more acute. As David Wheeler has argued, Home's *Douglas*, first performed in Edinburgh in 1756, emerges out of a renewed critical interest in the emotional response of the audience that also animates Hurd's *Letters on Chivalry and Romance*.[51] We have already noted how the Gothic medievalism of Hurd's text infuses the Mischianza, and I would argue Home's tragedy provides another site through which to allegorize the present moment.[52] Thus, the analysis that follows attempts to account for the singularity both of this deployment of ancient dynastic struggles and of the performing company's manipulation of pathos.

The play was performed frequently by British officers at the Theatre Royal in New York from 1778 to 1782 under the command of Sir Henry Clinton, and there is reason to suspect that it was a favorite with him.[53] While Howe was occupying Philadelphia, Clinton—second in command of the British army in America—maintained the tradition of British theatricals in New York that Howe had commenced in 1777. The first production at New York authorized by Clinton was *Douglas*, and it played to much acclaim on 6 and 9 January 1778.[54] By the time Clinton saw the play again in Philadelphia after the Mischianza, much had changed. France had entered the war as an ally of the colonists in March, Howe was officially recalled, and the newly promoted Clinton was to oversee the evacuation of Philadelphia in order to better defend New York. He received these orders in May while in Philadelphia when he officially became commander in chief. The succession of command from Howe to Clinton was rife with acrimony. During the year and a half of fighting before the change of command, Clinton's actions were repeatedly frustrated by Howe's inaction. In 1776,

> after becoming second in command and leading an abortive expedition to the Carolinas, he also failed to persuade Howe, the new commander-in-chief, to accept plans for trapping and destroying the continental army at New York. And in 1777, after a brief winter's leave in England, during which he learned the government's plans, Clinton was unable to convince

> Howe that he was expected to co-operate with a British army advancing south from Canada in a summer campaign along the Hudson. Howe, ignoring Clinton's arguments and the government's plans, took his army to Pennsylvania by way of Chesapeake Bay. He left Clinton to hold New York city and to do what he could to favour the British forces from Canada. When in early October Clinton made a bold dash up the Hudson, Howe promptly stripped him of the troops he was employing to open the river. Clinton, thoroughly frustrated with Howe, asked to resign as soon as he learned that the Canadian army had surrendered.[55]

The government did not accept Clinton's resignation but instead had him replace Howe. Thus, Clinton's participation in the Mischianza and his attendance at the theatre for *Douglas* the next evening need to be understood as part both of a fraught transition of power and of a shift in policy aimed at prosecuting the war on a global level. Howe's orders had been to deal with rebellious colonists widely understood to be more like brothers than enemies. Upon assuming his position as commander in chief, Clinton "had temporarily to subordinate the American war to a wider war with France."[56]

The circumstances of command are important here because John Home's tragedy is not only deeply concerned with matters of succession but also with the very fine dynastic distinctions that separate the men in the play. Because so much of the theory of tragedy on which Home is drawing is concerned with the power of affective response, the bulk of the reception of *Douglas* revolves around the remarkable character of Lady Randolph. But it is important to remember that it is a thoroughly soldierly play. As Sandro Jung notes, *Douglas* was "inspired by the old Scottish ballad *Gil Morrice*," and Home embedded "his tragedy within a vague framework of patriotism for Scotland in which the Scottish chiefs defend their native soil against an invasion of the Danes."[57] This Danish threat looms everywhere in the tragedy but actual warfare is projected into the future beyond the tragedy's denouement. What this means is that the conflicts that drive the action do not involve "foreign foes" but rather arise among "a people similar, / As twins are to each other."[58] Lady Randolph's distinction between foreign and civil wars comes early in act 1 and refers specifically to Scotch and English wars, but as the play unfolds, the audience is forced to consider conflict within the ostensibly selfsame. In fact, one could argue that it is the unstable definition of sameness that made this tragedy so resonant in its initial productions during the Seven Years' War and makes it so applicable to the situation in Philadelphia in May 1778.[59]

The play's characters come from three dynastic clans: the houses of Malcolm, Douglas, and Randolph. The play's main character, Lady Matilda Randolph, is the daughter of Malcolm and married to Lord Randolph, the play's senior military figure. But unbeknownst to Lord Randolph, his wife was previously married in secret to Douglas. Matilda had been introduced to the younger Douglas by her brother Malcolm, who carries his father's name. The marriage was secret because of enmity between Malcolm and Douglas's father, who is also named Douglas. The doubled names of the fathers and sons emphasize the distinction between the houses, and clearly the secret marriage forms an alliance against the wishes of the patriarchs. Matilda and Douglas have a child, who inherits Douglas's name and who embodies the hybridization of the two houses. He is quite literally the reconciliation of dynastic conflict. However, before any of this can play out in public, not only are Matilda's husband Douglas and her brother Malcolm killed in battle but also the child is lost and believed dead. So, at the outset of the play, both the homosocial bond between Malcolm the younger and Douglas younger and the heterosexual bond between Matilda and Douglas are cut short. Into this vortex of grief comes the house of Randolph, kinsmen to Malcolm. Shortly after the death of Douglas and the disappearance of her child, Glenalvon, Lord Randolph's heir, attempts to rape Matilda. She is rescued by Lord Randolph and she, out of duty and respect for his moral character, agrees to marry him. Now Lady Randolph, she brings all of the fortune of the house of Malcolm into the marriage, but none of the affection or love shown for her former husband. The Randolph's childless marriage is a pathological state in which the wife mourns objects known only to her and in which the husband's masculinity becomes a perverse manifestation of excessive bellicosity. The corruption is further signaled by the fact that the former rapist, Glenalvon, remains the heir to the family fortune and plots all through the play to kill Randolph and ravish his Lady.

At the beginning of the play, therefore, on the eve of the Danish invasion, the Scots are represented only by Lord Randolph and Glenalvon, able yet fundamentally flawed soldiers. The representatives of the houses of Malcolm and Douglas are dead, and thus the Danish threat appears that much more fearsome. The complexity of the relationship between clans—they all have stakes in Lady Randolph—is narrated more than enacted until the appearance of a young stranger in the second act. He is of course Lady Randolph's son by Douglas, although neither character knows this until acts 3 and 4, respectively. Saved by Old Norval and raised as a shepherd, young Norval exhibits extraordinary bravery by saving Randolph from Glenalvon's assassins. He also demonstrates an unusual aptitude for warfare. Well before his birth is revealed, Norval embodies the martial bearing of a true noble. That revelation, staged for the audience in a sentimental scene between mother and son, is only belatedly conducted for Randolph. Recognizing a rival when he sees one, Glenalvon plots against both Norval and Randolph simultaneously by inciting Randolph's jealousy. Glenalvon's poison words make Randolph misrecognize secretly maternal and filial affection for adulterous desire.[60] The ensuing eruption of violence is precipitous. Glenalvon and Norval kill each other, Lady Randolph commits suicide after losing her son yet again, and Lord Randolph reengages his bellicosity with the hope of dying in battle. Whether this death will be honorable is unclear at the end of the play, for it seems to emerge as an expiation of his own guilt rather than as an expression of selfless patriotism. But most importantly, the audience is left at the end with no heir to the legacy of any of the houses. Glenalvon, both Malcolms, and all three men named Douglas are dead. Lord Randolph, the surrogate husband, promises to fight the Danes to his death, but the future of Scotland, both in war and in love, appears in jeopardy.

The complexity of *Douglas*'s back story is belied by the simplicity of the tragic action. Basically, Norval is introduced in order to kill and be killed by the corrupt heir to Lord Randolph. As the embodiment of civic virtue, he is presented in order to be mourned.[61] However, his brief transit from obscurity to death is witnessed by Lady Randolph and her servant, and above all it is the alternative future that he represents that is of utmost concern. Immediately upon his appearance, he is cast as the great warrior hero who will save Scotland from the Danes, the true heir to Douglas's fortitude. Lady Randolph's grief for his loss both as a child and as a man is as much about the loss of her child as it is about the loss of her nation's future. Reaction to the appearance and loss of this alternative future is condensed in the extreme emotional responses of Lady Randolph. It is not an exaggeration to suggest that her performance of loss is aimed at consolidating audience response to what appears to be a political dead end for the nation. She is the only character who knows that Glenalvon is not a suitable heir to the house of Randolph and of Scotland, because he is cruel, vicious, and traitorous. Behind the mask of soldierly virtue, Glenalvon is a perverse internal threat to the unity of the Scottish cause. This is exacerbated by the fact that the play so insistently destroys homosocial and heterosexual ties between the houses: the friendship between Malcolm the younger and Douglas is prematurely cut off by their deaths, the new line emerging from Matilda and Douglas's marriage is prematurely cut off when Glenalvon stabs Norval in the back, and the Randolph marriage is childless. Paula R. Backscheider succinctly states that "the fulfillment of hope seems within a character's reach, then is cruelly and suddenly denied. Home has designed the play so that nearly every theatre-goer—wife, father, mother, youth—can be touched by the experiences of the characters."[62]

How do we read the production of this tragedy for this audience at this historical moment? Captain André was undoubtedly involved with the design and painting of the Gothic forests and castles in which the play is set, but he may have acted a part as well. We have relatively few details about the actual cast except that the men were played by officers stationed in Philadelphia and that Lady Randolph was likely played by the mistress of a British officer. But even these scant details, when considered in relation to the Mischianza and the succession of command from Howe to Clinton, are resonant. For all its success on the stage, the role of Lady Randolph in *Douglas* was widely scrutinized on moral grounds. Her distress was deemed by many critics to be preposterous and her relationship to both her husband and restored son was disturbing to many viewers.[63] Thus, to see this role performed by someone of dubious moral character is itself intriguing, especially when what the audience was watching was a loyal colonial mistress expressing grief for her dead husband and desire for her returned son.

If we understand the colonial relation as a marital allegory, then what we have is loyal America grieving for a lost relationship with Britain. Further, she is currently trapped in a loveless relationship to a bellicose kinsman whose heir is actively attempting to kill him and take her by force. It would seem that Lord Randolph is an apt allegory for the bellicosity of Lord North and his Ministry, and Glenalvon figures quite well for the rebel colonists. Furthermore, the rape fantasy is perfectly in keeping with the deployment of sexuality in the Mischianza discussed in the previous section of this chapter. When faced with these alternatives, Lady Randolph transfers her lost desire for her dead husband onto Norval, the true heir to the house of Douglas, who she argues in act 4 will be restored to his rights and will lead the Scots to victory over the invading Danes. In terms of the marital allegory, this amounts to a desire for a true heir to Britain's glorious imperial past. The implication is, I believe, clear: what Britain needs is someone capable of restoring the virtuous relationship between metropole and colony forged against the French during the Seven Years' War—a relationship forged by men like George and William Howe and which included heroic soldiers such as Wolfe and George Washington.

In much the same way that loyalist women are conscripted into an erotic fantasy of supremacy in the Mischianza, the unidentified woman playing Lady

Randolph in the production of *Douglas* is caught in an impossible trap. Her loyalty, as expressed both in her actual relationship to a British officer and in her performance, generates a perverse relationship to her "husband" whether that be understood as the officer in question, Randolph or Britain, because it operates outside the codes of normative conjugal relations. Her relationship to Lord Randolph/North and to Glenalvon/rebel colonists is always that of potential victim. And her relationship to her "true son" is both a misrecognition of the future for the past—that is, her son for her husband—and a fruitless passion. When the new Douglas is destroyed by the collusion of Glenalvon and Randolph, of rebellion and bellicosity, what the audience was witnessing was the death of Howe's dream of conciliation between Britain and the colonies, for that too was based on a prior attachment between Britain and America generated during the battles against the French in the Seven Years' War. With France's entry into the war, this dream was no longer viable.

This is a contentious reading of the performance, but its deployment of the actual bodies of colonial women matches that which was so laboriously exercised during the Mischianza on the previous evening. Furthermore, the allegory is given even more traction by the very question of succession posed by the play. Put bluntly, Howe was replaced by someone who was willing to prosecute the war in a fashion more in line with the dictates of North's Ministry. In this, Clinton bears a close resemblance to the Scottish commander Randolph. As noted already, Douglas never appears in the play that carries his name, and his son is cut down before he can fully accede to his potential. Does this not allegorize Howe's present position? He is politically dead and yet hoping to return with honor intact. At this point, it is useful to remember the motto to the ticket to the Mischianza: "I shine in setting; I shall rise in greater splendor." When Lady Randolph reveals to Norval his true identity, it is through the splendor of a specific stage property. Through her servants, Lady Randolph intercepted Old Norval, who has a set of jewels that were secreted with the child and attest to the former glory of his father. When she presents them to Norval, he states "I saw them once, and curiously enquir'd / Of both my parents whence such splendor came? / But I was check'd, and more could never learn" (4.1.43). The splendor of these jewels becomes a sign of the virtue of both father and son and of their blood relation. I would suggest that it is this past and fleetingly possible future for martial subjectivity that André and his fellow officers were bringing into performance. But they staged this possibility not to venerate it but rather to mark its passing. After all, Norval dies, and his death forces Lord Randolph to reconsider his actions, to rethink his relation not only to his wife but also to his country.

Could we not argue that this bizarre succession ceremony was staged to transform the subjectivity of the commander in chief by turning his attention away from his dead wife and relations—that is, the loyal and the rebellious colonists—toward the external threat posed by foreign powers? *Douglas* thus becomes an allegorical motor for turning attention from civil disagreements to true enemies, from narrowly colonial to global concerns. The honorable second Douglas prepares the ground for Randolph to go to war against the foreign threat by eliminating the traitorous Glenalvon.

For this audience, in this space, at this time, that external threat is clearly France. I would argue that the self-sacrifice of the colonial woman in this allegory merely pushes the erotic dynamic of the Mischianza one step further in order to grapple with the new global significance of the American conflict. In the Mischianza, the colonial women were deployed as the exchange objects needed to guarantee the homosocial bonds of the officer class. In this supplementary production of Home's tragedy, Lady Randolph is sacrificed in order to provide an occasion for the officers to feel the emotion that attends the loss not only of the governmental relation between colony and metropole but also of the fantasy of civic virtue on which this obsolete notion of governmental harmony was based. What fascinates me here is that Lady Randolf's suicide resolves the problem of political agency for Howe, André, and their associates by eliminating the problem of America altogether. Read allegorically, loyal America kills itself upon its recognition that the embodiment of civic virtue is dead. Rebellious America has already been distanced from virtue by associating it with Glenalvon's attempts to rape and assassinate Lady and Lord Randolph—the loyal colony and the bellicose metropole. This clearing of the colonial ground ensures that the tradition of republican governance based on civic virtue would not migrate from Britain to America. In this allegorical schema, there are quite literally no heirs to republican political thought on American shores, and thus this deployment of Home's *Douglas* interrupts the historical process mapped by J. G. A. Pocock in *The Machiavellian Moment.*[64] And with this interruption, attention shifts away from the question of virtue altogether so that the audience is left contemplating not only Lord Randolph's capacity to repel the invading Danes but also Sir Henry Clinton's, and by extension the Ministry's, capacity to wage a global war.

Nestled within the allegorical link between Lord Randolph and Sir Henry Clinton is a subtle critique of the Ministry because the play intimates that Lord Randolph's future actions may themselves be suicidal. In this regard, Lord Randolph's desire to die in battle is reminiscent of Marcus's death in Joseph Addison's *Cato.* Like Marcus he is "bent on death."[65] This is significant in light of the roughly contemporaneous performance of *Cato* by Washington's soldiers at Valley Forge on 11 May 1778—eight days before Howe's company's production of *Douglas.* The complex meaning of the production of *Cato* at Valley Forge has been admirably discussed by Randall Fuller and Jason Shaffer,[66] and I would like to suggest further that the divergent definitions of patriotic performance among American and British soldiers could be understood as a contrast between the republican ideals espoused and enacted in *Cato* and the emotions inculcated by *Douglas.*[67] As Shaffer argues, "Washington's attendance at the Valley Forge Cato . . . affirmed both his concern for the welfare of his men and his command over them, meanwhile acknowledging the stoic 'republican' virtue demanded of the army at Valley Forge."[68] And yet in a striking revision of *Cato,* the suicide of the hero is downplayed in light of a future where "the Continental Army might be able to embrace both liberty and life."[69] In contrast, the representative of civic virtue in *Douglas* is killed, and the emotions generated by his death are channeled into the histrionic mourning and eventual suicide of Lady Randolph. Howe is leaving, and his replacement is figured as Lord Randolph. In other words, the performance of *Cato* at Valley Forge, contrary to the plot of the play, imagines a future where republican thought can stay alive, whereas the performance of *Douglas* at Philadelphia propels its audience into an uncertain future disconnected from models of governance based on civic virtue. The former fantasy maintains a connection between past models of governmentality and future life, whereas the latter opens up a gap between the past and the future that is registered as a kind of sublime pain. In this context the generic differences between the two plays become decisive. *Cato*'s Augustan adaptation of Aristotelian principles "inculcates specific moral and ethical doctrines through pity and fear," whereas *Douglas*'s purpose, as understood by its apologists, was "the exercise and strengthening of the spectator's general faculty for sympathy."[70] Thus, for Washington's soldiers at Valley Forge, emotion was generated to inculcate republican virtue, whereas Howe's soldiers, through their deployment of the colonial woman in the role of Lady Randolph, were strengthening their sympathetic bonds to that which had been lost.

CHAPTER FOUR

"THE BODY" of David Garrick

Richard Brinsley Sheridan, America, and the Ends of Theatre

> What Shakespeare says of *ACTORS* may be better applied to the purpose of *PLAYS*; they ought to be "the abstract and brief Chronicles of the times." Therefore when history, and particularly the history of our own country, furnishes anything like a case in point to the time in which an author writes, if he knows his own interest, he will take advantage of it.
>
> Richard Brinsley Sheridan, *The Critic*, 2.1.1–7

At almost precisely the same moment that readers in London would be pondering the significance of the representation of the Mischianza in the *Gentleman's Magazine*, they were confronted with a remarkable letter from Admiral Augustus Keppel proclaiming victory over the French fleet at Ushant. The letter appeared first in the government publication the *London Gazette Extraordinary* and was reprinted in all of the newspapers on 4 August 1778. From the outset, it was the subject of intense scrutiny, because of the strange manner in which he described the crucial decision to not pursue the French fleet:

> The fleets, being upon different tacks, passed each other very close: The object of the French seemed to be the disabling the King's ships in their masts and sails, in which they so far succeeded as to prevent many of the ships of my fleet being able to follow me when I wore to stand after the French fleet; this obliged me to wear again, to join those ships, and thereby allowed of the French forming their fleet again, and range it in a line to

> leeward of the King's fleet, towards the close of the day, which I did not discourage, but allowed of their doing it, without firing upon them, thinking they meant *handsomely* to try their force with us the next morning; but they had been so beaten in the day, that they took the advantage of the night to go off.[1]

The adverb "handsomely" provoked repeated commentary in the weeks and months after its publication, in part because the word is so multivalent—it is synonymous with readily, appropriately, skillfully, elegantly, and, in a strictly nautical sense, carefully—and in part because very few of the papers were willing to allow the French any capacity for handsomeness. Britain was in the midst of a palpable invasion scare because the French had joined the American cause and were threatening the southern coast of England. Keppel, a much-lionized naval hero and Whig parliamentarian, had been hastily called forward to lead the poorly maintained channel fleet. The nation was preoccupied with news from the camps at Coxheath and daily reports of preparations for war with France, so it should come as no surprise that news from Ushant was much anticipated.

But the scrutiny of Keppel's letter, which briefly reported on the naval action of 27 and 28 July, was curiously stylistic. For example, in the same column of the *Morning Chronicle* in which Keppel's letter appeared, we get the following:

> Admiral Keppel's letter, in yesterday's London Gazette Extraordinary, is one of the most singular that ever was written as an official dispatch. It neither mentions where the action was fought, where the French fleet are gone to, nor in what kind the hard blows received by our ships were repaid. The latter may certainly be ascertainable as to the precise quantum of the injury done the enemy, but surely the brave Admiral might have given us some better expression to guess by, than the vague declaration that they were "*so* beaten."[2]

Questions of usage are here standing in for a full array of anxieties and recriminations. In the weeks and months that followed, the papers are replete with indictments of Keppel's failure to fully describe the battle in naval language, and insinuations that he failed to fully engage with the French fleet. For commentators hostile to Keppel, this smacked of evasion or, worse, of a willful attempt to mislead the public. Less factionalized reports argued that the lack of clarity and precision allowed for the deliberate or innocent misconstrual of events vital to the nation. Keppel's letter became a narrative enigma that prompted the proliferation of accounts of the battle: the papers printed accounts from subordinate

Don't you think my good Friends this a comical Farce is,
To see two Great Admirals fight with their A——,
Mons! squirts Soup-meagre across K—p—ls back,
But he in return, gives a far harder Smack,
What a Smoak & a Stink! & yet neither prevails
For how can it be? when they both turn their Tails.
July 177
Price 6
Keppels Court Martial, Jan 1780

officers and, more divisively, reprinted radically contradictory reports from France that celebrated French victory over the British fleet in the same battle.[3] These reports, of course, were rebutted and provided the occasion for invective against the perfidious French. Inflammatory prints such as the anonymous "The Engagement between D'Orvilliers and Keppel," whose appended verse concludes "What a Smoak and a Stink! & yet neither prevails / For how can it be? when they both turn their Tails," refigured the battle as a vortex of excrement in which both admirals were running from each other (fig. 4.1).[4] Like the letter itself, the Battle of Ushant very quickly became an event whose historical interpretation was dangerously inconclusive and thus had to be worked through at every level of its signification. The *Morning Post* captures the nature of the event when it referred to the battle as "that dark transaction off Brest."[5]

This double enigma—the battle and Keppel's representation of it—instantiates one of the crucial narratives of the American war, a narrative whose political significance is well known but whose cultural import remains underexplored.[6] From August 1778 through February 1779, the interpretive struggle to resolve the enigmas surrounding Keppel's actions and his text moved through various fields. In the summer and early fall, much of the engagement with the issue took place in the papers, and they played a decisive role in the institutional response to the issue. Throughout August, September, and October, the papers printed highly technical accounts of the action, signed by correspondents with names such as Nauticus Sr., that attempted to piece together the events of the battle from the reports printed in the papers. And they also printed a host of rumors aimed at undermining both the government's and the opposition's representations of the war itself. But the resolution of the enigma took a dramatic turn, when, on 15 October, Vice-Admiral Hugh Palliser, Keppel's second in command, was publicly impugned by one of Keppel's supporters aboard his own flagship in the *General Advertiser* for failing to obey orders and join Keppel in pursuit of the French fleet.[7] Within the week Palliser attempted to exculpate himself, again in print, but Keppel refused to contradict, in print, the attack on Palliser.[8]

This war of words, like the battle itself, remained inconclusive and threatened to destabilize the command structure of the navy. As the *Morning Chronicle* stated,

Figure 4.1., opposite Anonymous, "The Engagement between D'Orvilliers and Keppel," etching (1780). BM 5626. Department of Prints and Drawings © Trustees of the British Museum.

> It is much lamented by all true friends to their country, that there should exist such a matter as party aboard a fleet, fitted out like that sent to sea under the command of Mr. Keppel, on the most important of all possible occasions, the immediate defense of the kingdom, and the chastisement of her most perfidious and most powerful foe. Admiral Keppel and Sir Hugh Palliser are both allowed to be able seamen and brave officers, what a pity it is that two such respectable characters should be under the influence of either political or personal pique. When the service of their country is the business, every little passion should give way to the greater impulse, and all parties in employ should unite, hand and heart, in the discharge of their duty.[9]

On 9 December, Palliser brought charges against Keppel; they were accepted by Lord Sandwich, the lord of the Admiralty, and one of the most explosive trials of the eighteenth century was set underway. Keppel declared in Parliament that he would not serve with Palliser, and it became clear that the political divisions over the American conflict had the potential to undermine the solidarity of the military. Keppel's court-martial was the focus of intense conflict in Parliament throughout December, and literally dominated print culture for its duration from 9 January to 11 February. Politically, the court-martial was a disaster for the Ministry and especially for Sandwich. At a moment when it was extremely difficult to critique the government, the opposition was presented with a political gift. At the same time that it was defending one of its own—Augustus Keppel was a prominent member of the Rockingham faction and second cousin to Charles James Fox—the opposition could attack the Ministry on a variety of fronts. It is not an exaggeration to say that the rhetorical advantages gained during the Keppel affair provided much of the traction for subsequent parliamentary critique of the war effort.

All twenty-eight days of the court-martial were reported in intense detail, and Keppel's acquittal resulted in mass celebrations or mass rioting, depending on one's political perspective, throughout England. As Roger summarizes, "According to reports in the London and provincial press over 160 demonstrations were staged in his favour, coupled in most instances with the burning or hanging of Palliser in effigy. Comparable in scale to the Wilkite demonstrations, the Keppel affair rivaled the radical in popular engagement. It was one of the causes célèbres of the decade."[10] And yet even after Keppel's acquittal, anonymous satirical prints such as "Who's in Fault? (No Body) A View off Ushant" (fig. 4.2)[11] emphasized that the question of who was at fault in the Battle of Ushant and

Figure 4.2. Anonymous, "Who's in Fault? (No Body) A View off Ushant," etching (1779). BM 5570. Department of Prints and Drawings © Trustees of the British Museum.

even of what precisely happened in the Channel remained unresolved. Clearly the rendering of Keppel without a body in the satirical print attempts to get at this problem less through equivocation than through a direct pun on the word "nobody" and the direct assertion of cowardice when it states that Keppel's "Heart was in his Breeches."

In the satirical prints from the postacquittal period, Keppel becomes a head or, more specifically, a face. And certainly we have to be struck by the rejuvenation of Keppel's face in these satires. "Who's in Fault? (No Body) A View off Ushant" does not give us an aged Keppel, but rather supplies us with the new face of a younger, less experienced man. There is evidence that a similar facialization of Keppel was also true of the theatrical illuminations that accompanied many of the celebratory declamations in the theatres. These disembodied heads are significant because they effectively separate the martial hero from his body and thus implicitly pose the question of how and when the fragmented body of the hero will be reconstituted. Interestingly, "Who's in Fault? (No Body) A View off Ushant" attaches the faces to the same signs of power deployed in the postacquittal celebrations—namely, Keppel's uniform and his sword. But here their very status as mere signs is set in damning contrast to the representation of the battle itself on the right side of the picture—a battle, I might add, that is completely obscured by smoke. From this perspective, I think it is possible to recognize an important distinction between the hyperembodiment of Palliser and Sandwich in the celebrations themselves—effigies of both men were often attacked or burned by the crowd—and the decorporealization of the "hero." With the body of Keppel melting into air, the anonymous engraver of "Who's in Fault? (No Body) A View off Ushant" seems to put time into reverse in search of a body to attach to a rejuvenated face. This print is asking the viewer to think through the implications of celebrating Keppel's victory over the Ministry rather than celebrating his victory over the French, which amounts to asking why the nation was beset with internal conflict during a period when it faced direct threat from external forces. This harsh historical question, or a version of it, threads its way through all of the performances I discuss in the next three chapters. Sheridan, Cowley, Colman, and directors of the Handel Commemoration all develop strategies for addressing this question, and in each case a tactical deployment of the body of the national hero becomes crucial for countenancing the time to come.

To say that the Keppel-Palliser affair dominated the press would be both an understatement and, in some senses, a misconstrual of the press's role in the event itself. There is no question regarding the sheer column inches devoted to the debates and the court-martial, but the papers themselves were very much aware that they played a generative role in the crisis.[12] Here is the loyalist *Morning Post*'s reflection on the papers' role on the eve of the court-martial:

> The present unhappy divisions between our two Admirals, are the baneful effects of party-zeal. The little success attending our arms off Brest, gave rise to a thousand conjectures; burned, sunk, and destroyed, not making, as usual, a part of the Gazette, gave rise to murmurs and discontent; and the novelty of a sea-engagement without its usual consequences, led the people to surmise, that all was not right at bottom. The Minority threw some oblique hints to the disadvantage of Sir Hugh Palliser, and both parties alternately expressed their surprise at Admiral Keppel's suffering the French fleet to form, on the vague supposition, that they intended fighting it out *handsomely* the next morning. The very expression (handsomely) was a standing joke on both sides, and on all occasions; but the affair now become too serious for a subject of wit, or ridicule. The mistaken ——,

> therefore, which has caused such an unhappy conflagration, should subside, nor aggravate contradictions already too complicated; a continuation of which can only foment a professional discord among a set of brave men, whose country, at this period particularly, demands their utmost care and attention.[13]

Despite the *Morning Post*'s almost de rigueur slur on the minority party—that is, the Whigs—this is a remarkably accurate representation of how the enigma generated narrative effects. Because the papers were themselves so factionalized, "Party zeal" expressed itself in the struggle for dominance in the commercial print public sphere. The *Morning Post* is particularly important here because it argued from the outset that the opposition was actively impugning the reputations of both Keppel and Palliser in order to embarrass the Ministry.[14] Suggesting that the opposition was attacking Sandwich's friend Palliser was simply politics as usual, but charging the opposition papers, and in particular the virulently critical *General Advertiser*, with assassinating the reputation of one of their own heroes amounted to saying that the opposition was willing and able to eviscerate itself in order to destroy the best efforts of the government. This was tantamount to saying that Britons who were partial to the colonists' critique of imperial rule were exhibiting a form of self-loathing aimed ultimately at destroying Britain itself. This was sedition in its most profound form, and it was a highly effective way of containing the political efforts of not only the pro-American elements of the British populace but also those factions within Parliament that were deeply concerned about North's management of the war. In other words, this stream of anti-opposition rhetoric argued quite explicitly that the opposition critique of the Admiralty is simply the most egregious example of a kind of masochistic desire within the nation itself to tear itself to pieces. Resisting this kind of self-mutilation becomes a key progovernment trope, and thus much of the discourse surrounding the Keppel court-martial is aimed at restoring unanimity within the officer corps of the navy and, by extension, within the nation itself.

The Keppel-Palliser affair brought into unmistakable visibility the palpable disunity of not only the military but also the state at this crucial juncture in the war. Officer would not serve with officer, and certain officers would not follow orders because of political allegiances to entities other than the state. That disunity was frequently represented, especially by the progovernment papers, as a contagion destroying the patriotic vigor of the nation. And the contagion of factional politics was not simply a matter of parliamentary disagreement but rather was concretized by the papers themselves. However, this concretization carried with it a number of disturbing corollary effects relating specifically to their commercial circulation. The papers were both conduits of information and sources of entertainment. The porous relationship between news and entertainment is implicit in the *Morning Post*'s appraisal of the crisis, because it is seeking, rather belatedly, a restoration of the distinction between "facts" and "wit" that never existed in the first place. The coverage always already blended ostensible eyewitness accounts, public documents, opinion pieces, letters to the editor, bon mots, poems, and pedestrian commentary into an amalgam of printed materials aimed at keeping the story alive. The repeated reactivation of the enigma was a perfect mechanism for driving consumption of the papers themselves.

Illuminating the "darkness of the transaction off Brest" took narrative time, and narrative time in the world of the newspapers is a commodity whose exchange value only increases with the proliferation of points of view. The factionalization of the daily papers ensured that the story of the battle would be told in conflicting ways, and thus readers were confronted with the narrative pleasure of adjudicating between narrators. Thus, the entire struggle within the public sphere for the interpretation of the facts of the case aspired to the condition of the most complex experiments in prose fiction. It would be inaccurate to describe the entire newspaper archive as a novel, but the daily collocation of radically disjunctive narratives pertaining to the same story brings the problem of disunity or faction directly into the experience of reading. And that means that the very issue of faction is not only internalized but also formally reinforced by the medium itself. The very contagion that generated so much anxiety in the progovernment papers was formally propagated by the print public sphere of which they were a vital part. The charge of attempting to dismember the nation from within, which was so regularly directed by progovernment voices at the opposition during this period, is simply a specific case of a wider problematic that not only envelopes all parties but also permeates the political itself, especially when politics are actuated in the public sphere of print.

It was against this backdrop that Richard Brinsley Sheridan attempted to come to grips with the passing of David Garrick and the loss of one of the cultural icons of eighteenth-century Britain. The first envoi came on 1 February, just before Admiral Augustus Keppel's acquittal, at David Garrick's funeral. Richard Brinsley Sheridan was designated chief mourner for the man whose name was synonymous with theatre itself, and Sheridan's performance in the streets of London marked the end of a theatrical era. The procession and interment in Westminster Abbey quite literally overwhelmed London, and it was perhaps the only event capable of interrupting the barrage of Keppel-Palliser news in the press. This was supplemented by another performance roughly six weeks later within Drury Lane theatre. Working with De Loutherbourg, Sheridan wrote and staged an elaborate eulogy entitled "Verses to the Memory of Garrick, spoken as a Monody" which combined declamation, music, painting, and sculpture to mourn Garrick yet again. Sheridan wrote the poem, which was spoken by Mrs. Yates; Linley wrote the music; and De Loutherbourg designed the set, incorporating a strange portrait of Garrick by Sir Joshua Reynolds. These two performances are obviously linked by their pretext, Garrick's death, and much of this chapter aims to comprehend the curious relation between these events and their complex place within the historical crisis of the American war. The final farewell, on the surface, seems unconnected to Garrick's passing, but I argue that the premiere on 30 October 1779 of *The Critic*, Sheridan's last great play, engages not only with the loss of Garrick earlier in the year but also with the impending loss of the Atlantic empire. This chapter explores the relationship between these two losses. Garrick was definitely over, the American war was not, but both losses, one finished and one ongoing, raised fundamental questions about closure, tragedy, and continuation that I wish to explore in this chapter.

After Garrick

On 20 January 1779, David Garrick died from kidney failure. If the nation was suddenly confronted with the loss of arguably its greatest cultural icon, it was also routinely intimated that the Admiralty had lost much of its authority and reputation. When Garrick's death was reported on 21 January, Palliser's case had reached its lowest point: much of the log evidence was in disarray, and it was clear that Keppel would be acquitted. With the tide turning in favor of Keppel, most of the opposition had made its way to Portsmouth to witness Palliser's humiliation and to celebrate Keppel's victory. Many of the primary members of the opposition, including Richard Brinsley Sheridan, Garrick's close friend Edmund Burke, and Charles James Fox, left Portsmouth on the evening of 30 January, attended the funeral on the morning of 1 February, and hastily returned to Portsmouth to be present for Keppel's triumphant denunciation of the charges the next day. Sheridan's movements here are particularly important because he organized much of the funeral from afar and returned on the day to perform as the surrogate mourner not only for Garrick's family but also for the nation as a whole. Sheridan's movement from the site of the trial to Garrick's house at the Adelphi through the streets of London to Westminster Abbey and then back to

Portsmouth again physically traces a powerful psychic divagation from scenes of martial crisis.

I use the word divagation advisedly here because Garrick's funeral operates as a kind of metaleptic loop that momentarily interrupts the powerful narrative drive of the Keppel court-martial. For a day, the most powerful men in the land, the foremost practitioners of culture, and a large portion of London's inhabitants, watched what the papers referred to in bold letters as "THE BODY" move from its former domicile to the national pantheon.[15] Garrick's corpse moved in procession from his house on Adelphi Terrace up to the Strand and then westward to Charing Cross and along Whitehall Street to the Abbey: "There were upwards of thirty mourning coaches, followed by twice the number of gentlemen's carriages."[16] The "Order of the Procession" that was printed in all but a couple of the papers not only lists and categorizes the mourners but also keeps a careful tally of the porters, supporters, and physical accoutrements of the hearse and carriages. The hearse was very elaborately decorated with feathers and surrounded by four porters with staves, twelve pages, and twelve horsemen. It was followed immediately by the pallbearers including the Duke of Devonshire and Lord Camden. Sheridan, as chief mourner, followed the pallbearers in a coach of his own, which required two train bearers. Then came various members and associates of the family, gentlemen of the theatre Drury Lane, gentlemen of the Covent Garden theatre, gentlemen of the Literary Club, and intimate friends. Each of these groups was separated by two men on horseback with cloaks. All in all, a list of 38 unnamed attendants and 138 named figures, followed by a host of empty coaches with their footmen, slowly moved through the streets.

According to the papers, the crowds that attempted to see Garrick's body before the funeral and those attending the procession were extraordinarily large. The *Morning Post* reported that approximately fifty thousand "gentlemen and ladies" went to the Adelphi to see the remains on the day before the funeral, and this already large influx of people was matched by a huge crowd of less exalted personages: "A prodigious concourse of the lower class of the people likewise assembled before the house the whole day, and finding they could not gain admittance, became so troublesome, that an officer's guard was obliged to be sent for from the Savoy, which with great difficulty prevented their committing some acts of outrage."[17] Because the crowds at the funeral the next day were both unprecedented and predictably unruly, "as usual it was, in its progress, attended with some confusion; many pockets were picked, and some persons were hurt by the pressure of the crowd, which was enormous, there being more people present in the windows, and on the tops of houses, in the streets and the avenues of the Abbey, than were ever remembered to have been collected since the coronation."[18] Perhaps because of the difficulties the day before the funeral, the procession was preceded by a party of guards. When the procession approached the Abbey, two further bodies of armed guards "formed a lane for the ceremony to pass through."[19]

The fact that Garrick's funeral required an armed guard is not especially significant. To all reports, the event was marked by the utmost solemnity, but the size of the crowd and its relation to this particular space should give us pause. At a midway point between Adelphi and the Abbey lay the Admiralty office and the Houses of Parliament. None of the papers say anything about these sites as zones of political contestation, but it is difficult to imagine that observers were not aware of the strange spectacle of key opposition figures, recently arrived from the Keppel court-martial, walking before a large crowd outside the Admiralty office. In two weeks, members of this same crowd would be attacking the building and burning Palliser in effigy in this very same spot. No doubt the restraint in the press was a mark of respect for Garrick himself. But the lack of explicit partisan demonstrations or commentary does not mean that the funeral did not have its own political valences. As we will see, the funeral's reception was imbued with a complex critique not of Garrick but of the nation he was called on to represent.

Social Insecurity

As elaborate as this event might seem to us, perhaps the most fascinating thing about the funeral is the relative lack of commentary in the papers. All of the papers print a few paragraphs on the event, and most provide a detailed list of the mourners, including the order and nature of their procession. But after this spate of coverage the day after the event, references to Garrick's death are drowned out by the Keppel news. The only remnants of his passing are the consistent appearance of brief elegiac poems and epitaphs in the dailies for roughly a month after the funeral and the curiously detailed transcription of his will that appeared in papers and magazines alike. Furthermore, it is difficult to read the accounts of Garrick's funeral and not think of the profound response to Thomas Betterton's death some sixty years earlier. One could argue that Garrick's great innovations in Shakespearean performance were aimed at displacing performance protocols established by Betterton and James Quin.[20] And yet this comparison simply does not register either in print or in performance.

This lack of connection is important, because it allows us to consider Joseph Roach's famous account of the effigy in *Cities of the Dead* in a new light. According to Roach, the body of the actor plays a crucial role in the continuation of national ideology:

> [The effigy] fills by means of surrogation a vacancy created by the absence of an original. Beyond ostensibly inanimate effigies fashioned from wood or cloth, there are more powerful effigies fashioned from flesh. Such effigies are made by performances. They consist of a set of actions that hold open a place in memory into which many different people may step according to circumstances and occasions. I argue that performed effigies—those fabricated from human bodies and the associations they evoke—provide communities with a method of perpetuating themselves through specially nominated mediums or surrogates: among them actors, dancers, priests, street maskers, statesmen, celebrities, freaks, children, and especially, by virtue of an intense but unsurprising paradox, corpses.[21]

Of crucial importance to his analysis of Betterton's interment in Westminster Abbey is the relationship between the body of the actor and the body of the king. Because Betterton's fame, like Garrick's, was built on his representation of characters such as Lear, Hamlet, and Macbeth, his burial in Westminster Abbey in 1710 registered for observers such as Richard Steele and Colley Cibber as a surrogative burial of the king. In Roach's analysis, Betterton's body, and the performance history associated with it, occasions styles of remembering aimed at stabilizing national fantasy in a time of rapid growth and change in Britain's social and economic history. Through a subtle analysis of Betterton's own theorization of how to speak with the dead in the Ghost scenes from *Hamlet*, Roach argues that the actor "explored and codified an explicit mode of conduct governing conversations with the dead. By its protocols, the secular reverence appropriate to social memory in the Enlightenment could be extracted from the residual fear and worship of once omnipresent ancestors."[22] Betterton's great innovation in the role was to forego the excessive vociferation of earlier actors in favor of the embodiment of decorous, manly, control. It was the very epitome of self-governance that would come to figure for British governmentality. And it was this dignity of comportment that provided the figural ground for Richard Steele's meditation on the nondistinction of the imaginary and the real monarch in the grave.[23] In this argument, Roach suggests that these protocols were entirely apposite to Britain's consolidation of imperial power in the circum-Atlantic world.

However, this influential argument is not simply generalizable, because, with the unfolding of time, empires and the effigies that support them change.

Despite the manifest similarities between the interment of Betterton and Garrick's funeral, it is important to remember not only that Garrick, in the same scene from *Hamlet*, severely revised the performance protocols for conversing with the dead father expected by the audience but also that, in the seventy-year period between these events, Britain's status as an imperial power had gone through extraordinary transformations. In the winter of 1779, the circum-Atlantic empire, so forcefully consolidated at the close of the Seven Years' War, was unraveling before the eyes of its constituents, and the primary theatrical memory of most British onlookers of how to speak with the dead, and hence how to think through the problem of cultural continuation in a time of crisis, involved none of Betterton's stoicism. What I want to do here is utilize the distinction between Betterton's and Garrick's performances as a heuristic for understanding Garrick's funeral as a moment in which the nation turned to question its own imperial aspirations.

The archive of materials pertaining to Garrick's performance technique is extremely rich, and we are blessed with a range of accounts from all the different phases of his career. As one reads through descriptions of his performances, which are often separated by decades, it becomes clear that once a set of strategies was first worked up, it was repeated again and again. Garrick's famous performances of Hamlet are a case in point, but I concentrate here on Georg Christian Lichtenberg's description because it is both highly specific and based on performances from 1775, only four years before Garrick's death. Lichtenberg's famous account of the Ghost's appearance is markedly different from the Cibber passage cited by Roach:

> Hamlet appears in black . . . Horatio and Marcellus, in uniform, are with him, and they are awaiting the ghost. . . . The theatre is darkened, and the whole audience of some thousands are as quiet and their faces as motionless, as though they were painted on the walls of the theatre; even from the farthest end of the playhouse one could hear a pin drop. At his words, Garrick turns sharply and at the same time staggers back two or three paces with his knees giving way under him; his hat falls to the ground and both his arms, especially the left, are stretched out nearly to their full length, with the hands as high as his head, the right arm more bent and the hand lower and the fingers apart; his mouth is open: thus he stands rooted to the spot, with legs apart, but no less of dignity, supported by his

friends. . . . His whole demeanour is so expressive of terror that it made my flesh creep even before he began to speak. The almost terror-struck silence of the audience, which preceded this appearance and filled one with a sense of insecurity, probably did much to enhance this effect.[24]

As Lichtenberg emphasizes, the staging and Garrick's actions collaborate to generate a "sense of insecurity" in the audience. Some of the actions here are conventional—the falling hat, for instance—but other gestures would have deeply unsettled an audience that was highly cognizant of the corporeal signs formerly established by Betterton and replicated by actors such as Quin in the intervening years. Garrick's asymmetrical arm motions and, above all, his off-balance recoil are the very opposite of Betterton's self-control. Establishing the sense of insecurity in the audience was crucial to Garrick's adaptation of the play, because he wanted the audience to feel the degree to which Denmark, under the corrupt rule of Gertrude and Claudius, had descended into a realm where both space and time were out of joint.

Similarly, Garrick reintroduced violence into the scene and thus shattered the careful articulation of equipoise in the face of the dead that Betterton had inculcated. Again Lichtenberg's remarks are resonant:

At last he speaks, not at the beginning, but at the end of a breath, with a trembling voice: "Angels and ministers of grace defend us!" The ghost beckons to him; I wish you could see him, with eyes fixed on the ghost, though he is speaking to his companions, freeing himself from their restraining hands, as they warn him not to follow and hold him back. But at length, when they have tried his patience too far, he turns his face towards them, tears himself with great violence from their grasp, and draws his sword on them with a swiftness that makes one shudder, saying: "By heaven! I'll make a ghost of him that lets me!" That is enough for them. Then he stands with his sword upon guard against the spectre saying: "Go on, I'll follow thee," and the ghost goes off the stage. Hamlet remains motionless, his sword held out so as to make him keep his distance, and at length, when the spectator can no longer see the ghost, he begins slowly to follow him, now standing still and then going on, with sword still on guard, eyes fixed upon the ghost, hair disordered, and out of breath, until he is lost to sight.[25]

I have presented these oft-quoted passages at length, not only to emphasize Garrick's departures from Betterton's enactment of control but also to recognize the complex relationship between Garrick's violence and Horatio's and Marcellus's attempts to restrain him. Garrick's Hamlet draws his sword first on his friends and then holds it on guard against the Ghost. In the process, the audience watches his body struggle to regain its composure after a sudden outburst of violence. In this light, Garrick elicits a liminal state where things could go either way, and this is completely in keeping with the scene itself, where the audience is asked to contemplate the liminal state between life and death, present and past. Composure now registers, not as a permanent attitude but rather as a sign of self-preservation, occasioned by his predicament, in which Hamlet protects himself against present complacency and the revenant past. This is, after all, the play in which the past ruler, in the form of the Ghost, quite literally instantiates a critique of the present regime. In Garrick's interpretation of the role, that critique is totalizing—that is, it encompasses even the misplaced protective desires of Hamlet's friends—and deeply unsettling because it is aimed not at quelling insecurity but rather at fully recognizing the unviability of the social insecurity of the present times.[26]

Could this scene with the Ghost not only offer a way of understanding the political crisis enveloping Britain at this point in the American war but also allow us to comprehend the cultural crisis precipitated by Garrick's death? The obvious move here would be to build a comparison between the British Empire in 1779 and the corrupted state of Denmark under the rule of Claudius and Gertrude. For the opposition of all stripes, and for the rebellious colonists, this would hardly be a stretch. For these observers, something truly was rotten in the state, and the Keppel court-martial provided evidence of this corruption on a daily basis. In terms of cultural memory, it is important to remember that Hamlet's Ghost was conventionally understood to have been played by Shakespeare, and thus Garrick's unsettling negotiation with the Ghost validates the importance of contemporary culture's relation to the Shakespearean past by activating an anxious appreciation of its potential loss.[27] What this means is that Garrick's critique of the present is carried out on Shakespeare's behalf. In other words, it was through the enactment of insecurity that the desire for Shakespeare's patrimony—and, by extension, Garrick's cultural power—was fully activated.[28] With his death, British culture was confronted with a crisis of succession that resonated with the political crisis in the Atlantic, and like that conflict, this cultural crisis would require successive recalibrations of subjectivity before a new future could be envisaged.

As noted earlier, the media response to the funeral is surprisingly terse, but the *Morning Chronicle* offers a lengthy interpretation of the funeral's excesses that, I would argue, fulfills the twofold imperative to recognize social insecurity and critique the present state that I believe is encoded in Garrick's revision of Betterton's Hamlet.[29] Immediately after declaring that the crowd at Garrick's funeral was the largest "collected since the coronation," the correspondent makes a crucial comparison: "Lord Chatham's funeral had not near so many spectators."[30] Whereas Steele had compared Betterton to "real monarchs in the grave," the invocation of Chatham is both more specific and more pointed, because his name is almost synonymous with Britain's circum-Atlantic empire. Chatham, or Pitt the Elder, the much-lionized parliamentarian and personal friend of Garrick, had died nine months earlier on 11 May 1778. Parliament had agreed to an elaborate funeral in Westminster Abbey, which was preceded by two days' lying in state. Great crowds came to view the body, but only a handful of peers attended.[31]

But there is more at stake here than simply similarly crowded funerals. Chatham was given a state funeral because of his leadership before and during the Seven Years' War. With British imperial fortunes at a low point following the loss of Minorca to the French in the summer of 1756, Pitt took up the office of the secretary of state. After attempting to stabilize foreign affairs, Pitt was confronted with the problem of what to do about the execution of Admiral Byng. Byng was a flashpoint for public opinion regarding the humiliation at Minorca. Pitt argued for mercy but was overridden by the tide of public opinion. In later years, especially during the Keppel court-martial, Pitt's position was vindicated, but in 1757 his intervention in the Byng court-martial contributed to his dismissal from office. Later that year, however, he was reinstated in a new coalition with the Duke of Newcastle, and from then on his name was to be associated with the extraordinary turn around in the war with France in both North America and India. In the public imagination, Pitt was largely responsible for the glorious victories of 1759 that marked the highpoint of British imperial domination in the eighteenth century. He was revered as a great war minister in spite of demonstrable lapses in his later political career. This gave him particular stature in Parliament when he returned in the spring of 1777 to critique the North Ministry's management of the American war. As one of his biographers states: "After the startling news in December of defeat at Saratoga, Chatham, in enthusiastic co-operation with the Rockinghams, took the lead in furious criticism of the 'disgraces of the war'—so contrasted with 'the fame and renown' of the last war—and pointedly returned to the pervasive evil of secret influence."[32] Chatham broke with the Rockinghams over the question of American sovereignty and succumbed to his final illness in the midst of a speech reiterating the right of imperial sovereignty over the American colonies.

In other words, this comparison between Garrick and Chatham raises at the very least three key issues that animated the public in early 1779: the spectral presence of the Byng court-martial and the humiliation at Minorca during the Keppel court-martial, nostalgia for the great victories of 1759, and more recent opposition to the Ministry's mismanagement of the American war. Significantly, the Byng court-martial and the nostalgia for 1759 were regularly invoked in the months before Garrick's death by the opposition as key rhetorical points in its critique of the government's handling of the Keppel affair. Invoking Chatham at this historical juncture effectively calls into question the efficacy of the state and reminds the public of how more capable hands had turned an earlier set of reversals into a time of national and imperial glory. One could make a similar argument about Garrick's mythic relation to past glory. Just as Chatham was associated with the patriotic nostalgia for the military victories over the French in the Seven Years' War, Garrick was associated with the patriotic investment in Shakespeare and the cultural victory over French neoclassicism.

But the *Morning Chronicle* calls up Chatham's ghost in order make a different set of negative comparisons:

> The undertaker, we are told, was left to his discretion as to expense and decoration. . . . The coaches were covered with eschutcheons, and the horses loaded with mournful plumes; in both which points we are given to understand, that the customs of funeral procession were violated, and the ornaments over-charged. A correspondent, versed in heraldry, assures us also, that the form of the procession, number of banners, &c. &c. were out of all order; how far is right or wrong we pretend not to determine, but although we are ready to agree that too much respect could not be paid to the memory of so singular a genius as Mr. Garrick, we are a little scrupulous in opinion, as to what is really a token of regard, and cannot refrain expressing our abhorrence of useless ostentation; we know of none more ridiculous than that shewn at a funeral, unless indeed where the solemnity is (as in Lord Chatham's case) meant to be a monument of national honour.[33]

This is a complex intervention because it is simultaneously a critique and an endorsement of ostentation that both screens and indicts Garrick. Ostentation is appropriate when the dead body merits national honor. According to the *Morning Chronicle*, Chatham warrants such a funeral on the basis of his patriotic credentials and Garrick does not, and this is why the correspondent suggests later that a less public interment presided over by Johnson, Burke, and other literary figures would have been more appropriate. The gap between statesman and artist is forcefully maintained. Lurking behind this critique of ostentation is a familiar attack on luxury and the feminization of elite culture. But the paper very shrewdly ascribes this ostentation not to Garrick, or even to his superiors, but to a tradesman, the undertaker, and furthermore suggests that the undertaker was pandering to the disproportionate crowd in attendance. Suddenly the problem is a social one: the excesses of Garrick's funeral demonstrate a devolution in the citizenry whose members need to be reminded, by an unnamed correspondent to the paper, that the heraldry and funerary protocols "were out of all order." This critique is broad-based and damning because it suggests not only that mourners of all ranks fail to see the difference in value between a patriot statesman like Chatham and mere actor like Garrick but also that the very signs of aristocratic power encoded in the form of heraldry have become unreadable. This allows us to see the strange deployment of heraldry in the Mischianza in a different light, because it too was incoherent. In other words, there is nostalgia here for more than past martial supremacy; there is nostalgia for a mythic pre-bourgeois social order whose stability would reinvigorate the nation. In this scene, it is the mysterious "correspondent, versed in heraldry" who acts as the revenant.

Like Garrick's Hamlet, the paper yearns for a nation where the time is no longer out of joint, and where corruption has been cleansed from the land. And it is here that Garrick's scene becomes so instructive. Rhetorically, the *Morning Chronicle* follows Garrick's lead by turning the conversation with the dead into an occasion in which one can both read the present as a terrifying, almost Gothic, symptom and then act accordingly. Garrick's playing of the Ghost scene instantiates action not only toward one's friends and foes but also toward the past. What this means is that, at least in the case of the *Morning Chronicle*, the observer should be overwhelmed by the profound insecurity of the present moment, where the Admiralty seems bent on replicating the disaster of the Byng court-martial, where the government is repeating the errors in supply that disabled the British forces in the early phases of the Seven Years' War, and where the "people" no longer know the difference between the statesman and the actor. Unlike Steele's famous reaction to Betterton's death, the problem here is not the dissolution of distinction in death but rather the deeply unsettling dissolution of distinction in life. The liminality that Roach locates in the threshold between life and death in the reading of the Betterton funeral has, under Garrick's influence, moved fully into the realm of life, and thus violence is always on the verge of erupting into the scene. This was Garrick's legacy in the role, and perhaps we can see its trace in the threat of violence surrounding his funeral, for as the procession slowly marched past the Admiralty office and Parliament, the papers quietly inform us that guards were necessary—to keep the crowds from doing what exactly?

Monumental Tears

The preceding argument suggests that Garrick's funeral failed to do the cultural work necessary for ensuring the continuation of the social order, but rather set the stage for what amounts to a painful, even tragic, renovation of the present that involved a complex gleaning of the past for new models of political and cultural organization. That gleaning operation is necessarily involved with Garrick's emblematic relationship to Shakespeare, and it is tied to an explicit recognition of the social insecurity of the empire in the post-Saratoga era.

As noted earlier, Sheridan was very much involved in the organization of the funeral spectacle despite the *Morning Chronicle*'s attempt to impugn the undertaker for its excesses. But in the enactment of the spectacle, Sheridan's role was that of a silent but iconic mourner. His carriage was specially equipped with trains that required the attention of two pages, and thus he was a conspicuous figure. As Garrick's successor as manager of Drury Lane, he figures for the continuation of the theatrical enterprise and, by extension, the cultural patrimony. Like the figure of the poet in many elegies, he had the potential to declare his ascendancy. But he did not. Sheridan did not speak but rather reserved his public expression of grief for the "Verses to the Memory of Garrick, spoken as a Monody," that was first declaimed on 11 March 1779, again not by Sheridan, but by Mrs. Yates before a crowded house in the theatre all but synonymous with Garrick's name. The "Monody" was performed as an afterpiece to Richard Cumberland's *The West Indian*, a detail of theatrical history that poses some challenging questions for the place of Garrick's passing in the circum-Atlantic world.

In the six weeks between Garrick's funeral and the first performance of the "Monody," Keppel was acquitted, and virtually every metropolitan region in England was overwhelmed by pro-Keppel celebrations. Palliser was burned in effigy throughout the land and the Admiralty was attacked in every conceivable venue. As Nicholas Roger has argued, the newspapers were awash with discussions of the celebrations, of the Admiralty's actions, and of the opposition's ascendancy. Myriad tributes to Keppel were rushed into print and performance. Victory odes were performed both with and without musical accompaniment in all of the theatres.[34] It is not difficult to see these cultural artifacts as compensatory expressions of patriotism in a time when there was little to celebrate, and such a reading is substantiated by even a cursory look at two other developments in this six-week period. First, there is a rather singular spate of performances of Handel's patriotic oratorios all through the weeks between the funeral and the "Monody's" first presentation. *Samson, Judas Maccabeus, Messiah,* and *Alexander's Feast* are offered repeatedly at one or other of the theatres during this period. It is as though Handel's oratorios, which were so closely aligned with patriot ideology from an earlier era, were being mobilized either to shore up a crumbling polity in a time of martial crisis or to celebrate a renovated sense of national potential consistent with the enthusiasm for Keppel's victory. Second, almost every day the newspapers printed or reprinted brief elegies and epitaphs for Garrick. With the exception of Anna Seward's substantial "Prize Monody on the Death of Mr. Garrick," these poems are remarkably slight, perhaps a further sign of the failure to effectively eulogize the actor.

If the newspaper verse disappoints, Seward's poem does not, and it serves as a useful bridge between our previous discussion of Garrick's performance in *Hamlet* and Sheridan's complex deployment of Shakespeare in his "Monody." The poem's subtitle is "For the Vase at Bath Easton, February 11, 1779," and the eponymous vase becomes a crucial prop in the poem. Seward's poem is broken into four verse paragraphs and the first two are integrally connected to Garrick's performance of Hamlet. The poem's first image is of Horatio weeping over the vase:

> Dim sweeps the shower along the misty vale,
> And Grief's low accents murmur in the gale.
> O'er the damp vase Horatio sighing leans,
> And gazes absent on the faded scenes;[35]

By figuring Horatio as a surrogate mourner, Seward blurs the distinction between representation and reality and implies that Garrick will be mourned above all by Shakespeare's characters. This transposition of loss effectively renders Garrick as one of Shakespeare's creations and thus subtly cancels his mortality by investing in the memory of his transient performances. This rhetorical gesture is given further elaboration in the second verse paragraph when Seward reviews Garrick's great Shakespearean performances and argues that his audience understood Garrick to be Shakespeare:

> Shakespeare's great spirit, in its cloudless blaze,
> Led him unequal'd thro' th' inventive maze;
> 'Midst the deep pathos of his melting themes,

Thro' the light magic of his playful dreams.
He caught the genuine humour glowing there,
Wit's vivid flash, and Cunning's sober leer;
The strange distress that fires the kindling brain
Of feeble madness on the stormy plain;
Or when pale youth, in midnight shade,
Pursues the steel-clad phantom thro' the glade;
Or, starting from the couch with dire affright,
When the crown'd murd'rer glares upon the sight
In all the horrors of the guilty soul,
Dark as night that wraps the frozen pole.
—Our subject passions own'd the sway complete,
And hail'd their Garrick as their Shakespeare great. (13–28)

This passage starts with Shakespeare leading Garrick through the "inventive maze" of the plays and concludes with the audience so subjected to Garrick's performance that it can no longer distinguish between the living actor and the dead playwright.[36] That subjection, complete with its implied rupture of the temporal continuum, is ascribed to Garrick's performance, first, of Lear's madness on the heath and, second, of Hamlet's negotiation with the ghost of his father and the confirmation of Claudius's guilt. In other words, the revenant disclosure of the Shakespearean past into the present of Garrick's audience is linked to the precise scenes where the actor's capacity to become a cultural effigy was enacted. This effectively styles Garrick as an emblem of transience capable of bringing Shakespeare's "great spirit" to bear on the present.

But after this remarkable assertion, the next verse paragraph turns on the very notion of transience itself by emphasizing that Garrick's voice and his gestures are irrevocably gone. In light of the preceding verse paragraph, this common place of both elegy and discourses on acting takes on an important, and rarely articulated set of ramifications, because the real loss mourned by the poem is not Garrick but rather the audience's subjection to his performative power. In other words, Garrick's death implies a loss of Shakespeare, a curtailment of the audience's transient access to the national past encapsulated in his plays. Because the poem opens by equating Garrick the actor with Hamlet, Seward is ruthlessly following the logic that attends the death of both actor and character: namely, that with the death of Hamlet, the Ghost—often conflated with the historical figure of Shakespeare—will not reappear.[37] Could there be a more devastating statement of the failure of the effigy to ensure cultural continuation?

And the poem explicitly recognizes why this continuation does not occur: there is neither an actor nor an audience adequate to the task of subjection articulated in the second verse paragraph. In other words, the failure is a function of the historical moment. The culture, now allegorically figured by Genius and the Muses, is suddenly cast into a state of suspension marked by the repetition of the word "still":

> Breathe, Genius, still the tributary sigh,
> Still gush, ye liquid pearls, from Beauty's eye,
> With slacken'd strings suspend your harps, ye Nine,
> While round his urn yon cypress wreath ye twine. (39–42)

This state of suspension is both placating and fearsome, because "still" implies both continuation and stasis, and thus the reader is left contemplating when and if there will be access to the Shakespearean legacy that Garrick was so instrumental in disclosing to his audience.

Seward's poem offers a both a cogent, if perhaps apocalyptic, statement of the historical predicament facing British culture in the early months of 1779 and an illuminating point of comparison for Sheridan's much more famous "Monody." Sheridan too would be addressing the question of Shakespeare's legacy in a time of historical crisis through a consideration of the transience of the actor's art, but the "Monody" is complicated by its own enactment. A straightforward comparison of Seward's and Sheridan's texts, although they were at times printed side by side,[38] fails to account for Sheridan's collaboration with other artists in the construction of the "Monody." As noted earlier, the actual declamation of the words was ably handled by Mrs. Yates, but her performance was fashioned with De Loutherbourg's set design in mind, because at key moments in her declamation she not only embraced the giant urn placed in the center of the stage but also pointed to a painting by Sir Joshua Reynolds that had been incorporated into the set. Furthermore, a range of musicians and composers were called upon to supplement the spoken word, such that for a number of observers the staging of the event was akin to an oratorio.

The "Monody" unfolded in three declaimed sections, each of which was framed by orchestral and vocal performances. The *Morning Post*'s redaction of the performance gives a clear sense of its structure:

> The curtain rising to slow music, discovered in a cypress shade the mausoleum of our departed Roscius, on which were the figures of Melpomene

and Thalia mourning his loss; over whom appears Time supporting a Medallion with his portrait. Mrs. Yates in the character of the Recording Muse, is seen in the center of a temporary orchestra, reclining on an urn, with her hair dishevelled. The Introductory strain of music ceasing, she advanced, and recited an invocation to the audience, to pay their tribute to his memory before any other offering was made to it; then the Chorus sing—

His fame requires, we act a tenderer part;
His *Memory* claims the tear you gave his *Art*!

The unequal effects of the different arts of *Poetry, Painting,* and *Sculpture,* are then beautifully described, in the course of which an elegant compliment is paid to the superior genius of Sir Joshua Reynolds, the *Raphael* of the present age: these arts however are represented as yielding objects; but not so the *Actor's* art, for

Feeble tradition is his memory's guard.

Here succeeds a forcible, and marking description of Mr. Garrick's acting powers, which the poet says were

All perishable like the electric fire,
But strike the frame, and as they strike—expire!
Incense, too choice, a bodied flame to bear,
Its fragrance charms the sense, and blends in air!

Here a Trio of Mrs. Wrighten, Mr. Webster, and a young Lady, &c. succeeds; after which a second Poetic Exhortation is made to the audience, and the Monody concludes with a classical description of an intended Shrine, which the mournful Muse shall guard,

And with soft sighs disperse th'irrev'rend dust,
That Time shall shake upon his sacred bust.[39]

The printed versions of the "Monody" do not indicate which sections of the poem were sung, nor do they indicate where the musical interludes were placed. What the *Morning Post*'s description allows us to see is the degree to which the placement of the vocal and orchestral performances highlighted the poem's two separate exhortations to the audience. If we look closely at these moments, what we discover is a particularly rich moment of deixis that forces the audience to question its own capacity to effectively mourn for Garrick.

The first exhortation is a remarkably strange utterance, whose conditionality puts into question not only the very act of mourning that the "Monody" presumes to enact but also the practice of theatre itself:

If dying EXCELLENCE deserves a Tear,
If fond Remembrance still is cherished here,
Can we persist to bid your Sorrows flow
For fabled Suffe'rers, and delusive Woe?
Or with quaint Smiles dismiss the plaintive Strain,
Point the quick Jest—indulge the Comic Vein—
Ere yet to buried ROSCIUS we assign—
One kind Regret—one tributary Line![40]

The opening question of the first four lines is quite complex. The repetition of the word "if" in the first two lines forcefully establishes the conditional mood so that the audience is asked to consider whether the related acts of rememoration and commemoration are "still" practiced "here." "Here" specifies both present time and present place and thus hails the audience into this loaded consideration, because the doubt occasioned by the conditional mood threatens to call the auditors to account. I would argue that the rest of the poem strives to put the anxiety generated by these opening two lines into abeyance, for, by suggesting the slightest possibility that "Remembrance" is no longer cherished, the opening lines hint at a terrifying disarticulation of the present from the past. As the sentence unfolds, it becomes clear that the question of whether "excellence deserves a tear" or "Remembrance still is cherished here" is primarily rhetorical; lines 3 and 4 reorient the question such that the conditional terms register as the initial terms in an "if-then" construction. If, as we know, excellence deserves a tear, then can we continue to attempt to elicit sorrow in tragedy, or mirth in comedy for that matter, before Garrick is sufficiently mourned? This gesture establishes the purpose of the "Monody": it must satisfy the demands of "Remembrance" so that theatre, with all its capacity for surrogation, can operate. In other words, the question of cultural continuation is put front and center.

How the "Monody" is going to satisfy the demands of "Remembrance" involves a fundamental parsing of players from audience. Just as line 3 carefully separated "we" the players from "you" the audience, the couplet sung by the chorus places the responsibility for cultural continuation in the hands or, more precisely, in the eyes of the audience:

His Fame requires we act a tenderer Part:—
His MEMORY claims the Tear you gave his ART! (9–10)

The fact that these lines are not spoken by Mrs. Yates but rather are sung by the chorus that surrounds her on stage means that they operate as if they were a response to the complex set of questions declaimed in the opening eight lines. In this sense, the "we" of line 9 takes on a more capacious sense than that of the "players." In the context of this choral response, it is as though his fame requires that the nation, as figured by this community on stage, acts a tenderer part, which will elicit singular bodily responses from the audience. The verbs "require" and "claim" are part of a larger discursive construction, which understands the audience's relation to Garrick as one of obligation or debt.

This becomes abundantly clear in the verse paragraph immediately following the choral exhortation:

> The general Voice, the Meed of mournful Verse,
> The splendid Sorrows that adorned his Hearse,
> The Throng that mourn'd as their dead Favourite pass'd,
> The grac'd Respect that claim'd him to the last,
> While SHAKESPEAR's Image from its hallow'd Base,
> Seem'd to prescribe the Grave, and point the Place—
> Nor these,—nor all the sad Regrets that flow
> From fond Fidelity's domestic Woe,—
> So much are GARRICK's Praise—so much his DUE—
> As on this Spot—One Tear bestow'd by YOU. (11–20)

In this passage, which was singled out for special praise,[41] the speaker reviews the honors accorded Garrick between his death in late January and the performance of the "Monody" in mid-February—the general public acclaim, the outpouring of elegiac verse, the splendor of his hearse, the crowd at the funeral, the private expressions of domestic sadness, and, above all, his placement in Westminster Abbey near the statue of Shakespeare—and subordinates them to the tears of the audience elicited here and now by this poem. These bodily signs are both singular and multiple, because "One Tear" is bestow'd by the multifarious group of spectators designated by the plural pronoun "YOU." This doubleness is significant because it implies that it is through this shared emotional response to the present performance that the community will be reconstituted, and that reconstitution will allow theatre and, by implication, all the other arts invoked by the poem to carry on their task.

That task is specified in the second exhortation of the audience late in the poem. After an extended distinction between the transience of acting and the permanence of painting, sculpture, and poetry, Mrs. Yates's declamation is once again interrupted by a group of singers this time singing as a trio, rather than as a chorus:

> Where then—while sunk in cold Decay he lies,
> And pale Eclipse for ever veils those Eyes!—
> WHERE is the blest Memorial that ensures
> Our GARRICK's Fame?—whose is the Trust?—'tis YOURS. (79–82)

The legal and financial connotations of the word "Trust" establishes an important temporal relationship that will be explored at length in the exhortation proper. In its legal definition, a trust is: "The confidence reposed in a person in whom the legal ownership of property is vested to hold or use for the benefit of another; hence, an estate committed to the charge of trustees."[42] Suddenly, the distinction of players and audience has great significance, because the speaker is stating unequivocally that the audience has all the privileges and responsibilities of a trustee. It is the audience's job, not that of the players, both to memorialize Garrick and to ensure the safety and value of the cultural patrimony for the future:

> And O! by every Charm his Art essay'd
> To sooth your Cares!—by every Grief allay'd!
> By the hushed Wonder which his Accents drew!
> By his last parting Tear, repaid by you!
> By all those Thoughts, which many a distant Night,
> Shall mark his Memory with a sad Delight!—
> Still in your Heart's dear Record bear his Name;
> Cherish the keen Regret that lifts his Fame;
> To YOU it is bequeath'd, assert the Trust,
> And to his WORTH—'tis all you can—be JUST. (83–92)

This foregrounding of the audience's agency declares that it holds the cultural property of the nation in its hands, and that the audience must manage it with the same care and reverence exemplified by Garrick himself. In short, just as Garrick managed the theatre for the benefit of his audience, so the audience is being called on to manage the culture and, by extension, itself, so that it will benefit not simply itself but those in whose name they operate—that is, the Britons beyond the walls of the theatre and, most vitally, those yet to come. This is an explicit call not simply to memorialize Garrick but also to step forward and assert the Trust of nationhood in a time of great social anxiety.

But this declaration of a species of national trust is tied to a very particular set of performance protocols both on the stage and in the audience. As noted previously, the proof of able trusteeship is visible to one and all. It is marked by the tear elicited by the "Monody," and thus Sheridan pulled out all the stops in this performance:

> With regard to the representation, pains have obviously been taken to render it great in effect. The Monody is divided into three parts, between each of which, and at the conclusion, solemn airs are sung by Mr. Webster, Mr. Gaudry, a Young Lady, and Mrs. Wrighten, supported by a band of choristers. The stage is formed in somewhat like the same shape that it assumed when Mr. Garrick was wont to speak his Ode to Shakespeare, excepting only, that now, instead of an air of hilarity and chearfulness which then pervaded it, an air of solemnity and awful woe is cultivated. In the center of the perspective, amidst a thick grove of bays and cypress, stands a monumental pyramid representing the funeral pile of Mr. Garrick. The figures of tragedy and comedy appear as if in basso relievo, in positions expressive of their loss, while fame is mounting the skies with a medallion of Mr. Garrick, and little Cupids are weeping o'er his urn beneath. The ground work of the basso relievo is decorated with the torch of Hymen, comic masks and symbols, tragic bowls, chains, &c. Before the pyramid Mrs. Yates with dishevelled hair and in a flowing robe of purple sattin, speaks the Monody. The singers are ranged on each side in compartments railed off with a balustrade.[43]

De Loutherbourg's scenography explicitly conjures up Garrick's beloved performances of the "Ode to Shakespeare," and thus, in attending to Mrs. Yates's words, the audience would be continually reminded of the variance from the hilarity of past performance (fig. 4.3).[44] Her performance here both cites and cancels a specific moment of Garrick's performance, which itself played with the actor's relationship to the cultural patrimony of Shakespeare.[45] When one recognizes that Garrick's performance of the "Ode" was a supplement that both continued and canceled the Shakespearean legacy, then it becomes clear that the "Monody" aims to elicit an anxious cascade of references that testify to both the presence and absence of Shakespeare's ghost. In this context, Mrs. Yates's disheveled hair could well call up the famous fright wig Garrick employed in the Ghost scene of *Hamlet*.

What we have then is an assemblage of deictic moments signaled first by the poem itself when it states that "Shakespeare's Image . . . / Seem'd to prescribe

Figure 4.3. John Lodge, "Mr Garrick delivering his Ode, at Drury Lane Theatre, on dedicating a Building & erecting a Statue, to Shakespeare," etching (1769). BM Ee,3.163. Department of Prints and Drawings © Trustees of the British Museum.

the Grave" and then enacted by Mrs. Yates when she cites Garrick's past performances either of the "Ode" or of *Hamlet*. These deictic moments are also thematized by the poem's repeated investment in the capacity for pronouns such as *we* and *you* to shift meaning according to their moment of utterance. The act of pointing that is so crucial to reference here is a fundamental problematic in the "Monody" because it goes directly to the heart of the doubt elicited at the poem's outset. Can we point to performance? The question is troubling because it necessarily raises questions about memory, forgetting, and the inexorable passage of time. Is fond remembrance still cherished here? Everything is calculated to heighten the anxiety generated by Mrs. Yates's negotiation both with precursor performances, and with the nonliving props that surround her, in order to make the audience feel the precariousness of cultural memory.

The subtle invocation of Garrick's performances of the "Ode" and of the Ghost scene suggest a citational relation to the dead, but this relation is amplified and problematized by Mrs. Yates's negotiation with the nonliving objects on the stage. As the preceding passage indicates, a great deal of thought was put into the stage properties, and the poem itself theorizes their function. The poem's third verse paragraph discusses the capacity of painting not only to memorialize its subject but also to withstand the ravages of time. In doing so, it praises Reynolds, whose painting of Garrick is the object of both Mrs. Yates's and the audience's gaze and thus uses the object itself to confirm the argument of the verse. The poem points to the painting and the painting points back to the poem, thereby implicitly confirming the capacity of both arts to "rehearse" the past.[46]

Similarly, the fourth verse paragraph argues that sculpture, once it achieves a rendering of its subject, is augmented by the defects inflicted by time, and thus the speaker's call for the yet-to-be-constructed shrine to the memory of Garrick in the final verse paragraph is not that distant from a form of investment advice. The trustees—that is, the audience—should invest in a physical memorial because it will only accrue value over time for those in whose name it was built:

> With thoughts that mourn—nor yet desire Relief,
> With meek Regret, and fond enduring Grief;
> With looks that speak—He never shall return!—
> Chilling thy tender Bosom clasp his Urn;
> And with soft Sighs disperse the'irreverend Dust,
> Which TIME may strew upon his sacred Bust. (107–12)

In the printed version of the "Monody," these final lines are accompanied by an image of Mrs. Yates embracing De Loutherbourg's urn (fig. 4.4), which suggests the degree to which these lines were enacted in the "Monody."[47] But in their enactment, an important difference is articulated. Mrs. Yates embraces the urn, but this urn does not contain Garrick's body, nor is it even a permanent funerary monument. It is a mere prop, and its temporary status is emphasized as a way of stressing the need for a permanent record, because the record elicited in performance is written on the heart (89) and thus, like any other living thing, subject to death. In this light, the objects surrounding Mrs. Yates become paradoxical examples of the transience of living things: the urn is a theatrical object whose transience amplifies both the sense of life's impermanence and the desire for sculpture to alleviate some of this sense of decay.

Significantly, Sheridan's two allusions to the relative permanence of architectural sculpture were singled out for praise in the reviews: "Throughout the composition, the soul and spirit of true poetry exist manifestly; all the thoughts are good; that of Shakespeare's monument, pointing out the grave of Garrick is admirable, and that of architectural ruins giving the architect's fame additional grace from their decay, truly excellent."[48] But if the idea of a monument carrying out its deictic task was welcome to some reviewers, the temporary monument

Figure 4.4. Frontispiece, Richard Brinsley Sheridan, *Verses to the Memory of Garrick, spoken as a Monody* (London, 1779). Courtesy of the Thomas Fisher Rare Book Library, University of Toronto.

built by De Loutherbourg unraveled the claims for painting and sculpture's effective rememoration in the poem: "The *coup d'oeil* of the whole is good, but the monument, whether from its colouring, or from some other cause, does not produce the desired effect. The medallion also, which we understand to be an original picture of Mr. Garrick by Sir Joshua Reynolds . . . is scarcely distinguishable; we mean so distinguishable that the audience, did not the occasion tell them, could discover who it represented."[49]

The failures of Reynolds's painting and of De Loutherbourg's monument are effectively those of reference. For the reviewer, there is nothing in the likeness that ensures reference, and thus Reynolds's painting points to Garrick only by virtue of its spatial and temporal location in the theatre on this particular evening. In their attempt to memorialize or capture Garrick, both painting and monument end up pointing at some indistinguishable figure. It is the same shedding of specificity that lay behind the designation of Garrick's corpse as "THE BODY" in the newspaper accounts of the funeral. This disfiguration helps to explain why in the final line of the poem, Sheridan reintroduces the notion of doubt that opened the "Monody." In the final couplet, "And with soft Sighs disperse the'irreverend Dust, / Which TIME may strew upon his sacred Bust" (111–12), the verb "may" raises the question of whether Time will act upon the projected memorial sculpture. What remains in question here is whether there will be a bust to be ravaged by Time, and as we have seen the existence of such a piece of art relies on the fulfillment of the trustees' obligation to the nation. This is a curious proleptic moment because it projects the audience forward in time to witness its yet-to-be-constructed memorial to Garrick's passing into antiquity. Within the logic of the poem, this simultaneously drives the audience to translate its subjective reaction to the "Monody" into a "permanent" object and forces them to recognize that even this attempt to represent and reconstitute the past "may" fail.

Imperial Obsolescence

But why that attempt to build the requisite memorial shrine might fail is left curiously unstated. It simply registers as a possibility. In spite of their tears, the erstwhile sign of their commitment to remembrance, the audience and the nation may yet fail to mourn Garrick. This possibility is, I believe, directly tied to the larger context within which the "Monody" was composed and spoken. According to the papers, there were calls for a national monument to Garrick almost immediately after his death, but Parliament and the public were preoccupied with a host of interrelated issues pertaining to the Ministry's execution of the war.[50] With the war now taking on a global scale, naval matters were of particular importance, and thus the Keppel affair was a national obsession. Invasion scares were rampant and the newspaper-reading public kept careful track of the strange goings-on at the encampments at Coxheath.[51] But closely related to both the camp news and the Keppel court-martial were the almost daily accounts of the West Indian fleet. Important campaigns were being fought in the Antilles all through the summer and fall of 1778 and the winter of 1779. The French had captured Dominica in early September of 1778, and in December the British had conquered and successfully defended St. Lucia against a French counterattack. The French would go on to capture St. Vincent and Grenada in June and July of 1779. One of the primary concerns that surfaced in the Keppel court-martial was the safety of the West Indian fleet, whose commercial value to the nation was paramount. Many of Keppel's actions in the Channel were aimed at securing safe passage for ships to and from the West Indies. With the war in the thirteen colonies going extremely badly, British attention was focused on maintaining control of the Caribbean and the lucrative trade in sugar and slaves.

It is one thing to point to a general sense of anxiety regarding the West Indian campaigns, but quite another to conclusively link the sense of doubt in the "Monody" to these historical events. But the first performance of the "Monody" was staged as an afterpiece to Richard Cumberland's comedy *The West Indian.* As manager of Drury Lane, this bit of scheduling fell to Sheridan. At the time of this production, the Caribbean colonies were under continual threat, so we need to ask how the audience would understand the play in light of the difficulties faced by the West Indian fleet. And we need to consider how the interval between the mainpiece and the afterpiece sets up a historical dilemma that resonates with the figuration of historical rupture within the "Monody" itself. It could well be that the pairing of the "Monody" and *The West Indian* is purely circumstantial, but I want to momentarily explore the interpretive possibility afforded by their sequential performance.

The West Indian was one of the great theatrical successes of the prewar period. First produced by Garrick at Drury Lane on 19 January 1771, it had a run of more than thirty performances in its first season and quickly became a mainstay of the stage in the last quarter of the eighteenth century. The play was very much the product of the Seven Years' War in that key plot elements are directly concerned with the flow of goods and people in the post-1759 circum-Atlantic empire. The story of an intemperate young planter's misadventures in London relies on widely held beliefs about the influence of tropical climate on character. From Belcour's tumultuous landing to the revelation that his friend Stockwell is actually his father, the comedy figures the Caribbean as a space of unbridled yet innocent desire and London as zone of more restrained yet also more corrupt sociability. The prosperous merchant Stockwell's own Caribbean past is marked by sexual freedoms that would have damaged his reputation in London, but within the time frame of the play, he operates as an exemplar of commercial and moral rectitude. As Belcour slowly progresses toward the revelation of Stockwell's paternity, so too does the play engage in a complex disciplinary procedure. Belcour's "tropical" propensities are constrained in order to make him not only a suitable match for Louisa Dudley but also a prudent enough heir to Stockwell's fortune. At the same time, Belcour's "natural" innocence is used as a foil to frustrate and reveal the avarice and cruelty of Lady Rushport. Thus, the colonial figure is deployed to critique errant aristocratic behavior. This critique results in the affirmation of a familial alliance between the planter and the merchant, on the one hand, and between the planter and the soldier's daughter, on the other.[52] Louisa Dudley's father and brother are active military men who have served or will serve in colonial venues throughout the circum-Atlantic. The fact that the play's resolution also results in Captain Dudley's access to a posting in Africa often goes unnoticed. In this comedy, the drive toward marriage entails the disciplining of the impetuous colonial subject, the consolidation of circum-Atlantic capital, and the validation of both past and future military action in zones of commercial interest to Britain. In other words, it offers a fulsome fantasy of metropolitan control of the Atlantic imperium that is grounded in the marriage plot itself.

To see how this would have operated in its first season of performance is not difficult, but it is worth considering how the historical events of the rebellion of the American colonies would impinge on the play's reception. The relationship between metropole and colony was frequently figured as that between father and son or that between brothers. Belcour's intemperance, although generally benign, is not at all distant from the figuration of American rebels as impetuous. In fact, the entire discourse of civility that is so crucial for Cumberland's play is also an important trope for distinguishing rebellious colonists from more judicious imperial rulers. Perhaps this is why in the winter of 1777, King George III commanded a series of performances of *The West Indian* at Covent Garden to shore up the fantasy of metropolitan control at a moment when it was beginning to dissolve.[53] Equally important was the fact that General Clinton's officers staged the play for the first time in America on 15 January 1779. The audience for this performance was the largest house that had ever attended a play in the New York theatre, and it was immediately revived. The fact that it failed miserably on its third revival in New York by the same players may indicate that wishful thinking has a limited shelf life.[54] *The West Indian* played throughout the war with a particularly heavy scheduling at both Drury Lane and Covent Garden in the 1778–79 and 1779–80 seasons.[55] After this the play continued to run intermittently at Drury Lane as part of the standard repertory, but all but disappeared from the boards of Covent Garden until the end of the war. I discuss its revival in the postwar period in chapter 5, but I would like to suggest here that during the highly unstable days of 1779 the play had the potential to operate either as a nostalgic diversion from the present crisis or as an anxious articulation of what could be lost if the Ministry and the military did not turn things around. In fact, it is through the suturing of nostalgia and anxiety that the play could overcome the generic obsolescence of its sentimental structure.

Just as Garrick's funeral was preceded by Chatham's lying-in-state, so the "Monody" was preceded by another success of the prewar era that may now be obsolete, both in substance and in structure. In 1779 a comedy where the differences between colony and metropole are ameliorated by the sentimental resolution of virtuous commerce and conjugal desire would seem at variance with the violent struggle for power that had enveloped the empire. *The West Indian* would play on the London stage for the rest of the century, but as we will see in chapter 5, its signification changed irrevocably with the Peace of Paris. For our purposes here, it is enough to recognize that the war was an engine of obsolescence. Sheridan, I believe, explores the possibility that historical forces, beyond the control of art, may render the surrogative potential of performance null and void. Rather than continuation, the effigy, to use Roach's term, would turn on the present and signal its alienation from the past. It is this fear of alienation that seeps into the theatre between the mainpiece and the "Monody," and which the "Monody" both dramatizes and attempts to circumvent. But this attempt at circumvention amounts to a challenge to the audience to assert its historical and cultural agency.

The historical aporia between mainpiece and afterpiece on the evening of 11 March 1779 is akin to the aporia between the tears elicited by the "Monody" and the anticipated memorialization of Garrick. It is this stutter step in the time of mourning, whether it be for an evaporating sense of imperial control in the Atlantic world or for an evanescent sense of contact with Shakespeare through Garrick's art, that Sheridan recognized and dramatized in the "Monody." Its radicality lies in the implicit sense that the gap between one historical moment and another could simply expand in a way that consigns the culture to a state of entropic decline. In both cases, performance temporarily bridges the gap—De Loutherbourg fashions a surrogate urn to figure for the missing monument of the future, and Sheridan fashions a poetic spectacle to shift attention away from the historical rupture from the stable imperial world of Cumberland's play—but it does so in a way that warns the audience that such a bridging function may not work if the chasm becomes too wide. If the present, by force of political events in the Atlantic world, becomes disconnected from the past, then the proleptic desire of the nation to have a recognizable future may not be realized.

After Hamlet

In the months after the first performance of the "Monody," the sense of torpor that had enveloped the nation from at least the news of Burgoyne's loss at Saratoga reached an almost unbearable state. Spain declared war on Britain in June 1779, and thus the Spanish fleet joined the French in the English Channel. The historical analogue to Spain's earlier threat of invasion was palpable, but there was widespread fear that it would be repetition with a horrible difference. In June 1779 King George himself referred to the defeat of the Spanish Armada in an effort to rouse his subjects to the needed effort to defend his kingdom. "It was the vigour of mind shown by Queen Elizabeth and her subjects," he wrote in June 1779, "added to the assistance of Divine Providence, that saved this island when attacked by the Spaniards."[56] Invoking the glorious year of 1588 was not simply a royal prerogative. The deployment of past glory either to prop up patriot ideology or to critique present insipidity was a prominent feature not only of political reporting but also of two wildly popular plays from the fall of 1779: Thomas King's musical spectacle *The Prophecy, or Elizabeth at Tilbury* at Sadler's Wells and, of course, Sheridan's satire *The Critic* at Drury Lane. I am going to be looking at the plays in some detail later in this section in order to understand how the problem of historical rupture and repetition broached in the "Monody" was turned on the audience in even more heightened form by Sheridan's comedy.

If anything, the question of what it means to come after, to be tragically belated, is felt with even more intensity in Sheridan's third envoi to the theatre staged some six months after the "Monody." *The Critic* takes many of the concerns articulated in the "Monody" and reworks them into a biting satire not only of monumental history but also of the theatrical enterprise itself. If, as I have argued earlier, Sheridan's staging of Garrick's funeral failed to ensure a sense of cultural continuity, and his "Monody" dramatized the possibility of rupture and cultural decline, then there was no shortage of supplemental attempts, by far less able hands, to reconstitute patriot ideology. As Robert W. Jones argues, these attempts were keyed to the threat of invasion:

> The threat of invasion infected every aspect of political and cultural life: troops were mustered, debates raged in the Lords and Commons, angry

> letters in newspapers bemoaned the state of His Majesty's ships, and poets and dramatists exploited the mood of the times. In his "Ode to the Warlike Genius of Great Britain," William Tasker urged Britain to rouse herself to defeat the aggressors; in the summer of 1778 Richard Cumberland's tragedy *The Battle of Hastings* told a tale of forlorn Saxon daring and love in troubled times; at the Haymarket George Colman revived John Fletcher's *The Tragedie of Bonduca*, cleverly revising the play to reflect new anxieties about invasion and colonial conquest; and at Sadler's Wells in 1779 Tom King's extravagant pageant, *The Prophecy; or, Queen Elizabeth at Tilbury*, tried to rouse spirits by appealing to past glories.[57]

One can add to this list the Handel mini-explosion in the winter of 1779, much of the verse on Garrick's death, and specifically William Tasker's own "Elegy on the Death of David Garrick," which was advertised as a companion to his "Ode to the Warlike Genius of Great Britain." As is well known, these failed attempts at monumental history themselves became the target of Sheridan's critical history: all of these productions were burlesqued in *The Critic*.[58] Numerous critics, most notably Morwood, Jones, and Russell, have examined Sheridan's satire on the failures of patriot performance in both *The Camp* and *The Critic*.[59] Russell's work in particular has underlined the importance of the gender insubordination of fashionable society and martial masculinity in her writings on camp culture.[60] My intention here is to come at this issue from a different direction by exploring the play in light of the radical possibilities opened up by the "Monody." And in order to do so, I want to replicate my earlier deployment of Seward's poem, this time with Tasker's "Elegy," in order to indicate the importance of Garrick and Shakespeare to Sheridan's critique.

Warlike Genius

The antiquarian William Tasker's "Elegy on the Death of David Garrick" is almost a catalog of clichés that barely sustains critical interest, except for two rather strange elements of its initial printing, which appears to have occurred in the early fall of 1779. Tasker was a scholar of Latin and Greek, and beneath the thicket of classical tropes and references, the poem reveals a remarkable obsession with Sheridan's public responses to Garrick's death. This is signaled immediately by the insertion of the same illustration of Mrs. Yates grasping De Loutherbourg's urn that graced the first edition of Sheridan's "Monody" (fig. 4.4). The illustration even replicates the final lines of Sheridan's poem. When one enters the poem proper, it becomes clear that much of the substance of the poem is simply an elaboration on the themes and images of the "Monody"; therefore, the replication of the illustration acknowledges a fundamental state of indebtedness. Like the "Monody," Tasker's speaker calls for a memorial statue, honors Reynolds, and elaborates on De Loutherbourg's physical invocation of Melpomene and Thalia. Furthermore, those elements of the poem which do not directly reference the "Monody" are little more than rehearsals of other Garrick memorials. The poem's references to the interment in the Abbey call up the newspaper accounts, and the litany of Shakespearean characters, now dead, is clearly derived from Seward's "Prize Monody on the Death of Mr. Garrick." This is elegy warmed over for expressly commercial purposes.

But the other significant aspect of its printing should give us pause. Immediately on the title page, the reader is informed that the "Elegy" is "By the Author of the Ode to the Warlike Genius of Great Britain." Beyond mere authorship, these two poems are linked by their willingness to capitalize on national and cultural anxiety and by a rather startling inattention to how the later poem undoes many of the rhetorical objectives of the earlier poem. As its title suggests, the patriotic rhetoric of "The Ode to the Warlike Genius of Great Britain" turns on the repeated figuration of the "Genius of Britain," whose vengeance strikes terror into her foes and elicits virtuous pride from her sons and daughters. Predictably, Tasker offers a nostalgic catalog of past heroes (including Keppel) who have channeled this warlike genius. But when "genius" is invoked in the "Elegy," the speaker is more concerned with its future status. The final stanza of the "Elegy" directly thematizes the notion of cultural continuation:

While Science fires her Sons on Earth,
While BRITAIN gives to Genius Birth,
  His praise no bounds shall know;
The Stage while buskin'd Actors tread,
While Taste shall SHAKESPEARE's Drama read,
  While Avon's stream shall flow.[61]

By repeating the word *while* five times in six lines, the boundless praise afforded Garrick and the continued reverence for Shakespeare's texts are here pegged to the continual birth of British "genius." Because the precise nature of this genius goes unspecified in the poem, it signifies doubly: it can incorporate not only the artistic genius implicitly alluded to in the poem's celebration of Garrick, Shakespeare, and Reynolds but also the "Warlike Genius" alluded to on the poem's title page. There was nothing novel here: Garrick himself had made a similar gesture in the "Ode on Shakespeare" when he compared Shakespeare's art with the martial prowess of Alexander the Great.[62] The problem here is that the repetition of *while* begs the question of history's relation to this national destiny. It would appear that both artistic and warlike genius will replicate themselves for as long as the Avon will flow, but this does not square with the fact that in the seventh stanza, just as in Sheridan's "Monody," the act of memorialization has been forestalled. There is a gap between the transient expressions of grief, both enacted and referenced by the poem, and their manifestation as cultural monuments. This is exacerbated by the fact that Tasker's invocation of the Avon resonates with precisely those passages in Garrick's "Ode on Shakespeare," which indicate that it took well over 150 years for Shakespeare to be physically commemorated.[63] What Tasker isolates here, perhaps in spite of himself, or perhaps because his method is so citational, is the perilous nature of performance to ensure continuity. Lines such as the following underline both the psychic and commercial value of surrogation and the temporal alienation that attends its failure:

> Britannia's Sons the Tomb shall raise,
> And, sacred to her ROSCIUS' Praise,
>   The sculptur'd Marble stand;
> The Worth of him, who lies below,
> The fair recording Verse shall show,
>   Wrote by the Muse's hand. (37–42)

Tasker's assertion of future stability and his replication of Sheridan's topoi signal an anxious attempt to replace the question posed by the "Monody" with a fantasy of national supremacy that is at odds with the present state of affairs.

In contrast, Sheridan faced the threat of failed surrogation head-on in *The Critic*, but in doing so, he also recognized the cost of success. Significantly, his critique aimed at both the psychic damage and the commercial opportunities afforded by loss. In the face of national crisis, Sheridan stages a ruthless critique of nostalgia and of the often-profitable rememorative processes that subtend patriotism. The three-act play is broken into two sections. The first act, which garnered most of the reviewers' praise, is set in the critic Dangle's house, and aside from lampooning Richard Cumberland quite directly in the caricature of Sir Fretful Plagiary, much of the dialogue revolves around the commercial print press. Newspapers figure prominently in act 1, and their place in Sheridan's critique is extremely important. The second section of the play, comprising the second and third acts, is a rehearsal of Puff's tragedy "The Spanish Armada," which, like the play itself, is set in Drury Lane theatre.[64] The play is both an adaptation of the Duke of Buckingham's *The Rehearsal* and a pastiche of a host of recently performed patriotic plays, most notably Cumberland's lugubrious tragedy *The Battle of Hastings*, originally staged in the summer of 1778, and *The Prophecy, or Elizabeth at Tilbury*, an extremely popular musical spectacle that ran at Sadler's Wells from August 1779 through much of the fall.[65] I discuss these two sections in turn because the critique of the newspapers quite literally sets the stage for the more complex theatrical critique in the final two acts. Interestingly, the ready wit of act 1 immediately met with public approval, whereas it took a number of weeks for audiences to fully understand Sheridan's objectives in acts 2 and 3.[66] This lag time in the approbation of the play was itself an indication of the necessity of Sheridan's intervention.

Sheridan's analysis of the role of the newspapers in national fantasy unfolds in two stages in act 1. The play opens with newspapers strewn all over the Dangle's breakfast table. Mr. Dangle's opening speech famously captures the perilous state of national affairs and subordinates them to the theatrical intelligence:

> DANGLE: (*reading*) "BRUTUS to LORD NORTH."—"Letter the second, on the STATE OF THE ARMY."—Pshaw! "To the first L dash D of the A dash Y."—"Genuine Extract of a Letter from ST KITTS."—"COXHEATH INTELLIGENCE."—"It is now confidently asserted that SIR CHARLES HARDY."—Pshaw!—Nothing but about the fleet, and the nation!—and I hate all politics but theatrical politics.—Where's the MORNING CHRONICLE?[67]

The *Morning Chronicle's* close attention to theatrical affairs makes it Dangle's "gazette of choice," and Sheridan is clearly going after the state of denial that was enveloping the nation. All of the cited stories can be traced to the papers, and each one testifies to the unsatisfactory progress of the war. Lord North's inactivity, Lord Sandwich's humiliation during the Keppel affair, the perilous state of the West Indian fleet off of St. Kitt's, the continuing farce of aristocrats playing soldier at the encampment at Coxheath, and Sir Charles Hardy's reprise of Keppel's ineffectual engagement with the enemy fleet in the English Channel are signaled in turn. It is a catalog of ineffectual leadership, poor management, ministerial conspiracy, elite dissipation, political factionalism, and plain allegations of cowardice that had been raging from at least the time of the Keppel affair, and which continued for much of the war.

In the face of such a devolution in the state and its military leaders, Dangle decides to invest his time in the theatre, and Sheridan implies that the *Morning Chronicle* is similarly delusional. Even for those who profess to want to know about the state of the nation, news is a species of entertainment:

> MRS. DANGLE: . . . you never will read anything that's worth listening to:—you hate to hear about your country; there are letters every day with Roman signatures, demonstrating the certainty of an invasion, proving that the nation is utterly undone—But you never read anything that will entertain one. (1.1.28–33)

This is denial of a different order. Here the political has become simply another flight of fancy where emotions are elicited, but actual historical consequences are not fully grasped. It is difficult to say which form of denial is more dangerous, for at least Dangle recognizes that the time is out of joint.

But it is only with the arrival of Mr. Puff that the full extent of the nation's denial and its self-delusions are made apparent. In his famous adaptation of Touchstone's speech on lying from *As You Like It*, Puff offers a careful anatomy of the art of puffing that concludes with a discussion of political mediation:

> MR. PUFF: . . . Here are too some political memorandums I see; aye—To take PAUL JONES, and get the INDIAMEN out of the SHANNON—reinforce BYRON—compel the DUTCH to—I must do that in the evening papers, or reserve it for the Morning Herald, for I know that I have undertaken tomorrow, besides, to establish the unanimity of the fleet in the Public Advertiser, and to shoot CHARLES FOX in the Morning Post,—So, egad, I haven't a moment to lose! (1.2.314–22)

Many critics have noted that Sheridan at this time was himself involved, with Fox, in the production of *The Englishman*, but the specificity of Puff's remarks here are crucial. Here at the end of the first act, the audience is drawn back to the very issues that Dangle had attempted to evade in his opening speech. Puff is about to go and invent stories about the navy for papers from the opposite sides of the political spectrum. Almost all of Fox's parliamentary oratory during this period pilloried the Admiralty and Lord Sandwich's failure to bring unanimity of purpose to the navy following the divisive Keppel court-martial. So Puff here is writing one story arguing that the navy is unified in the Whiggish *Public Advertiser*, and another attacking Fox in the pro-Ministry *Morning Post*. Puff is working both sides of the issue on opposite sides of the press in order to stir controversy regarding the Ministry's management of the war, not because he is concerned with the fate of the nation, but because factional controversy sells papers. The problem here, much in evidence in the reporting of the Keppel affair, is that commerce and factionalism spur each other on and completely hijack the resolution of narrative enigmas vital to the state of the nation. As we will see, this specter of factionalism in the navy, inherited from the Keppel affair and kept alive by Hardy's failed efforts of August 1779, haunt the remainder of the play, because it is precisely this lack of unanimity that troubles Puff's use of the Elizabethan past in "The Spanish Armada."

Sheridan's exploration of the generative force of commercial culture in act 1 extends into his theatrical critique in acts 2 and 3. Richard Fitzpatrick's prologue to *The Critic* promised that, like Buckingham's *The Rehearsal*, the afterpiece would attack the degradation of theatre in present times. Tragedy and comedy are now so insipid that audiences are faced with dullness rather than bombast. The play focuses its attention on the pitiful state of tragedy by attacking Cumberland's *The Battle of Hastings*. As Morwood has argued, Cumberland's play "sets grand romantic passions against a backdrop of national crisis and puts a grotesquely elevated diction in the mouths of its characters."[68] Sheridan does precisely the same thing in "The Spanish Armada" and by his repetition ridicules the absurdity of Cumberland's diction and of the play's structure.[69] Sheridan's critique of Cumberland's Shakespearean phraseology is devastating but, I would argue, of less importance than his critique of Cumberland's deployment of the past. In the summer of 1778, there were commercial and patriotic gains to be made by invoking the Battle of Hastings on the stage, but, as many reviewers complained, the play does not allegorize the present but rather attempts to pass off a rather cumbersome love plot as a confirmation of British national resolve. In other words, its use of the past is unknowingly cynical, and thus, in its attempt to shore up British nationalism, it actually hollows out the sense of historical continuity implied by the title.

Significantly, Sneer and Dangle make the same complaint about Puff's "The Spanish Armada," but Puff's response indicates that he is well aware of the commercial value of this kind of cynicism:

> PUFF: It is a received point among poets, that where history gives you a good heroic out-line for a play, you may fill up with a little love at your own discretion; in doing which, nine times out of ten, you only make up a deficiency in the private history of the times.— Now I rather think I have done this with some success. (2.2.11–15)

In other words, the past has been rewritten to suit the audience's presumptive desire for a love plot and thus ensure the play's commercial success. It is important to recognize that Sheridan's attack, while aimed at *The Battle of Hastings*, could be equally directed at other more exalted productions. Garrick's famous rewriting of act 5 of *Hamlet* did not inject a spurious love plot, but it fundamentally reconfigured the play's closure in order to pander to audience desires; and Garrick, much like Puff, wrote widely about the success of his alterations.[70]

But aside from this explicit critique of the commercial and patriotic appropriation of the past, Sheridan's most biting satire was encoded into his complex treatment of *The Prophecy, or Elizabeth at Tilbury*. Significantly, all of the major papers applauded King's musical spectacle for its use of history:

> The new musical piece, performed here on Monday evening for the first, under the title of THE PROPHECY, or Queen Elizabeth at Tilbury, is not only a very allowable, but a very commendable use of an historical event, which happily suits the circumstances of the present times. While from the stage decoration, and the stile of exhibition, it serves to entertain within the theatre, it may also contribute to the enlivening the spirits, and to stimulating the zeal of those on whom the defence of this country rests, in the present hour of difficulty and danger.[71]

There is an implicit assumption here, as in George III's remark cited earlier, that the nation has lost its vigor and that its citizens need to be roused into action. What better than a spectacular reworking of the narrative of Elizabeth's victory over the Armada off of Tilbury? Only that does not quite describe *The Prophecy*, nor does it fully convey the use and abuse of the future at Sadler's Wells:

> The main incident is too well known to need detail of it; the manner in which it is used at the Wells, is as follows:—When the curtain rises, the scene discovers a part of the country near Tilbury, an excellent representation of that important Fort, with part of the adjoining river terminating the perspective. An old woman and her two daughters come on, and we learn from their converse, that, like the rest of their neighbours, they are gadding to Tilbury to see their Queen, who is expected there; they are presently joined by two countrymen, and after some humourous songs, on the report of martial music, they stand aside, in order to make away for the procession which precedes her Majesty, who at length approaches riding on a fine palfrey richly caparizoned; all present join in a loyal chorus, at the end of which the Queen thanks her subjects in recitative for their af-

fection, and in an air set to spirited music assures them, that relying on Heaven and them, she laughs at the Spanish Armada. Slow music is then heard, and presently a cloud descends to earth, from out of which the Genius of Britain issues, and after telling Elizabeth she has nothing to fear from the perfidious House of Bourbon, promises to present her with a view of what shall happen in the reign of mighty George, in an airy mirror; on waving his oaken sceptre, the cloud rejoins the sky, and a striking spectacle is exhibited, in which the navy of England appears riding triumphant on the seas, and the fleets of France and Spain, broken, dismasted, and vanquished. The prophecy is, "That England will ever be victorious, if Britons are true to themselves." And the whole concludes with a parody on the famous song, beginning with the words *On Thursday is the morn, &c.*[72]

The newspapers reprint the lines of both the opening songs between mother and daughters and Queen Elizabeth's song of thanks to her subjects, and it is significant that the first section of the play is dominated by women. The sailors and soldiers who fought in the Channel and at Tilbury are subsumed into their leader, and this effectively leaves them unrepresented on the stage, except in Elizabeth's words and in the painted backdrop. Thus, when the masculine Genius of Britain steps out of the cloud and ruptures the temporal continuum by magically displaying the future victory of the British navy over Spain and France in the English Channel, the play not only enacts the patriotic desires of the audience but also figures forth a form of masculinity capable of achieving this task. And it is here that the production confronts some of the key problems with its own generic conventions. The Genius of Britain may be borrowed from Tasker and speaks for George III, but in performance he shares a great deal with Harlequin. His oaken scepter operates much like Harlequin's flapper, and his entrance and exit through the cloud are conventional pantomime tricks.

This strange undercutting of the Genius of Britain's status is not an isolated element of the play. The question of whether there are men capable of achieving the eponymous prophecy inheres because the defeat of the Spanish and the French has not yet occurred. The futurity of the prophecy stubbornly undoes much of the play's invocation of the past. This is most evident in "Elizabeth's Reply to her People":

Thanks loving subjects! In whose loyal hearts
My hopes I place—nor need I fear the arts
Or arms, indeed, of an insulting foe.
When honour calls what cannot Britons do!

AIR: (*To Arms ye brave Mortals away*)
Turn your minds back to great Arthur's days,
From thence trace our brave British story;
With wonder reflect and with praise,
Your forefathers were all sons of glory.
CHORUS—*Our free fathers were all sons, &c.*

See the thousands on Cressy's proud field;
Let Agincourt still be before ye,
To Britons their standards they yield,
They're conquer'd by sons of true glory.
CHORUS—*They're conquered by sons, &c.*

To herself then let England be true,
In spite of each threat and bravado:
Protected by Heaven and you
I laugh at the *Spanish Armada.*
The last Verse in Chorus.[73]

The song is clearly designed for the audience to sing along, and each verse links success over the Spanish to moments of past glory. But both the first and final verses point toward the future and underline that Elizabeth's confidence is contingent on England being true to herself—that is, to her past history of valor. The song proclaims a continuity of purpose both in 1588 and, by extension, in 1779, but the play's final prophecy modifies the song when it states "That England will ever be victorious, if Britons are true to themselves." What are we to make of that "if"? It is a curiously double-edged utterance because it could equally indicate that Britain will be defeated if its warriors are not true to their patrimony. My sense is that this is not simply an oversight on the playwright's part, or an overreading on my own. The play both activates and alleviates anxiety regarding the future, and it is precisely this two-pronged effect that hails the audience from a state of torpor into a posture of patriotism. In short, it is precisely the play's equivocal address to the future that makes its use of the past potentially capable of "stimulating the zeal of those on whom the defence of this country rests."

Lurking beneath this inculcation of patriotic response lies something even more complex, which I believe is crucial for understanding the full implications of Sheridan's practice in *The Critic.* For audiences responding to the play's advertisement, which promised "A New Musical Piece consisting of Airs, serious and Comic, Recitatives, Choruses, etc. . . . In the course of which will be displayed a Transparency, representing the destruction of the Spanish Armada, and a moving Perspective View representing the present GRAND FLEET,"[74] some surprises were in store. First, there is no record of the promised transparency of the defeat of the Armada: this past event appears to have been subsumed into the as-yet-unrealized, but nevertheless represented, destruction of the French and Spanish ships currently threatening the Grand Fleet in the Channel. It is not difficult to recognize the structure of desire in this retroactive anticipation. The past event has quite literally been transformed—in this case, canceled and projected forward—to fulfill the desire for what has not been achieved.

Sheridan's lampoon of *The Prophecy* goes after this expression of patriotic desire by simply presenting what the proprietors of Sadler's Wells had initially advertised. *The Critic*'s closing spectacle is in part a rehearsal of the promised destruction of the Spanish Armada that was obviated by the magic of the "Genius of Britain":

> *Flourish of drums—trumpets—cannon, &c. &c. Scene changes to the sea—the fleets engage—the music plays "Britons strike home."—Spanish fleet destroyed by fire-ships, &c.—English fleet advances—music plays "Rule Britannia."—The procession of all the English rivers and their tributaries with their emblems, &c. begins with Handel's Water Music—ends with a chorus, to the march of Judas Maccabeus.—During this scene* Puff *directs and applauds everything—* (3.2)

De Loutherbourg's execution of the final naval spectacle was universally praised for its realism: according to the reviews, the motion of the waves was very natural, and the moving fireships were quite thrilling. As the *London Evening Post* stated, "The deception of the sea was very strong, and perspective of the ships, together with the mode of their sailing, truly picturesque. This great painter, in all his scenic productions, seems to *bring nature to our view*, instead of *painting views after nature*."[75] In other words, this was less of a rendering than a simulation.[76] And with this protodocumentary gesture, De Loutherbourg did something that *The Prophecy* did not achieve: it represented, with detailed specificity, the past event to which the present situation was being compared. In other words, it does not replace the past event with a present desire but rather fixes it before the audience on the stage. This act of fixing amounts to a form of countermemory aimed at dissociating the historical event from present fantasies of national identity. In this sense, *The Critic*'s objective is to challenge the ossified deployment of past greatness in order to salvage the nation from its own delusional sense of self.

That Sheridan and De Loutherbourg are engaged in an act of countermemory is evidenced by the supplemental pastiche of recognizable tropes of patriot representation. "Rule Britannia" had long since become a commonplace expression of loyalty, but it was originally composed for the masque *Alfred*, whose substance had been recrafted into a full-length tragedy and performed at Covent Garden in January 1778. The procession of rivers, as the *Morning Post* recognized, dramatized the catalog of rivers in Pope's "Windsor Forest."[77] Both Handel compositions were staged to commemorate crucial victories over French aggression in the early and midcentury.[78] Apparently this pastiche generated a patriotic response in the audience, but it is hard to see this collocation as anything other than a sign of desperation. Puff signals as much in the final speech of the play:

> PUFF: Well, pretty well—but not quite perfect—so ladies and gentlemen, if you please, we'll rehearse this piece again tomorrow. (3.2.290–91)

"Tomorrow" is the final word of the play, and I would argue that this is crucial, because the present rehearsal of the past, even in Puff's cynical eyes, has been insufficient. Just as *The Prophecy* projected the audience into the future desiring yet another assertion of naval success in the Channel, so Sheridan invites the "ladies and gentlemen," both on stage and off, to yet another blunt statement, that this kind of naval victory has been achieved, 180 years earlier. Each subsequent performance of *The Prophecy* only serves to fortify the delusional elements of the Armada allegory, whereas every subsequent performance of *The Critic* aims to reveal the historical discontinuity that is driving the desire for allegorical, rather than real, victory over the combined forces of France and Spain. In other words, the closing spectacle is a ruthless critique of the misrecognition of the present evidenced not only in the crowds that packed Sadler's Wells throughout the fall but also in those parts of *The Critic*'s audience that failed to grasp that the mock patriotism of these final moments of the play amounted to a proto-elegy for the nation. *The Critic*'s satire "constructs a countermemory—a transformation of history into a totally different form of time."[79] And this different form of time is linked to the temporal problems first elucidated in relation to the death of Garrick.

If, as Sheridan argues, the closure of *The Prophecy* amounts to little more than the symptomatic temporality of patriotic fantasy, I am equally interested in the way this play opens. As noted, *The Prophecy* begins with a dialogue song between a mother and two daughters on their way to see the Queen at Tilbury, which comically meditates on the general lack of concern with the future. Here are the daughter's first two verses and the Mother's final riposte:

Deborah.
Of life's busy round shou'd we take a survey,
And each mortal mark in his different way,
We shou'd find nine in ten think nought but today,
which no body can deny

Dorcas.
The fop more to dress than to pay for't inclin'd,
Let's nought, but time present take of hold of his mind,
Tho' to day free as air, he's to-morrow confin'd
Which nobody can deny. . . .

Mother.
'Bout present, or future, then no more ado,
One thing, when I think on't, will still make me rue,
There's no eating one's cake, and then having it too,
Which nobody can deny.

Chorus.
'Bout present, or future, then no more ado,
One thing when we think on't, will make us all rue;
There's no eating, &c.[80]

The prime examples of a lack of foresight—fops, lawyers, courtiers, and impatient lovers—constitute a typical list of the corrupt avatars of eighteenth-century masculinity, so this jaunty song fits into the ongoing critique of British masculinity that animated both the papers and Sheridan's *The Camp*. And these three women, like Mrs. Dangle in *The Critic*, are attempting to get men to forestall the gratification of their immediate pleasures and attend to their place in history. In this context, the introduction of the martial Queen Elizabeth not only calls up a moment of past glory but also registers the threatening forms of gender insubordination that were ostensibly corrupting elite culture. Like the figuration of the Genius of Britain as Harlequin, putting the Amazonian Elizabeth next to a critique of foppish masculinity heightens the sense of social insecurity addressed by the play. With the promulgation of insecurity comes the desire for the consolidation of community and, one might add, the desire for one more performance of *The Prophecy*.

The Dullest of All Dull Tragedies

As the papers were quick to point out, the political efficacy of *The Prophecy* rests on the allegorical link between the defeat of the Spanish Armada in 1588 and the desired destruction of the Spanish and French fleets in 1779. When Sheridan embeds Puff's tragedy "The Spanish Armada" in *The Critic*, the audience is forced to consider not simply the insipidity of recent tragedies such as *The Battle of Hastings* but more importantly the relationship between cultural production and historical events. This is why *The Prophecy* is so important, because Sheridan is drawing a set of historical and cultural parallels, which push his play beyond the ridicule of this or that bad play. If one takes the women's advice in *The Prophecy* and surveys "life's busy round" beyond the present, then an immediate parallel is drawn between the conclusive destruction of Spain's invading force in 1588 and the battle to be fought against the combined French and Spanish fleets in 1779. Unfortunately, the allegory amounts to wishful thinking because of the inconclusive interim battle at Ushant in which the Grand Fleet, under Keppel's command, failed to act decisively, and also because of Sir Charles Hardy's reprise of Keppel's excessive prudence in his nonengagement with the combined naval forces of France and Spain in August of 1779.

This sense of troubled allegory is explicit in Sheridan's play, but he expands the question of failed parallelism in a further disturbing direction when he starts to probe Shakespeare's relation to the present. The year 1599 was arguably Shakespeare's greatest: in the months before a second threatened Spanish invasion, he wrote two key explorations of patriotism and statecraft, *Henry V* and *Julius Caesar*. In the months after the dissolution of the second Armada fear, Shakespeare wrote *As You Like It* and *Hamlet*.[81] However, 1779 was not so auspicious: several months after not one but two inconclusive engagements in the Channel, Britons mourned the passing of Hamlet, in the form of "THE BODY" of David Garrick. Great victory would seem to generate the greatest of English tragedies, whereas "that dark transaction off Brest"[82] was followed by the loss of England's greatest tragic actor. If this was not a sufficient indication of social and cultural decline, one needed only to glance at *The Prophecy* to feel, not the proximity to past greatness, whether martial or theatrical, but rather its recession into the distant past.

If, as Tasker's "Ode" and Sheridan's own "Monody" implied, the only thing propping up the culture was the tenuous link to Shakespeare afforded by the memory of Garrick's performances, then we need to think carefully about the relationship between Shakespeare's plays and *The Critic*. In its first season,

The Critic was given fifty times; half of these performances paired the afterpiece with a Garrick adaptation of a Shakespearean play.[83] On only three occasions was a Shakespearean play offered without *The Critic*, and in these cases Sheridan chose to stage *The Camp*. The first production of Sheridan's afterpiece was staged after *Hamlet* and incorporated various elements of the mainpiece into "The Spanish Armada." James Morwood offers a comprehensive list of the parallels to Hamlet within "The Spanish Armada," and it is unlikely that the audience would have missed such obvious allusions as when Dangle declares that "the stage is 'the Mirror of Nature,'" and that "the actors are 'the Abstract, and brief Chronicles of the Time'" (1.1.724: cf. *Hamlet* 3.2.22, 2.2.518). Whereas *Hamlet* opens with two nervous and watchful officers on the guard platform at Elsinore, Puff's tragedy opens with "*Two Sentinels asleep*" at Tilbury Fort (2.2 SD). Similarly, Sheridan burlesques the declarative nature of the Horatio's exposition in the first scene of *Hamlet*, by having Sir Christopher Hatton and Sir Walter Raleigh go on at length to establish the already well-known historical situation. As Morwood emphasizes, "even Ophelia's mad scenes (4.5.21–71, 151–96) are mocked in Tilburnia's embarrassment of flowers (2.2.271–77) and her subsequent appearance stark mad—and crazily incoherent—in white satin (3.1.280, 293–301)."[84] That Tilburnia's white satin dress was precisely that worn by Mrs. Baddeley in her performance of Ophelia that very evening did not go unnoticed. These repetitions and parodies of *Hamlet* are not at all different from the attacks on Cumberland's *The Battle of Hastings*, so they radically expand the nature of Sheridan's critique. Is Sheridan arguing that *Hamlet* is similarly insipid? Morwood weakly argues that, in his control of language and in his treatment of themes of representation, Sheridan learned from Shakespeare and thus that *The Critic*'s send up of *Hamlet* is "good natured."[85] I think there is another possibility grounded in the historical situation of the play's performance.

Many of the papers were troubled by the play's implied criticisms of Shakespeare, but the *Morning Chronicle*, arguably the most sophisticated popular critic of theatrical culture, focused its attention on the fraught relationship between mainpiece and afterpiece:

> Whenever the public expectation is much roused by the reported or presumed excellence of a new after-piece, about to be performed, the managers of our theatres generally take occasion so far to advantage themselves of the publick curiosity, as to make the least alluring play in their catalogue serve the town for that evening, thereby through implication telling the audience that they shall pay for their eagerness to see the first face of

> the entertainment, by being obliged to sit out the representation of a piece, which they would not have come to see but for its accompaniments. Thus on Saturday evening at Drury-Lane Theatre, those who were desirous of being present at the first performance of Mr. Sheridan's *Critic,* were under the necessity of patiently hearing HAMLET, *altered by Garrick,* which (the present state of the stage considered) is beyond dispute the dullest of all dull tragedies. The performers, to do them justice, endeavoured to excite the publick attention. Mr. Smith played the closet scene with his mother with great warmth and energy. Mrs. Baddeley's Ophelia was interesting and pathetic, but in some of the lesser points of character, she fell short of much less capable actresses. Her dress looked rather fantastical.[86]

What are we to make of the distinction between the obligation articulated here and that prescribed in the "Monody?" In Sheridan's "Monody," the audience had a national duty to honor Garrick and revere Shakespeare. Only seven months later, the audience is under the almost unbearable obligation to sit through Garrick's adaptation of *Hamlet* in order to ensure a seat to see Sheridan's attack on the insipidity of "slow Melpomene's cold numbers."[87] As the *Gazetteer* reported on the day of the performance, the opening time for the theatre was pushed back to a quarter after five for the rest of the season, so an already long evening at the theatre—*The Critic,* at three acts, was widely censured for being too lengthy for an afterpiece—would have felt that much longer.[88]

As is well known, tedium is one of *The Critic*'s chief targets and, according to the papers, one of its primary faults in production. It was not until 5 November that the usually perceptive *Morning Chronicle* acknowledged, "The humour of the Mock Rehearsal being better understood, is much better relished than at first."[89] But it was the *Morning Post* that explicitly recognized that the satire works via boredom and therefore exhibits all the paradoxes of an imminent critique, noting that "when it is considered that burlesque is nothing more than the heightening to extravagance a ruling character in composition, it should seem to demand no common exertion of talent to make a burlesque on insipidity capable of furnishing continuance of entertainment."[90] For this reason it is important to consider that dullest of all dull tragedies, not Cumberland's *Battle of Hastings,* but rather the *Hamlet* being staged after Garrick's retirement from the stage.

The problem, of course, lies with Garrick himself, for his excellence in the central role cast a very long shadow. During Garrick's lifetime, no one would imply that *Hamlet* was boring. But after his death, theatregoers were left not only with less able performers attempting to replicate his Hamlet but also with Garrick's rather unsatisfying version of the play. Garrick's virtuosity overcame the shortcomings of his adaptation, but with actors such as William Smith playing Hamlet, some of the absurdities of Garrick's emendations and additions became all too visible. This was exacerbated by the fact that more correct reading versions of the play—in particular Johnson's edition—were in circulation. *Hamlet* without Garrick was a very tedious affair, and, as George III himself recognized, the nation had descended into a state of torpor. Audiences obliged, for whatever reason, to patiently sit through a *Hamlet* without Hamlet, as it were, would have found themselves in a position where the passing of Garrick would be acutely felt. The historical disjunction feared in the "Monody" would be registered not by tears but rather by yawns and, perhaps worse, by a creeping realization of the absurdity of the very project of bringing Shakespeare to bear on the present. This latter point is registered in the *Morning Chronicle*'s disdain for "Garrick's alteration," and it is rehearsed explicitly in *The Critic*. For Sheridan, it is this proliferation of torpor that warrants a tear, not simply for a belated player but for a nation on the verge of obsolescence. To put this more pointedly, a nation where *Hamlet* has become "the dullest of all dull tragedies" may not be worth reviving or fighting for.

I would argue that *The Critic* recognizes this predicament in order to militate against its final irrevocable realization, and it does so not by venerating Shakespeare, but rather by attacking the audience for whom this veneration has been bled of meaning. And this attack, like the attack on *The Prophecy*, is conducted through an imminent critique of the audience's pleasures in the theatre. Just as the anticipatory desire promulgated by *The Prophecy*'s staging of a naval victory yet to be achieved was attacked by De Loutherbourg's careful staging of past events, so too does Sheridan attack the audience's desire to experience Shakespeare without Garrick's mediation between the living present and the distant past. He does this by reinforcing the fact of Garrick's nonpresence, by making the audience fully aware of his death. Garrick garnered much early fame in the role of Bayes in *The Rehearsal*,[91] and thus it is not difficult to read Puff as a parody of the former manager of Drury Lane. This accounts not only for the necessity of the metatheatrical deployment of the playhouse but also for *The Critic*'s strong affiliation with Buckingham's earlier play. The harshness of this act of countermemory is evident in the ruthlessness with which he critiques the performance of Garrick's adaptation of *Hamlet* that immediately preceded the first performance of the play.[92] The parodies of *Hamlet*'s overly expository first scene, and of *Hamlet*'s rather simplistic plot, may be good-natured, but the ridicule aimed at Ophelia's mad scenes is not, because it is conducted with savage specificity. Mrs. Pope, in the role of Tilburnia, dons the "rather fantastical" white satin dress worn by Mrs. Baddeley only hours before in the role of Ophelia. It is useful to recall the *Morning Chronicle*'s equivocal response to Mrs. Baddeley's performance: "Mrs. Baddeley's Ophelia was interesting and pathetic, but in some of the lesser points of character, she fell short of much less capable actresses."[93] Mrs. Baddeley may not have fully realized Ophelia, but Sheridan is actually far more interested in her dress. This object physically ties the plays together, and it is as though this thing carries with it a kind of contagion of dullness. Emblematic of surplus affect and dead convention, the white satin dress becomes an icon of obsolescence.

In this context, the dress becomes a strangely antiquarian object: it physically links the afterpiece to the mainpiece as a potsherd links the present to the long-buried past. But the question it poses is whether this link, this emblem of continuation, is of value. Clearly, for Sheridan, it was not. To borrow the *Morning Chronicle*'s phrase, such emblems of continuity are, at this historical moment, "rather fantastical" and thus disconnected from the present crisis. And these failed or parodic connections to the past, whether theatrical, social, or political, proliferate throughout *The Critic*, because, as a few papers recognized, the entire play is composed of nothing but reworked elements of past cultural artifacts, some barely worth remembering and others so central to the patrimony of the nation that their presence in this pastiche is extremely disturbing. That said, Sheridan is not advocating a descent into nihilism or iconoclasm. Sheridan is saying not that *Hamlet* is no longer playable but that there will be a gap before it can signify properly again. Garrick's death, likewise, precipitated a hiatus in the cultural life of the nation: a gap in which the performance protocols for negotiating with the icons that moor national identity needed to be recalibrated, or even reinvented. The dead object, like the dead language that permeates "The Spanish Armada," had infiltrated the realm of performance, and *The Critic*'s difficult task is to make its audience aware of a different life. This is why the play is so resolutely aimed at the future, and why the play, in addition to critiquing commerce, also testifies to the productive force of commerce.[94] The drive to make money is at the heart of both the imperial and the theatrical enterprise, and Sheridan built a wildly successful play out of the scraps of a failing institution. The implication of course is that capital has the capacity to reconfigure the empire from the wreckage of the American war. As Puff states at the play's conclusion, a more "perfect" performance may be rehearsed "tomorrow" (3.2.291).

The strange temporality of tomorrow's rehearsal, its anticipation of a more perfect retroaction, is staged as a counter to the kind of retroactive anticipation exemplified by the patriotic fantasy of *The Prophecy*. This temporality also turns out to be a defining thread not only in Sheridan's three attempts to deal with Garrick's passing but also in his perception of the nation's rapidly transforming imperial identity. What Sheridan brings to the question of appropriate action at this juncture in the war is a sense of how the American conflict demands a revaluation of the values that define British subjectivity. Countermemory not only transforms our sense of historical time but also forces a reconsideration of the grounds of subjectification. Joseph Roach's analysis of the surrogative force of the performance effigy carries with it an implied argument about the value of continuity for the British imperial enterprise. I would argue that any theory of cultural continuity and, hence, of surrogation requires a more nuanced theory of value that can more accurately reflect the divergent interests of the nation's constituents.

The Critic demonstrates that continuity is a double-edged sword. When culture is corrupted or unmoored from its roots, then continuity only compounds the degradation. This understanding of political devolution can be found in Montesquieu, and it is certainly a part of Burke's thinking about the empire in the 1770s. This is what is at the heart of the American cause and what drives its supporters toward a radical critique of the value of liberty. For liberty, the defining element of British identity, to flourish, it needed to separate itself from its heritage. This paradoxical rupture, a discontinuation of present relations aimed at preserving a different kind of continuity for the future, describes both the war itself and the kind of action staged by Sheridan in the limited confines of Drury Lane theatre. In this sense, *The Critic* needs to be understood partly as a pro-American performance—this was already evident in its explicit critiques of the Ministry—and partly as a radically post-American intervention. The play's propulsion of the audience into the future is nothing short of a demand to reinvent British culture in a way that can revitalize its relation to the past, without demanding a slavish repetition of the performance protocols, which configure the relations between the living and the dead. And it is clear that these performance protocols need to be developed from the experience of the audience itself, from their intense sense of loss, both for Garrick and for their past imperial confidence. It may not be solely attributable to *The Critic*, but it is important to remember that, by the close of the 1779–80 season, Garrick's once popular adaptation of *Hamlet* would be consigned to oblivion, and thus one particular negotiation with the dead would be at an end.[95]

PART III

Celebrations

CHAPTER FIVE

Which Is the Man?

Remediation, Interruption, and the Celebration of Martial Masculinity

> Newspapers may be considered as literary Gladiators; and an invitation to battle is to them a welcome summons: they will take care to make the contest entertaining to their readers—the only object in which they are really interested.
>
> *Gazetteer*, 1 November 1779

After an unusually long court-martial of twenty-seven days, Admiral Augustus Keppel was unanimously acquitted and the charges against him were declared "malicious and ill-founded."[1] After Palliser's endless examination of witnesses, Keppel's defense was comparatively short, and like his earlier performance in Parliament, an exercise in grace and resolution that turned on the assertion of his "essential" courage.[2] But far more interesting than Keppel's actual remarks were the effect the acquittal had both in performance and in the press.[3] As Nicholas Roger has discussed, Keppel's acquittal generated some of the most extensive and complex crowd violence in the late eighteenth century. The celebrations took a variety of forms and very quickly swept the nation. The speed was due to the remarkably quick dissemination of the news in the papers. William Parker, the publisher of the *General Advertiser*, received the news within six hours, and thus celebrations in London occurred on the day of the acquittal. But the alacrity of the celebration was also due to a great deal of advance preparation. The strongly pro-Keppel *General Advertiser* was jubilant:

> The preparations that are making in the three towns of Portsmouth, Gosport, and Common, for the celebration of the joyful occasion of Admiral Keppel's acquittal, are amazing. All the ships at Spithead, and in the harbour, to the amount of an hundred sail, are to be dressed, and intend to fire a *feu de joyé* on the instant it transpires. Every ship has prepared Sir H—— P—— in effigy, (the Formidable and the Robuste not excepted [Palliser's ships]) whose death is to crown the transport of the day. The sailors have been contriving by the most curious expedients, to get liquors on board, running all hazards of detection, that they may carouse on the happy event. By one consent the three towns are to be illuminated for three nights successively; and we hear there are to be three balls given on the occasion; one by his Royal Highness the Duke of Cumberland; a second by the Admirals of the Navy; and a third by the Captains. Sir H—— P—— will be shot in every street, corner, and alley of the towns, and a most grand display of fire-works is to crown the celebration of the event.[4]

If the final sentence here exaggerated the extent of the symbolic violence, its portrayal of the action did not. Celebrations extended over multiple nights, and as Nicholas Roger demonstrates, the provincial celebrations were carefully staged, highly hierarchical events.[5] The most important of these occurred immediately after the acquittal and the return of Keppel's sword. At about twelve o'clock, the grand procession left the court led by "A band of musick playing 'See the conquering Hero comes' " from Handel's *Judas Maccabeus,* followed by Keppel and a host of dignitaries including the Duke of Cumberland and key opposition figures such as the Duke of Portland and the Marquis of Rockingham, and an array of officers:

> They all walked with their hats in their hands (in which were blue cockades, stamped in gold letters, KEPPEL) to Admiral Keppel's house, in High-street; after which, every merchant ship in the harbour, and at Spithead, gave a grand salute of nineteen guns each, the bells were set a ringing, and the evening concluded with bonfires, illuminations, guns firing, and other demonstrations of joy.
>
> A magnificent entertainment was prepared by the Captains of the western fleet, to which the Admiral, and the Members of the Court-Martial were invited; and yesterday, they gave a ball to the ladies. The streets were all illuminated, and an universal joy and festivity reigned amongst every rank of people.[6]

Figure 5.1. Anonymous, "The Fate of Palliser and Sandwich," etching (1779). BM 5537. Department of Prints and Drawings © Trustees of the British Museum.

The catalog of participants and events here are meant to invoke fashionable sociability: the Duke of Cumberland was a noted bon vivant, and the reporting on the ball is designed to convey civility. But in spite of the *Morning Chronicle*'s attempt to represent the aristocratic control over these highly choreographed events, they could not be dissociated from more violent forms of protest, especially in London. Palliser's effigy was attacked and burned in numerous towns, and in London a violent mob completely destroyed his house and eventually made moves on Lord Sandwich's residence. An anonymous celebratory print entitled "The Fate of Palliser and Sandwich" gives a clear indication of the tenor of these protests (fig. 5.1).[7] Similarly, opposition papers printed a vast array of attacks on Palliser just before and immediately after the acquittal, but these were simply a byway to the more damaging attacks on Sandwich that dominated the press and Parliament for the rest of February and much of March.

The *Morning Post* argued, in defense of the government, that the opposition had been and continued to be abetting both criminal and treasonous acts: "The wanton and cruel designs of faction in their late riots, have all been defeated by the prudence and temper of Administration; who, instead of devoting the hired mobs of opposition to the bayonet, which their employers anxiously hoped for, and expected, suffered rather the poor deluded rioters to enjoy their temporary frolic, knowing they must be convinced of their error on the return of reason."[8] In subsequent reporting, the same paper criminalized pro-Keppel celebration by tracking it through the "Bow Street Intelligence" and promulgated conspiracy theories alleging opposition treason. Significantly, this focused readers' attention on events in London, where the celebrations had proved more violent and more politicized than in the provinces. The allegations of abetting treason took the form of everything from poems such as the following "Extemporare, On the Late Illuminations" to complex denunciations of the predicament of government itself:

> Our Mob huzza!—with candles we must treat'em:
> The French huzza!—because we could not beat'em.
> Hail, noble Chief! Whose well-poised valour knows,
> To please at once thy *Country*,—and thy *Foes*.[9]

For one correspondent to the *Morning Post*, there was nothing the government could do that the opposition would not twist to its own ends, but the same author also recognized that "British Ministers ever [have] been more or less violent, as the spirit of the times hath been more or less depraved" and thereby argued that such depravity warranted suppression.[10]

With the *General Advertiser* actively promoting either celebration or demonstration and the *Morning Post* making the case for the criminalization of both the celebrants and their opposition supporters, the rest of the press navigated a middle ground that simultaneously applauded Keppel and denounced the rioting and William Parker, the editor of the *General Advertiser*, in particular. The *Morning Chronicle* is typical in this regard:

> Admiral Keppel's honourable acquittal is certainly in itself a matter highly satisfactory to every well-wisher of his country, but all who are not totally destitute of understanding, must confess that encouraging the mob to commit riots, and to exercise their licentious dispositions in defiance of law, decency, and even common humanity, is in the highest degree unwarrantable, and those who are instrumental in forwarding so bad a purpose, deserve the execration of the publick in general.[11]

By characterizing the more politicized acts of violence as a form of "patriotick phrenzy," the *Morning Chronicle* and other papers effectively drove a wedge between celebrants by deploying an all-too-familiar distinction between patricians and plebeians.[12] To all accounts, this was an effective containment strategy.[13] One could argue that the explosion of pleasure that swept across the land upon Keppel's acquittal is generated by the fulfillment of narrative desire, but to do so would be to suggest that, for at least some portion of the observing populace, Keppel's acquittal heralds the elimination of an aberrant administration. In this context, the violence of the mob, rather than simply being the outpouring of licentiousness, is an expression of God's will to harmonize the nation and the state after a period of misrule. Temporally, this releases Keppel and his public into a heavenly space somewhere in the future where the current conflict not only with America and France but also with Lord Sandwich and the government has been resolved. And that resolution is phantasmatically effected by a defeat of both the Whig "nation's" military combatants abroad and its political antagonists at home. It is a defeat that did not happen in fact, but whose very phantasmatic possibility allowed for a recuperation of Keppel and for the eventual ascendance of the Rockingham faction.

And we do not have to look too far to see this sentiment folded right into the forms of celebration that were not denounced by the press. After all, the choice of Handel's chorus "See the conquering hero comes" from *Judas Maccabaeus* is far from a neutral expression of national allegiance. I am going to be discussing the deployment of Handel's oratorio at length in chapter 6, but a brief discussion of its allegorization of both internal and external conflict is helpful for understanding the complexity of this performance of patriotism. *Judas Maccabaeus* was originally, and continued to be, understood as an allegory for George II's victory over the Jacobite Rebellion of 1745, but, as Ruth Smith has argued, it is an exceedingly complex and ambivalent expression of patriotism.[14] At the center of Thomas Morrell's libretto is the counterintuitive allegorical connection between the Maccabees story and the Jacobite Rebellion in Handel's oratorio. In order to understand the allegory, it is crucial to recognize that the Jacobite Rebellion was widely understood to be part of a larger French threat to English political and religious liberty. In this allegory, the Duke of Cumberland maps onto Judas, and the alliance between Scottish Jacobites and the French becomes comparable to that of the alliance between the Hellenized Jews and their Syrian rulers. So in its original context, *Judas Maccabaeus* allegorizes the Jacobite Rebellion in order to repudiate the larger threat of French aggression and to argue for the necessity of purging not only schism but also forms of political reform that threaten to make incursions on traditional notions of English political liberty. What becomes portable, therefore, in subsequent performances of the oratorio, is its ability to call forth the anxious specter of French aggression and the supposedly dire consequences of political apostasy or reform. And it is precisely this dramatization of disaster averted that fuels the oratorio's most patriotic moments.

In its deployment in the procession from the courthouse, "See the conquering hero comes" perfectly captures the anti-Gallic sentiments of virtually all of the observers, and the implicit critique of apostasy fits the opposition representation of the divisive nature of Palliser's charges. But the affiliated argument against reform is a particularly Whig bulwark against radical pro-American factions such as those abetted by the *General Advertiser*. In other words, this selection from *Judas Maccabaeus* allegorically attacks both Tory supporters of Sandwich, Palliser, and the Ministry and radical constituencies that want to use the Keppel trial to further their reformist agenda. It is doing battle on two fronts in order to consolidate Whig resistance to threats from both the Ministry and from the radical forces of street politics. As Roger has demonstrated, this has the important political effect of placing Whig objectives and desires in an ostensibly moderate middle position, and thus this kind of construction is crucial to the legitimation of the Rockingham critique of both the Ministry and the more rebellious pro-American factions in London.[15]

Despite the claims of his Whig supporters, Keppel's acquittal in January 1779 did not resolve the problem of disunity in the Royal Navy; if anything, the raucous celebrations pushed the supporters of the Ministry into more firmly entrenched positions. Admiral George Bridges Rodney's defeat of the Spanish fleet under Don Juan de Langara off Cape St. Vincent in 1780 was the first major naval victory after the Keppel-Palliser affair and should have been the object of illumination and mass celebration—especially because the unexpected capture of the Spanish fleet was evidence of a crisis averted. But Rodney's victories in 1780 generated little in the way of crowd response, except among supporters of the Admiralty and the Ministry. However, they did provide the occasion for a scathing critique of past celebrations, particularly those associated with Keppel's acquittal. Indeed, everything about the circulation of Rodney's victory in the public imagination was in dialogue with Keppel's enigmatic engagement with the French fleet in the summer of 1778.

This chapter explores the relationship between topicality and patriotic celebration in order to understand Hannah Cowley's innovative response to the problem of patriotic masculinity in this era. I consider one night at the theatre when a performance of Hannah Cowley's *The Belle's Stratagem* was interrupted by celebrants of Rodney's victory. Both the mainpiece and the afterpiece were modified to speak directly both to the king and queen, who were in attendance, and to an unspecified crowd that burst into the theatre during Cowley's play.

Thus, this performance offers an occasion to explore the power of topicality to mediate between the theatrical and the political world. What I hope to demonstrate is that analysis of this single performance opens new avenues for considering important plays both from the final phase of the war and from the period in the 1780s when Britain was reimagining its place in the Atlantic imperium. I offer a brief reading of Cowley's remediation of *The Belle's Stratagem* in her remarkable comedy *Which Is the Man?* in order to bring the question of its title to bear on the general sense of defeat following the fall of Yorktown in the autumn of 1781. And I conclude this chapter with a more extensive analysis of the kind of imperial future projected by George Colman's *Inkle and Yarico* by attending to the spectral presence of Admiral Rodney in the reconsolidation of masculinity in the postwar years.

Strategic Interruptions, or the Power of the Present
The Sky at Night

With some sense of how the opposition deployed the Keppel court-martial in its attack on the Ministry, the following occasional verse from the *Morning Post* for 2 March 1780 offers an important counternarrative in which the sky speaks, this time on behalf of the Ministry:

> Occasioned by the strong AURORA BOREALIS that appeared on Tuesday night
>
> EPIGRAM
>
> WHEN KEPPEL triumph'd, alias *ran away*,
> What fires were kindled for that noble day!
> When *Spain* is crushed, there's not a single blaze!
> 'Tis well—our citizens know when to praise;
> I view their sottishness without a sigh,
> For Heav'n, more just—*illuminates the* SKY![16]

The poet here is speaking of Admiral Rodney's victory at Cape St. Vincent on 16 January 1780, which had been first reported on 26 February, and which had received a full Gazette Extraordinary on 29 February.[17] As the poem indicates, news of Rodney's defeat of Don Langara was met with muted response in London. Parliament did not confer honors on the admiral, and illumination was sparse. That in itself was curious because the fate of Gibraltar, which was weathering one of the most vicious sieges in British military history, was in the balance.

Without Rodney's relief, Britain would have lost Gibraltar to the combined forces of France and Spain and, with it, access to the Mediterranean.[18]

Into this celebratory vacuum, one poet took it upon himself to thank Rodney and indict Keppel yet again:

> RODNEY we thank thee, and altho' too brave,
> You shunn'd no shore, and fear'd no angry wave
> Altho' not waiting for the coming light,
> You fought it *handsomely* that very night;
> Tho' no fat citizen should yield you praise,
> No senate thank, no flattering window blaze;
> Unenvying leave, secure of endless fame
> To KEPPEL, and his friends their burning *shame*![19]

By citing the phrase "handsomely" from Keppel's dispatch, the poet demonstrates that nothing at this stage in the war escaped factionalization.[20] As the poem suggests, the general lack of illumination—the traditional mode of celebration for naval victory—was even more palpable in light of the extraordinary celebrations for Keppel's acquittal, and the anti-Whig *Morning Post* was quick to interpret the contradiction as a sign of a social pathology:

> To the People.
>
> Friends and Fellow Citizens,
>
> You have now a glorious opportunity to celebrate the praise of your brave Admiral Sir George Rodney, who has obtained a signal victory over the Spanish fleet. You have lately thrown the city of London into a blaze for victories *lost*, surely then you cannot refuse the honours due to victories *won*. . . . Having thus far but superficially treated on this subject, I shall now tell you very plainly, that Sir George's behaviour exacts a very particular notice at this time from you; for between faction, luxury, timidity, your country is brought to so low an ebb, that you are not only the scorn of nations from the British spirit being lulled into a lethargy, but are on the eve of being victimized among yourselves, by your open public divisions, and private animosities. For many years you have boasted of being rulers of the seas; but within a short time behold how you have fallen. . . . till now that Sir George Rodney has rescued the British flag from infamy.[21]

The inability of the public to distinguish between "victories *lost*" and "victories *won*" is presented as a symptom of national lethargy, and all the familiar themes from the Keppel-Palliser affair are reengaged. Most importantly, the correspondent to the paper emphasizes that Britons are "on the eve of being victimized by yourselves," thus arguing that Whig critiques of the Ministry and the Admiralty during and after the Keppel trial and the lack of public support for Rodney betray a lack of true patriotism.

The next day, the same paper pushed the attack even further by using Rodney's victory and the muted celebrations as a salutary contrast to the Mischianza's celebration of Howe's dubious achievements. The anonymous correspondent takes the reader to a moment just after Rodney's smaller victory over the Spanish at Cape Finisterre on 8 January, but before his decisive battle with Don Langara on 16 January. Rodney's orders were for the Caribbean, but on the way he was ordered to relieve Gibraltar. His two engagements near the mouth of the Mediterranean were thus vital to the British resistance during the great siege of Gibraltar and preliminary to future engagement in West Indian waters. The correspondent is being quite specific about timing in order to emphasize not only the prematurity of the Mischianza but also the fact that the public has still not adequately commemorated Rodney's recent victory:

> Mr. Editor,
> I most heartily rejoice in Admiral Rodney's success; and think he has given us the best Gazette of any we have read since the commencement of the rebellion. But suppose that Sir G. Rodney, at his arrival at Gibraltar, on the credit of his having with eighteen ships, beat a squadron of eleven, had instituted for himself or got his Officers to institute for him, a *triumph*; in which, after decorating his ships, and manning all his shrouds, he had landed under the salute of cannon, and marched with all his officers in solemn procession, along a grand avenue formed by all the colours of the King's regiments, and lined with all the troops of the garrison, through two triumphal arches, adorned with all kinds of naval trophies;—a *Neptune* standing on top of one, and a *Fame* on the other, holding out from her trumpet, in letters of light, *Thy laurels are immortal*, should we not be justly concerned, that so much merit should be disgraced by such a spectacle of vanity and folly, and wonder how a man of common sense could have been led into it? Yet all this farce of a triumph, and ten times more, was [acted] by the *two* HOWES at Philadelphia, in honour of themselves, without their having done any thing for the real service of their country.
> Yours, &c. A.B.[22]

For this critic, something was amiss in both the content and the timing of the Mischianza: the celebration of victory lost had eclipsed the celebration of victory won, and thus his remarks resonate with the attack on the Keppel celebrations. This is important because, as I have already argued, both the Mischianza and the Keppel celebrations constitute critiques of the Ministry's prosecution of the war. In the former case, John André was subtly deploying the tropes of aristocratic sociability to suggest that Howe was being recalled too soon and that the entire approach to the rebellion was far too bellicose. In the latter case, Keppel's supporters were anything but subtle in their critique of the Admiralty. Taking their case to the streets, opposition constituencies marked their sympathy with the American cause. In a complex act of counterperformance, the Whigs presented themselves, through processions and through oratory, as a middle road between the Tories and those who would recognize not only American sovereignty abroad but also an expansion of the franchise at home.[23]

Rodney's victory over the Spanish at Cape St. Vincent, therefore, allowed conservative voices in the *Morning Post* to link together seemingly disparate events as signs of a social pathology at variance with both the interests of the nation and the dictates of providential election. According to the previously quoted epigram, the "sottishness" of those who celebrated Keppel, but ignored Rodney, implies a kind of affective disorder in which the ability to make true value judgments is impaired. This undermines the task of government, and the speaker of the epigram takes solace in the fact that heaven recognizes Rodney's valor as evidenced by the aurora borealis on the evening of 29 February.

29 February 1780

It is to that night that I now wish to turn in earnest. That evening a theatregoer was presented with two options. Drury Lane was reviving *A Maid of the Oaks* after a three-year absence from the stage with Fanny Abington as Lady Bab Lardoon. Sheridan paired the play with *The Critic,* and thus the audience would have been subject to an essay of sorts on the manipulation of public opinion in the papers. The most famous scenes in both the mainpiece and the afterpiece involve detailed critiques of how the newspapers work both sides of a story to generate both private and public scandal. If Lady Bab and Puff offer mutually supporting sites for media archaeology, it is important to recognize that the plays' patriotic gestures are often at cross-purposes. As we have seen, *The Critic* is in many ways an attack on the kind of patriotic prophecy staged in plays that have their roots in Burgoyne's spectacle of nativist election. One way of reading this particular pairing of mainpiece and afterpiece is to suggest that Sheridan was actively deploying his own play to undermine the ostensible patriotism of

Burgoyne's now obsolete generic hybrid and was thus contributing to the public attack on Burgoyne that was still raging in Parliament and the press in the aftermath of Saratoga.

Or Sheridan was simply mobilizing his biggest moneymakers—Fanny Abington was sure to generate receipts, and *The Critic* was one of the most successful plays of the era—in order to counter the theatrical juggernaut currently running at Covent Garden: Hannah Cowley's *The Belle's Stratagem*. As Russell points out, Drury Lane was running as many of Fanny Abington's "Fine Lady" roles as possible all through the month of February 1780 in order to compete with the success of Cowley's comedy.[24] With Sheridan's election to Parliament as the member for Stafford in 1780, Hannah Cowley became the most significant writer of comedy for the remainder of the war. With a string of hits from *The Belle's Stratagem* (1780) to *Which is the Man?* (1782) to *A Bold Stroke for a Husband* (1783), her plays were in almost constant performance in this period. Her critical and commercial success bears comparison to Sheridan's own cluster of great comedies from *The Rivals* (1775) to *The School for Scandal* (1777) to *The Critic* (1779). And yet it is only recently that we are beginning to comprehend her stature. That stature was never lost on her contemporaries: the reviews of her plays are among the most favorable in the century, and her plays had a mass audience. Cowley's comedies of the latter years of the American war not only engaged with the crisis enveloping the empire in innovative ways but also offered an important set of criteria for imagining postwar sociability and subjectivity.

Hannah Cowley's *The Belle's Stratagem* opened on 22 February 1780 to great acclaim, four days before the first news of Rodney's victory at Cape St. Vincent and seven days before the night of the aurora borealis.[25] That night is significant not only because their Royal Majesties commanded a performance of *The Belle's Stratagem* with Arthur Murphy's *The Upholsterer* but also because the show was interrupted by one of the only recorded instances of celebration for Rodney's victory.[26] In short, it is an evening when the world outside the theatre permeated the world within, and the complex amalgam of sociability and representation bears close scrutiny. Here is the *Gazetteer*'s account of the interruption:

> The universal joy with which the public received the news of Admiral Rodney's victory, with the material additions which appeared in the Gazette Extraordinary, was particularly conspicuous at Covent Garden theatre on Monday evening, in the presence of their Majesties: Mr. Quick, in the new comedy, amongst other instances of his prescience, affirmed,

> agreeable to the humourous stile of his character, that he had *foreseen*, if Admiral Rodney came up with the Spanish fleet he would play the devil with them. This was received with tumults of applause, in clapping and huzzaing, with mingled cries of distress from those who had rushed into the theatre, though the croud without-doors was still more numerous than those within. At the conclusion of the act the audience called for Rule Britannia, which was immediately played. Their Majesties and the royal children appeared to be particularly delighted with the scene; and our amiable Queen seemed hardly able to restrain herself from joining in the chorus. The event of Prince William's receiving the sword from the Spanish Admiral was mentioned by Mr. Lee Lewes, in the character of Razor in the Upholsterer, and received with equal warmth.[27]

Perhaps the most important aspect of this passage is its equal interest in what happens on and in front of the stage. By recording how the entire house was infused with the joy attending Rodney's victory, the paper provides a brief glimpse of the political possibility of the present moment of performance.

The first clause of the passage asserts something that by now should be clear about theatrical experience itself in this period: namely, that the play is put on by and for readers of the daily papers. In this regard, the *Gazetteer* is extremely precise because it specifies that the "joy" felt among the audience arose from the news of victory and was heightened by the publication of the Gazette Extraordinary, which gave the specifics of the battle, earlier that day. Aside from firmly locating the source of topical knowledge and acknowledging its ubiquity among the spectators, this detail also reminds us of the degree to which *The Belle's Stratagem* itself deals with the circulation of information in the print media. In fact, much of the play's first scene involves the rake Courtall imparting the "news" to Saville—"the representative of noble old English manners"[28]—and he immediately declares that it would fill three Gazettes.[29] While Saville is clearly looking for political and business news, Courtall condenses the society news into a tight whorl of scandal and insinuation that resembles nothing more than the *Morning Post*. The second scene goes further to recognize how the papers influence private reputation by unleashing Crowquill, a correspondent for something like the *Town and Country*, and clearly reminiscent of Snake in *A School for Scandal* or even Pamphlet in *The Upholsterer*, on Doricourt, who has just returned from the Continent, who, much like Dupeley in *The Maid of the Oaks*, is fascinated by foreign manners and beauty. By staging Crowquill's offer to buy gossip about Doricourt or his associates, Cowley, no less than Sheridan or Burgoyne, thematizes the perilous relationship between commerce, truth, and reputation in the daily and monthly press.

These details help us to establish what is arguably the most important quality of *The Belle's Stratagem.* It is a play resolutely about the present that is constructed from recognizable precursor scripts. Its strict adherence to the present moment is encoded directly into the sets themselves. The set paintings of Lincoln's Inn in act 1, the auction room in act 3, and, above all, the Pantheon in act 4 were all praised for their verisimilitude. In fact, the last-named was deemed too accurate by some observers: "The Pantheon is a very fine scene though it partakes too much of that cold and correct air, inseparable from so regular a building, and is by no means so well adapted to give the joyous sensations of a scene illuminated in a more familiar stile."[30]

The critic here is arguing that the attempt to replicate the Pantheon was doomed to fail and thus becomes a distraction.[31] That distraction should give us pause because the impetus to document the present pleasures of the metropolis operates in tension with the pleasure of afforded by the play's reworking of its famous precursors in the field of comedy. As its title announces, it is based on George Farquhar's *The Beaux's Stratagem*; its primary plot device—the stratagem—is adapted from *She Stoops to Conquer*; and it replicates characters and situations from *The School for Scandal* and *The Maid of the Oaks.* As Lisa Freeman and others have argued, this means, at the very least, that audiences for Cowley's plays were continually negotiating the history of English comedy itself.[32] And, as Erin Isikoff has argued, this negotiation is crucial for Cowley's particular style of intervention in the public sphere.[33] In her overview of the play, Russell states, "From its outset, . . . *The Belle's Stratagem* signals that it is concerned with the same social phenomena as *The School for Scandal*—the expansion and feminization of public culture, particularly through print, and the implications of this for the institutions of marriage, the family and the state—and that it will be exploring these topics through a remediation or remaking of the tropes situations and character types of Sheridan's comedy."[34] Put simply, Sheridan's comedies work primarily in the zone of critique, and they are aimed at the excesses of gender performance associated with the fashionable world. Cowley takes many of Sheridan's situations and reorients them to generate affirmative possibilities. As Russell, Kowaleski-Wallace, and Anderson argue, these affirmations are clearly aimed at opening up potential spaces for women's agency in the public sphere, and for that reason Cowley's plays represent the very sites of cultural opprobrium—the masquerade and the rout—as zones of sociability where women can modify the gender roles ascribed to them.[35]

Recent scholarship has done much to further our understanding of how Cowley's work contributes to the debates surrounding women's roles in the public sphere, but far less attention has been paid to the men in her plays. Anderson carefully documents the progress of Cowley's nationalism across the full panoply of her plays, and, as she demonstrates, national character is essential to the erotic economy on stage. After all, Letitia Hardy's stratagem is aimed at correcting the fashionable Doricourt's taste for foreign women; thus the play's most patriotic moments, like those of *The Maid of the Oaks*, are all enacted in the realm of eros. What is fascinating is that Cowley, in *The Belle's Stratagem*, deploys masquerade as a site for exploring specifically nonpatriotic identities. In act 4, Letitia not only condenses exotic French and Italian femininity in her performance as the Incognita but also indicates that, in order to clinch the desire of her beloved,

> then, I'd be any thing—and all!—Grave, gay, capricious—the soul of whim, the spirit of variety—live with him in the eye of fashion, or in the shade of retirement—change my country, my sex,—feast with him in an Esquimaux hut, or a Persian pavilion—join him in the victorious war-dance on the borders of Lake Ontario, or sleep to the soft breathings of the flute in the cinnamon groves of Ceylon—dig with him in the mines of Golconda, or enter the dangerous precincts of the Mogul's Seraglio—cheat him of his wishes, and overturn his empire to restore the Husband of my Heart to the blessings of Liberty and Love. (4.1.59)

Beth Kowaleski-Wallace has read this passage as an important expression of late eighteenth-century cosmopolitanism, and it would seem to presage a great deal about the performativity of late eighteenth-century subjectivity. But it is important to recognize first that Letitia's stratagem and the putative malleability of her personality are persuasive devices aimed at forcing Doricourt, and, by extension, Letitia to choose true English femininity. In other words, by demonstrating that she is both willing and able to be "any thing," Letitia separates herself from the very "things" she replicates. That these things are all on the periphery of the empire and in each case under dubious control—raising Pontiac's rebellion and the least secure Indian holdings is hardly comforting—should not go unnoticed, because when we get to the final act and Letitia restages this offer to be "any thing," suddenly the question of secure ownership becomes paramount.

Because of her prior assertion that she would adopt any manner of alterity, the revelation in act 5 that Letitia and the Incognita are one and the same forces the audience to consider the relationship between nation and empire in extraordinarily intimate terms. And it also turns the entire problem of self-other relations into a question of choice:

LET: You see I *can* be any thing; chuse then my character—your Taste shall fix it. Shall I be an *English* Wife?—or, breaking from the bonds of Nature and Education, step forth to the world in all the captivating glare of Foreign Manners?

DOR: You shall be nothing but yourself—nothing can be captivating that you are not. I will not wrong your penetration, by pretending that you won my heart at the first interview; but you have now my whole soul—your person, your face, your mind, I would not exchange for those of any other Woman breathing. (5.5.81)

Letitia accrues erotic value, first, by performing otherness in the dress of the Incognita and, then, by declaring that she will go further and cross the social, cultural, and racial distinctions that distinguish Britons from their colonial subjects. But strangely it is precisely this capacity to perform as the other that will "restore the Husband of my Heart to the blessings of Liberty and Love" (4.1.59). Her value lies not simply in the capacity for exotic performance, but rather in her capacity to restore agency to her lover. When Letitia asks Doricourt to choose her identity and he decides that he will attach himself to an English wife, he opts for an identity that subsumes all others. Because she can be "any thing," she is now valuable to him as English. This is why he expresses his desire in such curiously negative terms: "You shall be nothing but yourself—nothing can be captivating that you are not." In terms of national identity, this statement allegorically resolves the divergent meanings of imperium itself. As Pocock has argued, the distinction between empire as defined by the borders of the kingdom and that defined by the reach of British power across the globe was the source of recurrent anxiety throughout the century.[36] Although here rendered in terms of love, Cowley's solution to the problem is as elegant as it is timely: the future of desire lies in the acquisition of the commodity that can be all commodities. The English wife is the global feminine, and Doricourt accedes to the position of possessing all. The only way for that to work is for the empire to be subsumed into the national self. It is at once a Whig fantasy of the propagation of Liberty and a Tory fantasy of national election. One could argue further that both are species of retroactive anticipation in which the present moment is linked to the era of British imperialism after 1759. As we will see, this resonates with the selection of the afterpiece for this night at the theatre.

What this reading of the stratagem and its resolution suggests is that Cowley's play is already deeply involved in the debates surrounding the American war. But her focus is less on the prosecution of the war than on the mutually constitutive relationship between styles of sociability in the metropole and visions of the imperium that might support them. As Russell concludes, "By invoking the specific contexts of the Pantheon and the cosmopolitanism associated with it, Cowley is also able to amplify this fantasy in terms of a discourse of empire, locating the masquerade woman, and implicitly fashionable sociability, as emblematic of imperialism's imaginative energies and outreach. As such, she counters representations of fashion and luxury as signs of imperial decadence."[37]

This is why the interruption of *The Belle's Stratagem* on the evening of 29 March is so important, because suddenly a play, which allegorized the complexities of imperial rule in terms of erotic value, was directly addressing specific events and people. Now this intervention was no doubt in the hands of the players themselves, but their choice of how this intervention should be staged is startling. The first direct discussion of Rodney's victory is also the first key moment in the Masquerade scene. After a brief encounter between unnamed Masks and a Mountebank, which establishes that the Masquerade can be a place where one speaks truth to power, act 4, scene 1, opens with the play's most explicitly patriotic and topical speech:

Enter Hardy, in the Dress of Isaac Mendoza

HARDY: Why, isn't it a shame to see so many stout well-built Young Fellows, masquerading, and cutting *Couranta's* here at home—instead of making the French cut capers to the tune of your Cannon—or sweating the Spaniards with an English *Fandango?*—I foresee the end of all this. (4.1.50)

This scene was one of the most famous in the play, and this is the place where John Quick would most likely have inserted Hardy's prophecy regarding Rodney's victory over Langara.[38] According to the *Gazetteer,* Hardy's prophecy generated "tumults of applause, in clapping and huzzaing."[39] With a crowd primed by the Gazette Extraordinary earlier that day, perhaps the mere mention of Rodney was enough to set off the audience. But there is something deeply unsettling here. Hardy's character, in the words of one reviewer, "is drawn a very whimsical and comic assemblage of short-sightedness and imaginary foresight."[40] Hardy is a false prophet, rarely able to see what is before him; thus his prescience regarding Rodney, if judged by his other predictions, should be in error.

To complicate matters further, Hardy is speaking in the guise of Isaac Mendoza, a role that Quick had made his own in Sheridan's *The Duenna*. So we have an elaborate metatheatrical joke in which a character from Sheridan's comic opera speaks in the masquerade of Cowley's comedy. The joke is made possible by the casting of Quick in the part, and I think there is much to be made of his performance here. As noted previously, if this particular speech was simply spoken by Hardy, it would be mired in error and thus would signify the opposite of what it suggests: namely, that the men at this masquerade would be incapable of vanquishing their foes and that Rodney would not succeed against the Spanish fleet. But in the guise of Mendoza, Hardy makes an unabashed call for "Young Fellows" to give up social pleasures in favor of martial endeavors and then predicts their success by declaring what everyone already knows, that Rodney has been victorious. In other words, the stability of both Hardy's patriotic invocation and his encomium to Rodney relies on the adoption of the Jewish dress and mannerisms of a character from Cowley's competitor's play.

Before addressing what it means for a Jew to express patriotic prescience, we need to consider what it means for Cowley to bring Sheridan back to the stage in this remediated form. In *The School for Scandal* and *The Camp*, Sheridan had aligned the excesses of aristocratic sociability with the poor showing of Britain in the American war. Thus, to have one of his characters suddenly turn up at a masquerade in the Pantheon ventriloquizing his own position is ironic enough. It implies that only at a masquerade will the truth of Sheridan's critique be expressed. Furthermore, during the Keppel-Palliser affair, he was among the most conspicuous of Keppel's advocates. At this point, Sheridan is in Parliament, a Whig critic of both North's Ministry and the Admiralty, and as such he voted against conferring special honors for Rodney. Thus, he is one of the politicians under attack by the *Morning Post* and, I would argue, by the cast of *The Belle's Stratagem* on the evening in question. The full power of that attack relies on a recognition of what it means for Quick to be performing as Mendoza. As many critics of *The Duenna* have recognized, Mendoza practices a style of foresight all of his own. In his actions, he consistently brings about the opposite of what he intends, and in his speeches, he reveals to the audience a future about which he is completely unaware.[41] As Charles Dibdin notes, "Shewing beforehand how clearly he shall himself be taken in by his different attempts to deceive others, is the most artful species of anticipation that ever was practised, and shews a judgement of theatrical effect powerful, new and extraordinary."[42]

So what does it mean for the expression of patriotic sentiment and the certainty of victory to be coming from someone the audience associates with ironic self-entrapment? I would simply suggest that Hardy's tendency toward false prophecy is replaced by Mendoza's propensity to reveal unwittingly the true future that he does not understand. The species of anticipation, when deployed by Cowley in *The Belle's Stratagem* allows her to lampoon Sheridan's theatrical critique of aristocratic sociability. The addition of new lines by Quick prophesying what the audience already knew to have happened was a way to attack Sheridan and, by extension, his friends' critique of the Ministry and Admiralty. The sophistication of the temporal game is notable: it is not only anticipation itself as a theatrical and political device that is being deployed in such effective ways but also the patriotic desire for a future already known that is enacted here.

This helps to explain the divided response to Quick's intervention, for, as the *Gazetteer* notes, the applause was accompanied by "mingled cries of distress from those who had rushed into the theatre, though the croud without-doors was still more numerous than those within."[43] It is a shame that we cannot give a more detailed account of this distressed crowd; the papers are silent on any kind of demonstration or street celebration in the environs of Covent Garden. What interests me is that this encounter between the world outside and the world within the theatre coincides with Quick's intervention, which in itself blends the theatrical and the extratheatrical in such a way that the cascade of theatrical reception trumps the world of politics. Or, to be even more biting, theatrical Sheridan is momentarily staged to attack Sheridan and his political associates. That this all results in momentary victory for Cowley, Covent Garden, and supporters of the Ministry is perhaps best indicated by the fact that the entire masquerade scene, the play's most theatrical moment, is supplemented by a call for "Rule Britannia," which was immediately played and sung, by among others, the queen.[44] There is nothing special about such a call or such a response, but the timing is significant. Quick's remark comes at the inception of the masquerade, but "Rule Britannia" is called for at the masquerade's close not at the moment in act 5 when Doricourt declares that Letitia will be an English wife, nor at the moment when the play ends and Doricourt rejects "*foreign Graces*" in favor of "the Grace of [English] Modesty" (5.5.82). This implies that it is not simply the reference to Rodney, or the implicit lampooning of Sheridan, that prompts patriotic demonstration, but rather the enactment of the masquerade scene itself. Furthermore, this substantiates Russell's claim, and my expansion on it, that Cowley's play counters representations of fashion and luxury as signs of imperial decadence by making specific scenes of fashionable sociability "emblematic of imperialism's imaginative energies and outreach."[45] Quick's supplementation of Cowley's script pushes the argument one step further by suggesting that Cowley's style of comedy and specifically her remediation of Sheridan have the capacity to sublate political and theatrical adversaries to such a degree that they can restore "Liberty" in its time of crisis.

We have seen this sublation before. It is effectively the same gesture that gives the "Epigram Occasioned by the strong AURORA BOREALIS that appeared on Tuesday night" its rhetorical force, only in that case it was God who remediates the illuminations of the Keppel celebration into a natural expression of approbation for Rodney. And the less-than-subtle transition from artificial illumination to the natural heavenly glow of the aurora borealis has its counterpart in the highly complex shift from theatrical utterance to political performance when Quick supplements Cowley's lines. Suddenly, Cowley's performative struggle with Sheridan, which turns on competing forms of futurity and irony, transforms into a political act whose force lies in the fact that the future has momentarily come true in this room in the present.

Staging a Gazette Extraordinary

And yet, as the *Gazetteer* and the players themselves recognize, that present is thoroughly the construct of a mediated past whose "reality" lies in the material fact of the publication of the Gazette Extraordinary that morning. As noted earlier, *The Belle's Stratagem* is deeply concerned with remediation both in print and in the theatre, but on this particular evening at Covent Garden, by command of their Royal Majesties, this issue was heightened more than usual because the afterpiece was Arthur Murphy's *The Upholsterer.* As discussed in the introduction, Murphy's farce is about a pathological relation to the news and specifically news arising from the early anxious moments of the Seven Years' War. Its main character, Quidnunc the Upholsterer, goes bankrupt because he is obsessed by political rumor and gossip pertaining to the fate of British actions on the Continent, in India at Chandernagore, and in North America. Quidnunc's obsession is abetted by Razor the barber and Pamphlet the hack journalist, but he is saved by his long lost son Rovewell, who pays down his father's debts and arranges for his friend Bellmour to marry the upholsterer's daughter. Significantly, Murphy's play postulates a form of retirement where one could simply pursue the news, without any economic and social obligations. When the play was revived, it was generally to satirize the excessive influence of the daily press, and thus the details of Razor's reports would be changed to fit the present moment. The performance of *The Upholsterer* on the night of 29 February 1780 was no different, for Mr. Lee Lewes, who had played the foppish Flutter in the mainpiece, in the role of Razor narrated "the event of Prince William's receiving the sword from the Spanish Admiral."[46]

The important thing about this move on Lee Lewes's part is that the news being reported, namely the conferral of Don Langara's sword to Prince William, which had been printed in the Gazette Extraordinary that morning, is fundamentally different from the kind of information passed on by Razor in Murphy's play. Everything Razor imparts to Quidnunc is hearsay, and all of it suggests that the papists will get the better of Protestant Britain in the Seven Years' War. This is because Razor suffers from a kind of pathological patriotism in which he is always imagining "Dear Old England" suffering at the hands of the House of Bourbon, and he is likewise certain of its demise: "Luxury will be the ruin of us all."[47] He is hardly a reliable messenger of news of naval victory, and yet this is precisely who is called on to narrate the formal sign of Spanish defeat of Cape St. Vincent.

Again it may be that simply any reference to Rodney's victory would generate applause, but this is a play in which the West Indies figures quite prominently. At this point, it is important to remember that Rodney was en route to the West Indies when he received orders to relieve Gibraltar. His victory over the Spanish is inextricably tied to British naval operations in the Caribbean. Quidnunc's son Rovewell has made his fortune as a planter. His return renders his father's financial embarrassments moot, and he persuades Quidnunc to give his daughter to Bellmour. In other words, the play's economic and sexual complications are resolved by the injection of capital from the West Indies and by a strong assertion of the familial connection between colony and metropole. Significantly, the revelation of this stabilizing colonial influence is figured in terms of masquerade:

> QUID: Why, you have my blessing Boy, I am heartily glad to see thee—I did not know you again, you're in such a Kind of Disguise—mayhap now, you can tell—why you look very well—I'm glad to see thee, *Jack*, I am indeed—pray now—mayhap, I say, you can tell what the *Spaniards* are doing in the Bay of *Honduras*? (2.4.48)

Like Letitia in *The Belle's Stratagem*, Rovewell is disguised as himself, for he is both Planter and Englishman, protector of the father and the father's son, foreigner and family. In the context of its performance in February 1780, Rovewell's stabilizing influence, with its implicit assertion of the security of the relation between Britain and its colonial holdings in the Caribbean, amounts to wishful thinking. But it is a fantasy of stability firmly linked to a past pattern of initial setback and final victory over the French and Spanish in North America and the West Indies twenty years earlier.

It is difficult to overlook the topicality of Quidnunc's speeches in this context. The audience, like Quidnunc, had been scouring the papers in the days prior to discover how the Spaniards were doing at sea. By the time they were watching this play, they were well aware that Gibraltar had been relieved, an outcome vital not only to the security of the British Isles but also to the Caribbean theatre of the war. Rodney's victory ensured that naval operations in the Caribbean, which would play a crucial part in the closing phases of the war, would focus on the French. Rovewell keeps putting Quidnunc off and will not answer questions such as "How many ships of the Line has the Admiral with him" (2.4.48), and thus the question of the Caribbean is forestalled to a point after the events of the play, when Quidnunc will retire into a state where he does nothing but contemplate the news. This is because it is crucially the future of the war currently being fought. By staging *The Upholsterer* on this day, a different kind of prophecy from either Hardy or Mendoza's is put into gear: one that asserts naval supremacy over the Spaniards in the present, which retroactively looks back to a moment of uncertainty after the execution of Admiral Byng when the Royal Navy was about to assert its dominance, and, I would argue, which optimistically looks forward to that which cannot yet be declared, namely a new era of naval supremacy in the Caribbean.

So why not have Rovewell celebrate Rodney's victory and narrate the conferral of Don Langara's sword to Prince William? The answer has to do first with the politics of anticipation. If this declaration is made by Rovewell, the play is less able to activate the anxiety that it will then later quell. The news of Rodney's victory needs to be separated from the resolution of the marriage plot and the cancellation of Quidnunc's debts. Fortunately, the play's other business—namely, Quidnunc's interactions with Razor and Pamphlet—provide ample opportunity for a different kind of intervention. The players opted for a strategy based on the politics of mediation that this chapter has been at pains to argue is integral to this period of theatre history. By having Razor speak the news, Murphy's critique of mediation comes to the fore, except it is turned inside out. Rather than being a force eating away at the vigor of the nation, the papers, through their mediation of the news, are able to consolidate national character. But where and how this consolidation takes place is crucial. My sense is that when Lee Lewes stands before the audience and relates the events from that day's Gazette Extraordinary in the character of the pathological patriot, an identificatory mechanism is activated that temporarily supersedes the claims of faction. For audience members critical of the Ministry, he embodies the man concerned with "Dear Old England"; for audience members loyal to the Ministry, he is a source of solid information vindicating the prosecution of the war. What is crucial is that Razor's obsession is tied to that of his audience not by anything he does or expresses, but rather by the fact that the audience itself had a preexisting affective relation to Rodney's victory, which has its source in the print media.

The players at Covent Garden, on the evening of the aurora borealis, were able to supplement two scripts already attentive to the power of remediation in such a way as to focus the specific patriotic emotions already generated by the press. Razor's mania for England is shared by the audience because of its mania for reading, but significantly its expression lives and dies in the performative moment where the audience recognizes its shared emotional investment in the news. The moment of performance is a nodal link that demonstrates a cohesiveness that could only ever be fleeting in print. It is here that the medial distinction between print and performance is most acute: the latter can momentarily counteract the atomizing qualities of the former, but the very autoethnographic qualities that these plays are exploring rely on the information made accessible by commercial print culture. The night of 29 February 1780 offers a particularly charged example of the recursive loop linking the present moment of political performance and representation's historicality, and the reason why such moments of performance are recurrently necessary. They are the aesthetic moments where the public can feel, not just postulate, its cohesion.

Venus and Mars, or Our Future Needs

The Belle's Stratagem is a play in which the future of the empire is allegorized as a question about desire. For Doricourt, the central question he must resolve is, "Which is the woman?" As we have seen, that question turns out to be highly complex not only because Cowley's dramaturgical practice is so citational but also because the play is so attentive to the performance of subjectivity. The question, "Which is the woman?" provokes anxiety, and hence comic interest, because the object of Doricourt's desire has the capacity to be "any thing." That anxiety is staged in order for it to be subsumed into a fantasy of English femininity capable of sublating all difference into itself—in short, a phantasmatic construct that allows Doricourt to have everything by owning just this one thing: Englishness. In the winter of 1780, the resolution of the anxiety at the heart of the question can serve, as Russell argues, as a ground for optimism.

One year later, when Cowley staged the cognate question *Which is the Man?*, all such optimism was gone. Cowley's comedy opened at Covent Garden on 9 February 1782 shortly after news of the fall of Yorktown reached London. In a series of disastrous strategic decisions, the British military lost the advantage gained by its capture of Charleston by attempting to cut off the Continental army in Virginia. Rear Admiral Sir Thomas Graves's strategic loss to the French at the Battle of the Chesapeake in early September 1781 meant that Cornwallis's troops at Yorktown were effectively stranded. The British surrendered more than five thousand troops to the combined American and French forces on 19 October 1781. Britain would pursue no further significant military activity in the thirteen colonies, and the war was effectively lost. All that remained was the repulsion of now imminent threats to British holdings in the Caribbean. North's Ministry fell, and all attention was focused on achieving the least disadvantageous peace terms not only with the Americans but also with the French and the Spanish. In this section of the chapter, I want to briefly look at why Cowley chose to present her encomium to British military masculinity at the height of its abjection. As critics recognized at the time, Cowley's comedy was a remediation of *The Belle's Stratagem*, and thus she was bringing her citational practice to bear on her own work. The *London Courant* called her heroine, Lady Bell Bloomer, the "second part of Miss Hardy."[48] What I want to suggest is that by reactivating the character types and situations from *The Belle's Stratagem*, Cowley was not only offering an autocritique of wishful thinking but also sketching a new path for the consolidation of masculinity for the postwar years.

Misty Anderson's authoritative reading of the play carefully demonstrates that "the economic and ideological implications of this post-revolutionary but not yet postwar moment fracture Cowley's nationalism."[49] Anderson is very attentive to how the play continually points to the preferable treatment of women in France and argues that the play's marriages fail to resolve the societal tensions they allegorize. I concur with this reading but want to pursue the question posed by the title further. *Which is the Man?* is explicitly aimed at parsing martial from foppish masculinity. As the *London Courant* emphasized, the play's ostensible hero, Lord Sparkle, was "Lord Foppington modernized."[50] Sparkle styles himself the most fashionable man in London and he has designs on the widow Lady Bell Bloomer. A woman of fashion, the mourning Lady Bell is yearning to put her weeds aside and remarry. This transition from mourning widow to potential bride is staged in the fifth act in which Lady Bell throws a rout to mark her second coming into society. Lady Bell makes her availability well known, and, as one might expect, Lord Sparkle not only assumes that he is her most obvious and valued suitor but also is assured that his acquisition of her hand will be enacted for all of society at the party.

Cowley's exploration of Sparkle's predatory narcissism is both reminiscent of myriad fop roles through the century and a highly innovative construction, because his character is carefully aligned with errant governance.[51] Much is made in the early scenes of his corruption, but his suspect qualities go beyond gender insubordination and impinge on the affairs of state.[52] Anderson notes that "his unscrupulous election procedures and sexual conduct signify a breakdown of the English political system."[53] The excessive gaming of Sparkle and his similarly dissipated aristocratic friends threatens the very notion of landed property and all that this entails for the stability of the British social structure. Rarely had the fop role been deployed in this way, and some papers even suggested that Cowley was satirizing the profligate Prince of Wales. Nothing in the script makes this clear—such a move clearly would not pass the Lord Chamberlain—but numerous papers commented on Sparkle's costume and declared the connection to the Prince.[54]

This brings a political overtone to the entire erotic economy of the play that suddenly renders Lady Bell's widowhood quite topical. If she is Letitia Hardy continued, then she has lost her Doricourt. The dissolution of this relationship, here figured by the dead Lord Bloomer, allegorizes the loss of the American colonies for post-Yorktown Britain. When we consider how the marriage between Letitia and Doricourt resolved the conflicting claims of imperial and national sovereignty, it is revealing to discover that Lady Bell's prior marriage was not a happy one.[55] Despite the loss of her first husband, and the insinuation that the relationship would have broken her heart, Lady Bell's desire—whether we understand it in sexual or imperial terms—is not reined in, nor does Cowley stage a retroactive critique of women's fashionable sociability. Rather, it is through Lady Bell's fashionable pursuits and her erotic agency that she is able to discern the man with which she can build a future.

That man is not Lord Sparkle. He is rather Lord Sparkle's protégé Beauchamp. Full of fantasies of martial grandeur culled from the ancients, Beauchamp desires to be a soldier, and Sparkle procures a commission for him. This largesse is carefully calculated to make Beauchamp obligated to Sparkle, and even though he knows that Beauchamp is in love with Lady Bell, Sparkle torments him by making Beauchamp act as his go-between with her. Likewise, Lady Bell torments Beauchamp—both in his interview with her in act 4, scene 1, and in act 5—in order to humiliate Sparkle, but in the process discovers that she loves the earnest soldier and ultimately chooses him as her husband.

What interests me is the way that Cowley settles the marriage and the question of property, for it is a precise reversal of the closing scene of *The Belle's Stratagem* in which Letitia asks Doricourt to choose her identity from the panoply of options she represents. In *Which is the Man?*, Lady Bell first chooses Beauchamp over Sparkle, and then is presented with a second choice. Fitzherbert, the Saville character in this play, offers to make Beauchamp his heir:

> FITZ: Incorrigible man!—But I have done with *you*.—Beauchamp has answered all my hopes, and the discernment of this charming woman, in rewarding him, merits the happiness that awaits her; and that I may give the fullest sanction to her choice, I declare *him* heir to my estate. This, I know, is a stroke your Lordship did not expect.
>
> BEAUCH: And was it then to you, Sir!—The tumults of my gratitude—
>
> FITZ: Your conduct has completely rewarded me; and in adopting you— (5.1.54)

If we understand Sparkle to be the embodiment of aristocratic dissipation and governmental corruption, then the conferral of property from Fitzherbert to the soldier Beauchamp amounts to a validation not only of Beauchamp's enactment of civic virtue but also of the military. And that validation locates the blame for the loss of the American war firmly in the realm of politics.

This is why Lady Bell's interruption of this homosocial link between "noble Old England's" representative and the meritorious young soldier is so important:

> LADY BELL: (*interrupting*) Oh, I protest against that!—our union would then appear a prudent, *sober* business, and I should lose the credit of having done a mad thing for the sake of the man—my heart prefers.
>
> FITZ: To you I resign him with pleasure: his fate is in your hands.
>
> LADY BELL: Then he shall continue a soldier—one of those whom Love and his Country detain to guard her dearest, *last* possessions.
>
> BEAUCH: Love and my Country! Yes, ye shall divide my heart!—Animated by such passions, our forefathers were invincible; and if we wou'd preserve the freedom and independence they obtain'd for us, we must imitate their virtues. (5.1.54)

Lady Bell, like Doricourt, determines the identity of her spouse, and her decision is complex. As Anderson recognizes, by keeping him as a soldier she places him in a position of economic inferiority.[56] But this does not attend to Lady Bell's reason for her decision: she needs someone to guard the dearest, *last* possessions of both Love and Country, namely herself and what Pocock refers to as the limited realm of Britain itself. In other words, what is needed are soldiers, not gentry. At this point in history, when Britain has lost the Revolutionary War but is still prosecuting the global war with America's allies, the chief object is to ensure a favorable peace and protect the nation itself. As the second Letitia Hardy, Lady Bell figures for Britain, but now one severed from some portion of its empire; and thus "Love" and "Country" are mutually constitutive objects of desire. In fact, they are figures for one another. Therefore the division that appears to surface in Beauchamp's speech is actually an amplification. I would argue that it is this amplification that opens onto Beauchamp's invocation of the civic virtues of his forefathers.

In the face of Britain's uncertain position, Cowley signals the brittleness of national ideology and the disturbing uncertainty of the future of the empire. The play concludes with Sparkle still able to wreak havoc on the social fabric, and it is not at all certain that Beauchamp will be successful. But she also isolates two key styles of political agency, which must come together in order to meet the future needs of the nation and its empire. Lady Bell must retain the capacity for choice, so that she can finish her accession to political and social responsibility. And her future husband must attempt to give substance to his adoption of the tropes of civic virtue. This latter point is crucial because Beauchamp is all potential. Disconnected from the reverses sustained by the British military throughout the war, he represents simultaneously a new beginning and a wishful link to a more glorious past. For all his classical posturing, Beauchamp is untried in war, and he must prove that he can imitate the virtues of his invincible forefathers. But Cowley has established both the situation and the desire for the subsumption of soldier and politician into such a stance. In a remarkable act of restraint, she did not overstep her historical situation and precipitously bridge the gap between potential martial hero and true statesman. Rather, the play projects a very specific chronology for the future: the desire for civic virtue can be satisfied only by the enactment of martial heroism, and only then can the hero accede to the status of statesman. In the final section of this chapter, I want to follow the theatrical afterlife of this desire into the Caribbean itself by looking, first, at the representations of Rodney's West Indian career and, second, at his spectral presence in one of the most successful plays of the 1780s, George Colman's *Inkle and Yarico*. Colman not only answers Cowley's question "Which is the Man?," but also explores precisely what must be done to fulfill the potential encapsulated in Beauchamp. As we will see, Colman's prosthetic strategies come with a number of disturbing corollaries.

West Indian Futures
Spoken from the Sky

In the dying phases of the American war, one event was able to generate unabashed celebration in every town and city in Britain. Admiral George Bridges Rodney's spectacular victory over Admiral de Grasses at Les Saintes on 12 April 1782 was both tactically innovative and strategically crucial. Breaking the French line preserved British colonial holdings in the West Indies and thus established a breakwater of sorts against the overwhelming tide of defeat in the Atlantic. And this victory over the French navy gave the British a modicum of bargaining power in the negotiations that ended the American war. Timothy Jenks has recently discussed the importance of naval celebration to national identity in the late eighteenth century, but it is hardly an exaggeration to state that the widespread illuminations and public demonstration of loyalty for Rodney's heroism not only allowed Britons to reconfigure overall defeat as a momentary victory but also provided the groundwork for the political reconstitution of the navy in future years.[57] However, there was an ancillary development that was no less important to the recalibration of imperial identity. The preservation of the West Indies as colonies of Britain meant that Britain was in full possession of an exemplary site of political and moral shame, which would prove extraordinarily useful, if not necessarily profitable, over the next twenty years. As Christopher Leslie Brown has brilliantly argued, the struggle against the slave trade and its eventual abolition in 1807 were tied to a complex reconfiguration of Britain as a morally exemplary power.[58] By abolishing the trade, Britain could claim moral superiority over precisely the political constituency that had so forcefully called the morality of Britain's imperial rule into question. In short, the retention of the West Indian colonies provided a space for social and cultural reconstitution, a place where empire in the Atlantic can or could be imagined in a new way. These islands were revalued precisely because their history of horrific oppression offered a background from which to figure forth the future.

Admiral George Rodney's fame is inextricably tied to his service in the West Indies from 1779 to 1782. His victory at Les Saintes at the end of this period played a decisive role in how he was remembered, because the early phase of command was marked by controversy and recrimination. A notorious gambler, Rodney spent much of the war plagued by debt, and much of his action was perceived through this lens. Although he was following orders, his capture of St. Eustatius from the Dutch at the end of 1781 was widely criticized as nothing short of avarice.[59] Fellow officers and the daily papers accused Rodney of subordinating strategic concerns to his desire for prize money:

> The capture of the island and the ending of the trade had been a priority of the government. Shining success that it seemed to be, the capture quickly soured the relationships of Rodney and Hood, and Rodney was accused of losing all sense of the strategic priorities of his command in the dazzle of the wealth that had been captured. The burden of Hood's argument centred on the stationing of ships—Hood's squadron—to intercept any French reinforcement from Europe. Hood wanted to be far to windward of Martinique, Rodney wanted to keep Fort Royal blockaded to prevent any attack on the homeward convoy of booty from the island. In the event the covering of Fort Royal proved illusory for much of the wealth that Rodney acquired in the West Indies was lost to the French when the convoy on which it was shipped was intercepted by La Motte Picquet in the western approaches.[60]

Critiques of Rodney's command accelerated in the ensuing months not only because the capture of St. Eustatius was ultimately fruitless but also because of three crucial errors of judgment:

> While it was common practice to remove ships from the Caribbean with the approach of the hurricane season, and it was known that De Grasse intended to send a force to North America, Rodney failed to anticipate De Grasse's move or to make an informed estimate as to the force he would take. Second, there was a singular failure to send adequate and timely intelligence to Thomas Graves, the naval commander in North America. Finally, the reinforcement eventually sent was small in number and late in dispatch. Twenty-two ships of the line were potentially available but this number was dissipated to fourteen.[61]

These errors directly contributed to De Grasse's victory at Chesapeake, which in turn was integrally tied to the defeat of Cornwallis at Yorktown. In short, Rodney was in part responsible for two of the worst reverses of the American war.

Significantly, Rodney was in England when news of the defeat of Chesapeake Bay and the surrender of Yorktown reached London. In ill health, Rodney had left the Caribbean theatre on 1 August 1781 and was convalescing in Bath. He was immediately enveloped in the ensuing recriminations, and as Breen notes, "His claims to ill health as the cause for his return were not well received—'had it come about,' wrote the *Public Advertiser*, 'thru action then everyman would have regretted the impaired health of the Admiral; but none finds himself interested in the fate of the storekeeper' (24 Sept 1781)."[62] At this point in his career, the invalid admiral was associated, on the one hand, with disastrous failures of strategic judgment and, on the other, with a desire for prize money bordering on the corrupt.[63] Had Rodney not returned to the Caribbean later in the year, and had he not been so successful at Les Saintes, then he would likely have become of an exemplary figure for all that was wrong with the British navy during this period. But his action at Les Saintes prevented this from happening, and thus it needs to be understood as a moment of both personal and national redemption.[64] Rodney's redemption at Les Saintes involved the erasure of his association with corruption, debt, and loss and his subsequent reconstitution as the very figure of valor and selfless patriotism.[65] As we will see in our consideration of Colman's *Inkle and Yarico*, this substitution of a vigorous military man for the invalid merchant has immense ramifications not only for the figuration of imperial masculinity after the American war but also for the conceptualization of colonial space and imperial governance.

After his redeployment in the Caribbean in late 1781, Rodney's command, either because of past poor judgment on his own part or through the regular politicization of naval affairs, was continually under scrutiny. His second in command, Admiral Hood, had been involved in two inconclusive conflicts with Admiral De Grasse, and everything seemed to be going the way of the earlier misadventures in the Channel in 1778 and 1779. The conflicts between Rodney and his second in command, Admiral Hood, were well known and seemed all too reminiscent of the Keppel-Palliser affair. The threat of further disunity in the officer corps of the navy, and the record of nonengagement between Hood and De Grasse was also eerily similar to the Battle of Ushant. This was explicitly indicated after Rodney had defeated the French at Les Saintes in an anonymous print from 1782 entitled "Count de Grasse delivering his sword to the gallant Admiral Rodney" in which the defeated French Admiral reiterates yet again Keppel's infamous remark on the French intention to fight handsomely the next day, only here it is the French admiral attributing "handsomeness" to his British counterpart (fig. 5.2).[66] As one might expect, these problems and apparent repetitions generated intense criticism in Parliament from the Whig opposition. Fox and Burke quite regularly attacked Rodney and the Admiralty for

Figure 5.2. Anonymous, "Count de Grasse delivering his sword to the gallant Admiral Rodney," etching (1782). BM 5991. Department of Prints and Drawings © Trustees of the British Museum.

incompetence. After the dissolution of Lord North's Ministry in the spring of 1782, Rodney was replaced as commander of the Leeward Islands by Admiral Hugh Pigot. When news of Rodney's decisive victory came through in spring of 1782, the new Rockingham government found itself in the embarrassing situation of having replaced a hero.[67]

In part because of this sudden transformation of fortunes and in part because Rodney's situation replicated elements of the Keppel affair, the celebrations that attended Rodney's return to Bristol on 22 September 1782 recalled those following Keppel's acquittal.[68] And it was not simply the pervasiveness of public approbation that linked these events. In a very real way, Rodney's victory at Les Saintes put the questions concerning not only his command but the unanimity of the navy in abeyance in much the same way that Keppel's legal victory instantiated a very useful forgetting of less decisive outcomes. And in both cases, victory served the interests of the parliamentary opposition. As one of Rodney's biographers indicates, "many cities honoured Rodney with their freedom, including Huntingdon in which Sandwich made reference to the fact that Rodney's record was unsurpassed in that he had taken or destroyed sixteen ships of the line and captured the commanding admiral of each of the nations with which England was at war."[69] Celebrations were most intense in Bristol, but he was honoured repeatedly in the spring and summer of 1782 throughout Britain. As P. J. Marshall summarizes, news of Rodney's victory "produced frenzied celebrations throughout Britain on the scale of those in the 'year of victories' of 1759. The ambiguities of fighting the Americans had been replaced by a simple triumph over the French in which every section of British opinion could rejoice."[70] Misrecognizing 1782 for 1759 is a symptomatic gesture because it negates the fact that Rodney's victory was really a mitigation of profound loss. It prevented further disintegration of British colonialism in the Atlantic, rather than extending the nation's imperial reach. Nevertheless, celebratory songs were performed at Vauxhall Gardens, Astley's Amphitheatre replicated the action of Les Saintes in a shadow show, and illuminations were staged across several nights. Rodney was awarded a baronetcy and was the subject of panegyric in the House from the formerly critical Fox and Burke. And, of course, his victory was a recurring topic for verse in the newspapers.

Among the myriad poems celebrating Rodney's victory at Les Saintes, the following brief verse, entitled "On our late Successes in the West Indies," resonates with much of our discussion of the Keppel affair and of the experience of diffidence during the American war:

> Praying that o'er my drowsy Head
> Kind Nature would his poppies shed,
> Till Britain rous'd from Grief and Shame,
> Again should wake to ancient Fame:
> I slept—But soon the Cannons Roar
> Resounds, brave Britons sleep no more!
> The Spell's dissolved—The Thunder breaks
> Thro' lowering clouds—Tis RODNEY Speaks![71]

The sense of anodynal retreat, here figured by the poppies, is dissolved by a sudden utterance from the sky—this transmutation of Rodney's voice to the sky and his ability to rouse Britons from the unendurable sense of Grief and Shame. But most importantly, the sleep described here is explicitly understood to be the self-induced sleep of denial. The speaker states unequivocally that the nation's response to loss has been to step out of time into a static laudanum-induced reverie. Rodney's guns, the sound of which are conveyed by this poem, sound across the world and jolt the nation back into a time of agency. The metaphorical link between the cannons of the *Formidable* and Rodney's voice amounts to a prosthetic device—a rhetorical device applied to mitigate or obviate a sense of loss. The operation is akin to prosopopeia: relief in the form of Rodney's voice, rather than his face, is suddenly spoken from the sky. This substitution transfers the signs of bodily agency to the sky in order for the sound of new-found confidence to be articulated with and by nature.

A similar set of tropes accrues to many of the Rodney celebrations. The final verses of "A Naval Ode" sung at Vauxhall Gardens by Mr. Barthélemon recall the nation from its trance through a metaphorical link between the roar of cannons and the active voice:

Pride is rous'd, they try their Pow'r,
French and British Cannons roar;
Broadsides rage for many an Hour;
Hark! they cry they'll have no more.

In CHORUS
Scenes of Blood and Horrour rise!
Loud Huzzas salute the Skies.

4th Stanza.
Waken, Britons, from your Trance;
Spain ere this has felt a Blow;
Laugh at all the Pow'r of France;
Rodney's cool'd her Courage now.

In CHORUS
Hearts of Oak, for you we burn,
Long to hail your safe Return!

GRAND CHORUS.
From the East and the West
Good News, Boys, is come;
Each Heart be at Rest;
For Despair there's no Room.
A Truce with all Fear;
Let the merry Bells ring!
Peace soon may be here,
Sing, God save the King![72]

This sense of a nation roused from a trance is important because it indicates the importance not simply of Rodney's victory but, more importantly, of the Indies to the reconstitution of national and imperial purpose. The "News from East and West" alluded to in the Grand Chorus marks out what is essentially a compensatory fantasy of acquisition. Rodney's victory ensured the maintenance of British colonies in the sugar islands, but this song is also invoking similar "good news" from India. But this collocation of news from East and West is revealing because news from India that the second Mysore was not going to result in an unmitigated disaster operates in much the same way as news from the Saints. Just as news of a possible treaty with Mysore in the spring of 1782 allowed for a momentary cancellation of the humiliation of British forces at Pollilur, so too did news of peace negotiations after Rodney's victory allow for an ideological cancellation of the defeat of British forces at Yorktown. Both of these resolutions shifted attention away from the troubling conflict with the Americans onto the much less ideologically volatile global conflict with France. The reports of reverses at Pollilur and Yorktown had been almost simultaneous, so it is not surprising to see the specter of losses in both venues haunting this panegyric to impending peace.

The entire Rodney phenomenon—its cancellation of the immediate disaster of the American war, its resuscitation of the victories of 1759, and above all its redemption of the naval hero from the slur associated with the phrase "storekeeper"—was enacted on the London stage some five years later in George Colman's innovative production of *Inkle and Yarico.* What I hope to demonstrate is that the reformation of masculinity in that play, and in contemporary productions of Cumberland's *The West Indian,* not only gains new meaning in relation to the elevation of Rodney to the status of imperial hero but also relies on a cognate fantasy of whiteness. If Rodney can be understood to speak from the sky to rouse the anaesthetized nation, then we need to understand how domination can leap forth from the apparent representational blankness accorded to reconsolidated martial masculinity and normative white femininity in the performance of these two plays in the late 1780s.

Mercantile Deformities: George Colman's Inkle and Yarico

The incessant remediation of the Inkle and Yarico story in verse and in prose across the eighteenth century offers a particularly felicitous archive for a history of colonial thought in the period.[73] It is tempting to read the subtle modifications and elisions in the tale as one moves from version to version and from medium to medium as signs of history. I wish to take up that temptation in relation to the most culturally significant version of the narrative after Richard Steele's version of 1711.[74] Of all the late eighteenth-century comedies set in colonial spaces, none is as important as George Colman's highly successful comic opera *Inkle and Yarico* (1787) for understanding the relationship between shifts in imperial policy and the question of racialization on the London stage. These shifts of course are fundamentally concerned with reimagining the imperial enterprise in light of the newly configured Atlantic world. Of crucial importance is the apparent contradiction between the play's supposed abolitionist gestures and its explicitly racist representations of Africans and Native Americans. In his introduction to the play, Frank Felsenstein argues that "it is specifically this supreme ineptitude of the colonizing English in differentiating one racial group from another and the simultaneous tendency, conscious or otherwise, to barbarize the native that are the targets of Colman's lighthearted satire."[75] Whether this assessment is too generous to Colman is perhaps aside from the point, for I intend to demonstrate that these ostensible political contradictions and confusions regarding racial identity are in fact part and parcel of a larger recalibration of colonial relations that is thoroughly enmeshed both in the stabilization of the white middle-class body in the metropole and in the complex engagement with the end of the American war. It is my contention that this radical reorientation of the narrative's historical function can be excavated from a certain ambivalence in the play's reception history.

The early reviews and accounts of the first runs at the Haymarket in 1787 and Covent Garden in 1788 tend to focus on the performance of affect in the character of Yarico and how the feeling elicited by her character is mobilized in a condemnation of Inkle's mercantile greed. However, these understandings of the play as a critique of mercantilism are superseded by assertions that the play is an example of abolitionism avant la lettre. Later introductions to Colman's play tend to focus on the morality of Colman himself by applauding his prescient concern for humanity in chains. The most interesting instance of the latter revisionist position is Inchbald's laudatory introductory remark for the *British Theatre* (1806) in which she states:

> This is a drama, which might remove from Mr. Wilberforce his aversion to theatrical exhibitions, and convince him, that the teaching of moral duty is not confined to particular spots of ground; for, in those places, of all others, the doctrine is most effectually inculcated, where exhortation is the most required—the resorts of the gay, the idle, and the dissipated. . . .

> [The opera] was popular before the subject of abolition of the slave trade was popular. It has the peculiar honour of preceding that great question. It was the bright forerunner of alleviation of the hardships of slavery.[76]

The ascription of abolitionist intent should give us pause because at the time of the composition of Inchbald's remarks the general approbation of the moral argument against slavery is at its height, and hence Inchbald is making yet another argument for the moral value of the theatre. But this attempt to make *Inkle and Yarico* morally exemplary is strained by the critical contortions required to direct Colman's play at the African slave trade.

> A fault more important, is—that the scene at the commencement of the opera, instead of Africa, is placed in America. It would undoubtedly have been a quick passage, to have a fourth part of the western globe, during the interval between the first and second acts; still, as the hero and heroine of the drama are compelled to go to sea—imagination, with but little more exertion, might have given them fair wind as well from the coast whence slaves are *really* bought, as from the shore where no such traffic is held.*
>
> > *No doubt the author would have ingenuity to argue away this objection—but that, which requires argument for its support in a dramatic work, is a subject for complaint. As slaves are imported from Africa, and never from America, the audience, in the two last acts of this play, feel as if they had been in the wrong quarter of the globe during the first act. Inkle could certainly steal a native from America, and sell her in Barbadoes, but this is not so consonant with that nice imitation of the order of things as to rank above criticism.[77]

Inchbald's somewhat uncharacteristic recourse to the unities focuses attention on the "particular spots of ground" that I wish to consider in more detail.

As Inchbald notes, Yarico is not an African, and the first act is set in the Americas. The suggestion that this is a lapse in composition has merit only if one wants the play to be specifically about the African trade. In other words, it is Inchbald who is retroactively shifting the ground in imitation of the current order of things, and it is difficult not to read that gesture as part of a large-scale rewriting of colonial history following the American Revolution aimed at suppressing the prior relationship between the American and the Caribbean colonies. As Christopher Leslie Brown has argued, English abolitionist discourse itself constitutes a part of this historical redirection.[78] My suggestion is that Colman's *Inkle and Yarico* addresses a specific historical moment in colonial economics that has been superseded by the time Inchbald anthologizes the play. In subtle ways, Colman is much more concerned with a critical yet exculpatory reading of mercantile ideology that paves the way for precisely the kind of arguments against the slave trade that simultaneously highlight its economic obsolescence and its moral turpitude. Colman's play performs a sort of readjustment of the colonial encounter to fit emergent forms of biological state racism and, as such, plays a crucial mediating role between the constructions of race endemic to England's mercantile economy and those which come into full hegemonic force in the early nineteenth century.

For the purposes of this chapter, the dominant discourse network of the Inkle and Yarico archive mediates between an ostensible historical source and its sentimental literary elaborations.[79] Steele's sentimental version of 1711 is based on Richard Ligon's brief rendition of the story in his *True and Exact History of the Island of Barbadoes* (1657). Ligon's text provides historical legitimation and the source material for a very particular sort of eroticization in which the focalization shifts to Yarico's subjectivity. In Steele and in all subsequent versions, Yarico becomes a noble subject and the erotic play between Inkle and Yarico follows the conventions of metropolitan courtship. The following is a brief synopsis of Steele's version:

> Mr. Thomas Inkle, an ambitious young English trader cast ashore in the Americas, is saved from violent death at the hands of savages by the endearments of Yarico, a beautiful Indian maiden. Their romantic intimacy in the forest moves Inkle to pledge that, were his life to be preserved, he would return with her to England, supposedly as his wife. The lovers' tender liaison progresses over several months until she succeeds in signaling a passing English ship. They are rescued by the crew, and with vows to each other intact, they embark for Barbadoes. Yet when they reach the island Inkle's former mercantile instincts are callously revived, for he sells her into slavery, at once raising the price he demands when he learns that Yarico is carrying his child.[80]

Steele's text becomes a template of sorts, and later verse is often cast in Yarico's voice to maximize the pain of betrayal. This effectively incorporates the Inkle and Yarico story into contemporary constructions of femininity and heterosexuality, but it is important to recognize that in the process Yarico's racial otherness is subsumed in the constitution of gender normativity. When the narrative makes its way onto the stage in Colman's opera, this subsumption of racial difference into normative femininity is put into crisis not only because the theatre demands an embodiment of this contradiction but also because femininity is itself beginning to be understood as incommensurable with nonwhite bodies. How does Sarah Kemble's performance of femininity in the role of Yarico impinge on the historical consolidation of whiteness on the late eighteenth-century stage? Is it whiteness or some vaguely defined otherness that constitutes the character's feminine desirability? Answering these two questions ultimately reveals the degree to which the twofold racialization and sexualization of the opera's characters participates in the consolidation of the emergent white middle-class body of the early nineteenth century.

Like all the post-Steele versions, Colman's *Inkle and Yarico* is suffused with sentimental affect, but the opening-night review from the *General Magazine* saw the relation to Steele as a liability: "The story as related in the *Spectator*, is universally known and is not greatly promising of dramatic incident. The genius of the author has happily supplied this deficiency."[81] Jeremy Bagster-Collins's illuminating summary of the play describes Colman's alterations to the tale:

> Colman's first act follows the Steele tale fairly closely: Inkle and Trudge, his pun-loving clerk-factotum, abandoned by their shipmates in the forest, find and fall in love with Yarico and her maid Wowski, respectively. The ladies are responsive; after offering protection from the other natives they join their voices with those of the men in a pair of love-duets, made possible, most fortunately, by the English they had learned from a shipwrecked sailor. The act ends on these happy notes. Thereafter, however, Colman diverges from his source in varying degrees. Inkle, Yarico, Trudge, and Wowski reach Barbadoes, but Inkle's indecision here in the matter of getting rid of Yarico is made much less mercenary by Colman's giving him a different object for his voyage—namely, marriage with Narcissa, daughter of Sir Christopher Curry, Governor of Barbadoes. Swayed by his interest, he decides at first to sell Yarico, who is *not* with child, and offers her, unknowingly, to Sir Christopher, who roundly denounces his inhumanity on learning the circumstances. Eventually, Inkle repents and marries Yarico. Thus Colman nullifies Steele's moral but substitutes one of his own.[82]

Inkle's betrothal and the fact that Yarico is not pregnant alter the sexual economy of the play, and the introduction of Sir Christopher Curry directly impinges on how one reads the play's engagement with colonial governance.[83] It is my contention that the questions of sexual and political economy are folded into the same complex allegory, but before entering this argument it is important to highlight the contextual shifts that had occurred between 1711 and 1787 that directly impinge not only on how one reads the performance of femininity on stage but also on how one understands the relationship between the generation of Yarico's affect to the history of British colonial activity.

By the mid-1780s the American colonies had seceded from British rule, Adam Smith had published *The Wealth of Nations* with its scathing critique of mercantilism, Rousseau's noble savage was fast becoming a common cultural construct, and emergent forms of middle-class sexuality were beginning to gel. But in the eyes of recent scholarship these important developments are overshadowed by the fact that the play coincides with the first major political push to abolish the slave trade. As Felsenstein emphasizes, 1787 saw the establishment of the Society for the Abolition of the Slave Trade, the publication of Clarkson's *A Summary View of the Slave Trade and of the Possible Consequences of Its Abolition,* and the initiation of the parliamentary campaign against slavery by William Pitt and William Wilberforce.[84] Arguments for the play's protoabolitionist qualities usually rest on this coincidence and on the role played by Joseph Jekyll in the play's composition.[85] However, declarations of the play's abolitionist intent, whether they come from Inchbald or from recent criticism, suggest that the emotion elicited by Yarico's betrayal "promotes the abolitionist cause by tugging at people's heartstrings."[86] This assertion characterizes the political engagement of the play too narrowly and obscures a series of interventions in the British perception of colonial relations that are coded into the very additions that figure so prominently in the *General Magazine* review. The Wowski subplot, the persistent ridicule of the working-class characters that appears in no earlier version, the frequent interludes of singing and dancing, the introduction of Inkle's betrothed Narcissa, and Captain Campley's complicating love interest constantly threaten to overwhelm the play's sentimental critique. Furthermore, whatever political force one could glean from the play is thoroughly undercut by Colman's gratuitous racial slurs—especially those attributed to the play's principal working-class characters—and by his decision to supply a happy ending to the story in which Inkle repents and Yarico grants forgiveness. In short, Colman's "genius" spins the protoabolitionist and antimercantile gestures in the play toward an audience-pleasing exculpation of British colonial rule. What I wish to demonstrate is that the abolitionist aspects of the play do not exist in contradiction with its racist gestures but rather that both elements are folded into an emergent form of imperial domination that is deeply involved in the consolidation of the middle-class body in the metropole.

Crucial to this exculpation is the intervention of the state in the person of Sir Christopher Curry at key moments in the Inkle and Yarico tale. Curry, like other stereotypical representations of West Indian subjects such as Belcour in *The West Indian*, exhibits "a hot-tempered bluntness."[87] Significantly, during the period of *Inkle and Yarico*'s domination of Covent Garden's offerings from September 1788 through the winter of 1789, Drury Lane was repeatedly staging *The West Indian*.[88] This naked attempt to capitalize on West Indian themes should come as no surprise, but it is important to consider the subtle distinctions in how West Indian subjectivity was being presented during this period, for they clearly indicate the difference between British imperial activity in the period after the Seven Years' War and that after the American war.[89] In a sense, Drury Lane was countering Covent Garden's theatrically innovative articulation of the West Indian future with a nostalgic rehearsal of a past moment in the political and representational history of the circum-Atlantic

Unlike Belcour in *The West Indian*, Curry is not a man of commerce but rather a colonial administrator, and as such he retains a certain distance from the merchant class that comes under sharp scrutiny in Colman's play. Despite his official status in the play, the only instances we are given of Curry's governmental activities are confined to the marriage market. In a rush to marry off his daughter for profit, Curry mistakes Captain Campley for Inkle, and Narcissa is suddenly able to marry her true love. Narcissa's desire for a military man is fulfilled through her father's desire to marry her to a merchant. This confusion between soldier and merchant has historical resonance, for it reflects a complex transition in colonial policy as Britain replaces earlier forms of mercantile imperialism with a more militarily active acquisition of territory. All across the empire, the governance of colonial space is shifting from the hands of commercial bodies to the more direct rule of the state and its military apparatus. We should perhaps not be surprised that Drury Lane's nostalgic investment in *The West Indian* was thoroughly outpaced by Covent Garden's speculation on the future figured forth by Colman's generic and thematic innovations.

It is here that Admiral Rodney's legendary status comes into play, because the confusion between Captain Campley and Inkle is akin to the double reception of Rodney's own exploits in the Caribbean. His capture of St. Eustatius and the widespread suggestion that strategic issues were being subordinated to his desire for self-enrichment made him the very figure of mercantile greed. His victory at Les Saintes suddenly canceled this set of associations, and he became the exemplar of selfless martial virtue. In other words, from the spring of 1781 to the spring of 1782, Rodney is transformed from Inkle to Campley, from the epitome of corruption and loss to the emblem of British might. In a sense, by breaking the Rodney figure into two characters, Colman is simply enacting the supersession of one aspect of Rodney's history by another.

Significantly, this shift from "storekeeper" to confident warrior was accompanied by a shift from invalidism to vigorous agency. In James Gillray's caricatures from this period, such as "Rodney invested—or—Admiral Pig on a cruize" from 4 June 1782, Rodney's frame shows no signs of the decrepitude that had interrupted his service the previous year.[90] Victory at Les Saintes had not only redeemed his reputation and, by extension, the reputation of the navy but also seemed to reconstitute his body. The importance of this cannot be overemphasized because Rodney's ill health had dogged him from before his service in the Seven Years' War.

The reparation of Rodney's body is clearly articulated in Gainsborough's famous portrait that was painted during the height of Colman's success with *Inkle and Yarico* (fig. 5.3).[91] Rodney's defiant pose is, in a sense, directly attached to the source of his confidence, for Gainsborough has included a précis of the breaking of De Grasse's line in the background immediately adjacent to Rodney's forward thrusting leg. A similar fetishization of Rodney's leg occurs in Reynolds's contemporaneous portrait of 1788 (fig. 5.4).[92] If anything, the power of Rodney's leg is underscored by the visible signs of age in Rodney's face. This leg is important because physical disability is a key trope in Colman's play. The play's subordination of Inkle's mercantilism to Campley's martial masculinity not only replicates the redemption of Rodney from his earlier avaricious reputation but also turns on the same erasure of Rodney's prior invalidism in post-1782 representations of his body. It is through the careful management of the bodily expression of confidence as figured by notions of health and normativity that much of this ideological sleight of hand is secured. And this management of bodily signs, so crucial to the play's historical importance in the postwar period, is linked to the enactment of normative heterosexuality and to complex fantasies of racial distinction.

The replacement of mercantile coercion by territorial military intervention is aptly allegorized by the Narcissa marriage plot, with her body figuring as that which must be governed. Within the terms of the allegory, the hotness of the climate induces Curry to choose the military man as the most appropriate husband despite his repeated desire for an entrepreneurial connection. When Curry's "mistake" is revealed late in the final act, Colman not only marks the

Figure 5.3. Richard Josey, *George Bridges Rodney*, mezzotint (1784), after Thomas Gainsborough, *Lord Rodney* (1788), Dalmeny House, Edinburgh. NPG D4095. © National Portrait Gallery, London.

historical moment of war in American and Caribbean waters, which so directly impinges upon British colonial policy, but also ties together the classical allusion that gives teeth to his critique:

> CAMPLEY: I am a soldier, Sir Christopher; "love and war" is a soldier's motto. Though my income is trifling to your intended son-in-law's, still, the chance of war has enabled me to support the object of my love above indigence. Her fortune, Sir Christopher, I do not consider myself by any means entitled to.

Figure 5.4. Sir Joshua Reynolds, *Lord Rodney* (1788). The Royal Collection © 2010, Her Majesty Queen Elizabeth II.

SIR CHR: 'Sblood, but you must, though! Give me your hand, my young Mars, and bless you both together! Thank you, thank you for cheating an old fellow into giving his daughter to a lad of spirit when he was going to throw her away upon one in whose breast the mean passion of avarice smothers the smallest spark of affection or humanity.[93]

Campley's financial straits subtly recall Rodney's financial difficulties before and during his Caribbean tour of duty, but this is less important than the ensuing classical reference. Casting Campley as the Mars to Narcissa's Venus effectively emphasizes Inkle's role as Vulcan. The rhetorical move is telling for it picks up on the monstrosity of the earlier representations of the Inkle figure in Jean Mocquet, Richard Ligon, and Richard Steele but tempers it so that Inkle becomes ugly, lame, and frequently cuckolded.[94] This figural shift from monstrosity to deformity, from ungrateful and inconstant lover to cuckolded husband not only activates the Rodney allegory but also alters the terms of the critique of Inkle in culturally significant ways. Normative masculinity in the earlier versions of the tale is defined against inconstancy, whereas in Colman it is defined in terms of healthy marriageable bodies. In other words, the terms on which the question "Which is the Man?" will be adjudicated are changing, both in the realm of marriage and in the larger Atlantic world.

Intriguingly, Sir Christopher Curry's attempts to govern the marriage market do not stop with his daughter, for his role in Inkle's attempt to sell Yarico in the slave market also opens onto the marital realm. Curry is crucial to how the audience interprets the sale of Yarico and the condemnation of Inkle because, as the representative of the state, his arbitration of the play's chief sentimental scene thoroughly entwines the sexual and political registers of the play. The extent of this entanglement is evident from the beginning of the transaction in act 3, scene 2:

> INKLE: Then to the point: I have a female whom I wish to part with.
>
> SIR CHR: Very likely. It's a common case nowadays with many a man.
>
> INKLE: If you could satisfy me you would use her mildly and treat her with more kindness than is usual—for I can tell you she's of no common stamp—perhaps we might agree.
>
> SIR CHR: Oho a slave! Faith now I think on't, my daughter may want an attendant or two extraordinary, and as you say she's a delicate girl, above the common run, and none of your thick-lipped, flat-nosed, squabby, dumpling dowdies, I don't much care if— (3.3.103)

That Inkle's proposition is initially detached from the language of commerce leads Sir Christopher to interpret Inkle's desire as that of many a man who wishes to dispose of his mistress. The ambivalence here is one that runs throughout the play for Inkle *is* attempting to dispose of his mistress, but because of her racial difference and the space in which the transaction takes place, the commodification that underlies Sir Christopher's leering gibe can operate explicitly. The joke plays on the metaphorical linkage between extramarital sexual exchange in the metropole and commodity exchange in the colony.[95] What interests me is that value in either marketplace is assessed on related grounds. Inkle stresses that she is not common, and Sir Christopher immediately interprets this to mean that she is physically delicate and hence sexually desirable. The short transit from the assertion of class difference to sexual desirability is crucial because it structures the construction of Yarico's femininity not only in Colman's play but in every version of the tale following Steele, and because the linkage is immediately and forcefully supported by an important set of bodily signs that establish the physical parameters of undesirable racial and class others. This construction of delicate femininity at the expense of "thick-lipped, flat-nosed, squabby, dumpling dowdies" immediately opens onto Sir Christopher's critique of slavery that Inchbald found so admirable:

SIR CHR: I can't help thinking the only excuse for buying our fellow creatures is to rescue 'em from the hands of those how are unfeeling enough to bring them to market. . . . Let Englishmen blush at such practices. Men who so fully feel the blessings of liberty are doubly cruel in depriving the helpless of their freedom. (3.3.103–4)

The extraordinary speed with which the play is able to separate and maintain the process of racialization from the critique of slavery reflects the historical separation of the political drive to abolish the trade in slaves from their emancipation. Sir Christopher's protoabolitionist rebuke exhibits many key elements of the early arguments against the slave trade, most notably his construction of Africans as naturally helpless beings and his suggestion that such a contravention of individual liberty is an embarrassment to English national character.

But the sexual undertones and racial slurs of this protoabolitionist position unfold in remarkable ways when Yarico enters and finds herself between these two men. As in the scene of rebuke, everything starts with Sir Christopher's desiring gaze:

SIR CHR: Od's my life, as comely a wench as I ever saw!

(Enter YARICO, who looks for some time in INKLE's face, bursts into tears, and falls on his neck.)

INKLE: In tears my Yarico? Why this?
YARICO: Oh do not, do not leave me!

INKLE: Why, simple girl, I'm labouring for your good! My interest here is nothing. I can do nothing from myself—you are ignorant of our country's customs; I must give way to men more powerful who will not have me with you. But see, my Yarico, ever anxious for your welfare, I've found a kind, good person who will protect you. (3.3.106)

It is important to attend to temporal lag between Yarico's appearance on stage and her demonstration of emotional distress. As in the earlier scene when Inkle first meets Yarico, Colman stages a moment of looking in which the audience watches an English character overcome with Yarico's immediate desirability.[96] It is a moment verging on fetishization that gives way to the demonstration of intense emotional response. However, the moment in which Yarico looks at Inkle's face sets up a complex identificatory circuit. Because Sir Christopher's desiring gaze is a rehearsal of Inkle's earlier ascription of desire, the audience watches her sexual objectification and then passes into her subject position to feel the structure of betrayal. Her tears as much as the pastoral sentimentalism of her response to Inkle's duplicity perform crucial cultural work:

YARICO: Take me into yonder mountains, where I see no smoke from tall, high houses filled with your cruel countrymen. None of your princes, there, will come to take me from you. And should they stray that way, we'll find a lurking place, just like my own poor cave, where many a day I sat beside you and blessed the chance that brought you to it, that I might save your life. . . . Come, come, let's go. I always feared these cities. Let's fly and seek the woods, and there we'll wander hand in hand together. No cares shall vex us then. We'll let the day glide by in idleness, and you shall sit in the shade and watch the sunbeam playing on the brook while I sing the song that pleases you. No cares, love but for your good. And we'll live cheerily, I warrant. In the fresh, early morning you shall hunt down our game and I will pick you berries, and then, at night, I'll trim our bed of leaves and lie me down in peace. Oh, we shall be so happy! (3.3.106)

These are Yarico's most extended speeches, and their pastoral discourse folds this scene into a series of notable imperial scenarios, of which Pope's *Windsor Forest* is perhaps the most important predecessor. As Laura Brown has argued with regard to Pope's celebration of the Peace of Utrecht, the pastoral allows for both subtle and explicit modes of critique.[97] In Pope's poem, the pastoral landscape is deployed to celebrate the fruits of British imperial expansion, but he also uses the figure of the hunt to emphasize the cost of imperial prosperity. The famous scene of the dying pheasant figured as an agglomeration of commodities is one of the earliest literary critiques of mercantilism.

Colman's Rousseauian vision of presocial harmony engages the same trope but much more explicitly, in part because at this point in British imperial history the nature of the hunt is changing rapidly. Inkle's mercantile response to Yarico's pastoralism is arguably the play's most historically resonant moment:

> INKLE: This is mere trifling! The trifling of an unenlightened Indian! Hear me, Yarico. My countrymen and yours differ as much in minds as in complexions. We were not born to live in woods and caves. 'Tis misery to us to be reduced to seek subsistence by pursuing beasts. We Christians, girl, hunt money, a thing unknown to you. Here 'tis money which brings us ease, plenty, command, power, and everything; and, of course, happiness. You are a bar to my attaining this. (3.3.106)

Inkle's naturalization of the hunt for money is subject to rigorous critique on a number of levels. The figure itself reveals the violence at the core of the mercantile economy. Yarico's emotional speeches and the heart-rending scene of her grasping Inkle as he sells her simultaneously emphasize her constancy to Inkle and her extraordinary sacrifice for one so undeserving of her love. And these rhetorical and performative critiques of Inkle's economic view of happiness are substantially augmented by Sir Christopher's scathing condemnation. Inkle's lingering concern that her new owner adequately care for Yarico is met with nothing but scorn:

> SIR CHR: I never heard of such barbarity! . . . Liar! Cheat! Rogue! Imposter! Breaking all ties you ought to keep and pretending to those which you have no right to! The Governor disowns you, the Governor disclaims you, the Governor abhors you, and, to your utter confusion, here stands the Governor to tell you so! (3.3.107)

That Inkle's condemnation comes from the agent of state cannot be overemphasized for it significantly alters the judgment of Inkle's "ingratitude." In earlier versions of the tale, Inkle's actions are primarily understood to be dishonorable. Colman stages this aspect of the tale by moving into the rhetoric of dueling.

Inkle interprets Sir Christopher's scorn as an insult to his honor and threatens to seek justice with the governor. Because Sir Christopher is the governor, the interpretation of Inkle's honor is sealed, but this narrative twist carries with it the implication that Inkle's economic defense of his actions as what Christians naturally do is as abhorrent to the state as his avaricious character. In other words, Sir Christopher's judgment is both a private and a public critique of the mercantile hunt for money that defined the first British Empire's vision of its colonial activities.

This is where Colman's play suddenly veers into the realm of colonial policy and where the play picks up on resonances of a second discourse network that haunts the Inkle and Yarico tale. The story of Dido and Aeneas lurks behind a number of eighteenth-century versions of the tale. As Peter Hulme emphasizes, the narrative parallels are extensive between the two stories. The Trojans and the English are both shipwrecked in a storm on a hostile coast. Aeneas and Inkle are separated from the other sailors and passengers. In both cases, an amorous relationship develops between the travelers and a hospitable princess of the country, and in both cases the relationship is consummated in a cave. After a period of bliss, the traveler moves on, deserting the woman he had loved or perhaps deceived. The 1736 poem "Yarico to Inkle, an Epistle" draws attention to these parallels when it quotes Dido's anguished condemnation of Aeneas in its epigraph: *Quod genus hoc hominum? quaeve hunc tam barbara morem Permittit patria?* (What manner of men are these? What land is this that allows them such barbarous ways?).[98] In Colman's play, Dido's charge of barbarism comes not from Yarico but from Sir Christopher. The significance of this subtle shift lies in part in the reception of the *Aeneid* and in part in Inkle's remarkable attempt to defend his actions. As Peter Hulme emphasizes, it was always a problem for eighteenth-century readers of the *Aeneid* that Aeneas, the founder of Rome, deserts and is ultimately responsible for the death of Dido. Hulme rightly underlines that Dido's offer of hospitality operates on both an amorous and a political level. Aeneas's decision to desert Dido is conventionally understood as a victory of duty over passion necessary for the foundation of Rome. As we shall see, Colman uses the Dido and Aeneas resonance in a manner distinct from that of his predecessors, for he ultimately offers a critique of duty that has important economic implications.

Colman addresses the question of duty to the future of empire in Inkle's attempt to defend his actions. Inkle's speech resonates with the Dido and Aeneas story in a manner that activates not only a new vision of imperialism but also a redeployment of interracial sexuality:

INKLE: Then let me speak. Hear me defend a conduct—

SIR CHR: Defend? Zounds! Plead guilty at once; it's the only hope left of obtaining mercy.

INKLE: Suppose, old gentleman, you had a son—

SIR CHR: 'Sblood, then I'd make him an honest fellow and teach him that the feeling heart never knows greater pride than when it's employed in giving succour to the unfortunate. I'd teach him to be his father's own son to a hair.

INKLE: Even so my father tutored me from my infancy, bending my tender mind, like a young sapling, to his will. Interest was the grand prop round which he twined my pliant green affections, taught me in childhood to repeat old sayings—all tending to his own fixed principles—and the first sentence that I ever lisped was "Charity begins at home."

SIR CHR: I shall never like a proverb again, as long as I live.

INKLE: As I grew up, he'd prove—and by example: were I in want, I might e'en starve for what the world cared for their neighbours; why then should I care for the world? —men now lived for themselves. These were his doctrines. Then, sir, what would you say should I, in spite of habit, precept, education, fly in my father's face and spurn his counsels? (3.3.109)

The translation of charity for hospitality puts Inkle's actions in a historical frame here figured by the parent-child relation. According to Inkle, he behaves without gratitude to Yarico because he has been trained to look out only for himself. This casts his shame onto his father, and suddenly the play's critique of mercantilism takes on a more thoroughly historical register. Inkle's mistakes are really the mistaken principles of his father and, as such, they can be overcome. This familial trope figures for the complex political shift from the first to the second British Empire, and it involves an act of remarkable renunciation and exculpation.

In response to Inkle's question regarding his filial duty to the memory of his father, Sir Christopher identifies the paradox of duty and opens the door for Inkle to renounce the past:

SIR CHR: Say? Why, that you were a damned honest, undutiful fellow! Oh, curse such principles, principles which destroy all confidence between man and man, principles which none but a rogue could instil and none but a rogue could imbibe, principles—

INKLE: Which I renounce . . . entirely. Ill-founded precept too long has steeled my breast, but still 'tis vulnerable. This trial was too much. Nature, 'gainst habit combating within me, has penetrated to my heart, a heart, I own, long callous to the feelings of sensibility. But now it bleeds, and bleeds for my poor Yarico. Oh let me clasp her to it whilst 'tis glowing, and mingle tears of love and penitence. (*embracing her*) (3.3.109)

When Inkle renounces duty and is forgiven by Yarico, it is as though Aeneas returns to Dido and ditches his plans for Rome. The renunciation here is allegorically tied to a renunciation of British imperial activities based on the obsolete principles of mercantile trade. However, this is anything but an anti-imperial gesture tout court. What we see here is a modulation from one form of imperialism to another. The play's obsession with skin color, with interracial and interclass sexuality, and with questions of bodily health and deformity points toward the emergence of biological state racisms that undergird nineteenth-century models of British imperialism and emergent forms of middle-class self-stylization.

The close ties between the emergence of a racialized classed body and the renunciation of mercantilism are coded directly into Inkle's exculpation, for his image of the sapling bent to his father's will refers to the famous engraving from *Orthopaedia; or, the Art of Correcting and Preventing Deformities in Children* (1743) (fig. 5.5). We have already noted that Inkle is figured as Vulcan throughout the play and is thus linked to deformity and failed masculinity. Helen Deutsche and Felicity Nussbaum's remarks on the sapling image allow one to build an even more incisive analysis of Inkle's tearful renunciation of duty:

> In the engraving . . . a leafy curvaceous sapling . . . seems to be locked together with a rigid measure in a gentle but firm embrace. The fledgling tree thrives but requires training in order to fit itself to the standard by which it is judged. The pair exemplifies not only parent and child but also the marital couple. . . . Though the straight stake seems to represent the masculine member and crooked one the feminine, the viewer nevertheless awards aesthetic preference to the contorted trunk with its flourishing branches. Yoked together with the straight stick of wood to coax it into conformity, the healthy sapling's crooked nature will be rectified by the encircling rope. Though the engraving is intended to represent the art of correcting and preventing deformities in children . . . it also illustrates the eighteenth century attitudes toward another group of correctables,

Figure 5.5. From *Orthopaedia: or, the Art of Correcting and Preventing Deformities in Children* (1743). Courtesy of the Thomas Fisher Rare Book Library, University of Toronto.

> women, who charm because of their defects, while it depicts masculine science as offering moral and aesthetic criteria by which women and children are to be gauged.[99]

Deutsche and Nussbaum's emphasis on gender in their reading of the illustration is illuminating precisely because Colman's adoption of the image questions the terms of normativity in a fashion that directly impinges on emergent forms of masculinity.

In Inkle's account, "Interest was the grand prop round which [his father] twined my pliant green affections." Under the gentle but firm embrace of his father's—and fatherland's—obsession with commerce, Inkle becomes an exemplar of British mercantile interest, but what should be normative turns out to be monstrous at the historical moment following the secession of the American colonies. Inkle's renunciation of these codes of masculinity is accompanied by the onset of "feelings of sensibility" and the mingling of tears of love and penitence. The reformation of Inkle, as Sir Christopher calls it, involves a certain feminization that indicates that both Inkle and colonial policy are susceptible to correction (3.3.110). As both Inkle and Sir Christopher stress, it is the principle, that is, the straight rod, that needs to be modified. What is needed therefore are new precepts of masculinity and economics from which to build a more suitable governmental relationship between metropole and colony. These precepts are to be found in the military man Captain Campley and his wife Narcissa, the only non-interracial couple in the play, for they exemplify not only the normative white masculinity and femininity, against which the audience is to judge Inkle and Yarico, but also the militarization of colonial policy. The presence of this new military couple relegates Inkle and Yarico to a quaint bower of historical obsolescence. Furthermore, the figural connections between Campley and Narcissa and Mars and Venus and between Inkle and Yarico and Aeneas and Dido perform a remarkable deification of normative white heterosexuality.

Captain Campley and Narcissa's "straightness," therefore, is more than an incidental addition to the tale. A recognition of their examplarity allows one to read the complex hybridity of both Inkle and Yarico. Inkle's gender hybridity is matched by Yarico's racial hybridity, but full analysis of the construction of Yarico requires that we turn from figures of embodiment to the history of the body itself. In this case, we must turn to a specific body in a specific space at a specific time. Almost every contemporary account of *Inkle and Yarico* testifies to the centrality of Yarico's speeches in act 3, scene 3, to the theatrical power of the play. And that power was deeply tied to the power of emotion generated by Mrs. Stephen Kemble's physical presence on stage:

> Nothing was destined to soften the obdurate more effectively than the acting of Mrs. Stephen Kemble, the original performer of Yarico, whose presentational style is described in this typical eyewitness account: "Those sweet and pathetic tones and that exquisite plaintiveness by which Mrs.

> Kemble, in Yarico, brought tears into the eyes of the audience, defy the powers of panegyric." Shock waves of sympathetic emotion seemed to have dispossessed audiences of their self-control wherever Mrs. Kemble performed this character.[100]

The extraordinary level of emotional response elicited by Mrs. Kemble's performance style is intriguing because it would seem that the tears that overwhelm Inkle also overwhelm the audience. The identificatory relation established through the act of crying has its counterpart in the remarkable assertion of equivalence between Mrs. Kemble and the character of Yarico by James Boaden:

> The stage never in my time exhibited so pure, so interesting a candidate . . . her modest timidity—her innocence—the tenderness of her tones, and the unaffected alarm that sat upon her countenance—all together won for her at once a high place in the public regard. . . . I have often listened to the miserable counterfeit of what she was, and would preserve, if language could but do it, her lovely impersonation of artless truth . . . The FANCY may restore her, or be contented with its own creation. That of Steele, in one of its softest inspirations, first saw her about the year 1674, on the continent of America, fondly bending over a young European, whom she had preserved from her barbarous countrymen; she was banqueting him with delicious fruits, and playing with his hair. He called the vision Yarico.[101]

The terms of Boaden's infatuation are perhaps unsurprising. He fetishizes Kemble's performance of timidity and innocence in a manner that draws close parallels between the noble savage and the fantasy of feminine desirability. But the hyperbolic suggestion that Mrs. Kemble is Yarico personified or that she embodies Yarico makes explicit the degree to which Steele's and, by extension, Colman's Yarico is a phantasmatic projection of white femininity.

In terms of Colman's play, however, it is interesting that this phantasm is embodied by Mrs. Stephen Kemble and not by Mrs. Bannister, who played Narcissa in the first production. In other words, the fetishized white actress who plays the wronged native woman comes to embody the "engaging innocence and deep-toned pathos" of white femininity, while the ostensibly normative white woman becomes the object of neither erotic desire nor feminine identification but rather the example of "elegance, chasteness, and propriety."[102] This distinction between pathetic innocence and elegant propriety may seem slight, but its difference lies in its performance. Narcissa's erotic desirability, unlike that of

Yarico, is not presented through the staging of the masculine gaze but rather through her conjugal conversation with Campley. In short, Yarico is eroticized as a mistress, whereas Narcissa is always already a wife. The distinction involves two forms of commodification that impinge directly on how the audience consumes the two actresses' performance.

That consumption is very much conditioned by the way that Colman parses race and sexuality in the play. We have already seen how Yarico is carefully enveloped by a shroud of pastoral sentiment, but it is important to remember that the Inkle and Yarico dyad is always already accompanied by the pairing of their servants Trudge and Wowski. Indeed, the hypersexualization of Wowski and Trudge is the condition of possibility not only for the sentimental resolution of the interracial love plot between Inkle and Yarico but also for the ascription of normativity to Campley and Narcissa. Put simply, the exaggerated performance of racial difference in the lower-class characters is linked to sexual promiscuity, so that the relationship between Inkle and Yarico can be bled of all comparable sexual meaning on stage. Their relationship will be contained in a discourse of love, not sex, and thus the potential for miscegenation is quietly set aside. In this context, it is only in the Campley-Narcissa union that a future for reproductive heterosexuality lies, not because the play explicitly says this, but precisely because so little is said about their private lives. I have written extensively about this process elsewhere, but for our purposes here it is enough to look at one example of how the play deploys working-class characters to both critique the Inkle and Yarico relationship and establish the normativity of Campley and Narcissa.[103]

Late in act 3, scene 1, Trudge retells the story of the meeting of Inkle and Yarico to Patty. Patty is Sir Christopher's servant, and Colman locates the fear of interracial sexuality in her character. In response to Trudge's assertion of Yarico's beauty, Patty presses for a clarification:

PATTY: Well! And tell me, Trudge, she's pretty, you say: is she fair or brown or—?

TRUDGE: Um—she's a good comely copper.

PATTY: How? A tawny?

TRUDGE: Yes, quite dark, but very elegant. Like a Wedgwood teapot.

PATTY: Oh, the monster! The filthy fellow! Live with a black-a-moor?

TRUDGE: Why, there's no great harm in't, I hope?

PATTY: Fough, I wouldn't let him kiss me for all the world! He'd make my face all smutty.

TRUDGE: Zounds, you are mighty nice all of a sudden! But I'd have you to know, Madame Patty, that black-a-moor ladies, as you call'em, are some of the very few whose complexions never rub off! 'Sbud, if they did, Wows and I should have changed faces by this time. (3.1.98)

The trajectory of this exchange is notable, for Patty's abhorrence of interracial sexuality is countered by Trudge's invocation of one of the period's prevalent misogynist tropes. As the working-class woman asserts her racial privilege, Trudge launches into a critique of feminine artifice that is usually tied to charges of prostitution: "Pshaw, these girls are so plaguy proud of their white and red! But I won't be shamed out of Wows, that's flat. . . . After all the fine, flashy London girls, Wowski's the wench, for my money" (3.1.99). Trudge's gibe reengages the question of exchange and suggests that white working-class women don whiteness for the express purpose of increasing their value in the sexual market place. Trudge's "Black-a-moor ladies" have no recourse to artifice because they do not bring themselves to market but are rather forcibly commodified and because their value is ostensibly confined to the auction block. It is this latter point that Colman picks up on in particularly grotesque ways, first through Patty's ridicule of Inkle and then in Trudge's account of his constancy to Wowski.

Patty expressly refers to Inkle's relationship with Yarico as a "mistake" of a very particular sort. Her song in act 3, scene 1, reengages the hunting metaphor that runs through the play:

Song. PATTY.

Tho' lovers, like marksmen, all aim at the heart
Some hit wide of the mark, as we wenches all know,
But, of all the bad shots, he's the worst in the art
Who shoots at a pigeon and kills a crow—oho!
Your master has killed a crow. . . .
Love and money thus wasted in terrible trim,
His powder is spent and his shot running low,
Yet the pigeon he missed, I've a notion, with him
Will never for such a mistake pluck a crow—no, no,
Your master may keep his crow. (3.1.98–99)

This description of Inkle as one who is "unskilled how to level at wives" raises questions about his later remarks on hunting for money. The shared metaphor of the hunt draws attention to the fact that within the play's narrative and within British society at large the acquisition of a wife is a hunt for money. However, this understanding of marriage as a bond of familial and financial alliance is what pushes Inkle to sell Yarico in favor of Narcissa's standing. When he repents and decides to opt for love instead of duty, he is not only deviating from his mercantile duty but also from his duty to marry well. In this light, Patty's song advocates for a model of social relations that the play's sentimental plot ultimately rejects. That this advocacy comes from a working-class character is crucial, for Colman indulges in the racist discourse of the song and then, through a gesture of class containment, implies that this kind of discourse is part and parcel of subservience.

However, to stop reading the song at this point neglects the fact that the play contains two nonsentimental marriage plots. It is difficult to interpret precisely the final two lines of the song, but the pigeon in question is Narcissa, and Patty seems to be suggesting that Narcissa will not compete with Yarico for Inkle. She will instead cede Inkle to Yarico because, in "mistakenly" choosing a "crow," Inkle the merchant has shown himself to be unworthy of Narcissa's hand. It is Inkle who has lost his value—that is, spent his powder and his shot—in the middle-class marriage market. I would argue further that this devaluation is tied to the figuration of Inkle as Vulcan and emphasizes that Inkle's defect is ultimately one of class identity. This implies that interracial sexual desire constitutes an infraction against the codes of middle-class self-stylization. Foucault's prescient commentary on the racialization of classed bodies is apposite here for, as Ann Laura Stoler argues, the middle class is trying to train itself out of certain vulnerabilities.[104] Inkle's "defect," his sentimental interracial desire, therefore must be ejected but retained within view as an example. Interestingly, the question of what to do with Inkle at the close of the play was a fundamental problem for Colman. John Adolphus argues that "the thought of Inkle's repentance, which brings the piece to a satisfactory, if an awkward conclusion, was suggested by [Bannister]. 'But, after all,' said Colman, 'what are we to do with Inkle?' 'Oh!' said Bannister, 'let him repent'; and so it was settled."[105] The shaming of Inkle associated with the earlier versions of the tale has been effectively redeployed. What was earlier a moral lesson in gender propriety has become a moral and economic lesson in the cost of interracial desire and miscegenation to the emergent middle class. Inkle's exemplarity guarantees his retention in a nebulous zone of necessary counternormativity.

The argument I am presenting here gains some depth when we look at Trudge's answer to Patty's song, for it clarifies the intrication of class and interracial desire in the play:

A clerk I was in London gay'
    Jemmy linkum feedle
And went in boots to see the play,
    Marry fiddlem tweedle.
I marched the lobby, twirl'd my stick,
    Diddle, daddle, deedle;
The girls all cried, "He's quite the kick."
    Oh, Jemmy linkum feedle. (3.1.99)

As Sutcliffe notes, Trudge is "aping the affectations of high society" (99) in the theatre lobby. Such a reference to the social milieu in which the audience finds itself lends a certain urgency to the song's humor for an explicit comparison is being made between Trudge's imitation of Inkle and the social performance of class envy. While Inkle is not described as a young buck—he is far too engaged in the hunt for money for that—it is clear that Trudge's actions in the play frequently repeat those of Inkle. As noted earlier, the wooing of Wowski rigorously restages the conversation and duet of Inkle and Yarico. However, Trudge and Wowski are far too sexually experienced to perform an exact rehearsal. Likewise, Trudge's performance in the lobby for the "English" belles engages the same discourse of prostitution discussed earlier, but as the song continues and Trudge finds himself in America, the question of exchange value is fundamentally altered by Wowski's racial difference:

Your London girls with roguish trip,
    Wheedle, wheedle, wheedle,
May boast their pouting under-lip,
    Fiddle, faddle, feedle.
My Wows would beat a hundred such,
    Diddle, daddle, deedle,
Whose upper lip pouts twice as much,
    O, pretty double wheedle!

Rings I'll buy to deck her toes,
    Jemmy linkum feedle;
A feather fine shall grace her nose,

Waving siddle seedle.
With jealousy I ne'er shall burst,
Who'd steal my bone of bone-a?
A white Othello, I can trust
A dingy Desdemona. (3.1.99–100)

Trudge counters the bodily sign of female desirability here figured as the "pouting under-lip" of the London girls with one of the emergent signs of racial difference—that is, Wowski's full lips. It is tempting to read the facial expression of the London girls as signifying the fact that they are never happy with one such as Trudge, and I suspect the fact that Colman specifies that it is Wowski's upper lip that pouts twice as much is tied to a racist image of mental inferiority—there is no shortage of such gestures in the play. But the tenuous ascription of meaning here is superseded by the extraordinary closing verse of the song that emphasizes that Wowski is valuable to Trudge precisely because her racially coded body makes her undesirable to other white men. The racial inversion of the Othello-Desdemona pair makes this explicit, but the allusion has complex connotations when one considers the overall trajectory of the song. Othello's desire to accede to whiteness through the acquisition of Desdemona has its counterpart in Trudge's desire to reap the sexual spoils of class privilege in the theatre lobby. Trudge's class envy haunts his actions before meeting Wowski just as surely as Othello's jealousy haunts his tragic figure. But Trudge is comically reformed by Wowski. In this light, the reversal of race in the Othello-Desdemona pair figures a negation of class envy. Trudge's devotion to Wowski involves an explicit rejection of his earlier imitation of the whoring aristocrat in the theatre. That such a performance of class envy in the metropolitan theatre has been unsuccessful opens the door for a different imitation in the colonial realm. Trudge imitates Inkle and takes a "dingy dear," but the vector of class imitation reverses. Trudge is no longer playing the young buck but rather increasingly embraces his position in a fashion that would have warmed the hearts of those in the audience who are threatened by the very performability of class evident in the theatre lobby. Furthermore, it is Inkle now who imitates Trudge for, as we have seen, his decision to sell Yarico *and* repent places him in a liminal position somewhere outside the middle class.

Both sets of interracial couples are consigned to the constitutive outside of the middle class, but they function in different ways. Trudge and Wowski become increasingly connected to figures of domestic bliss as in the Finale:

TRUDGE: 'Sbobs, now I'm fix'd for life!
My fortune's fair, tho' black's my wife;
Who fears domestic strife?
Who cares now a souse?
Merry cheer my dingy dear
Shall find with her factotum here;
Night and day I'll frisk and play
About the house with Wows. (3.3.111)

Wowski's lack of sexual exchange value but surplus of sexual use value draw Trudge's working-class sexuality out of the public sphere and into a frisky zone of private play. In other words, Trudge and Wowski are subject to the regulatory fantasies through which the middle class consolidated first itself and then its class others. Inkle and Yarico become exemplars of conjugal love that are notably disconnected from both direct expressions of class and geographical location:

YARICO: . . . Doomed to know care and woe,
Happy still is Yarico,
Since her love will constant prove
And nobly scorns to shrink.
INKLE: Love's convert here behold,
Banished now my thirst of gold,
Bless'd in these arms to fold
My gentle Yarico.
Hence all care, doubt and fear,
Love and joy each want shall cheer,
Happy night, pure delight,
Shall make our bosoms glow. (3.3.111–12)

Yarico's—and Mrs. Kemble's—surplus of erotic desirability that so moved Boaden engages the sexual fantasies of the play's audience, but these same fantasies are quickly re-routed to bolster the redefinition of marriage as a site of conjugal devotion rather than economic affiliation. Inkle's final song in the finale points toward a bower of bliss beyond the reach of capital that is as ideological as the regulatory fantasies mentioned previously.

The play's normative couple, Campley and Narcissa, remain importantly undefined. They exhibit Inkle and Yarico's devotion and Trudge and Wowski's commitment to a heterosexuality confined to the domestic sphere, but they have not "taken black for white" and thus accede to normativity. What is clear, however, is that their union has the sanction of the state in the person of Narcissa's father and that the economic viability of the marriage is directly related not only to the continued growth of the military's role in British colonial affairs but also to a transference of the economic gains of mercantile hegemony to this emergent imperial vision. That this new vision is so insistently linked to the health of Campley's body—to Rodney's leg as it were—marks this play as a crucial turning point in the culture of British imperialism in the Atlantic world.

CHAPTER SIX

Days and Nights of the Living Dead

Handelmania

It is the winter of 1784. The American colonies have been irrecoverably lost. There is widespread understanding—sometimes stated explicitly—that Britain's political and martial elites were to blame. The damage to the British economy is extensive, yet disturbingly unclear. War in India is going poorly and, in many eyes, is turning into another potential humiliation. The East India Company's bellicosity and the excesses of Warren Hastings are eerily reminiscent of the errors leading to the reverses in North America. Ireland is beset with unrest. The Fox-North coalition has generated great ill-will, and the king's interference in the passage of Fox's East India Bill has elicited one of the worst constitutional crises in British history. The ensuing election of 1784 is the most divisive and fractious of the eighteenth century. What better time for a grand celebration.

The State of Denial: The 1784 Handel Commemoration

By any standards, the five-day Commemoration of Handel staged in the spring of 1784 ranks as one of the three or four most significant performance events in the eighteenth century. It was originally scheduled as a three-day celebration with concerts in Westminster Abbey on the first and third days and a concert at the Pantheon on the second day, but the king and queen commanded repeat performances of the first and third days' programs, thereby turning the Commemoration into a five-day event. The staging of *Messiah* in Westminster Abbey on the third day involved more than five hundred performers and drew an audience of over forty-five hundred people (fig. 6.1). As Claudia Johnson has argued, the Commemoration was very much about size: it involved the largest orchestra and largest choir ever convened.[1] And it was widely held that the vast numbers

Figure 6.1. "View of the Orchestra and Performers in Westminster Abbey, during the Commemoration of Handel." From Charles Burney, *An Account of the Musical Performances in Westminster Abbey and the Pantheon . . . in Commemoration of Handel* (London: Payne and Robinson, 1785), 107. Y,4.286. Department of Prints and Drawings © Trustees of the British Museum.

of performers, the immense audience, and the grand settings were particularly suited to the sublimity of Handel's music. Nothing had ever been attempted on this scale before, and its effect was to all accounts extraordinary. The musical sublime, which was so clearly the object of the performances, prompted the papers to indulge in increasingly sublime rhetoric. One could argue that the concerts provided a testing ground for the political effectivity of the sublime.[2]

The Commemoration generated highly detailed day-by-day discussion across the press and a book-length commentary by Charles Burney, which offered an account of Handel's life and described the genesis of the event and the effect of every piece performed on the program.[3] Burney wrote under the explicit patronage of George III, who did everything possible to align himself with Handel's music in this period. As many commentators have noted, Burney's text is a partisan account of an extremely important political ritual, which used the power of a vast array of performers to proclaim the emergence of a new era. As William Weber has argued, the Commemoration turned Handel into a national icon and instantiated a string of celebratory programs of Handel's music well into the 1790s.[4] For enthusiastic observers of musical culture such as Anna Seward and her circle, "Handel's oratorios stood for national music, and for the ecstatic possibilities of the religious sublime—as well as its opposite, lyric sensuality."[5]

Even reports skeptical of the Commemoration's aesthetic and political significance described the entire affair not only as the highest attainment of musical art but also as the most remarkable social gathering in living memory:

> We cannot in any adequate terms describe the grandeur of this festival. Habituated as we are to public exhibitions, and having had the opportunity of beholding whatever has engaged the notice of the metropolis for many years, we may be allowed to speak from comparison—on experience, therefore, we say, that so grand and beautiful a spectacle, with, at the same time, a feast so rich and so perfect, has not been presented to the public eye within our memory. The *coup d'oeil* infinitely surpassed that of the trial of the Duchess of Kingston in Westminster-hall—and the Jubilee of Garrick, from which the idea of the present was taken, though it filled the bosoms of men with equal enthusiasm, fell greatly short in the execution. On the trial of the Duchess of Kingston there was a heavy grandeur—the robes and etiquette of rank, aided by the gloom of the Hall, prevented us from enjoying the beauties of variety. Here we had all the youth, beauty, grandeur and taste of the nation, unrestrained by the regulations of a

court of law, and grouped in all the natural and easy appearance of the *pele mele*. The ladies were without diamonds, feathers, or flowers, and thus, in our mind, their charms were embellished.

—For beauty
Needs not the foreign aid of ornament;
But is, when unadorn'd, adorn'd the most.[6]

The lack of distinction between the events discussed here—all notable for their capacity to draw elite society into close quarters—is revealing. For the correspondent to the *London Magazine*, the Handel Commemoration was more aesthetically satisfying than the Shakespeare Jubilee and preferable to the trial of the Duchess of Kingston because fashion, and thus the exhibition of female beauty, was given more free rein.[7] That the trial in question was one of the scandals of the age does not even warrant commentary, but significantly the verse cited here, derived from James Thomson's *The Seasons* and made famous by its deployment in Joseph Addison's remarks on fashion in *Spectator*, no. 265, places the question of the exhibition of female virtue on the same plane as the cultural work necessary to crystallize Shakespeare and Handel as the iconic artists of Britain.[8] In this context, the word *foreign* in Thomson's lines carries ethnocentric connotations that permeate the press coverage of the Commemoration. What interests me here is that the correspondent is marking a historical difference from both the trial of the Duchess of Kingston and the Shakespeare Jubilee: in his eyes, both women and art—and, by extension, the nation—had changed since 1776 and 1769 respectively. And this change is figuratively linked to a supposed curtailment of ornament, here applied first to the women in attendance, but later—rather more incongruously—tied to the music of Handel.[9] This hypostatization of nature in both society and music comes to play a key role in the legacy of the Commemoration, for it had a significant impact on how virtue was conceived and culturally mediated in the period after the American war.

Music and Governance

The press focused its attention on three interrelated concerns: the sublimity of the music in this unusually grand setting, the demonstration of national pride as exemplified primarily in the royal family, and the capacity of the event—and specifically of Handel's music—to inculcate the virtue necessary for the renovation of the state. This last point is particularly important because it suggests that the entire event was both conceived and received as more than mere entertainment. William Weber has carefully demonstrated the relationship between the directors of the Commemoration and the emergence of an ostensibly "new order" led by the government of William Pitt. As he states, "The Commemoration put in ritual form the culmination of the country's political development over the previous three decades. The new harmony seen in the grand event suggested the reunion of Tories with Whigs and the growth of a new political community—a kind of establishment—that, despite the conflict over the war and the constitution, was broad-bottomed in its inclusion of faction and opinion."[10] Weber's analysis of the event is attentive to its immediate proximity to the constitutional crisis arising from George III's interference in the passage of Fox's East India Bill in early January 1784 and to the ongoing dispute over the Westminster election.[11]

If one consults the press coverage of the Handel Commemoration, one finds it often interspersed with the political wrangling over Fox's contested seat and with satirical remarks either on the king's abuse of his prerogative or on the Whigs insolvency and lack of patriotism.[12] Both of these issues are crucial to how we understand the reception of the Commemoration, because they are linked by a shared concern over the relationship between virtue and governance that ultimately impinges on the stylization of masculinity. If, like many Whigs, one was deeply troubled by George III's flirtation with absolutism, then one was sensitive to the recurrent deployment of tropes of despotism in this period. Figured as the despot, the monarch became simultaneously the embodiment of arbitrary power and effeminate lassitude. Some papers directly invoked the king's infringements on the constitution: "Under the patronage of his Majesty a most *harmonious meeting* will re-assemble on Saturday in the Abbey;—it is to be lamented that a similar spirit of *concord* cannot be diffused through *two* buildings in the *neighbourhood*:—but *secret influence* has seized upon the Government, and the safety of the State requires vigilance from the honest representatives of the people."[13] But the *Morning Herald*'s less-than-subtle excoriation of Pitt and the king and its invocation of Fox as the "man of the people" were in many ways minority opinions: the press was replete with anti-Whig sentiment. If, like many Tories, one was horrified by the ambition and immorality of Fox, then there was no shortage of satirical materials attacking Fox for his gaming, his profligacy, and his libertinism. The combination of excessive sexual and financial expenditure was most potently activated in tropes that figured the entire Fox-North coalition as voluptuaries running the nation into bankruptcy in order to pursue their pleasures and to cover their gambling debts. It was another version of the tropology of despotism that signaled a widely held belief that the notion of King-in-Parliament had devolved into a parody of itself.

In this context, some of the papers singled out specific individuals desperately in need of moral and political reform. Not surprisingly, the Duchess of Devonshire, who was widely satirized for campaigning for Fox in Westminster, figures prominently here.[14] The *Public Advertiser* reviewed the seating arrangements in the Abbey and indicated its desire for a new political order as follows: "The Duchess of Devonshire was close to Mr. Pitt; which we hope, presages a Contiguity to more decorous Politics."[15] A few papers gently chided the Prince of Wales for his Whig affiliations by dutifully reporting that he was not present at any of the sacred performances in Westminster Abbey and that he appeared at the Pantheon concert "incognito" or as "a private gentleman" separate from the royal entourage.[16] Aside from implying his distance from both the Church and the Crown, there is also a subtle critique of his dissipation in the suggestion that he is masquerading in the Pantheon like any other young blade. Fox is conspicuous by his absence. And the more factionalized papers are replete with reports of the frustration of "the Blue and Buff Division"; my favorite is a brief account of a "Chevalier d'Industrie," who, having already ruined the country, pathetically steals tickets for the Pantheon performance while other members of his "Order" steal watches "in order to be punctual to the proper Hour of returning."[17]

But there was more at stake than simply satirizing Foxite society. Perhaps the most revealing report takes aim at John Montagu, the 4th Earl of Sandwich, who was one of the principle leaders of the Commemoration. A man of exceedingly bad personal and military reputation—he was a notorious libertine, and his term as lord of the Admiralty during the American war was disastrous—his involvement in the affair became exemplary for the *Morning Post*:

> The Earl of Sandwich shews the first good example to the ruined adherents of the [Fox-North] Coalition, in betaking himself to an honest industrious calling.
>
> When the vigour of mind and body, and appetite for vicious indulgences are flown, mankind have recourse to devotion! So *Jemmy Twitcher*, after failing in every worldly pursuit, is now raising his eyes to Heaven; and, driven from the Admiralty and the Parks, is glad to take refuge at the foot of the altar![18]

The correspondent is particularly interested in the toll vice has taken on the body of the Earl of Sandwich and, despite the mildly satirical gibes regarding his desperation before the altar, has an investment in the renovation of bodily and mental vigor. This investment is constitutional in both senses of the term because this particular manifestation of Handel's music, according to many of the papers, not only has the hygienic capacity to cure both the aristocracy and the Crown but also promises to curtail corruption and to return government to its past dignity. This capacity is explicitly articulated by the *Gazetteer* right after the first full rehearsal in the Abbey:

> Such entertainments as the ensuing musical feasts in commemoration of Handel do the highest honour to the nation where they are encouraged, and give superior dignity to the Monarch who patronizes them, as well as those of the nobility and gentry who follow so laudable an example. How much better is the money so spent employed than that which is laid out in debauchery, dissipation, and luxury! The latter practice tends to enervate the mind, to enfeeble the constitution, and to waste the fortune; while the former exalts the soul, improves the judgement, and delights the ear of taste. Let reason and prudence make their choice.[19]

The choices presented here take the form of a historical ultimatum, which needs to be read in a broader frame than the immediate context of the constitutional crisis of 1783 and the election of 1784. These contemporaneous events represented a significant threat to the nation, but they were on the way to being resolved. What looms over this utterance is the failure of the state to retain the American colonies and the unresolved recalibration of the national and imperial economy. The person described in the penultimate sentence—enervated, enfeebled, and financially embarrassed—is a figure for the nation itself at this historical juncture, and the illness that has generated these symptoms did not come on overnight. The emasculated voluptuary here—and it was clearly formerly a man—has destroyed himself, and the readers of the *Gazetteer* are being hailed on the eve of the first performance into a new form self-stylization that turns on a combination of moral and aesthetic judgment. In fact, it is in the fusion of these forms of judgment that the vigor of the nation will be reconstituted. As we will see, this narrative of self-destruction and renovation is a crucial dynamic in the program of the Commemoration.

The next morning the *Public Advertiser* offered an even more explicit politicization of the Commemoration, which, despite its predictable ridicule of Whigs bankrupting the nation, in its language suggests that the event itself was generated by the British Constitution:

> The Patronage of Genius in such Magnitude as this unrivalled Composer is well worthy of such a Constitution as Great Britain!—and when some Historical Narrative of the Arts shall refer to the Publications of the Times, for the Accounts of this memorable Transaction, let the The PUBLIC ADVERTISER record, that it was little less than what may be called the Constitution which accomplished this great Effort—That his Majesty's Assent, spontaneous and hearty Assent was with it—That the Aristocracy also supported it—at least those among them who are not reduced to Bankruptcy by Gambling, and the yet more extravagant Villainy of bringing Beggars into Parliament—And last, not least in all Matters of Entertainment and Expense, by the *Majesty of the People.*[20]

Here the Commemoration is figured as a parliamentary bill that, unlike Fox's East India Bill, has received the support of the people or Commons, the aristocracy or Lords, and has been given royal assent. Fox's East India Bill received an overwhelming plurality in the House of Commons but was killed in the House of Lords after the king made it known that anyone who supported the bill in the upper house would be deemed his enemy. George III's interference directly precipitated the constitutional crisis and the fractious election of 1784. Read in this way, the Handel Commemoration becomes a surrogate governmental action: one that not only puts ongoing crisis in abeyance but also indulges in the fantasy of an abstract agent—the Constitution—generating its own recuperation.

Not everyone was so easily drawn into the fantasy of conciliation in part because those responsible for the perceived decline of British society were present in body if not in soul. William Cowper was deeply disturbed by the "canonization" of Handel in the Abbey and saw the entire event as the "profanation of a sacred building."[21] As H. Diack Johnstone has argued, Cowper's critique of the Commemoration was aimed primarily at the clergy, but his overall position is that the entire event is a further symptom of the decline of national morality.[22] This kind of diagnostic was not confined to evangelicals such as Cowper. The most biting critique comes in the pages of the *St. James Chronicle*, and I am particularly interested in the correspondent's notion of the "mingled Expression" elicited by the hypocrisy of the audience during the performance of *Messiah*:

> But all murmurs were silenced by the commanding, perhaps terrifick, Manner in which the Chorusses were performed.

> Agitated and affected as we were by them, we could not keep out of our Minds Ideas of Regret and sometimes Disgust, arising from the Nature, Character, and Views of the Assembly, and the aweful Subject of the Entertainment. It has been the diligent Study of men in Power in this Country for Twenty years, to discredit every principle that can render Man useful or respectable. Almost all the active Instruments of publick and private Vice were in our Eye when the Band broke out into—"Hallelujah! The Lord God omnipotent reigneth." And such a Scene would baffle the Skill of Homer; though the Finger of Heaven traces legibly the Characters of Iniquity on the human countenance. The Assent given to the Excellence of the Performances and the Resistance made to the terrifick Truth of the sublime Sentence, formed a *mingled Expression* more unpleasing and hateful than can be well imagined. This Circumstance has long induced us to avoid Oratorios, as they are performed exactly in the Manner of Parodies, to ridicule and insult the moral and religious Sentiments they were meant to promote; and it will make us deem the Commemoration of Handel as *signal Proof of the musical Proficiency, and the abandoned Profligacy of the present Period.*[23]

The correspondent here, unlike the writers for the *Gazetteer* and the *Public Advertiser* previously cited, is all too conscious of how vice inheres in the "countenance" of the nation and how the staging of Handel's sublimity is lost on those who have not the capacity to hear it in spite of the "terrifick" power of choruses more than two hundred singers strong. The face figured forth here is remarkable not only because it is disfigured by a long history of iniquity but also because its "mingled expression" intersperses assent to musical pleasure with resistance to religious and moral sentiment. The implication is that what has remained constant among the elite audience assembled in the Abbey is a commitment to pleasure. In light of the preceding notices in the press and the passage's own explicit critique of the political health of the state, it is difficult not to hear political overtones in the words "Assent" and "Resistance." From this perspective, the Commemoration's very size and the sublimity of Handel's music become signs of the moral deafness and hypocrisy of the "Instruments of publick and private Vice." As the last sentence in the passage emphasizes, aesthetic judgment has broken with moral judgment, and the latter remains foreign to the assembly. Significantly, the correspondent does not mark the party affiliation of these assembled "Instruments" but rather forcefully implies that they have not only ruled for the last "twenty years" but also remain in power. It is a universal indictment of the elites who have ruled and continue to rule Great Britain.

Although the *St. James Chronicle*'s correspondent is the most vituperative of the commentators, his recognition that musical consumption may not lead to any kind of moral reform in the listeners marks a certain anxiety associated with music itself that appears elsewhere in the press. That anxiety has to do with the enervation and emasculation conventionally associated with the reception of Italian music and specifically opera. And these anxieties had a notable influence on overall arc of the Commemoration's program. Handel's formidable operatic works were represented by brief selections at the Pantheon, and that performance was sandwiched between two "sacred" concerts at Westminster Abbey. Furthermore, when the king and queen commanded repeat performances of the Commemoration, the program of Handel's Italian arias was conspicuously absent.

In order to counteract conventional wisdom that associated musical pleasure with dissipation, much of the press made explicit links between musical reception and fantasies of governmental prowess, between aesthetic pleasure and virtuous rule. The most extreme instance of this kind of rhetoric was articulated immediately preceding the first day of the Commemoration, and it argues that music, and specifically Handel's music, constitutes a fundamental component of martial and political subjectivity:

> His is the muse for the English character. He writes to the masculine genius of a free people, and it was only by such an execution that the true majesty of his composition could be demonstrated. It has been attributed to music that it enervates the mind. How far this may be true of the refinements of the Italian school, or even of simple melodies, we do not think ourselves competent to determine; but the most refined and most martial people of antiquity, the inhabitants of ancient Greece, whose achievements both in arts and in arms fill the mind with astonishment and incredulity, were so enamoured of the charms of harmony, that they deemed a proficiency on some musical instrument an essential embellishment to the character of the statesman, the general, and the oratour. And surely, if any thing can more than ordinarily invigorate the mind; if anything can arouse the faculties, and coagitate the masculine passions of the soul, it is the music of Handel, performed by such a band as are now engaged in his commemoration.[24]

Again there is a predictable antithesis between "the masculine genius of the free people" of England and the enervation associated with the Italian school. But there is a more complex argument here as well—a very tendentious antithesis proffered between melody and harmony. Melody is very subtly aligned with Italian refinement, enervation, and emasculation. In contrast, harmony is forcefully aligned with the martial prowess of ancient Greece, and it is this elevation of harmony over melody that makes musical proficiency essential to the statesman, the general, and the orator. With the invocation of this triad of masculine leaders, the correspondent is attempting to articulate the specific importance of Handel to the state and that seems to lie in harmony's capacity to bring disparate elements into an apt arrangement of parts. Handel's genius for harmony is being put forward as a figure for or as a model for the right disposition of men and things: in other words, as a trope for military and political governance.

How Haven't the Mighty Fallen

That this argument is so strongly affiliated with martial achievements from the ancient world is significant, because, as the correspondent for the *London Magazine* was well aware, the "sacred" concert scheduled for the next day was an exceedingly bellicose affair. The program for the first performance was widely published, and it carefully interweaves some of Handel's most famous anthems with fragments from the oratorios.[25] All of the chosen compositions explicitly praise the king and the Hanoverian line, but it is worth attending to which works were presented in their entirety, which were abridged, and the overall order of the program. As Ruth Smith has persuasively demonstrated, the reception of Handel's music, and particularly the oratorios, was extraordinarily attentive to topical allegory. There is no reason to assume that the audience's tendency to read Handel's music for political allegory would have abated from the midcentury or earlier; if anything, the explicitly political motives of the directors, well documented in the press, would have prepared the audience for a complex negotiation with history mediated through the words and music of the selected works.

After the king and the royal family were greeted with the *Coronation Anthem of Zadok the Priest*, a very specific historical narrative unfolds. Part 1 adds the overture to *Esther* to a full performance of the *Dettingen Te Deum*—the only work, aside from the performance of *Messiah* on the third and fifth days, given in its entirety. The *Dettingen Te Deum* is not a conventional Te Deum but a grand martial panegyric that "celebrated the national success against the forces of Catholic absolutism."[26] In June 1743 George II led an alliance of British, Austrian, and Hanoverian troops to a decisive victory over the French in the War of

Austrian Succession. It was the last time a reigning British monarch led a British force into battle, and importantly it was a war with little or no colonial theatres or consequences. As "Composer of the Musick to the Chapel Royal," Handel was commissioned to compose a Te Deum and an anthem for a day of public thanksgiving on George II's return from the Continent. As one might expect, it is martial in almost every sense of the term. Charles Burney's account of the Commemoration gives a hint of its most prominent features by listing the chief instruments: "I shall only observe that as it was composed for a military triumph, the fourteen trumpets, two pair of common kettle-drums, two pair of double drums from the Tower, and a pair of double-base drums, made expressly for this Commemoration, were introduced with great propriety; indeed, these last drums, except the destruction, had all the effect of the most powerful artillery."[27]

Within the closed space of Westminster Abbey, the effect of the drums in the first chorus of the Te Deum must have been almost overwhelming. But there was more than a figural link between these drums and artillery. Hypernationalist elements in the press stressed that they came from the ordnance stores, and their provenance is revealing:

> On each side of the Organ . . . are the Kettle Drums, a pair of which was made of unusual dimensions, in a very spirited manner, by Mr. Aspridge at his own expence on this occasion; and another pair of equal fame with the circumstance they are now produced to celebrate; they were brought from the Tower yesterday by permission of his Grace the Duke of Richmond, being a part of the ordnance stores, and the instruments taken from the French at the battle of Malplaquet, by the Great Duke of Marlborough.[28]

Everything here would appear to be overdetermined. The drums used to rehearse George II's victory at Dettingen turn out to be material artifacts from Marlborough's earlier victory at Malplaquet. Two historical instances of heroic British victory over the French on the Continent are brought together in the Abbey, but the act of rememoration here is aimed at forgetting the more recent and pressing defeat in America. This is surrogation in its most basic form: a form of denial predicated on the mobilization of compensatory narratives.

But the problem here is that surrogative narratives are always already unstable either because they do not adequately cover the historical wound or because their excessive visibility draws attention to what is hidden below. The bandage either does not fit or draws too much attention to itself. The former problem is made evident by the press's interest in the material provenance of the drums. On 11 September 1709 the allied forces of Britain, Holland, and Austria under the command of the Duke of Marlborough defeated the French at Malplaquet, but they lost twenty thousand men, almost twice that of the enemy. It was the bloodiest battle not only of the War of Spanish Succession but of the entire eighteenth century. And it may well have been a strategic victory for the French, in that the loss of life prevented an allied assault on Paris. News of the carnage and of the inconclusiveness of the battle traumatized the nations of Europe. These particular drums are evidence of Pyrrhic victory and have the potential to activate as much anxiety as triumphalism. Alternatively, one could argue that their deployment is folded into an overarching strategy of surrogation aimed at assuaging a whole constellation of traumatic events in Britain's recent military past. If the musical sublime has the potential to generate a revisionist history where Britain only ever wins over the French, then why not throw in the disturbing slaughter outside Mons for good measure. The two events—the American war and the Battle of Malplaquet—are linked by the disturbing fact that martial superiority does not necessarily translate into victory or divine election.

A correspondent for the same paper that invoked the memory of the "Great Duke of Marlborough" on the eve of the first performance recognized both the stakes and the potential for surrogation to go awry when it came time to report on the repetition of the same program on the fourth day: "We cannot help thinking that the drums were by much too powerful for the other parts of the band.—They stunned and dumbfounded, but did by no means fill the mind with those sentiments of terror which are the effect of the musical sublime. They were least offensive in the Dead March in Saul, where perhaps their sepulchral tones were most admissable. The *thunder of music* should always be proportioned to its *still small voice*."[29] This suggestion that the drum parts in the performance of the *Dettingen Te Deum* stunned audience members rather than terrified them is crucial because it is through terror that the sublime opens onto awe and reverence. To be stunned is to be returned to the moment of historical trauma, and, in this case, the affiliation between the carnage of Malplaquet and the humiliation of Yorktown only deepens the sense of powerlessness. The key distinction here lies in the temporality of these aesthetic effects. Sublime terror carries with it a certain futurity that is folded into the act of reverence; being stunned keeps one in a damaged state, waiting for some kind of release.

The directors' choice of the *Dettingen Te Deum* was, I believe, aimed at avoiding precisely these kind of connotations, and the fact that the press nevertheless makes these connections is significant. Handel's decision to employ battlefield instruments to enhance the sense of jubilation and the emphatic treatment of the opening six verses is not subtle. As Donald Burrows argues, "Handel's style in the more extrovert sections of the Dettingen Te Deum, as with all such powerful rhetoric, requires the listener to share rather uncritically in the emotions of the moment. . . . Celebration and judgement are the two topics that remain in the memory of the listener at the end of the Te Deum."[30] Nevertheless, Charles Burney felt it was necessary to specifically obviate the potential for a sorrowful interpretation of what should have been a fairly straightforward passage:

> There is some reason to suspect that Handel, in setting his grand *Te Deum* for the peace of Utrecht, as well as this [the *Dettingen Te Deum*], confined the meaning of the word *cry* to a sorrowful sense: as both the movements to the words—
>
> *To thee all angels* cry *aloud,*
>
> are not only in a minor-key, but slow, and plaintive. It contrasts well, however, with the preceding and subsequent movements. Indeed, the latter glows with all the fire and vehemance of Handel's genius for polyphonic combinations and contrivances.[31]

Drawing the reader's attention to the "fire and vehemance" of the surrounding movements is not surprising, as this is precisely what the *Te Deum* itself does; but worrying over the meaning of "cry" overemphasizes its sorrowful connotations in order to dispense with them. As Burrows argues, this verse's potential for plaintiveness was already well contained: "Even in the more lyrical and restrained, 'To thee all Angels cry aloud' [Handel] was unusually careful to avoid any possible ambiguity by marking the voice parts 'tutti' at the opening accolade and the first entry: he wanted *all* the angels on duty."[32] "Cry" here is an occasion for unifying utterance, not sorrow. Burney's prophylactic remarks on the performance reveal the other problem with surrogation: it requires vigilant surveillance and containment of possible divergent readings. It is as though sorrow must be kept at bay, because it is everywhere threatening to permeate the proceedings. This is perhaps why part 2 of the first performance not only turns explicitly to the question of death but also so stringently manages the work of mourning.

If the drums generated equivocal associations in the *Dettingen Te Deum*, they were universally praised in the Dead March from *Saul*, which opened the second part of the first performance, in part because there is a demonstrable shift from matters of war to a more complex—and perhaps mystifying—political narrative.

Part 2 takes two of Handel's most famous treatments of death, segments them, and sutures them together. The program unfolded as follows:

Overture, with the DEAD MARCH in SAUL
Part of the FUNERAL ANTHEM. [for Queen Caroline]
When the ear heard him.
He that delivered the poor that cried.
His body is buried in Peace.
GLORIA PATRI, from the JUBILATE [for the Peace of Utrecht].[33]

At one level, this sequence simply features some of Handel's best-known and best-loved compositions. Winton Dean notes that "the Overture and Dead March . . . were among the most popular of Handel's instrumental pieces and appeared frequently in concert programmes."[34] The *Funeral Anthem of Queen Caroline* was redeployed by Handel under a different title—"The Lamentation of the Israelites for the Death of Joseph"—as the first part of *Israel in Egypt* and thus, like the excerpts from *Saul*, operated in the patriotic economy of the Israelite oratorios. And the Gloria Patri from the Utrecht Jubilate was not only frequently performed as church music throughout the century but also prefigures a similar passage in *Messiah*.[35] So listeners would have been on exceedingly familiar ground.

But with familiarity comes knowledge, and this particular grouping lends itself to a political reading because each element was widely understood either as part of a grand patriotic allegory or as an explicit statement of national election. In the ensuing paragraphs, I want to explore at least one reading of how these allegories operate, and everything I would argue flows from the selections from *Saul*. Charles Jennens's libretto takes a rather confusing and repetitive narrative from Samuel and refashions it into a highly dramatic tragedy. Act 1 opens immediately after David's victory over Goliath. King Saul first welcomes David to court and even offers him the hand of his daughter Merab. But this period of admiration is short-lived, and Saul is eventually overwhelmed by jealousy. Significantly, his son Jonathan recognizes this as a return of Saul's "old disease" but can do nothing to stop Saul from repeatedly attempting to murder David. As act 2 unfolds, Saul descends further into violent madness and eventually kills his own son. In the third act, Saul regains sanity, recognizes his hubris, but nonetheless continues to pursue David, this time with the assistance of the Witch of Endor. The witch summons the ghost of the prophet Samuel, who foretells Saul's death at the hands of the Amalekites because he disobeyed God in an earlier conflict with the Amalekites in which he was enjoined to slaughter the remaining survivors as a sacrifice to God. Saul is killed in a battle on Mount Gilboa, and the bodies of Saul and Jonathan are carried in to the strains of the Dead March. The march is followed by a remarkable elegy for both Saul and his son Jonathan. David is declared the new king and the final chorus urges him to "retrieve the Hebrew name."

Winton Dean's discussion of the libretto's thematic coherence underscores the overall arc of the narrative from rejoicing to mourning. He emphasizes that

> the finest achievement of this remarkable libretto is its handling of the great central theme—or themes, for there are two: the moral tragedy of Saul himself and the religious and political struggle of a small people beset by enemies. The progressive deterioration of Saul's character, confused and halting in the Bible account, is admirably clear. We are shown in turn the noble and generous King; the onset of jealousy and mental derangement (its suddenness mitigated by the information that it has happened before); the resort to physical violence. . . . culminating in a public assault on his own son at a religious festival; and a final ironical return of sanity when the obsession has played itself out, leaving him no remedy save the invocation of evil. But though morally this is his lowest point, artistically it enobles him. A dangerous lunatic is repulsive; a man who refuses to bow when fate has him beaten is a tragic figure.
>
> With Saul's decline is bound up at all points the fate of the Jewish people, as the chorus remind us at intervals. Here lies the significance of the great scenes of rejoicing and mourning that frame the oratorio, and of the turning from past to future in the final chorus.[36]

The narrative is tragic in the fullest sense of the term because it dramatizes the purging of the nation and the figuring forth of a new covenant. For our purposes, it is important that we recognize the significance of Saul's public assault on his son: it is the lowest point of Saul's violent frenzy and carries with it the most disturbing allegorical potential for the audience of the Commemoration, because it so forcefully raises the question of violence directed toward the family and the nation.[37]

Sitting in the Abbey in 1784, one hears only the Overture and the Dead March: the overall movement is from rejoicing to mourning. But it is a form of mourning that opens onto a new and ostensibly virtuous future. But for whom or what is one expected to be mourning? In the immediate political context, George III was widely excoriated for contravening the law of the land in his interference in the India Bill. The entire constitutional crisis of 1783–84 turns on the question of the king's relation to the law, and charges that his lawbreaking autocracy threatened the legacy of the Glorious Revolution were commonplace. There was also no shortage of rhetoric describing the war with America not only as a sign of derangement but also as an instance of the father's taking up arms against the son.[38] In a number of disturbing ways, George III bears resemblance to Saul, and the war on Mount Gilboa can be read as a figure for the war in America.

Now, I recognize the tendentiousness of this reading. As William Weber has argued, the directors of the Commemoration were explicitly interested in countering Whig factions and their support for the king and a broad-bottomed establishment was explicit. But what if this set of associations is part of a larger allegorical gambit that focuses on the transition from the past to the future? What we may be seeing here is the parsing of George III's kingship into two parts. We have a pre-1784 period where his bellicosity and his desire for autocracy were justifiably punished by God by a series of military losses and political crises. In this allegory, the entire period from the triumphant victory in the Seven Years' War, leading up to the conflict in America, is understood as a period that moves, as *Saul* does, from rejoicing to mourning. The death of Saul at the hand of the Amalekite now takes on very specific resonances, because in scripture the Amalekites, like the French, are the eternal and permanent enemies of Britain's proxy, the Israelites. But in this case, Saul's wounds are largely self-inflicted: the Amalekite only finishes off the job, and his function is to fulfill Samuel's prophecy. The upshot here is that, as Ruth Smith argues, "even God's anointed cannot escape the consequences of breaking God's Law."[39]

Such an allegory then opens the possibility for a renewed kingship for the post-1784 era, and specifically for the era following the constitutional crisis, that threatened to bring the disintegration already evident in the colonies home to the metropole itself. It is here that *Saul*'s other topical allegory kicks in, because the oratorio was written at the height of the opposition's attempt to bring down the Whig Ministry of Robert Walpole. Saul's madness springs from envy, and it was one of the vices most frequently associated with Walpole himself. As Smith argues, "For a contemporary audience the Saul-Walpole parallel would have been unmistakable. . . . It is worth noting in this connection that according to opposition writers, David is not only Saul's righteous successor; being the chief poet of the Scriptures, he is the archetype of all virtuous (that is, opposition) writers. It is of course *while he is singing and playing* that Saul tries to kill him, and this incident forms a central episode of the libretto."[40]

What I would suggest is that many of Saul's qualities are also those associated with another Whig minister routinely assailed for corruption and immorality. In the spring of 1784, Charles James Fox was regularly lampooned for envying the king's and Pitt's power. Even the daily reporting of the Commemoration cannot help joking about his destitution and his jealousy following his temporary defeat in the Westminster election. In this context, Fox is the dead leader and Pitt and the king emerge as the new David ready to reinvent the nation. This helps to explain why both the press and the king himself, through his patronage, affiliate themselves with both virtue and music in the Commemoration. In this figural economy, one George III is put to rest and another is called forth as his own successor. George III becomes the surrogative figure for himself and sits through a Dead March that consigns to oblivion not only his past self and all the attendant shortcomings of elite rule during this period but also Fox's challenge to the monarchy in the turbulent postwar years. And it is from here that we can retroactively understand the performance of the *Coronation Anthem of Zadok the Priest,* which opened the performance, as a reinauguration of the monarchy.

But this complex maneuver requires a very important supplementary gesture. The Dead March cannot be followed by Handel's remarkable elegy from *Saul* because it would demand not only a fundamental separation between the "dead" and the living king but also a reckoning with the death of the son. The opening chorus of the elegy is too much about the cost of war:

> Mourn, Israel, mourn thy beauty lost,
> Thy choicest youth on Gilboa slain!
> How have thy fairest hopes been cross'd!
> What heaps of mighty warriors strew the plain!

And Michal and David's lamentations over the death of Jonathan lend themselves all too readily to the antiwar rhetoric that consistently figured American patriots as sons and brothers who were acting on the very sense of political liberty that defined the parent country. In lieu of the elegy on the death of Saul and Jonathan, the audience is presented with three verses of the *Funeral Anthem for Queen Caroline* that focus on the mourned royal figure's enactment of virtuous government. Some sense of the importance of the anxiety concerning the death of Jonathan can be gleaned from the fact that it is doubly avoided, both in the suppression of the elegy from *Saul* and in the cutting of key verses from the *Funeral Anthem.* The repeated refrain "How are the mighty fallen," which is the emotional linchpin of the *Funeral Anthem* and which is derived from David's lament over Saul and Jonathan in 2 Samuel, is consistently elided from the Commemoration performance.

Ruth Smith has argued that the *Funeral Anthem* was the greatest collage anthem of Handel's time and that the strategic selection of fragments of scripture with little concern for context or even textual integrity prefigures Handel's practice in the oratorios.[41] Ranging across scripture with little concern for order, tense, or even person, the power of the anthem derives from the way the collage brings disparate elements of the Bible together in new and sometimes startling ways. For example, much of the patriotic spine of the anthem derives from an adaptation of verses from Lamentations that refigures the captive City of Jerusalem as the dead queen.[42] This gesture, along with the repeated invocation of the death of Jonathan from 2 Samuel, affiliates the particular loss of the queen with national crisis. Some sense of the allegorical force of tying the fate of the biblical nation of Israel to that of Britain via the dead body of the queen can be gleaned from the opening two choruses:

> CHORUS:
> The ways of Zion do mourn and she is in bitterness. [Lamentations 1:4]; all her people sigh [Lamentations 1:11] and hang down their heads to the ground [Lamentations 2:10].
>
> CHORUS:
> How are the mighty fall'n [2 Samuel 1:19]. She that was great among the nations, and princess of the provinces! [Lamentations 1:1].
> How are the mighty fall'n—[43]

It is in this second chorus that Handel links the queen and the City of Jerusalem, and the sense of mourning activated throughout this minor key section is quite complex. As Donald Burrows emphasizes,

> At the end of the first section the voices, gathered together, descend into gloom as they "hang their heads to the ground": the reaction in "How are the Mighty fall'n" comes as a protest as much as a lamentation. This text must have needed careful treatment, if the minds of the original listeners were not to be diverted towards a more worldly interpretation relating to Caroline's constant political support for Robert Walpole. . . . The fallen city from the Book of Lamentations perhaps bore some comparison with the passing of Queen Caroline, as a general parallel could be made in relating present desolation to the recollection of past glories.[44]

Both the specific and the general political interpretations are significant, because in the Commemoration virtually all of these passages in minor keys are elided. In other words, the sense of political and national desolation that Handel was so at pains to construct through his selection of scripture and through his complex movement from minor key to minor key is avoided in the Commemoration program. And this elided segment would have been exceedingly familiar to listeners because it constitutes the opening of the first act of *Israel in Egypt*.

The Commemoration program enters the *Funeral Anthem* immediately after this intense expression of specific and national loss. The focus now is resolutely on the celebration of past glory, but through a series of careful modifications, these same glories lose their pastness. Here is the section of the *Funeral Anthem* with the performed verses highlighted in italics:

SOLI & CHORUS:
When the ear heard her [him], then it blessed her [him], and when the eye saw her [him], it gave witness of her [him] [Job 29:11].

CHORUS:
How are the mighty fall'n [Samuel 2, 1:19]. She that was great, great among the nations, and princess of the provinces! [Lamentations 1:1]

CHORUS:
She [He] delivered the poor that cried, the fatherless, and him that had none to help him [Job 29:12]. Kindness, meekness, and comfort were her [his] tongue [Ecclesiasticus 36:23]; if there was any virtue, and if there was any praise, she [he] thought on those things [Philippians 4:8].

CHORUS:
How are the mighty fall'n [2 Samuel 1:19]. She that was great, great among the nations, and princess of the provinces! [Lamentations 1:1]

SOLI & CHORUS:
The righteous shall be had in everlasting remembrance [Psalms 112:16], and the wise will shine as the brightness of the firmament [Daniel 12:3].

CHORUS:
Their bodies are buried in peace; but their name liveth evermore [Ecclesiasticus 44:14].

The elisions here are crucial not only because they suppress any direct expression of loss—"How are the Mighty fall'n" is elided twice as are past-tense expressions of former greatness—but also because they keep almost the entire sequence in the major key. This is mourning in the major key, and the paradox inherent in that statement speaks to the strange alteration in the pronouns. With the switch from her to him throughout, the performance not only more firmly invokes *Israel in Egypt*, where this transposition had already taken place in order to focus attention on the death of Joseph, but also invokes the king. In light of our earlier reading of the deployment of the Dead March from *Saul*, what emerges here is an act of mourning for someone—and, by extension, something—who remains alive, because only his past is in the process of being buried. This is why there is little need for the minor key: in this rendering of the anthem, the mighty quite literally *have not* fallen.

The two verses from Job, which are now the focus of the performance, are those in which Job rehearses his past rectitude and the universal regard in which he was held as political official before he was stripped of everything. With the broader context of desolation and loss eliminated from the anthem, the verses and the music celebrate virtuous government. The tension now lies in the inherence of two key problems: Job is afflicted in spite of his virtue; and even if this virtue could be unequivocally celebrated, it has to be linked to the present to prevent the entire performance from lapsing into nostalgia for past glory. This is why the shift to "Their bodies are buried in peace; but their name liveth evermore" from Ecclesiasticus is so important. It both recognizes and contains this problem by transmuting the bodies of the dead (in this case, the forefathers of the nation) via the figural capacity of language—and, in this case, music—to move the listener from grief over a particular body to a generalized abstract notion of peace. The first section of this verse is the only section of the entire adaptation of the anthem that operates in a minor key. It is the carefully contained moment of grief, now rendered so general that it is politically safe, necessary for getting beyond mortality and all the implied, but never directly elicited, sense of loss. In the original text, this chorus "functions as a transitional stage in the subject and mood of the anthem. Although the subsequent movements are in minor keys, the cloud of mourning has lifted: 'How are the Mighty fall'n' does not occur again."[45] It should perhaps then come as no surprise that in the Commemoration program this transitional gesture opens not onto an elegiac minor key meditation but directly onto the Gloria Patri from the Jubilate celebrating the Peace of Utrecht, a passage that not only gives thanks to God for British imperial supremacy but also expansively resonates with one of the most famous sections of *Messiah*. Through careful selection, segmentation, and suturing, the work of mourning has been transformed into a remarkable declaration of national election that attempts to suppress the recent history of loss in the empire and surrogatively refigure the Paris Peace Treaty of 1783 as the Peace of Utrecht. Not only has loss has been tendentiously refigured as gain, but the political and economic turbulence of the present peace has been figuratively quelled.

Both the necessity and the extremity of this move to the Jubilate can be gleaned from Charles Burney's account of audience reaction to the performance of the second part of the first performance:

> Each of the three movements from the *Funeral Anthem*, seemed to excite such lively sensations of grief, as reminded all present of the ravages which death had made among their particular families and friends, and moved many to tears. . . . This Chorus, from the *Jubilate*, which Handel set at the same time as the grand *Te Deum*, for the peace at Utrecht . . . being in his grandest and most magnificent style, received every possible advantage in the performance, from a correct and powerful band, and the most mute and eager attention in the audience.[46]

Burney is working directly for the king, but I would argue that this passage reveals more than it conceals.[47] Despite the careful elision of all signs of desolation in this adaptation of the *Funeral Anthem*, it is the historically specific sense of affliction, the particular bodies of the dead that cannot be so quickly consigned to oblivion, that not only reactivates the sense of individual and political loss that animates the anthem but also demands a return to the overwhelming power of the *Jubilate*. Burney's attempt to make the emotion expressed by the audience simply a matter of familial or personal grief runs counter to the manifestly nationalist allegory in both the selections from *Saul* and the *Funeral Anthem*. Any suggestion that the mourning, even in its celebratory major-key manifestation, is for the nation risks drawing attention not only to the process of surrogation that so permeates this section of the program but also to the fact that surrogation requires constant supplementation and maintenance. What interests me here is that the entire mechanism of part 2 allows for a carefully modulated evocation of past loss but privatizes the affect generated by Handel's allegorical treatment of national crisis. This both separates responsibility for the crises that beset the nation after the triumph in the Seven Years' War from the ruling elites and propels the listener toward a celebration of virtuous rule that is here affiliated with past prosperity. The problem of pastness continues to haunt the entire figural economy, but the crucial task of generating a political future for a reinaugurated king and Ministry, if not completed, is at least put in motion. In this context, the "mute and eager attention" described by Burney sounds like a desire for future hegemony after a period of disastrous turbulence.

In this light, the third part of the program is all too apt because it is all about turbulent waters. It pairs the fourth Chandos Anthem, a setting of fragments of Psalms 96 and 93, and the concluding sections of *Israel in Egypt*, which dramatize the drowning of Pharaoh's army in the Red Sea from Exodus. Aside from the obvious celebration of the power and righteousness of God, both selections are intimately connected to raging seas and were particularly well suited to the size of the orchestra and the chorus in the Abbey. But the turbulence evoked here moves the primary focus of the program away from the complex negotiation with the past, which preoccupies the first two parts of the performance, toward the relationship between God, the nation, and the future. The fourth Chandos Anthem interrupts its setting of Psalm 96 with a single verse from Psalm 93: "The waves of the sea rage horribly; but yet the Lord who dwells on high is mightier."[48] As Burney notes, the music that accompanies this verse is extraordinarily violent:

> Handel, in the accompaniment of this boisterous air, has tried, not unsuccessfully, to express the turbulence of a tempestuous sea; the style of this kind of Music is not meant to be amiable; but contrasts well with other movements, and this has a spirit, and even a roughness, peculiar to our author. . . . The solemnity of [the ensuing] movement may, perhaps, seem as much too languid to the admirers of the preceding air, as that may be too turbulent for the nerves of those partial to this. The truth is that both verge a little on the extreme.[49]

The violence of the setting of Psalm 93, verse 5, and the extremity of the transition to verse 9 of Psalm 96 both shocks the audience with the initial storm and provides a moment of intense calm before the full power of the orchestra and choir is mobilized in the final movement. As Burney states, "In the last movement of this Chorus, when all the instruments are busied, such a commotion is raised, as constitutes one of Handel's most formidable hurricanes."[50]

But this formidable hurricane is given a very specific interpretation by the usually restrained Burney; he offers the following modified quotation from Addison that ultimately cites a key passage from Dryden's translation of the *Aeneid*: "Bellowing *notes* burst with a stormy sound. ADDISON."[51] The cited passage ultimately points to a moment of intense carnage in book 9 of the *Aeneid*, and it is worth a momentary digression. With Aeneas away from the Trojan camp, the Rutulian armies are on the verge of overwhelming the Trojans. The passage from Dryden that Burney cites comes immediately after a particularly horrible reverse in the Trojan's fortunes in which a tower collapses and the trapped soldiers are slaughtered. Mezentius mocks the Trojans watching from the ramparts by calling them women, and Ascanius responds by killing one of the Rutulians. This reassertion of Trojan masculinity prompts a long intervention by Apollo in which he declares Ascanius

> Offspring of Gods thyself; and Rome shall owe
> To thee, a Race of Demigods below.
> This is the Way to Heav'n: The Pow'rs Divine
> From this beginning date the *Julian* line.
> To thee, to them, and their victorious Heirs,
> The conquer'd War is due, and the vast World is theirs.[52]

In other words, Burney brings us to a moment not only where Trojan masculinity is first put into question and then reconsolidated but also where the transition from Trojan nationhood to the future empire of Rome is prophesied. With this divine intervention, the Trojans unleash a storm of battle that Burney likens to the sound of the final chorus of the fourth Chandos Anthem:

> The Trojans, by his Arms, their Patron know;
> And hear the twanging of his Heav'nly Bow.
> Then duteous Force they use; and Phœbus' Name,
> To keep from Fight; the Youth too fond of Fame.
> Undaunted, they themselves no Danger shun:
> From Wall to Wall, the Shouts and Clamours run,
> They bend their Bows; they whirl their Slings around:
> Heaps of spent Arrows fall; and strew the Ground;
> And Helms, and Shields, and ratling Arms resound.
> The Combate thickens, like the Storm that flies
> From Westward, when the Show'ry Kids arise:
> Or patt'ring Hail comes pouring on the Main,
> When *Jupiter* descends in harden'd Rain,
> Or bellowing Clouds burst with a stormy Sound,
> And with an armed Winter strew the Ground.[53]

The specificity of Burney's citation here is important for two reasons. First, it marks a moment that is simultaneously the lowest point of the Trojan fortunes and the point from which their transformation into the forebears of empire is articulated as a matter of divine election. And it is the specific fact that some of the Trojans go on to found Rome that is so crucial here, because it speaks directly to the narrative of renewal that permeates the entire first performance. Second, it explicitly casts the resurgent violence of the Trojan forces and the declaration of Ascanius's role in the founding of the Roman Empire as a compensation for the suggestion that the Trojans are, to quote Dryden, "less than Women, in the Shapes of Men."[54] As we have already seen, this fear of emasculation was a prominent feature of the rhetoric concerning the failed American war, and it surfaced explicitly in the press's discussion of the effect of the music of Commemoration. I would argue that the historical allegory that attends Burney's citation is quite straightforward. At a particularly low point in the fortunes of the British Empire and the nation, the Commemoration is not only figuring forth the generation of a new Rome but also putting allegations of compromised masculinity among the ruling elites into abeyance. This issue of gender insubordination becomes a prominent concern in the second performance of the Commemoration at the Pantheon, but here it is only fleetingly evoked by Burney and then only to be overcome.

As noted earlier, the raging seas of the fourth Chandos Anthem are sutured to the final two choruses and recitatives of *Israel in Egypt* that also use the full potential of the enlarged orchestra and the chorus to render the drowning of the Egyptians in the Red Sea. As the audience is moved from one moment of scriptural turbulence to another, the program concludes with some of the most dramatic music in Handel's repertoire, and it is explicitly aimed at reinforcing the notion that Britain, like the Israelites, once in captivity, was delivered because it is God's elect nation. This topos infuses all of the Israelite oratorios, and its appearance here rather directly liberates the reconsolidated nation and points it toward a glorious future. But it is worth considering how the chosen materials not only build on the storm first evoked in the fourth Chandos Anthem but also continue the complex act of historical erasure or revision that we have already excavated in the second part of the program. The storm in the Chandos Anthem is invoked only to demonstrate that God "who dwells on high is mightier" than the raging sea. It is the distinction between the divinity of heaven and the worldliness of the earth that is important here, because Psalms 93 and 96 are explicitly calling for the Israelites to see past worldly or historical events and open themselves to worship their Lord because it is through his awesome power that they will prevail. As a precursor to the selected passages from *Israel in Egypt*, the drowning of Egyptians and the Israelites' rejoicing amount to a specific example of God's awe-inspiring power.

But it is worth noting how the overall trajectory of the program limits the articulation of God's power: the audience is presented with the aftermath of the

Red Sea overwhelming the Egyptians. When we recognize that the segments of the *Funeral Anthem* from part 2 are the major-key components of the first part of *Israel in Egypt* and that the final section of part 3 is the conclusion to the third part of the same oratorio, then it becomes apparent that *Israel in Egypt* plays a vital structuring role in the entire program—and not just for the first day's performance. What is remarkable is that, in the movement from the elements of "Lamentations of the Israelites for Death of Joseph" to the final elements of "Moses's Song," the program elides all of part 2 that narrates both the myriad afflictions with which God besets the pharaoh on behalf of the Israelites and the deliverance of Moses and his people. The verses detailing scenes of affliction are performed during the Commemoration, but in the following program, in the Pantheon where their meaning is radically altered. In this strangely truncated and interrupted performance of the oratorio in the Abbey, one could argue that these signs of God's fearsome power are replaced by the far more general "raging seas" in the fourth Chandos Anthem which evoke similar sentiments of awe, but which have far less specific resonances in Handel's music. As Ruth Smith argues, "Moses' redemption of the Israelites and their passage to the promised land through the Red Sea, like many national myths in the eighteenth century, had a history as contested ground, but in this case the terrain was mainly occupied by the opposition [to Robert Walpole's Ministry]."[55]

In her reading of the oratorio's political allegories, Smith argues persuasively that the libretto, and especially the verses that render the period of Israelite slavery, was susceptible not only to patriotic readings aimed at restoring national integrity by ousting the corrupt Whig oligarchy but also to more radical Jacobite readings aimed at wresting the monarchy from the Hanoverian line. In 1784 there is no fear for the succession, but any possibility of allowing the "slavery" figure to migrate toward George III's absolutist tendencies—in short, any possibility that he could be figured as Pharoah by disgruntled Whigs, dissenters, and emergent radicals—had to be obviated. Otherwise, it would be all too possible to read the disaster of the American war as a plague visited upon the nation for the autocracy of the king and for the government's betrayal of fundamental notions of British liberty. In this figural economy, the colonists emerge as the formerly enslaved elect nation, and it is Britain—and specifically the navy—that is consigned to the depths of the sea. Hardly a stretch in this historical setting. Because the librettos to Handel's oratorios were so consistently read as political allegories, this figural possibility had to be contained. Here this is achieved by simply transferring the performance of verses such as "He smote all the first-born of Egypt, the chief of all their strength" and "He gave them hailstones for rain; fire mingled with the hail ran along upon the ground" to the Pantheon performance where they become examples of punishment befitting perversions of masculinist notions of national character, and not possible typologies for misrule.

The Palace of Love and the Temple of Mars

With the second performance in the Commemoration schedule came a deeply significant shift in performance space and repertoire. The celebration moved from Westminster Abbey to the most auspicious site of elite sociability—the Pantheon—and the program consisted chiefly of excerpts derived from Handel's Italian operas and his chamber music. But careful scrutiny of the program also indicates that the airs from often-obscure operas were intercut with extremely famous passages from well-known Israelite oratorios: namely, *Joshua, Israel in Egypt*, and *Judas Maccabaeus*. The *London Magazine* noted that "this evening's entertainment, though perhaps not equal in point of grandeur to that of the preceding day, was in every respect worthy of the occasion. It consisted of Handel's lighter compositions, with several of his most sublime chorusses."[56] The press's coverage of the second performance is less extensive than the reporting on the performances held in the Abbey, and aside from the repeated acclamation of Madame Mara's and Mr. Harrison's singing, comparatively little is said about the music.[57] But the papers offer detailed discussions of the architect James Wyatt's decorations, and I would suggest that this intense interest in the space of performance allows one to speculate on the stakes or significance of this performance in the overall Commemoration.

As Gillian Russell has extensively documented, the Pantheon, which opened in January of 1772, was almost immediately celebrated as the most eroticized space in London. Architecturally, Wyatt's original design for the building was replete with amorous references both to the heathen past and to the exotic East. As she states,

> A foreign nobleman was said to have commented that the building evoked "the enchanted palaces of the French romances," and that it was "raised by the potent wand of some Fairy.": "In short, the building seemed the Palace of Pleasure, inhabited by the Loves and Graces; all was beauty, gaiety and elegance." A hybrid of Roman and Byzantine styles, the Pantheon consisted of fourteen rooms in total. Its centrepiece was the rotunda or dome, based on the mosque of Santa Sophia in Constantinople.

> Niches below the dome contained statues of heathen gods and goddesses, on the model of the Roman Pantheon, illuminated by numerous lights in gilt vases.[58]

The intersection of the amatory fantasies of classicism and orientalism conveniently figured forth by the great dome was matched by a very particular style of fashionable sociability that was controversial from the outset. The entertainments at the Pantheon were attended by people of fashion, and that meant it was not a site where virtue was always manifest. In fact, it was the presence of demireps and their libertine suitors, along with the remarkable opportunity for erotic display, that constituted the Pantheon's greatest draw. Because it was also run as a commercial operation outside the control of the licensing procedures that regulated other sites of fashionable sociability, such as the theatre or the pleasure gardens, it was always perceived as a suspect site. As Russell demonstrates, the sexual politics of the Pantheon's eroticization of spectatorship needs to be understood within a larger framework where elite women such as Teresa Cornelys, through the sponsorship of musical entertainments in private domiciles, were threatening the highly masculinist economy of entertainment in London. The fact that the Pantheon was modeled on these entertainments opened its original proprietors to charges of effeminacy and vice.[59] What is important for our purposes here is that all through the 1770s and 1780s the physical elements of the building itself, the conduct of its patrons, and the character of its management were all associated with gender insubordination and sexual misconduct. Therefore, the movement of the Commemoration from Westminster Abbey to the Pantheon amounts to a shift from a rememorative space of national glory to a suspect space of elite dissipation.

And that movement required fundamental modifications to the Pantheon itself, which ultimately had to do with the spectacle of the royal family. As the *London Magazine*'s description of Wyatt's modifications indicates, the Pantheon on this evening was transformed into a space resembling one of the patent theatres on the night of a command performance:[60]

> No exertions of art were wanting to prepare the grand saloon for the most perfect accommodation of the subscribers. A spacious projecting gallery, on painted columns, in imitation of the porphyry ones which support the building, was erected over the great door, for the reception of their Majesties, and the rest of the royal family. In the centre of it appeared a state gallery, with seats for the King and Queen, under a lofty canopy, adorned with crimson and gold decorations, the dome of which was richly gilt, and

relieved by the royal arms. Elegant compartments of the same box were reserved for the Princess Royal, and the junior branches of the family; large piers of plate glass were fixed behind it, which heightened by various reflecting lustres, gave the whole an appearance truly magnificent! . . . A gradual elevation of benches was made in all the galleries, and likewise through all the recesses underneath them. The dome was illuminated with buff coloured lamps, disposed in small squares, which, with the addition of numberless lustres, added peculiar brilliancy to the scene! the orchestra remained in its usual place and form; but in the gallery over it was erected an organ, on the top of which shone in transparency an irradiated bust of the immortal HANDEL![61]

What we have here is a careful layering of the performance space. The introduction of the projecting gallery reorients what was previously a circular space and the introduction of reflecting surfaces literally made the king and the royal family the focus of visual attention. In a gesture reminiscent of the deployment of mirrors in the Mischianza, one could also argue that the mirrors and lustrous surfaces intensified the autoethnographic character of the event. Similar optical effects were deployed to draw attention to the transparency of the bust of Handel. If we look at published illustrations of the architectural modifications, it becomes clear that Wyatt effectively concealed eroticized scenes of heathen love by playing up, first, the classical elements of the building—especially the columns—which were themselves a quotation of the Roman Pantheon and, second, the royal arms (fig. 6.2).[62] There is even evidence in the papers that much of the erotic imagery that decorated the dome and other surfaces was temporarily concealed.[63] Out of a space of intense erotic spectatorship formerly associated with elite dissipation and, by extension, national decay emerges a disposition of bodies and architectural elements that cannot help but equate the state of Britain and imperial Rome. The Palace of Love was transformed into the Temple of Mars. And it is this maneuver that allows us to read the program of the second performance. As we will see, this fantasy of renewed empire, which was coded directly into the physical space of performance, also emerged in the performance itself, but in order for this to happen, the corresponding enactment of amorous passion in the music had to be similarly contained.

I would like to suggest that that movement from the first to the second performance, from the Abbey to the Pantheon, is not simply a matter of contrasting sacred and secular music, or—from a slightly different view—war and love, but rather constitutes a strategic gesture aimed at countering allegations of emascu-

Figure 6.2. "An inside view of the Pantheon exhibiting their Majesties Box &c as fitted up under the direction of Mr. James Wyatt, for the Commemoration of Handel." From *European Magazine and London Review*, May 1784, 324–25. 1978,U.1911. Department of Prints and Drawings © Trustees of the British Museum.

lation that lie at the heart of much of the consternation following the American war. To put this in its most extreme form, the program for the second performance can be read as having a pedagogical imperative whose ultimate aim is prophylactic: it explores suspect sexuality in order to protect an already compromised nation from replicating the sociability that ostensibly contributed to its recent defeat. As we have already noted, the problem of emasculation among the social elites was a recurrent topic in the press coverage of the Commemoration. Here is the *Morning Chronicle* reporting on the announcement of Dr. Burney's intention to write a history of the Commemoration:

> We have heard it asserted that in the same proportion a nation becomes attached to the fine arts, in the same proportion the minds of the people become enervated, and regardless of their political liberty, and that music, more than any other science emasculates the mind. Whether this position be true or false we have not leisure to examine, though we are ready to

> grant, that where music becomes the *business* of a people, it may and perhaps does produce the effect alluded to, but where it is taken up as in England by way of relaxation from the more weighty concerns of the statesman and merchant, no evil consequence can possibly (in a national point of view) attend our attachment. On the contrary, Concerts assist in forming the manners of our youth, by giving a polish to their behaviour, not often met with among a people, where music does not constitute part of their public amusements.[64]

The pedagogical imperative that closes this passage seems straightforward, but how are we to understand music's role "in forming the manners of our youth"? The correspondent does not disagree with the assertion that music enervates and emasculates the mind but argues instead that these deleterious effects have to do with dosage. If music is consumed as an intermittent diversion from the demands of the state and the market, then it becomes a valuable tool for the inculcation of civility. Because all of this is staged as a question of national character, English masculinity is here defined by a rationing of pleasure. But this begs the question of the proper balance between policy, business, and entertainment.

Rationing, I would argue, is what the program of the second performance is all about, and this is evident from its structure. The operatic airs are carefully intercut with selections from the oratorios that prevent a coherent narrative of passion from unfolding. Passion instead is fragmented and contained within each air: the audience is not allowed to follow the development of any particular character's desire. The program's refusal of narrative is an argument against the central dramatic tenet of Handel's Italian operas. It would be granting a great deal of force to this one performance, but it is worth noting that, with the exception of an unusual run of a pasticcio of *Giulio Cesare in Egitto* in 1787, Handelian opera is effectively silenced for more than one hundred years.[65] Furthermore, the Pantheon as a site of elite entertainment declined in popularity as the 1780s unfolded. In this context, the oratorio selections become doubly significant because, in form, language, and subject, they exist in contrast to the arias and duets on the program. We could argue that, like the decorations that Wyatt introduced into the space of the Pantheon, the choruses, by virtue of their sublimity and their subject matter, effectively put the Handel of erotic operatic entanglement in abeyance.

The choice of choruses is apt. The choruses from *Joshua* and *Judas Maccabaeus* are among Handel's most direct expressions of national election. The two choruses from *Israel in Egypt,* referred to in the previous section, detail the plagues that afflict the Egyptians immediately before the Israelites' liberation from captivity. If we understand the deployment of "He smote all the first born" and "He gave them hailstones for rain" as part of the larger tactic of segmenting and reactivating *Israel in Egypt* in the Commemoration as a whole, then these verses from Exodus have the capacity to figure forth God's retribution for disobedience. Disconnected from the overall narrative of the oratorio, they can stand as particularly powerful expressions of God's displeasure. This of course implies that Pharaoh's misrule is being temporarily or strategically affiliated with past instances of British autocracy. It would be an exaggeration to simply suggest that the central allegory of part 2 of *Israel in Egypt* is being decisively reversed in order to critique the political errors and social conditions that led to the American debacle. But in the physical environs of the Pantheon and among the very people often directly involved in these historical events, it is difficult not to at least contemplate the possibility that a program of social and political reform was being articulated for and by the elites themselves.

The nature of this reform can be gleaned from the way two of the most famous airs from Handel's so-called magic operas frame the operatic elements of the program. After an introductory performance of Handel's "Second Hautbois Concerto," the vocal part of the evening opened with Signor Tasca's performance of "Sorge infausta una procella" from Handel's 1732 opera *Orlando. Orlando* was the first of three operas Handel derived from Lodovico Ariosto's *Orlando Furioso,* and its narrative is intriguing in this context. Anthony Hicks's synopsis sets out the key predicament as follows:

> The opening scene is the countryside at night, with a view of a mountain on which Atlas is seen supporting the heavens. Zoroastro contemplates the constellations, obscure in meaning to ordinary mortals, but which tell him that Orlando will one day return to noble deeds. Orlando himself appears, torn between conflicting desires for love and glory. Zoroastro rebukes him for his devotion to love, and illustrates the dangers of that emotion by causing the distant mountain to change to the Palace of Love, where heroes of antiquity appear asleep at Cupid's feet. He urges Orlando to follow Mars, the god of war. Orlando, at first shamed by the vision, decides that glory can be obtained in pursuit of love.[66]

Orlando is in love with Angelica, but she is in love with Medoro. After numerous twists and turns, Orlando's pursuit of love ultimately leads him into a state of jealousy and madness from which he is rescued by the necromancer Zoroastro.

In the aria performed at the Pantheon, Zoroastro implores Orlando to accept the betrothal of Angelica and Medoro, and immediately afterward a statue of Mars rises as Orlando "proclaims victory over himself."[67] Zoroastro's aria therefore is explicitly about not only regaining control of one's passions but also renewing reverence for marriage. It is clear from both the overall narrative of the opera and the immediate context for the song that with control comes martial prowess. Here is Burney's translation of the aria:

Though furious storms awhile may rage,
And darkness ev'ry hope deny,
The Sun, at length, shall fear assuage,
And calm at once the heart and sky.

So men, endow'd with virtue rare,
The lures of vice sometimes decoy;
Yet, freed from such insidious snare,
Conversion brings unbound joy.[68]

Performed in this space at this historical moment, the audience, even if it was unfamiliar with the narrative of *Orlando*, would have been confronted with metaphorical linkages not only between past stormy darkness and the pursuit of vice but also between newfound calm and the conversion to virtue. It is a song that lends itself to an allegory of recent British history, but more significantly it reiterates in more specific terms the argument of the preceding program in the Commemoration.

Zoroastro's critique of Orlando's excesses deploys the same figural economy that animates the storms of the third part of the first performance in the Abbey, only here the argument concerning the lures of vice is more pointed because it is articulated in a space routinely associated with social and sexual misconduct. It is in this context that Burney's reading of the fourth Chandos Anthem, in which he invokes the scene from the *Aeneid* where allegations of emasculation are the prelude to both renewed martial prowess and the prophecy of future empire, is so resonant. If his reading—or my reading of it—seemed strained in our earlier discussion, then it is only too apt when linked to the performance of this song within a building that was itself modeled on Hadrian's architectural paean to a syncretist understanding of imperial rule. Could we not argue that both the modifications to the building and the specific import of this opening song constitute a critique of past excesses that both fleetingly recognizes that punishment was due and that future glory nevertheless awaits? What interests me here is that the critique is aimed directly at the social and sexual excesses of the elites but only indirectly implies that the historical setbacks of the 1770s and early 1780s—conveniently the period of the Pantheon's greatest fame—were the result of errant governmental and military policy. Making that connection relies on an argument that sees bad governance as the result of debased and specifically effeminate masculinity. In other words, vice and effeminacy need to be set aside, and one way of reading the Commemoration's work in the Pantheon is to suggest that the battle against vice is being waged at its source.

Whether the audience was ready for such a conversion is another matter. Burney's analysis of part 2 of the Pantheon performance has to deal with the only instance in his account of the Commemoration where the audience clearly loses interest in the music. The selections throughout this section are various, but with the exception of the final air from *Alcina*, they are unified by themes of honor, virtue, and the restraint appropriate to considering the possibility of departed glory. The central vocal piece in the program, Caesar's accompanied recitative over the ashes of Pompey from *Giulio Cesare in Egitto*, was singled out by Burney as "the finest piece of accompanied Recitative, without intervening symphonies, with which I am acquainted."[69] Its "brooding modulations evoke the cold shadow of departed glory, and give the episode an extraordinary sombre power";[70] for the audience assembled in the Pantheon on 27 May 1784, however, it generated boredom:

> But though delivered by Signor Pacchierotti, with the true energy and expression of heroic Recitative, for which he is so justly celebrated in Italy by the best judges of his poetry and musical declamation of that country, had not the attention or success it deserved here, detached from its place in the Opera, and printed without a translation. Indeed, the audience, fatigued with the struggles for admission, the pressure of the crowd in their seats, and relaxed by the accumulated heat of the weather and company, were neither so attentive to the performers, nor willing to be pleased by their exertion, as in Westminster Abbey.[71]

Significantly, he goes on to argue that this lack of interest was not always the case; Burney compares the original performance of this recitative to an earlier Italian performance where the words "occasioned such agitation in all who heard it, they trembled, turned pale, and regarded each other with fear and astonishment."[72]

These supplemental remarks suggest that the problem is not simply one of audience discomfort and the lack of translation. It suggests that the audience has lost the capacity to fully comprehend the import of Caesar's soliloquy, or that the historical moment is not right for such a harrowing account of the mutability of power. Here is Burney's translation of the recitative:

These are thy ashes, Pompey, this the mound,
Thy soul, invisible, is hovering round!
Thy splendid trophies, and thy honours fade,
Thy grandeur, like thyself, is now a shade.
Thus fare the hopes in which we most confide,
And thus the efforts end of human pride!
What yesterday could hold the world in chains,
To-day, transform'd to dust, an urn contains.
Such is the fate of all, from cot to throne,
Our origin is earth, our end a stone!
Ah wretched life! how frail and short thy joys
A breath creates thee, and a breath destroys.[73]

In the opera, these lines operate as a cautionary utterance articulated during Caesar's and Rome's ascendance; in the Pantheon, these lines had the potential to capture quite powerfully the decline of Britain's influence in the world. I think it is symptomatic of the entire program that the selection from *Giulio Cesare* does not partake of that opera's celebrated exploration of the intensity of worldly sexual desire, or its remarkably joyous scene of peace that attends the nonmarital sexual union of Caesar and Cleopatra and the political union of Rome and Egypt. Instead, the program's final negotiation with the problem of love activates a narrative of future vengeance and implies that the current humiliating peace will be followed by a return to war.

Like the opening aria from *Orlando*, the final operatic aria performed that evening in the Pantheon was "Ah! mio cor" from *Alcina*, Handel's last magic opera and the last one based on Ariosto. In other words, the evening opens and closes with songs sung by necromancers. But unlike Zoroastro's correction of Orlando's excessive amorous passion and the ensuing hypostatization of war, Alcina's aria moves from an expression of pathetic desolation at being deserted by her lover to an extraordinary outpouring of rage that explicitly puts grief aside and promises revenge:

But why let grief my soul devour?
I'm still a queen, and still have pow'r;
Which power my vengeance soon shall guide,
If still my kindness he deride.[74]

There is no hesitation over the mutability of power here, but rather an explicit statement of political continuity. As ruler of her own island, Alcina bears comparison to the king in both her desolation and her statement of unwavering rule in spite of the desertion of her lover/subjects. Madame Mara's performance of this aria drew the highest marks of praise from Burney and was the focus of much of the press coverage. The assertion of future vengeance fits nicely with all of the renewed martial vigor figured forth during the first performance in the Abbey; but listeners familiar with the entire opera would have been worried about where this vengeance would lead, because it operates at variance to the pursuit of virtue so insistently called for earlier in the evening. Unlike Zoroastro, Alcina abuses her magical powers and is ultimately undone by those made captive on the island. In other words, Alcina has the potential to signify not only both past and future rule but also the very suspect sexuality and errant femininity with which the Pantheon was associated.

Perhaps it is to keep this insistent problem at bay that the program turns so decisively to yet another Coronation Anthem, this time to Handel's "My heart is inditing," which was composed for the coronation of George II in 1727. This is not the grand anthem of *Zadok the Priest*, which figured so prominently in the first performance, but the anthem that accompanied the coronation of George II's wife, Queen Caroline. It is a remarkable insertion into this secular program because it is a piece of church music. But of all of Handel's Chapel Royal compositions, it is the most insistently concerned with the place of gender normativity in monarchical rule. As Jeremy Summerly notes,

> The second movement deals with the king's daughters and is a study in Baroque femininity, graceful and coquettish. In similar vein, the third movement contrasts the transparently textured demure queen with the lasciviously dense king's pleasure. After these gender stereotypes, the fourth and final movement unites kings and queens as nursing fathers and nursing mothers respectively, although Handel still cannot resist giving the highest choral note to the kings rather than to the queens.[75]

Throughout the Commemoration, the press was fascinated by the public display of the princesses' femininity and with the parental qualities of the king and queen,[76] but it is important to register the effect of verses such as "King's daughters were among the honourable women" and "Kings shall be thy nursing fathers, and queens thy nursing mothers" in this specific performance space. In the very space most famously associated with demireps and adventurers, with fashion and the eroticization of spectatorship, the audience was suddenly presented with an erotic and political spectacle from the past, which simultaneously put forward the queen and the royal princesses as models of honorable femininity and asserted the king's potency. One can hear the sexual restoration in Burney's closing remarks: "The fourth, and last movement, 'Kings shall be thy nursing fathers' is a full Chorus, big with all the fire, contrivance, rich harmony, and energy of genius, which Handel afterward displayed in his best Oratorio Choruses."[77]

If the first performance reconstituted the king as a martial figure, this recalibration not only of the king's fatherhood but also of his virility in the second performance reconstituted the sexual norms that informed past notions of the state as the patriarchal family. That this should happen on this particular territory is remarkable, but it is important to recognize that, by going into the space of the Pantheon, the stakes would have been that much more evident. At the end of the evening, sitting in the gently raked temporary seats of a now transformed room, one's eyes would be firmly directed toward the royal box above, one's ears would have suffused with music repeatedly associated with the masculine qualities of sublime power, and one would have been directed toward the future: a future of supposedly virile leadership, which may or may not enact revenge for past humiliations; a future ostensibly dedicated to the regulation of dissipation and excessive passion; but a future that certainly included "all the fire, contrivance, rich harmony and energy" of the *Messiah*.

Resurrection

The extended reading of the first and second performances presented in the preceding sections gives a detailed sense of how social and political anxieties were carefully activated and contained through complex acts of surrogation and selection. And it is important to recognize that these two days of performance open with one anthem and close with another, and that both were composed for the coronation of George II. The casting forward of this music, which was also used for George III's coronation, is part of a complex reinauguration of the monarchy necessary after a period of immense political and historical turbulence. As we have seen, in both the Abbey and the Pantheon, the audience was witness to an attempt to ideologically renovate Hanoverian rule, and I hope that both the complexity and depth of that attempt are more tangible following my admittedly speculative readings. But this phantasmatic reinauguration of the martial and political power of monarchy is incomplete without the third performance of the Commemoration: the massive performance of *Messiah* in Westminster Abbey (fig. 6.3). The

Figure 6.3. "View of the magnificent Box erected for their Majesties, in Westminster Abbey under the direction of Mr. James Wyatt, at the Commemoration of Handel." From *European Magazine and London Review,* June 1784, 478. 1867,1012.781. Department of Prints and Drawings © Trustees of the British Museum.

return to the Abbey is itself significant for all the reasons I have articulated. With the struggle with the social past of the Pantheon at least temporarily completed, the celebration can return not only to "sacred" music but also to explicit statements of national election and resurrection. As William Weber has demonstrated, the resurrection in question was arguably that of George III himself, and after the Commemoration he assiduously styled himself as the nation's foremost Handelian.[78] Furthermore, the return to the Abbey also involved a shift to the performance of a complete choral work, which by this time had "transcended Britain's religious divisions more universally than any other cultural phenomenon."[79] Weber's analysis of the political valences of the Commemoration indicates the importance of High Church religion to the overall project of the Commemoration, but *Messiah* is important because it had the capacity to speak to a diverse community and thus call forth a renewed nation under a Protestant god. Certainly the press was overwhelmed by the sublimity of the occasion.[80] This is not to say that everyone was convinced. With Cowper's encouragement, John Newton wrote a set of fifty sermons attacking Handel's oratorio. His resistance is one measure of its totalizing force.

But for the rest of the 1780s, Britain was seized by what Weber terms a kind of "Handelmania" that revolved around the person of the king. His patronage of the Concerts of Ancient Music and his part in Burney's account of the Commemoration was matched by a flood of commercial concerts and performances:

> Musical entrepeneurs put together for the theatres long pasticcios of numbers from Handel's works set to new words of biblical origin. Singers offered more and more numbers from Handel's operas in concerts. Critics began comparing composers of the time with Handel as the great master of opera. . . . In 1787 the King's Theatre went so far as to put excerpts from Handel's operas on stage, the first such production since 1754, in a pasticcio of arias compiled by Samuel Arnold from different operas under the title *Guilio Caesare in Egitto.* George III had not gone to the Italian opera as often as his two predecessors had done, and an aristocrat later claimed that the production was intended mostly to get the king back into the King's Theatre.[81]

These events abated by 1792, but I think it is culturally significant to consider the ways in which the political ritual of 1784 opened the door for the commercialization of Handel's works, especially in 1786 and 1787. For a brief period of time, Handel's music was most prominently represented in London by two bizarre pasticcios, both of which were composed by Dr. Samuel Arnold. Arnold was a very successful composer of comic operas for the patent houses—he composed the music for *Inkle and Yarico*—and also produced the first collected edition of Handel's music. His *Redemption*, which dominated the musical season of 1786 and which was performed well into the 1790s, offered a compilation of Handel's Israelite oratorios and used every typological possibility at hand to proclaim with nationalist fervor "our REDEMPTION" in Christ. Arnold's and Nicola Haym's version of *Giulio Cesare in Egitto*, although loosely based on Handel's opera of the same name, radically departs from the original by the "addition of a few fabulous incidents, introduced for the conveniency of the performance" and by the excision of key elements to "give the piece a dramatic consistency."[82] That it exhibits neither consistency nor clarity should come as no surprise, but I would like to suggest that the popularity of these two rather strange corruptions of Handel's work warrants attention and requires that we think about the very notion of pasticcio in a time of political transition and renovation. I will leave that reading for another time, in order to make way for what I take to be a highly symptomatic deployment of pasticcio, but this time staged at a considerable distance from London itself.

Projection, Patriotism, Surrogation: Handel in Calcutta

Unlike the 1770s and 1780s, the 1790s were a period of consolidation in the British Empire. Military victories over Tipu Sultan in Mysore and the establishment of the Permanent Settlement not only confirmed actual British domination in India but also provided an occasion for phantasmatic constructions of global supremacy.[83] I have written elsewhere about how these events were staged at Astley's Royal Amphitheatre and at Sadler's Wells, but in the concluding section of this chapter I am more concerned with the enactment of masochistic nationalism among Britons in Calcutta—that is, a nationalism that coheres in the pain of its mutilated members[84]—whose dynamics are deeply connected to the recalibration of British subjectivity after the loss of the American colonies. Masochistic nationalism may seem counterintuitive to our normative understanding of national character because masochism carries with it the connotation of perversion, a turning aside from truth or right, and specifically a turning from pleasure to pain. But it helps to explain the allegorical tactics employed in Calcutta on the particular evening I discuss here. Prior catastrophic losses both in Mysore and in America had a lingering effect on future actions in India, not only because the British could not afford further defeat but also because the primary

British actant in the Mysore Wars and the Permanent Settlement, Lord Cornwallis, carried his experience of defeat at Yorktown and other American campaigns to India when he was appointed governor-general of Bengal.[85] As an icon of both imperial humiliation and domination, Cornwallis plays an oddly double role in the celebration of victory over Mysore. Because the commemoration of Cornwallis's actions in India always carries the threat of reactivating traumatic memories of the American war, the performance of fragments from Handel's oratorios that I discuss in this section compulsively repeat and repudiate scenes of national humiliation. What interests me is the way both the actants and the audience members, who are largely indistinguishable from each other, tie their fantasies of national and imperial election to an unresolved cultural wound.

The checkered history of British conflict with the sultans of Mysore before the early 1790s activated deeply felt anxieties not only about the susceptibility of British subjectivity to Indianization but also about the viability of the imperial enterprise. As Linda Colley has reminded us, news of Britain's spectacular defeat at Pollilur in the First Mysore War reached London at almost precisely the same time as the news of the fall of Yorktown, and there was general consternation that the entire empire was going to collapse.[86] These anxieties were only exacerbated by heavily contested accounts of British atrocities in India, as well as by widely circulated captivity narratives from the 1780s that revolve around scenes of bodily degradation and mutilation. Many of Tipu's prisoners were enslaved and forced to fight against the British forces. These cheyla battalions were the site of intense anxiety because most of the cheylas, or slaves, were forced to convert to Islam and were circumcised. As Kate Teltscher states, "The British cheylas, marked with the stigma of Muslim difference but otherwise unconverted to Islam, were stranded in a doctrinal no man's land, and the texts reveal their sense of marginalization."[87] However, she is also quick to point out, following Mary Louise Pratt, that the very fact of the existence of the survival narratives performs a kind of inoculation of their dangerous contents.[88] Presented within the frame of a survivor's tale, the mutilation of the penis, and by extension of the religious and national subject, can be presented and contained. However, the line separating circumcision and castration is at times hard to discern in these texts because the mutilation, whether partial or complete, seems to instantiate a form of subjectivity that for all attempts at containment continues to inhere in the narratives and haunts even the most triumphant accounts of victory over Tipu in the early 1790s.

Projection, or the Volatility of Paternalism

Like earlier campaigns against the sultans of Mysore, the Third Mysore War did not start well for the British forces. The initial campaigns were conducted under the leadership of General William Medows, the governor of Madras. Medows served under Cornwallis in the American war and, despite his prior experience, made a number of tactical errors that reminded Cornwallis of his own miscalculations in Pennsylvania and South Carolina.[89] Tipu took almost immediate strategic advantage in the early phases of the conflict and forced Cornwallis to take over Medows's command in mid-December 1791. Cornwallis undertook one of the most massive deployments of men, animals, and artillery in British military history and eventually conquered the strategic fortress of Bangalore. However, insufficient supply lines and uncooperative weather prevented him from successfully taking Tipu's capital Seringapatam. The monsoon and other logistical problems forced Cornwallis to retreat.

The anxiety regarding the mutilation of the national subject was partially resolved by Cornwallis's victory over Tipu Sultan at Seringapatam some months later. However, the resolution was partial, because this conflict did not conclude with a decisive military annihilation but rather with an extraordinary diplomatic transferral of money, lands, and two of Tipu's sons as hostages to British rule. That transfer generated three successive performances of patriotism in Mysore and Calcutta, each of which had a supplementary relation to its immediate precursor. On 23 February 1792, Cornwallis himself engineered the first of these when he carefully staged a spectacle outside Tipu's fortress at Seringapatam involving elephants, artillery, and soldiers in full ceremonial costume, in which he publicly received Tipu's two sons, "dressed for the melancholy occasion in muslin adorned with pearls and assorted jewellry," with a gesture of paternal care. The *Gentleman's Magazine*'s account of the event is symptomatic:

> Lord Cornwallis received [Tipu's sons] in his tent; which was guarded by a battalion of Sepoys, and they were then formally delivered to his Lordship by Gullam Ally Beg, the Sultan's Vackeel, as hostages for the due performance of the treaty. . . . At length Gullum Ally, approaching Lord Cornwallis, much agitated, thus emphatically addressed his Lordship: "These children," pointing to the young princes, whom he then presented, "were this morning the sons of the Sultan, my master: their situation is changed, and they must now look up to your Lordship as their father." The tender and affectionate manner in which his Lordship received them, seemed to

confirm the truth of the expression. The attendants of the young princes appeared astonished, and their countenances were highly expressive of the satisfaction they felt in the benevolence of his Lordship.[90]

Teltscher argues that the representation of Cornwallis's acceptance of Tipu's sons as a scene of paternal benevolence contrasts with the popular accounts of Tipu's alleged mistreatment of British captives. After the defeat of Tipu in 1793, war between the East India Company and Mysore was now refigured as a tropological struggle between normative and errant models of paternal care. The wide circulation of visual representations of this scene, on everything from prints to tea trays, achieved the twofold effect of putting the prior atrocities into abeyance and of reinforcing British fantasies of colonial rule as a form of affectionate paternalism.[91]

This spectacle of military paternalism outside of Seringapatam was followed by elaborate celebratory performances in Calcutta. A Gala Concert was performed using amateur musicians and singers from the ranks of the East India Company, and an extraordinary number of illuminations or projected transparencies were displayed throughout the town. Precinematic transparencies had been used to powerful effect in other colonial locales, but in this case it is the screens themselves that are most important.[92] By illuminating the key offices of the East India Company, the celebrations in Calcutta took icons of the bureaucratic regulation of subject peoples and made them contiguous with Cornwallis's paternal care of Tipu's sons:

> The Government house as it ought, the swelling of "public cause of pride" surpassed in magnificence grandeur all the rest:—the symmetry and style of the whole building, was particularly favorable to the occasion, and it was seen and embraced by the ingenious contrivers on this occasion with felicitous effect, the balustrades along the wings were ranged with party coloured lights, and intervening pedestals with lamps in festoons. . . . A transparent painting of 32 feet high by 27 completed in its contrast an admirable idea of the whole spectacle; the scene bore a figurative allusion to memorable signature of the preliminary articles; and the introduction of the hostages to Earl Cornwallis on that occasion—three oriental figures in chief were the most remarkably distinguishable, and we think with propriety of judgement in the artist: They were the Vakeel and the Princes hostages presenting to Britannia, or her genius in the usual habiliment, a scroll—she appeared seated and behind her a figure of Hercules, emblematic of the great work so completely and speedily performed: above Fame

appeared with a medallion of his Lordship and in the background a perspective view of Seringapatam.[93]

The substitution of Britannia and Hercules for Cornwallis in this visualization of the hostage transaction has the curious effect of hollowing out his specific actions in favor of a fantasy of abstract national agency here projected onto the surface of company rule. Removing him from the scene and relocating him into an apotheosis of Fame simultaneously exemplifies Cornwallis and contains his heroism as a subset of Britain's "clement bravery."[94] But does the eruption of femininity into the scene in the form of seated Britannia reinforce the notion of benevolent rule or undermine the particular significance of paternity to this ideological construct? It is as though each subsequent allegorical gesture calls into question the self-confirming fantasy of benevolent paternalism.

One could argue that Cornwallis's history of defeat and victory in colonial warfare makes him a volatile emblem of patriotic paternalism. That volatility requires not only repeated reassertions of his paternality—as Teltscher demonstrates, this ideological assemblage is highly overdetermined—but also supplementation by a series of more complex phantasmatic constructions that both undo the tight ideological sutures achieved in the initial performance and raise questions about how the nation can be seen at this distance from the metropole. The colonial newspaper accounts devote extensive coverage to the technical achievements of the illuminations and, in so doing, subtly declare the cultural superiority of technological modernity. Throughout the newspaper coverage, there is a fascination with how the illuminations transform the quotidian spaces of Calcutta into "one continuous blaze" of allegorical splendor in which the very loci of formerly precarious rule emerge as classical emblems of virtue. The *Madras Courier* declared that "so general a display of beauty, splendor, and magnificence were combined to render Calcutta, and its vicinity, one of the most superb Coup d'oeil's it has ever exhibited."[95] This declaration of artifice is to the point because it both invests in the power of representation and recognizes its limitations.

As the papers literally take the reader on a walk about town something strange begins to occur. In attempting to catalog all the transparencies, the loco-descriptive act testifies to divergent visual interpretations of Cornwallis's victory. As the papers turn their attention from the official East India Company buildings to the private houses of its employees, "Cornwallis" is increasingly figured forth by his coat of arms, and the buildings become the surfaces on which a fantasy of pastoral peace is projected:

> Messrs Gibbon and Brown's house in the Cossitollah; the whole extent of their house on all sides was laid out in the same style of illumination as the government house, in front before the centre Window was displayed a neatly painted transparency, of his Lordship's arms, the coat of which extended considerably beyond the supporters, and over the crest, displayed the roof of a superb and splendid tent—the allusion was happy, apt, and finely impressive: above the tent was the [*Collar*?][96] and *George* and below the star with Laurels and Palms; the lower story of the house was in a similar style, the Gateway and avenue leading thru shrubbery was converted with great skill into a luminous Vista terminated by an alcove containing a temple dedicated to peace; within which was an urn inscribed to the memory of the brave dead; and without—the motto *Glorious Peace*—the perspective was so happily preserved, that nothing appeared out of proportion, and yet the object immensely distant.[97]

Like other projections of "Fame relinquishing War,"[98] this image carries out a crucial act of memorialization that simultaneously marks the dead, so that they may be forgotten, and projects the viewer forward into a state of peace that is not only precarious but also not fully achieved until almost a decade later. Tipu would not be killed until 1799.

If we think of Calcutta on that night as a precursor to the image city, then the emphasis on the illusion of perspective in the description of both transparencies is resonant, for it quite literally takes the present historical buildings and ruptures their very contemporaneity by giving them both spatial and historical "depth." In the case of government house, the view of Seringapatam puts observers in a position of elevated contemplation—quite literally, the lord of all they survey. In the case of the house of Gibbon and Brown, the everyday residence is literally and phantasmatically transformed into a picturesque pastoral scene of the kind that Britons were well acquainted with not only in the Georgic experiments of eighteenth-century poetry but also in picturesque visual representation. James Thomson's "The Seasons" is the most apposite exemplar of this kind of deployment of the prospect as a tool for representing good governance and eliminating all manner of social resistances.[99] As Beth Fowkes Tobin demonstrates, these same Georgic strategies were vital to William Hodges's almost contemporaneous picturesque erasure of warfare in his illustrations to *Travels in India during the Years 1780, 1781, 1782 and 1783*, which was published in 1793.[100] Significantly, the battles being veiled by Hodges's picturesque representation of captured Indian fortresses are precisely those troubling conflicts of the First

Mysore War, which generated so much anxiety among British observers. To employ John Barrell's resonant phrase, both Hodges's illustrations and the projections in Calcutta manipulate light to hide "the dark side of the landscape," only here it is not the rural poor who are occluded by representation but the ongoing social conflict between British imperial power and native colonial resistance.[101]

We should not be surprised to see geographically displaced Britons using the representational strategies of an earlier form of patriotic identification to project a rather different imperial vision. But what remains so resonant here is the very duplicity of the image, for the projection of metropolitan fantasy is literally cast on the contours of colonial space. One has the sense that one could look upon the house of Messrs. Gibbon and Brown and see conflicting images of triumph and ongoing struggle, past victory and present strife, the prospect of peace modeled on England's past and the portent of continuing conflict with Tipu that inheres in the very ground on which the viewer walks. And if this overlay of contradictory representations and ideological scenes is not complex enough, it is important to remember that perspective is understood as a technology suited not only to the representation of peace but also to the practice of warfare itself as conducted by Cornwallis. The British ability to effectively target Tipu's fortresses with artillery relies on precisely the same geometric abstraction of physical space as that employed in the transparencies. The very technology of war figures forth the fantasy of peace.

Mrs. Barlow's Songs, or Specters of France

Oddly enough, it is the parallel acts of walking and reading that ultimately give the image city its political purchase, but it is important to remember that this stroll does not climb up to an "eminence" but rather ends up in the theatre. Once inside the doors, the collocation of might, moderation, and precinematic visual wonder was similarly enacted in the Gala Concert held in the Calcutta theatre:

> Entering at the west door, the first object that rivetted the attention was a beautiful semicircular temple, of the Ionic order, dedicated to Victory, placed at the east end, whose dome reached within a foot of the ceiling. In this was placed a transparency, representing a bust of Lord Cornwallis on a pedestal, with the Goddess of Victory flying over it, with a wreath of Laurel in her hand, which she was in the act of placing on his Lordship's brows:—on the plinth of the pedestal was his Lordship's motto,

Virtus Vincit Invidiam.
And over the bust
Regna Assignata.

—and on each side of this was a nich,—in one of which a figure of Fortitude, and in the other, of Clemency, was placed. Over these, and extending the whole breadth of the temple, was a transparent painting of the action of the 6th of Feb. 1792, and beneath, the following four lines:

Still pressing forward to the fight, they broke
Through flames of sulpher, and a night of smoke,
Till slaughter's legions fill'd the trench below,
And bore their fierce avengers to the foe.[102]

The contiguity of the emblem of Clemency and the images of slaughter encapsulate a specific patriotic style that unites the illuminations and the musical entertainment. The projected lines are from Addison's *The Campaign*, which celebrates the victory of the Duke of Marlborough over the French at Blenheim in 1704.[103] This comparison is bolstered by other elements of the poem that represent valiant British troops breaching the defenses of hillside forts not unlike those Cornwallis encountered at Bangalore, Nundydroog, and Severndroog.[104] Equating Cornwallis and Marlborough is an extremely important gesture not simply because it consolidates Cornwallis's heroism but because it suggests that Cornwallis's treaty with Tipu, like the Treaty of Utrecht eighty years earlier, will establish a balance of power in the Asian subcontinent that will permanently check French aspirations to commercial and territorial empire. This allusion is effective because Tipu was widely supported by the French, and British observers generally saw war with Mysore as a subset of a larger global struggle with France. What the projection suggests is that with this victory, the British have entered a new phase of imperial domination. However, this involves a misrecognition of both the past and the future that gets played out in the musical celebration.

The accounts of the concert indicate that transparencies were illuminated and extinguished in order to direct audience attention to various patriotic emblems before the performance of excerpts from Handel's *Judas Maccabaeus*. Like the mobilization of the prospects in the city itself and the citation of Addison's *The Campaign*, the choice of repertoire here takes arguably the most famous example of patriotic discourse in the eighteenth century and modifies it to suit the present circumstance. Contrary to what one might expect, the members of the civilian cadre of the East India Company who put on the celebration decided not to perform the famous "liberty airs" or even the more direct celebration of martial victory, but rather focused on pastoral passages that drew attention to the terms of new-found peace. Act 1 takes the audience directly to an ambivalent moment from *Judas Maccabaeus* that both looks back at momentary victory and anticipates a return to war. This return, as well as its attendant anxieties, is averted by a surrogative shift to a passage from *Joshua* that focuses on the Israelite conquest of Canaan. This activation and containment of anxiety is repeated in the second act with even more intensity. Despite the celebration of conquest at the end of act 1, act 2 opens with the overture from *Samson* that calls forth the abject and dispossessed leader of the Israelites. This invocation of national weakness is answered by a return to the closing pastoral scenes of *Judas Maccabaeus*. Thus, like the Handel Commemoration of 1784, the evening's entertainment both segmented and sutured together often divergent patriotic images, texts, and oratorios into a hybrid performance that engages with and reconfigures the allegorical objectives of the primary source material. The depth of that engagement is breathtaking, for it returns to the very scenes of forced conversion, circumcision, and dispossession that crystallized British imperial anxiety in the 1780s.

Judas Maccabaeus was originally, and continued to be, understood as an allegory for George II's victory over the Jacobite rebellion of 1745, but as Ruth Smith has argued, it is an exceedingly complex and ambivalent expression of patriotism.[105] James Morrell's libretto is based on both books of Maccabees, but much of its larger argument is implied. In 175 BC Antiochus Epiphanes ascended to the Syrian throne and was immediately involved in expansionist campaigns against Egypt. The Jews under Syrian rule were divided into orthodox and Hellenized Jews, who were open to the Greek culture of their rulers. Through a series of accommodations between these Hellenized Jews, represented by Jason, and their Syrian rulers, steps were taken to turn Jerusalem into a Greek city with Greek institutions. More orthodox Jews came to fear that these developments would contaminate their religion, and the ensuing conflict between orthodox and reform factions within the Jewish population was interpreted by Syrian rulers as rebellion and brutally put down. Following a massacre of Jews and a profanation of the Temple, Antiochus effectively outlawed Judaism, including the act of circumcision. In 2 Maccabees these events are interpreted as a warning from God not to diverge from traditional religious practice: "Now I beseech those that read this book, that they be not discouraged for these calamities but that they judge those punishments not to be for destruction, but for a chastening of our nation" (2 Macc. 6:12). As Ruth Smith indicates, this passage is presented nearly verbatim early in part 1 of *Judas Maccabaeus* and needs to be understood as the condition of possibility for the oratorio's patriotism.[106] The period of national, ethnic, and religious division constitutes that which must be overcome to secure the political liberty of the Maccabees and, by extension, their British counterparts. This period of chastisement precedes the action of the oratorio, which focuses instead on the Maccabees' revolt against Antiochus's attempt to enforce pagan sacrifice among them. The patriarch of the family, Mattithias, refuses the edict, flees with his sons into the mountains, and upon his death establishes his sons, Simon and Judas, as the political and military leaders of a rebellion against Syrian rule.

The oratorio begins at this point in the story and the first two parts track Judas's victories over the Syrian forces. Significantly, Morrell and Handel relegate much of the military action to the intervals between the parts of the oratorio and present the audience with retroactive, largely choral, celebrations of victory. The spiritual and political center of the work occurs in the beginning of part 3 when Simon recovers the Sanctuary of the Temple—that is, the events still celebrated at Chanukah. In response to the recovery of the temple and the defeat of his general Lysias, Antiochus withdrew his repressive orders, and Jews could now live in accordance with their own laws. The oratorio thus shifts its attention from the struggle for religious freedom to the pursuit of Jewish independence and concludes with a treaty that guarantees independence for the Maccabees. This structure allows Handel and Morrell to indulge in some of the most resonant celebrations of political liberty in the eighteenth century, while downplaying a whole series of reverses in the historical account of the Maccabees rebellion.

When excerpts of this oratorio were performed in Calcutta in 1792, the audience was confronted with a cascade of allegories, each laid over the top of the other, and like any palimpsest, this act of layering erases as much as it figures forth. At the center of these layers is the counterintuitive allegorical connection between the Maccabees story and the Jacobite Rebellion in Handel's oratorio. In order to understand the allegory, it is crucial to recognize that the Jacobite Rebellion was widely understood to be part of a larger French threat to English political and religious liberty. In this allegory, the Duke of Cumberland maps onto Judas, and the alliance between Scottish Jacobites and the French becomes comparable to the alliance between the Hellenized Jews and their Syrian rulers. As Smith states,

At first sight, it might have seemed that the analogy would have appeared paradoxical or strained to its intended audiences . . . ; the Maccabean story of a successful rebellion in which the rebels were in the right was apparently being used to celebrate the suppression of a rebellion in which the rebels were in the wrong. But Morrell is careful not to transcribe from Maccabees the instances in which the Jewish opposition resembled the Jacobite campaign, and the parallel is not between Syrians attempting to suppress a rebellion by the native Jewish population and Britain suppressing a rebellion by the native Scottish population. Rather, in the light of the contemporary perception of the rebellion as part of France's plan to dominate Britain politically and forcibly to change its religion, Judas unifying a nation disrupted from within by hellenizers who co-opt foreign hellenizing Syrian forces is equivalent to Cumberland unifying a nation disrupted from within by Jacobites who co-opt foreign Catholic French forces. This factual analogy is given vitality by an emotional one: the purgation of hellenistic tendencies . . . parallels British affirmation of loyalty after the upsurge of popular anti-Hanoverian feeling in 1742–4.[107]

So in its original context, *Judas Maccabaeus* allegorizes the Jacobite Rebellion in order to repudiate the larger threat of French aggression and to argue for the necessity of purging not only schism but also forms of political reform that threaten to make incursions on traditional notions of English political liberty. As Sudipta Sen argues, this "natural liberty" was not only "enshrined in legislation that reflected the intimate connections between liberty, private property, and law" but also supported by the continuing constitutional investment in the Protestant monarchy.[108] What becomes portable, therefore, in subsequent performances of the oratorio, is its ability to call forth the anxious specter of French aggression and the supposedly dire consequences of political apostasy or reform. And it is precisely this dramatization of disaster averted that fuels the oratorio's most patriotic moments. However, the activation of these anxieties does not always result in their resolution. Their performance has the potential to resuscitate past reversals and humiliations without fully resolving them.

With some sense of the political allegory of *Judas Maccabaeus*, we can now return to the Calcutta theatre and sketch in the remaining allegorical layers. Addison's lines on the Temple implicitly compare Cornwallis's victory over Tipu to the Duke of Marlborough's victory at the Battle of Blenheim. What links the two historical moments, aside from some obviously wishful thinking that the treaty with Tipu will be another Treaty of Utrecht, is the fact that British forces prevail against alliances between Mysore and France and Bavaria and France, respectively. The inscription on the Temple globalizes the conflict in India by emphasizing French involvement in both conflicts and thus establishes the alliance needed for translating the Maccabean allegory to the Third Mysore War. This is crucial because the Mysorean uprising of the early 1790s, like that of the Scottish Jacobites in the 1740s, needed to be figured not as rebellions but as French aggression carried out by proxy native forces for the allegory to operate properly.

The parallels being drawn between Judas's war against Syria, Marlborough's campaign against the Franco-Bavarian alliance, Cumberland's suppression of the French-sponsored Jacobites, and Cornwallis's victory over Tipu Sultan all revolve around the specter of French interference in British affairs. Impending war with France in Europe is again setting up the political and emotional condition for the Maccabean allegory to have some purchase on the audience. The Calcutta papers were full of the news of revolutionary France, and the palpable evidence of English social and cultural schism in response to the French example was as much a topic of concern in the colonies as it was in the metropole. Just as the adverse incidents that beset the Jews in Syria prior to the Maccabean revolt are interpreted as temporary punishment—or "chastening"—for Hellenization, the staging of *Judas Maccabaeus* in Calcutta plays out the reverses of British fortune in the first two Mysore wars, not only as punishment for comparable prior examples of Indianization, in which some British colonial subjects adopted the cultural and social norms of India, but also as a warning against current sympathy toward the French Revolution among some British constituencies. In both the Maccabees story and the revisionist history implied by Cornwallis's reforms of the East India Company, any deviation from national and racial purity implied by openness to surrounding Syrian or Indian society is punished and then overcome. This historical comparison is crucial because it speaks directly to the current moment of social schism in Britain itself. In the face of increasingly polarized British reaction to events in France, my suspicion is that the celebrants in Calcutta are exorcizing the dangers of social and cultural apostasy by turning the defeat of Tipu into a phantasmatic victory over France. In other words, this performance both chastens the nation by invoking past humiliation in the time of political crisis *and* projects the future triumph of the reconsolidated nation in a larger geopolitical frame.

This fantasy of unification, and its allegorical support, may have had particularly strong purchase because many of the audience members would have been Scots—the East India Company was composed of an inordinate number of

Scottish employees. For these audience members, the entire allegorical economy is predicated on the historical ejection of forms of political affiliation perhaps not at all distant from some audience members' pasts. In very real ways, the loyal Scottish members are the normative counterexample not only to past rebels but also to current factions opposed to the actions of the state. One of the primary objectives of the Calcutta celebration is to crystallize this counterexemplarity in the very space where previous observers, including Cornwallis, bemoaned the openness of East India Company officials to Indian styles of sociability.[109]

In this context, the earlier British losses to Mysore with all their attendant narratives of abjection become evidence of Britain's voluntary descent into faction and apostasy in the late 1780s and early 1790s. The allegory is at its most insistent here because Tipu's forceable conversion of British soldiers to Islam is implicitly compared to Antiochus's demand that the Maccabees take up pagan worship. As noted earlier, the anxiety produced by forced circumcision and the intense resistance to such blurring of religious and ethnic identity is felt throughout subsequent representations of conflict in Mysore, and they mirror the Maccabees story in eerie and powerful ways. But the allegory replaces the Mysorean act of forced circumcision with Antiochus's prohibition of the act: that which is most terrifying is tropologically canceled yet nonetheless activated. This is because, in the chain of allegories, forced Indianization in Mysore is being used to figure the openness of both Whig and more radical British constituencies to French constitutional reform, and thus the voluntary desire for reform among Britons is being recast as French desire for the absorption of British society. The entire figural economy aims to cancel past and present forms of voluntary cultural hybridization that were routinely satirized as an adoption of Eastern and/or French effeminacy by positing an external tormentor who violates the cultural, social, and sexual autonomy of the patriot Briton. Thus, the ostensibly prior hollowing out of masculinity from the inside is replaced by a fantasy of violation that paradoxically reestablishes the "integrity" of the patriotic subject at a future date. Put bluntly, the disturbing evidence of consensual, dare we say seditious, deviation from normative masculinity is replaced by a fantasy of being raped by the other. This ideological manipulation of what Reik in his analysis of Christian masochism refers to as "adverse incidents" allows the audience not only to reconfigure past instances of abjection into prophetic signs of future imperial pleasure but also to effectively subsume the real threat posed by Tipu or France into a masochistic fantasy where the tormented remains fully in control of the scene.[110]

Because the Maccabean allegory is so concerned with establishing the threat posed by an alliance between an internal other and a larger external force, the entire event is traversed by fantasies of persecution and vulnerability. The Calcutta concert picks at this wound in revealing ways. The first act of the Calcutta performance takes a brief recitative and song from the beginning of the second part of *Judas Maccabaeus* that not only celebrates Judas's first victories over Syrian forces but also precedes a return to war. This return is negated by a sudden shift to a chorus from *Joshua* that focuses not on the contamination of the nation by foreign influence but rather on the triumphant subjection of foreigners. *Joshua*, unlike *Judas Maccabaeus*, is largely about the acquisition of territory—in this case, Canaan—through conquest. The surrogative effect of shifting from *Judas Maccabaeus* to *Joshua* is clarified by remembering the role of Canaan in seventeenth-century British theories of governmentality. In her analysis of *Joshua*, Smith argues:

> The partition of Canaan was for Harrington the origin of the Israelite 'agrarian,' the ordering of society based on land ownership which in his view formed the foundation of right government. . . . In other words, the division of Canaan by Joshua under God's direction was the birth of the Israelite nation, and since the division was based on principles of land ownership essential to the prosperity and stability of any society, it was or should be the pattern of all societies—including, for the audience of *Joshua*, their own. According to Harrington their agrarian law was the key factor which saved the Israelites from falling into typical eastern servility.[111]

This hypostatization of landed property as the source of governmental and social security is precisely what underpinned Cornwallis's implementation of the Permanent Settlement after the 1792 treaty with Tipu. And the Permanent Settlement was itself as an allegorical policy—one that utilized one form of social and economic relations to figure forth another.

When, in act 2, Mrs. Elizabeth Barlow, the wife of the very man who would attempt to reconfigure Indian property relations in terms of British notions of landed property,[112] and Captain Haynes sing the following lines, one is presented with the aural equivalent of what C. A. Bayly refers to as the Permanent Settlement's "massive effort in wishful thinking":[113]

> Oh! lovely peace! With plenty crown'd,
> Come spread thy blessings all around,
> Let fleecy flocks the hills adorn,

And vallies smile with waving corn!
Let the shrill trumpet cease;
No other sound
But Nature's songsters
Wake the cheerful morn![114]

In a significant alteration of Handel's oratorio, this song, originally scored for the Israelitish woman, is transformed into a duet with the countertenor Captain Haynes. Thus, the audience is presented with the civilian and the military wings of the East India Company singing in concert. Would it be too much to suggest that the duet refashions the pastoral moment such that the military man is tamed by the implied domestic relation between male and female singer? It is precisely this sublation of the soldier into the paternal, the military into the familial or bureaucratic, that informs both the treaty ceremony and many of the projections. Thus, the performance supplements the complex reorientation of Cornwallis as imperial icon such that the specter of castration is put into abeyance by the plenitude not simply of the imperial father but of the biopolitical imperatives of the middle classes.[115] This supplemental relation is revealing, for it emphasizes that the fantasy of benevolent paternalism and the Permanent Settlement are ineffective in and of themselves and thus require the deep micrological regulation of domestic relations that came to preoccupy British rule in India in the early nineteenth century. As Sen, Collingham, and others have recognized, sexual and racial deployments that the middle classes first utilized to consolidate their own power both at home and abroad became crucial norms for managing colonial populations.[116] It is precisely these deployments in the form of the singing conjugal pair that are grafted onto now obsolete figurations of pastoral peace and that reorient the ideological import of this patriotic performance.

The American Ghost

However, the full depth of this reorientation can be understood only when we look closely at how these pastoral lines are deployed. This happy fantasy in which India starts to look like England and the future French threat is conveniently consigned to allegorical oblivion is haunted by an American ghost. Act 2 of the Calcutta performance opens with the overture from Handel's *Samson. Samson,* like many of the Israelite oratorios, offers recurrent images of national weakness and opens with its hero collapsed on the ground, dispossessed by a foreign foe. As Smith argues,

> Samson and the Israelites, "no longer hero and inferiors but, at the crisis, equally powerless, wait upon God's aid, and there is no certainty that it will materialize. . . . The nation's setbacks, its oppression by an alien race, the only partly heroic career of its hero, its absolute dependence on divine favour which cannot be claimed to be merited, and its recognition of divine agency in every success—all these aspects of this oratorio, which recur throughout the librettos of the Israelites, even when taken with the many expressions of faith, strength and confidence which also recur, do not add up to triumphalism.[117]

Smith is highly attentive to how anxiety works in each of the Israelite oratorios and argues that their patriotism is often shadowed by fundamental moments of doubt regarding British national election. But the performance we are examining in this section fragments these patriotic texts and stitches them together such that "adverse incidents" are located in a very specific temporal structure. For audience members familiar with Handel's music, the overture would have engaged the anxiety attending Cornwallis's previous failures in America. Read in this way, the sudden return to the pastoral passages of *Judas Maccabaeus* quoted earlier would amount to nothing less than an attempt to bury some particularly bad memories. But why risk engaging the very nightmare of colonial defeat? As in the previous allegorical cascade, imperial setbacks are mobilized to highlight the act of overcoming them. But there is also something else at stake, which lies deep in the heart of the allegory itself and perhaps explains why everything about this performance seems so overdetermined.

When we consider the historical structure that allows the Maccabean allegory to function, what we encounter is a figure that cannot help but call forth the American disaster. After all, the historical situation that most powerfully resembles the Maccabees story is that of the American colonies in 1776. As Dror Wahrman and others have argued, the key problem for British subjectivity posed by the American crisis is that the people most like them not only take up arms in internecine strife but form an alliance with the French.[118] If we run this through the Maccabean allegory, the Americans become the Hellenized Jews, the French remain in the role of the Syrian oppressors, and the English find themselves cast as the orthodox Jews. Only in this story, no unification is effected; the orthodox Britons simply lose and are forced to reimagine Britishness without their American brothers. In this story, Cornwallis is desolate, alone, and dispossessed—a figure not unlike Samson who is in desperate need of recuperation. The nightmare of Yorktown becomes inextricably linked to the dreams fostered by the Mysorean treaty: a dream of Permanent Settlement and benevolent paternal rule, no less than a dream of global supremacy over France.

Could we not argue that by 1792 this dispossessed figure has finally become politically useful, not only literally in the sense that he has a job to do in India but also figuratively in the way he is invoked in the Gala Concert: as the chastened sign of history whose recurrent pain retroactively anticipates the pleasures of unrealized imperial domination. And it is the ultimate unpresentability of global supremacy either in fact or in fantasy that allows for its figural presentation in the person of Cornwallis. By invoking Lyotard's reading of Kant's famous notion of the "sign of history," I am trying to suggest that Britons at this moment of patriotic investment see human progress as a form of national election that is not susceptible to direct presentation but rather must operate through a complex temporal game in which patriotic enthusiasm—with all its recollected pain and forestalled pleasure—is itself an as-if presentation of supremacy.[119] As a "chastened" sign of history, it is a perversion of the very notions Kant was attempting to explore in the late historical and political writings, but it should not come as a surprise because British patriotic discourse claims "liberty" in a fashion altogether different from Kant's analysis of the French Revolution. Throughout this phantasmatic exchange, the particular term "Briton" trumps any universal notion of the human; English "liberty" overrules any abstract notion of freedom as the tendency toward the moral idea of the Absolute Good; and thus the story inexorably reverts to arrogant attributions of God's will. As Kaja Silverman states, all adverse incidents, all "sufferings and defeats of the fantasizing subject are dramatized in order to make the final victory appear all the more glorious and triumphant."[120] Imperial Britain's calamities in America and Mysore are transformed into exemplary and necessary punishments that presage a level of future supremacy only God can bestow, because it has not—and, we might add, will not—come to pass. But the supposed deviations from appropriate national character—Britons' flirtations with hybrid forms of sociability whether they be understood as Indianization or Francophilia—for which the nation has been chastened or is to be chastened will become all too evident in the emergent patriotisms of the early nineteenth century. They will become the negative ground from which racialized notions of national election are activated and maintained.

Coda

"In praise of the oak, its advantage and prosperity"

Chapter 1 opened with a performance in which military men dressed as druids sang "in praise of the oak, its advantage and prosperity." Such a panegyric to the oak is not unusual in the context of wartime writing in England in the eighteenth century. In both Pope and Whitehead, British oaks have a global reach either through their transformation into warships in the case of "Windsor Forest" or through a certain political extension in Whitehead.[1] Here is Whitehead writing as Laureate on the eve of the American war:

> Beyond the vast Atlantic tide
> Extend your healing influence wide,
> Where millions claim your care:
> Inspire each just, each filial thought,
> And let the nations round be taught
> The British oak is there.
>
> Tho' vaguely wild its branches spread,
> And rear almost an alien head
> Wide-waving o'er the plain,
> Let still, unspoil'd by foreign earth,
> And conscious of its nobler birth,
> The untainted trunk remain.[2]

But this figure of the spreading branches of the British oak—here extending across the Atlantic itself—is simply not possible after the fall of Yorktown in 1781. The loss of the American colonies imposed a certain restraint in this emblematic figure. But this spatial restraint is supplemented by a renewed investment in the oak's capacity to represent historical continuity: spatial extension gave way to temporal reach.

A similar combination of restraint and overdetermination can be found in what is perhaps the most significant mobilization of the oak metaphor in the late eighteenth century. I am referring of course to Burke's use of the oak to signify the British constitution in *Reflections on the Revolution in France*: "Because half-a-dozen grasshoppers under a fern make the field ring with their importunate chink, whilst thousands of great cattle, reposed beneath the shadow of the British oak, chew the cud and are silent, pray do not imagine that those who make the noise are the only inhabitants of the field; that of course they are many in number; or that, after all, they are other than the little shrivelled, meagre, hopping, though loud and troublesome insects of the hour."[3] As a figure for the nation or constitution, the important feature of this oak is the capacity of its branches to give shade, but the animalization of British subjects—whether they be revolutionary grasshoppers or loyal cattle—not only privileges the silence of the cows but also renders the entire political arrangement quite compact. The oak's protection is nativist; there is none of the extensibility that played such a key role in Pope or Whitehead. This marks a significant curtailment of the diffusion of British liberty beyond the shores of the British Isles. And we need to recognize that this constitutes a recalibration of imperial governance as much as it does a rejection of Whig suggestions at the time that Burke was writing the *Reflections* that the revolution in France had the potential to diffuse English models of liberty into the heart of Europe. Burke's supplementation of the oak figure with that of the cattle is aimed at ensuring that the oak does not become confused with a younger liberty tree.

It is for this reason that Burke's figure sacrifices extensibility to duration by intertwining the life cycle of the tree with the bonds of the family:

> Our political system is placed in a just correspondence and symmetry with the order of the world, and with the mode of existence decreed to a permanent body composed of transitory parts; wherein, by the disposition of a stupendous wisdom, moulding together the great mysterious incorporation of the human race, the whole, at one time, is never old, or middle aged, or young, but in a condition of unchangeable constancy, moves on through the varied tenour of perpetual decay, fall, renovation and progression. Thus, by preserving the method of nature in the conduct of the state, in what we improve we are never wholly new; in what we retain we are never wholly obsolete. . . . In this choice of inheritance we have given our

> frame of polity the image of a relation in blood; binding up the constitution of our country with our dearest domestic affections.[4]

This is a confusing passage precisely because the image of "a relation in blood" does not sit well with "the varied tenour of perpetual decay, fall, renovation and progression." Burke wants the constitution to be both an "incorporation of the human race" and something that shelters the polity of Britain. This strange hybridization of blood and oak, human and tree, through its very overdetermination, performs a rhetorical intensification that separates him from his predecessors. By collapsing the distinction between humans and plants, Burke has opened the door for a racial interpretation of the constitution: "In this choice of inheritance we have given our frame of polity the image of a relation in blood." And this racialization of governance lays claim to historical constancy by aligning itself with the durability at the heart of the oak figure. The tension between the symbolics of blood nascent in Burke's analogy between family and constitution, on the one hand, and the more subtle invocation of the tree, on the other, not only signals the struggle to redefine the oak figure for a new imperial era but also opens the door for—and perhaps even demands—a reevaluation of the relationship between extension and duration in the notion of British liberty.[5] Could we not argue that Burke's reactivation of the oak metaphor is the trigger that allows for a series of rememorative utterances that seek to address the imperial wound of 1781? We know that at least one poet responded to the *Reflections* in precisely this way and that his poetic meditation on the figure had a profound impact on Wordsworth, Coleridge, Clare, and others.[6] William Cowper's "Yardley Oak," which was written in response to Burke's text, explicitly addresses the reevaluation of extension and durability in the oak metaphor and, in so doing, recalibrates imperial and national relations in quite remarkable ways.

We need to go back to the global war of the early 1780s in order to move forward. In early December 1781, less than two months after Cornwallis's surrender at Yorktown, William Cowper sent an imaginary "sociable conversation" to his friend Joseph Hill in which Cowper articulated his thoughts on the American war. After stating that he knew of no one up to the task of leading Britain out of the conflict, Cowper offered the following summary of the state of the empire:

> If we pursue the war, it is because we are desperate; it is plunging and sinking year after year in still greater depths of calamity. If we relinquish it, the remedy is equally desperate, and would prove, I believe, in the end no remedy at all. Either way we are undone—perseverance will only enfeeble us more, we cannot recover the Colonies by arms. If we discontinue

> the attempt, in that case we fling away voluntarily, what in the other we strive ineffectually to regain, and whether we adopt the one measure or the other, are equally undone. For I consider the loss of America as the ruin of England; were we less encumbered than we are, at home, we could but ill afford it, but being crushed as we are under an enormous debt that the public credit can at no rate carry much longer, the consequence is sure. Thus it appears to me that we are squeezed to death between the two sides of that sort of alternative, which is commonly called a cleft stick, the most threat'ning and portentous condition in which the interests of any country can possibly be found.[7]

Of the myriad statements of imperial doom from this period, Cowper's remark stands out because the metaphor of the cleft stick captures the predicament of imperial subjectivity at this moment so vividly. To be cleft is to be split or divided to a certain depth, but the expression *a cleft stick* uses the notion of bifurcation to figure the two horns of a dilemma: as the *Oxford English Dictionary* states, it indicates "a position in which advance and retreat are alike impossible." For Cowper, the nation and, by extension, the imperial subject are entangled to the point of being unable to move. Disentangling the imperial subject from this painful, static, almost abject, position involves a phantasmatic reconfiguration of the political beyond the limits of specific policies and actions. In short, the predicament seems to call forth a new kind of political and poetic utterance perhaps best embodied by *The Task*, which was composed in the immediate aftermath of the war.

For Cowper and others, the reverses of the early 1780s, both in America and in other colonial locales, raised the simultaneous possibility that British culture may die and yet live on in a ghostly form elsewhere. Throughout this book I have attempted to show how the complex temporality of this ghosting procedure and the figural attempts to keep it under control permeated the performance cultures of the metropole during this period. In the final two chapters, I have given examples of how postwar culture mobilized the anxieties of the war years to construct new imperial fantasies. In this coda, I wish to return to Cowper as a kind of emblematic figure for cultural change, only this time I am not looking at *The Task* but rather at a lesser known poem, "Yardley Oak," which addresses the changes wrought on the oak figure in the age of revolution and which sums up much of what I have been trying to elucidate in the preceding chapters.

The political dilemma presented in Cowper's 1781 letter presupposes a strong sense of the integration of colony and metropole. For Cowper, the loss of America implies the ruin of England; his thoughts on the nondistinction of England and America emerge frequently in his letters but nowhere more explicitly than in the following missive to John Newton: "I consider England and America as once one country. They were so in respect of interest, intercourse, and affinity. A great earthquake has made a partition, and now the Atlantic Ocean flows between them. He that can drain that Ocean, and shove the two shores together so as to make them aptly coincide and meet each other in every part, can unite them again; but this is the work for Omnipotence, and nothing less than Omnipotence can heal the breach between us" (1:569–70).

What is strange about this account of the American war is that it forgets that the Atlantic Ocean has always separated the colonies from the British Isles. Cowper here imagines a prerevolutionary state that negates the very material structure of the globe. In this fantasy it is contiguity that matters most: the shores must "aptly coincide." It is a figure of an organic whole rent asunder, which in some ideal future state could be sutured together again by none other than God himself. God's role here is important because elsewhere in both the poems and the letters from this period, Cowper emphasizes that this fatal wound—here it is naturalized as an earthquake—is inflicted by Providence because England is a "sinfull Nation" (2:104). Like many other commentators at this juncture, Cowper felt that England had been hollowed out from within and held aristocratic dissipation and political corruption to be the undoing of both the empire and the nation. But, as in the cleft-stick passage, agency has been fully wrested from politicians and citizens and is transferred to a divine nonhuman process. Failed military and state policy not only are subsumed into a narrative of irrevocable decline and fall but also are corrected in a field where men have little or no active role to play.

Roughly ten years after Cowper's appraisal of the end of the American war, he found himself again contemplating the destruction of the nation, only this time he deploys a cultural rather than a natural trope for disintegration:

> I am entirely of your mind respecting this conflagration by which all Europe suffers at present, and is likely to suffer for a long time to come. The same mistake seems to have prevailed as in the American business. We then flattered ourselves that the colonies would prove an easy conquest, and when all the neighbour nations arm'd themselves against France, we imagined I believe that she too would be presently vanquish'd. But we begin already to be undeceived, and God only knows to what a degree we may find we have erred, at the conclusion. Such however is the state of

things all around us, as reminds me continually of the Psalmist's expression—*He shall break them in pieces like a potter's vessel,* and I rather wish than hope in some of my melancholy moods that England herself may escape a fracture. (4:426)

As a figure, the broken sherds of the nation implied by his allusion to Psalm 2:9 is more coherent than his strange cancellation of the Atlantic in his 1784 letter, but it still argues that God will break that which man has made, because Britain has set itself against God.

This same sense of providential retribution suffuses "Yardley Oak," but it is played out not only with more rhetorical force but also with more historical specificity:

Survivor sole, and hardly such, of all
That once lived here thy brethen, at my birth
(Since which I number threescore winters past)
A shatter'd vet'ran, hollow-trunk'd perhaps
As now, and with excoriate forks deform,
Relicts of Ages![8]

Cowper's address does two things. First, it establishes a relation of intimacy between this last surviving oak and the aged speaker. This is achieved by constructing the effect of physical proximity between speaker and oak: the poem's descriptive specificity is one of the poem's most prominent rhetorical strategies. And this effect of intimacy is intensified almost immediately by the syntactical ambiguity introduced by the parenthetical phrase in line 3. Cowper's sudden specification of the speaker's age suspends the syntax at the end of line 2 and thus allows "A shatter'd vet'ran" in line 4 to figure not only for the oak but also for the speaker. This figural ambiguity sets up the possibility for complex identifications between the speaker and the tree, which will have important political ramifications as the poem unfolds. At this point, it is enough to recognize that this establishes the potential for precisely the same collapse between the body of the subject and the arborial figure for governance that animated Burke's overdetermined deployment of the oak in the *Reflections*. As we will see, Cowper does not allow that collapse to occur.

But this is not all that is achieved here. The metaphorical comparison between the oak tree and "the shatter'd vet'ran" also activates the memory of past war—and not the triumphalism following the Seven Years' War, but rather the sense of loss characteristic of Cowper's remarks on the American war. I believe that this phrase evokes the wounded veteran of the American war and this oak is shattered like the potter's vessel alluded to in Cowper's 1793 letter. The full connotations of this metaphor are not activated until seventy lines later, but it is the central enigma of the poem. In what sense is the tree shattered, and in what way is it a veteran?

These questions are temporarily supplanted by an explicit statement of the desire to venerate the tree, which concludes the first verse paragraph:

> . . . Could a mind imbued
> With truth from heav'n created thing adore,
> I might with rev'rence kneel and worship Thee.
> It seems Idolatry with some excuse
> When our forefather Druids in their oaks
> Imagin'd sanctity. The Conscience yet
> Unpurified by an authentic act
> Of amnesty, the meed of blood divine,
> Loved not the light, but gloomy into gloom
> Of thickest shades, like Adam after taste
> Of fruit proscribed, as to a refuge, fled. (6–16)

This is a rather startling turn because it suggests that veneration of the oak is not only a form of pagan idolatry but also akin to Adam's attempt to hide from God's view after consciously breaking God's explicit proscription.

The allusion to book 9 of *Paradise Lost* is deeply significant because the "thickest shades" referred to here are not offered by oak trees. Adam expresses the desire to be "Obscured where highest woods impenetrable / To star or sunlight spread their umbrage broad" (9.1086–87) and ultimately chooses the banyan tree:

> So counselled he and both together went
> Into the thickest wood, there soon they chose
> The fig-tree: not that kind for fruit renowned
> But such as at this day to Indians known
> In Malabar or Deccan spreads her arms
> Branching so broad and long that in the ground
> the bended twigs take root and daughters grow
> About the mother tree, a pillared shade
> High overarched and echoing walks between.
> There oft the Indian herdsman shunning heat

Shelters in cool and tends his pasturing herds
At loopholes cut through thickest shade. (9.1099–1110)

As Balachandra Rajan has argued, the evocation of the banyan tree from Milton speaks directly to the question of shelter.[9] Adam chooses the tree because it provides shade or, in Cowper's phrase, "gloom." To venerate the oak for its shelter is to misrecognize it as the banyan, and the spiritual cost is, in Cowper's eyes, catastrophic: it is further evidence of the nation's alienation from God. In this context, the verb "might" in line 8 of "Yardley Oak" becomes crucial, for it signifies temptation and the speaker's resistance to it. The speaker might have worshiped the tree, except for his belief that to do so would be to be attempting to hide from one's responsibility before God. Furthermore, in shunning the "loopholes cut through thickest shade" (9.1110), the speaker is abandoning the famous "loop-holes of retreat" that afforded the speaker of book 4 of *The Task* respite, through the distancing effect of remediation, from the violence of imperial war.[10] In that sense, this poem involves a progression toward a performance of historical reckoning.

When we recognize that the capacity to provide shade is precisely the feature of the figure that is so appealing to Burke, then I think the full import of Cowper's intervention becomes clear. For Cowper, the loss of the American colonies and the predicted failure of the war with France amount to symptomatic signs of God's displeasure with the corruption of British liberty, at both a national and an imperial level. What is remarkable here is that Cowper's opening verse paragraph activates the entire historical predicament with such iconic specificity: the shattered oak, the banyan tree, the sense of a nation deformed and hollowed out from the inside. But, most importantly, their collocation suggests that all of these connotations are comparable to one another and to the speaker himself. This collocation implies that these figures, like India and Britain, are bound up in a global historical dynamic.

As the poem unfolds, the two primary elements of the oak figure—extension and duration—are scrutinized historically; and by this I mean that their figural potential is tested against the historical moment of 1791. Cowper's evaluation of this moment in Britain's history is dire, and the poem is suffused with a sense of past or passing glory. As one might expect, Cowper plays out the "mutability in all / That we account most durable below" (70–71) and traces "thy growth / From almost nullity into a state / Of matchless grandeur, and declension thence / Slow into such magnificent decay" (87–90). The pun on "state" bolsters the direct assertion that Britain is in a condition of irrevocable, but nonetheless magisterial, decline.

But Cowper's description of the tree focuses our attention on the tree's boughs and on the hollowing out of its trunk:

Time made thee what thou wast, King of the woods.
And Time hath made thee what thou art, a cave
For owls to roost in. Once thy spreading boughs
O'erhung the champain, and the num'rous flock
That grazed it stood beneath that ample cope
Uncrowded, yet safe-shelter'd from the storm.
No flock frequents thee now; thou has outlived
Thy popularity, and art become
(Unless verse rescue thee awhile) a thing
Forgotten as the foliage of thy youth. (50–59)

I want to look at the fate of the boughs and trunk in turn, because the loss of the former has an extraordinary effect on the latter, and because it is in the destruction of these elements that the reader gets a sense of precisely how and why this tree is a "shatter'd vet'ran."

After declaring the tree's "magnificent decay," the speaker brings the tree within the orbit of human affairs:

At thy firmest age
Thou hadst within thy bole solid contents
That might have ribb'd the sides or plank'd the deck
Of some flagg'd Admiral, and tortuous arms,
The shipwright's darling treasure, didst present
To the four quarter'd winds, robust and bold,
Warp'd into tough knee-timber, many a load.
But the axe spared thee; in those thriftier days
Oaks fell not, hewn by thousands, to supply
The bottomless demands of contest waged
For senatorial honours. (93–103)

It is hard not to think of Pope's "Windsor Forest" here, especially because Cowper's presentation of the oak's potential use in the construction of warships and merchant vessels tallies so well with Pope's double understanding—both military and commercial—of the rush of oaken timber around the globe. The oak addressed in this poem's opening line is a "sole survivor" not because it has been the object of symbolic veneration, but rather because its "brethren" have become the material basis for imperial wars that Cowper clearly signals have more to do with the hubris of politicians than the benefit of the state. Again Cowper is reiterating his frequently stated reservations about the failure of corrupt politicians to recognize the true interests of the nation. As the passage unfolds, it becomes clear that man destroyed the forest for ill-advised war, and now it is only a matter for Time to finish the task by "disjoining" atom by atom this "shatter'd vet'ran" (103–8) .

But nestled within this fairly explicit critique is a very subtle gesture. Imperial war is evoked by the pun on "tortuous arms," but by focusing the reader's attention on a fairly arcane element of shipbuilding—knee timber—Cowper consigns the "arms" figure to the notes only to activate it in a surprisingly brutal fashion in the next verse paragraph. At the most explicit comparison between the oak and the state, the speaker suddenly discloses that the tree affords no shelter because it has no limbs:

So stands a Kingdom whose foundations yet
Fail not, in virtue and wisdom lay'd,
Though all the superstructure by the tooth
Pulverized of venality, a shell
Stands now, and semblance only of itself.
Thine arms have left thee. Winds have rent them off
Long since, and rovers of the forest wild
With bow and shaft, have burnt them. Some have left
A splinter'd stump bleach'd to a snowy white,
And some memorial none where once they grew. (120–29)

The suspension of the tree's lack of limbs until this point is extremely shocking because it disjoins this particular tree from the usual political connotations of the emblematic oak figure. And yet the figure of the tree's arms reveals itself to be exceedingly complex. If we understand arms to signify the martial capacity of Georgian England, particularly its naval strength, then the poem recognizes that the diffusion of liberty that was so integral to early theories of empire relies on the felling of oaks such as the one being addressed by the speaker. But the corruption of ministers, and the implicit sinfulness of the nation, have generated a situation where "Thine arms have left thee" in both senses of the word. After the loss of the American war, one can no longer simply assume that Britain can protect its imperial holdings through force of arms, nor can one assume that the symbolic shelter afforded by the boughs of the constitution will protect the citizenry. The implication is that both the military and what Burke described as the frame of the polity have been "pulverized by venality." So the reader is presented with a particularly dangerous situation where the diffusion of liberty through empire—here figured by the propagation of ships from oaks—has undercut one of its fundamental principles—the notion that the state through its laws will, like the oak, shelter the people. It is the same organic loop that allowed Cowper to understand the loss of America as equivalent to the loss of England.

With the loss of its arms, the tree's capacity to represent shelter has been permanently compromised. From this figural dismemberment comes a different possibility for metaphor. This tree becomes notable not for its arms but for its screaming mouth:

> Embowell'd now, and of thy ancient self
> Possessing nought but the scoop'd rind that seems
> An huge throat calling to the clouds for drink
> Which it would give in riv'lets to thy root,
> Thou temptest none, but rather much forbidd'st
> The feller's toil, which thou could'st ill requite.
> Yet is thy root sincere, sound as the rock,
> A quarry of stout spurs and knotted fangs
> Which crook'd into a thousand whimsies, clasp
> The stubborn soil, and hold thee still erect. (110–19)

This oak tree tempts no one because it offers no shade and provides no suitable timber for arms. With the capacity to subdue enemies and to provide shelter for the polity shorn away, the tree becomes a remarkable figure for the poet. It becomes a mouth calling for sustenance from the sky so that it can sustain the only thing worth sustaining—its roots.

It is in this sense that the tree is a "shatter'd vet'ran" and why the syntactical ambiguity that allows the phrase to also refer to the speaker in the opening verse paragraph is so important. Cowper is laying the groundwork for a different kind of relationship between patriotic poet and national figure. There is an analogy between tree and speaker here, but it does not conform to Burke's "philosophical analogy" between constitution and blood. The analogy does not rest on the capacity for autogeneration nascent in Burke's naturalization of the constitution but rather on the capacity for mediating between sky and soil that Cowper aligns not only with expressivity but also with patriotic Christian humility. This mediating function in the face of physical, spiritual, and national decline is the ultimate task of the poet in the time of national and imperial crisis, when the oak can no longer protect anyone owing to ill usage.

It is in this light that the poem's truncated ending—the poem remained incomplete—gains its resonance. At the very moment that the speaker declares that the tree is bereft of arms and un-memorialized, he also insists that the tree endures:

> Yet life still lingers in thee, and puts forth
> Proof not contemptible of what she can
> Even where Death predominates. The Spring
> Thee finds not less alive to her sweet force
> Than yonder upstarts of the neighbour wood
> So much thy juniors, who their birth received
> Half a millenium since the date of thine. (130–36)

The question that remains is what is to be done with this "sweet force" in the face of decrepitude. What is the dismembered tree/nation/poet to do? The "yonder upstarts of the neighbour wood" are presented as signs of the future. The fact that the poem does not specify their species is, I think, important because "upstarts" may be referring to the revolutionaries of a neighbouring nation—especially at the time when this poem was composed.

But whether Cowper is referring to France or to new patriots in Britain is not crucial. What follows in both the canceled and the retained versions of the poem is an explicit adoption of a pedagogical stance. Because the "shatter'd vet'ran" can no longer speak, its double, the oracular poet, must perform:

> But since, although well-qualified by age
> To teach, no spirit dwells in thee, seated here
> On thy distorted root, with hearers none
> Or prompter save the scene, I will perform
> Myself, the oracle, and will discourse
> In my own ear such matter as I may. (137–42)

The way "Myself" is stranded at the beginning of line 141 is for me one of the differential marks through which we could define Romanticism, for it is here that an entire political narrative, an entire political symbolics, is suddenly transformed into an example of what not to do. History's dismemberment of the oak has allowed the poet to suddenly and boldly speak to and for the figure in what is described as a theatrical space. But he does so while "seated here / On thy distorted root." He does not become the tree, but rather contends with disfiguration. It is in this light that the poem's obsession with the contorted structures of the ruined tree, its distorted roots and tortuous arms, is so important. The figure has been disfigured, and that spectacle demands a performance where private desire and public discourse intersect in a profound engagement with the past. In retrospect, could we not simply state that Cowper's sense of dismemberment, traceable to the global crisis that would reconfigure the Atlantic imperium and reorient the entire project of empire, has called forth the performance of Romanticism? That the poem sputters out at this point without fully articulating this prophecy is apt, not only because the September massacres would so radically call into question the hope expressed for the "Spring" but also because Cowper had cleared the ground, or allowed future readers such as Wordsworth and Clare to see how the ground was cleared for their future utterances.

Notes

Introduction: *Entertainment, Mediation, and the Future of Empire*

1. Samuel Johnson, *A dictionary of the English language: in which the words are deduced from their originals, and illustrated in their different significations by . . . The fourth edition, revised by the author*, vol. 1 of 2 (Dublin: Thomas Ewing, 1775).

2. As William B. Warner emphasizes, entertainment has its roots in the French word *entre* and thus always carries with it the condition of "between-ness." See *Licensing Entertainment: The Elevation of Novel Reading in Britain, 1684–1750* (Berkeley: Univ. of California Press, 1998), 231.

3. This notion of release is easily aligned with theories of "laughing comedy." For a discussion of the issues implied here, see Lisa Freeman, "The Social Life of Eighteenth-Century Comedy," in *The Cambridge Companion to British Theatre, 1730–1830*, ed. Jane Moody and Daniel O'Quinn (Cambridge: Cambridge Univ. Press, 2007), 73–86.

4. See Stephen Conway, "From Fellow-Nationals to Foreigners: British Perceptions of the Americans, circa 1739–1783," *William and Mary Quarterly* 59.1 (2002): 65–100, for a detailed account of the modulations in identification and for an exhaustive catalog of the scholarship on this issue.

5. For a provocative discussion of theories of empire that attempted to deal with emergent problems after the Seven Years' War but that failed to gain traction during the American Revolution, see Brendan McConville, *The King's Three Faces: The Rise and Fall of Royal America, 1688–1776* (Chapel Hill: Univ. of North Carolina Press), 220–316. See also Paul Downes, *Democracy, Revolution, and Monarchism in Early American Literature* (Cambridge: Cambridge Univ. Press, 2002).

6. This problematic has been admirably discussed by Stephen Conway in *The British Isles and the War of American Independence* (Oxford: Oxford Univ. Press, 2003). See also Bruce Lenman, *Britain's Colonial Wars, 1688–1783* (Harlow: Longman, 2001), 195–225, for a brief summation of many of the key issues posed by the loss of the American colonies. Kathleen Wilson's "Empire of Virtue: The Imperial Project and Hanoverian Culture c. 1720–1785," in *An Imperial State at War: Britain from 1689 to 1815*, ed. Lawrence Stone (New York: Routledge, 1994), 128–48, offers a very lucid synopsis of the cultural dynamics that attended these transformations in imperial identity.

7. The examples of social unrest here have all been studied through the lens of crowd violence. Most of these discussions take their cues from George Rudé, *The Crowd in History: A Study of Popular Disturbances in France and England, 1730–1848* (New York: Wiley, 1964); and E. P. Thompson, "The Moral Economy of the English Crowd in the Eighteenth Century," in his *Customs in Common* (New York: New Press, 1993), 185–258. For canonical discussions of Wilkite actions, see Rudé, *Wilkes and Liberty: A Social Study of 1763 to 1774* (Oxford: Clarendon, 1962); John Brewer, *Party Ideology and Popular Politics at the Accession of George III* (Cambridge: Cambridge Univ. Press, 1976), 163–200; Kathleen Wilson, *A Sense of the People: Politics, Culture and Imperialism in Britain, 1715–1785* (Cambridge: Cambridge Univ. Press, 1995), 206–36; and Brewer, "Theatre and Counter-Theater in Georgian Politics: The Mock Elections at Garrat," *Radical History Review* 22 (1979–80): 7–40. For a detailed analysis of social dynamics of the Gordon Riots, see Nicholas Roger, *Crowds, Culture, and Politics in Georgian Britain* (Oxford: Oxford Univ. Press, 1998), 145–75.

8. For a detailed account of British reaction to the American war in political pamphlets and sermons, see Eliga H. Gould, *The Persistence of Empire: British Political Culture in the Age of the American Revolution* (Chapel Hill: Univ. of North Carolina Press, 2000), 106–214.

9. Colin Mercer, "Entertainment, or the Policing of Virtue," *new formations* 2 (1988): 51–71.

10. Mercer also seems more interested in the repressive strategies of entertainment, whereas I wish to push the Foucauldian reading of entertainment toward an analysis of its productive capabilities.

11. For a recent discussion of the effect of the Licensing Act on theatrical culture, see Matthew Kinservik, *Disciplining Satire: The Censorship of Satiric Drama on the Eighteenth-Century London Stage* (Lewisburg, Pa.: Bucknell Univ. Press, 2002), 95–133.

12. See ibid. and Jane Moody, *Illegitimate Theatre in London, 1770–1840* (Cambridge: Cambridge Univ. Press, 2000), for discussion of the complex relationship between generic integrity and licensing.

13. Susan Staves, "Tragedy," in Moody and O'Quinn, *The Cambridge Companion to British Theatre*, 87–102, and Michael Dobson, *The Making of the National Poet: Shakespeare, Adaptation and Authorship, 1660–1769* (Oxford: Clarendon Press, 1990).

14. The notion of legitimate theatre being transformed from within is most forcefully articulated by Jane Moody in *Illegitimate Theatre in London, 1770–1840* (Cambridge: Cambridge Univ. Press, 2000).

15. David Worrall's *Theatric Revolution: Drama, Censorship, and Romantic Period Subcultures, 1773–1832* (Oxford: Oxford Univ. Press, 2006) directs its attention to how state censorship impinges on production.

16. See Robert Donald Spector, *Arthur Murphy* (Boston: Twayne, 1979), 32–36, for a survey of Murphy's political journalism, and Howard Hunter Dunbar, *The Dramatic Career of Arthur Murphy* (New York: Modern Language Association, 1966), 34–36, for a discussion of his work on *The Test*.

17. After offering a useful survey of the Byng court-martial (19–40), Tom Pocock, in *Battle for Empire: The Very First World War, 1756–63* (London: Michael O'Mara, 1998),

argues that news of Byng's execution had direct impact on Admiral Pocock's decision to take more aggressive positions not only in the assault on Chandernagore (83–84), but also in the naval battle off Pondicherry in 1758 (129–30). The standard histories of Byng's career are John Charnock, *Biographia navalis; or, Impartial memoirs of the lives and characters of officers of the navy of Great Britain, from the year 1660 to the present time; drawn from the most authentic sources, and disposed in a chronological arrangement*, vol. 4 (Uckfield, England: Naval and Military Press, 2002), 145 to 179; Brian Tunstall, *Admiral Byng and the Loss of Minorca* (London : P. Allan, 1928); and Dudley Pope, *At Twelve Mr. Byng Was Shot* (London: Weidenfield and Nicholson, 1962).

18. This sense of pressure was exacerbated by the trial against George Sackville for his conduct at Minden in 1759. As in the Byng affair, the press played a key role in destroying Sackville's character, accusing him of everything from cowardice to sodomy. For a full discussion of this case and its importance for antiministerial propaganda during the American war, see Piers Mackesy, *The Coward of Minden: The Affair of Lord George Sackville* (London: Allen Lane, 1979).

19. *London Gazette*, 11 February 1758.

20. See Arthur Murphy, *The Upholsterer, or What News?* (London: Vaillant, 1758), 2.2.36–37. News of events in Chandernagore are printed in London from 11 February 1758 onward in a host of papers. All references are to act, scene, and page number.

21. *London Evening Post*, 20 December 1757, 3 and 21 March 1758, and *Lloyd's Evening Post*, 19 December 1757.

22. Murphy, *The Upholsterer*, 1.1.11.

23. The question of how the war was being funded was a topic of intense debate not only during the war but also during the aftermath of British victory. The policies undertaken by Lord North to deal with the extraordinary debt incurred during the Seven Years' War—the Townsend Acts, the Stamp Act—precipitated much of the colonial resistance to British rule. Murphy could not have known the future, but Quidnunc's calculations here, and his failure to achieve a solution, have a prophetic feel to them. See John Brewer, *The Sinews of Power: War, Money and the English State, 1688–1783* (London: Routledge, 1989), 93–108, for a detailed discussion of the problem of funding imperial war.

24. Samuel Weber, in his essay "Mass Mediaurus; or, Art, Aura, and Media in the Work of Walter Benjamin," in *Walter Benjamin: Theoretical Questions*, ed. David S. Ferris (Stanford: Stanford Univ. Press, 1996), 27–49, offers an illuminating translation of Benjamin's notion of *Aufnahme* as a mode of intermedial reception characterized by the movement of collection and dispersion.

25. For a full discussion of Wilkes, Junius, and the press, see Robert Rea, *The English Press in Politics, 1760–1774* (Lincoln: Univ. of Nebraska Press, 1963). For general introductions to eighteenth-century newspapers, see Jeremy Black, *The English Press in the Eighteenth Century* (London: Croom Helm, 1987); and Bob Clarke, *From Grub Street to Fleet Street: An Illustrated History of English Newspapers to 1899* (London: Ashgate, 2004).

26. Clarke, *Grub Street to Fleet Street*, 92.

27. Lucyle Werkmeister, *The London Daily Press, 1772–1792* (Lincoln: Univ. of Nebraska Press, 1963), 4.

28. See Niklas Luhmann, *The Reality of the Mass Media*, trans. Kathleen Cross (Stanford: Stanford Univ. Press, 2000), 25, for a discussion of the fictionality of the news.

29. Werkmeister, *The Daily London Press*, 5.

30. Ibid., 7.

31. Ibid., 8–9.

32. Ibid., 10.

33. Ibid., 11.

34. Mary Favret, "Everyday War," *ELH* 72.3 (Fall 2005): 605–33.

35. Matthew Kinservik, *Sex, Scandal, and Celebrity in Late Eighteenth-Century England* (London: Palgrave Macmillan, 2007).

36. Werkmeister, *The London Daily Press*, 7.

37. Lisa Gitelman, *Always Already New: Media, History and the Data of Culture* (Cambridge, Mass.: MIT Press, 2006), 4.

38. For a definition of media archaeology, see the introduction to Lisa Gitelman and Geoffrey B. Pingree, *New Media: 1740–1915* (Cambridge, Mass.: MIT Press, 2003), xi–xxii; and Gitelman, *Always Already New*, 1–24, 151–57.

39. I am adapting Thomas Crow's notion of the "The Intelligence of Art" in order to stress the value of working within these performance archives. Crow is attempting to come to terms with the necessary translation required to write about objects, but I think a similar set of concerns is raised by performance archives. Crow asks in *The Intelligence of Art* (Chapel Hill: Univ. of North Carolina Press, 1999), 5, "whether there can be objects of study . . . where the violent acts of displacement and substitution entailed in making any object intelligible are already on display in the art."

40. For Gillian Russell's innovative account of theatrical paratexts, see *Women, Sociability and Theatre in Georgian London* (Cambridge: Cambridge Univ. Press, 2007), 126–35.

41. Benjamin's negative definition of distraction can be traced back to his analysis of Brecht's epic theatre in "The Author as Producer," in Walter Benjamin, *The Work of Art in the Age of Its Technological Reproducibility and Other Writings on Media*, ed. Michael W. Jennings, Brigid Doherty, and Thomas Y. Levin (Cambridge, Mass.: Harvard Univ. Press, 2008), 89–91. By the time he writes the second version of "The Work of Art in the Age of Its Technological Reproducibility," distraction begins to take on much more complex and positive connotations. Benjamin's revised thoughts on distraction are concentrated in section XVIII of this essay (39–41). For a cryptic sign of this shift, look at the way Brecht is placed in Benjamin's "Theory of Distraction," in Jennings et al., 56–57. Jennings notes that Benjamin's term for distraction is *Zerstreuung*, which, in the context of both essays, can be translated as "entertainment" (57).

42. Long before Brecht theorized the pedagogical possibilities nascent in interruption, playwrights and managers in the Georgian theatre were exploring a wide range of disjunctive effects.

43. As Michael Jennings emphasizes in Benjamin, *The Work of Art in the Age of Its Technological Reproducibility*, Benjamin's interest "in the capacity of an artwork to encode information about its historical period (and, in so doing, potentially to reveal to readers and viewers otherwise unapprehensible aspects of the nature of their own era)" emerged

out of his ongoing dialogue with Alois Riegl's notion of the *Kunstwollen* (9–10). Jennings's summary is helpful: "With the concept of 'artistic volition,' Riegl sought to show how art tracked major shifts in the structure and attitudes of collectives: societies, races, ethnic groups, and so on. *Kunstwollen* is the artistic projection of a collective intention. . . . Works of art—or rather details within the work of art—are thus the clearest source of a very particular kind of historical information. They encode not just the character of the artistic production of the age, but the character of parallel features of society" (10).

44. Benjamin, *The Work of Art in the Age of Its Technological Reproducibility*, ed. Jennings et al., 14–15.

45. See Julie Ellison, "News, Blues, and Cowper's Busy World," *Modern Language Quarterly* 62.3 (September 2001): 219–37; Kevis Goodman, "The Loophole in the Retreat: The Culture of News and the Early Life of Romantic Self-Consciousness," *South Atlantic Quarterly* 102.1 (Winter 2003): 25–52; and Mary Favret, *War at a Distance: Romanticism and the Making of Modern Wartime* (Princeton: Princeton Univ. Press, 2010), 49–84.

46. See Ellison, "News, Blues, and Cowper's Busy World," 230, for documentation of the relationship between lines in the poem and specific numbers of the *Morning Chronicle* and the *General Evening Post*. For a discussion of the political performances surrounding Fox's East India Bill and their remediation in Elizabeth Inchbald's *Such Things Are*, see Daniel O'Quinn, *Staging Governance: Theatrical Imperialism in London, 1770–1800* (Baltimore: Johns Hopkins University Press, 2005), 125–63.

47. William Cowper, *The Task*, 4.5, in *The Poems of William Cowper*, vol. 2, *1782–1785*, ed. John D. Baird and Charles Ryskamp (Oxford: Clarendon Press, 1995), 187. All subsequent references to *The Task* are presented in the text by book and line number.

48. Jay David Bolter and Richard Grusin, *Remediation: Understanding New Media* (Cambridge: MIT Press, 1999).

49. Favret, *War at a Distance*, 61–62.

50. See Ellison, "News, Blues, and Cowper's Busy World," 230, for specific documentation of the relationship between lines in the poem and specific numbers of the *Morning Chronicle* and the *General Evening Post*.

51. See Ellison, "News, Blues, and Cowper's Busy World," 219–25.

52. See Luhmann, *Reality of the Mass Media*, 25, for this succinct definition of the news system. He traces the fictionality of the news to the seventeenth century. Clearly the eighteenth-century press and the topical theatre of the mid-eighteenth century are fundamentally defined as a system whose commercial viability relies on there being something new and worth consuming virtually every day.

53. See Russell, *Women, Sociability and Theatre*, 1–16.

54. By sheer coincidence, Garrick's famous retirement speech was given on the same day as Richard Henry Lee's admonition that Congress had to move to a formal declaration of independence from the British Crown.

55. Dunbar, *Dramatic Career of Arthur Murphy*, 259.

56. Arthur Murphy, *News from Parnassus*, in *The Works of Arthur Murphy*, vol. 4 (London: Cadell, 1786), 396.

57. Ibid., 406.

58. For a succinct account of the Nandakumar affair, see J. Duncan M. Derrett, "Nandakumar's Forgery," *English Historical Review* 75.295 (April 1960): 223–38. B. N. Pandey offers a more extended discussion in *The Introduction of British Law into India: The Career of Elijah Impey in Bengal, 1774–1783* (London: Asia Publishing House, 1967).

59. Murphy, *News from Parnassus*, 424.

60. On the naming of the Boston Tea Party, see Alfred F. Young, *The Shoemaker and the Tea Party: Memory and the American Revolution* (Boston: Beacon Press, 1999), 87–194.

61. J. G. A. Pocock, "Political Thought in the English-Speaking Atlantic, 1760–1790, Part 1: The Imperial Crisis," in Pocock, *The Varieties of British Political Thought, 1500–1800* (Cambridge: Cambridge Univ. Press, 1993), 257.

62. Ibid., 284.

63. Ibid., 259–60.

64. Ibid., 262.

65. Ibid., 275.

66. Ibid., 278.

67. Ibid., 301.

68. See C. A. Bayly *Imperial Meridian: The British Empire and the World, 1780–1830* (London: Longman, 1989); Sudipta Sen, *Distant Sovereignty: National Imperialism and the Origins of British India* (New York: Routledge, 2002); and H. V. Bowen, *The Business of Empire: The East India Company and Imperial Britain, 1756–1833* (Cambridge: Cambridge Univ. Press, 2008), for succinct accounts of the institution of new forms of governance for India. Catherine Hall's *Civilising Subjects: Metropole and Colony in the English Imagination 1830–1867* (Chicago: Univ. of Chicago Press, 2002) is an exemplary study of the implications of this shifting definition of coloniality in the Caribbean and the Antipodes for cultural histories of British imperialism.

69. Jean-François Lyotard, *The Differend: Phrases in Dispute* (Minneapolis: Univ. of Minnesota Press, 1988), 161–71.

70. See O'Quinn, *Staging Governance*, 43–73.

71. Dror Wahrman, *The Making of the Modern Self: Identity and Culture in Eighteenth-Century England* (New Haven: Yale Univ. Press, 2004), 238.

72. Ibid., 242–43.

73. Jay Fliegelman, *Prodigals and Pilgrims: The American Revolution against Patriarchal Authority, 1750–1800* (Cambridge: Cambridge Univ. Press, 1989).

74. Wahrman's argument owes a great deal to Mary M. Higonnet's essay "Civil Wars and Sexual Territories," in *Arms and the Woman: War, Gender, and Literary Representation*, ed. Helen Margaret Cooper, Adrienne Munich, and Susan Merrill Squier (Chapel Hill: Univ. of North Carolina Press, 1989), 80–98.

75. See Michel Foucault, *The History of Sexuality*, vol. 1 (New York: Vintage, 1980).

76. John Cartwright, "A Letter to Edmund Burke, Esq; Controverting the Principles of American Government" (London, 1775), 6–9.

77. For their accounts of both the political machinations and the actual military actions of the American war, I am much indebted to Piers Mackesy, *The War for America, 1775–1783* (London: Longmans, 1964); Ira D. Gruber, *The Howe Brothers and the American*

Revolution (Chapel Hill: Univ. of North Carolina Press, 1972); and Stephen Conway, *The War of American Independence, 1775–1783* (New York: St. Martin's Press, 1995).

78. Now crucially the divorce papers were served by one set of parties to another, and the Declaration of Independence itself plays a remarkable game with time and identity. As Derrida and Lee have shown in their readings of the document, the Declaration performs what it states and thus simultaneously declares sovereignty and invents a sovereign body capable of making such a declaration. This retroactive invention of the people relies on a temporal problematic within linguistic performance itself. Pragmatically the problem for the Americans is how to constitute the idea of a sovereign state without a speaker. As a speech act, the Declaration employs a very particular form of prosopopeia where the United States is formulated by a "we" who will be fully constituted as a "people" only when the Constitution of the United States is formulated twelve years later. As Lee has argued, it is the continuity of these performatives that shores up the figure of sovereignty. See Jacques Derrida, "Declarations of Independence," trans. T. Keenan and T. Pepper, *New Political Science* 15 (Summer 1986): 3–19; Benjamin Lee, "Performing the People," *Pragmatics* 5 (June 1995): 263–80.

79. In this observation, I concur with Lisa Freeman's important intervention in *Character's Theater: Genre and Identity on the Eighteenth-Century English Stage* (Philadelphia: Univ. of Pennsylvania Press, 2002), 1, which states unequivocally that theatrical character offers a site of resistance to the rise of the novelistic subject, on which in many ways Wahrman is basing his analysis.

80. For a careful discussion of the staging and reception of *Bonduca* at the Haymarket in July 1778, see Wendy C. Nielsen, "Boacidea Onstage before 1800, a Theatrical and Colonial History," *SEL* 49.3 (Summer 2009): 598, 604–7. I discuss the legacy of Cumberland's *The Battle of Hastings* in chapter 4.

81. This is adapted from Michel Foucault, "Governmentality," in *Power: Essential Works of Foucault, 1954–84*, vol. 3, ed. James D. Faubion (New York: New Press, 1994), 219–20.

82. Favret, *War at a Distance*, 82–83.

83. See Judith Butler's *Bodies That Matter: On the Discursive Limits of Sex* (New York: Routledge, 1993), 1–24, and *Excitable Speech: A Politics of the Performative* (New York: Routledge, 1997), 127–63; and Pierre Bourdieu, *The Logic of Practice*, trans. Richard Nice (Cambridge: Polity Press, 1990), 52–79.

CHAPTER ONE The Agents of Mars and the Temples of Venus: *John Burgoyne's Remediated Pleasures*

1. *Gentleman's Magazine*, June 1774, 262–65. The same gazette extraordinary is also published in the *Public Advertiser*, 11 June 1774, and the *Morning Chronicle*, 15 June 1774. All subsequent page references to the "Oak Gazette Extraordinary" are to the *Gentleman's Magazine* version and are incorporated into the text.

2. Joseph Addison and Richard Steele, *The Tatler*, 4 vols. (London: Rivington, Marshall, and Bye, 1789), 2:379.

3. Steele contrasts diversion with "the true and proper delight of men of knowledge and virtue. . . . The pleasures of ordinary people are in their passions; but the seat of this

delight is in the reason and understanding. Such a frame of mind raises that sweet enthusiasm, which warms the imagination at the sight of every work of nature, and turns all round you into picture and landscape." Ibid.

4.. For discussion of North's tea plan, see Benjamin W. Labaree, *The Boston Tea Party* (New York: Oxford Univ. Press, 1964). For discussion of resistance to the Coercive Acts both in the colonies and in the British Parliament, see Stephen Conway, *The War of American Independence, 1775–1783* (London: Edward Arnold, 1995), 15–18.

5. Edward Smith Stanley was elected to the House of Commons as the member for Lancashire in 1774 and was one of North's supporters in the prewar period. He became the 12th Earl of Derby in 1776 and drifted toward the opposition after the Ministry scapegoated his uncle for the devastating loss at Saratoga.

6. Cobbett, ed., *Parliamentary History*, 12:1271, quoted in Richard J. Hargrove Jr., *General John Burgoyne* (Newark: Univ. of Delaware Press, 1983), 62–63.

7. See Gerald Howson, *Burgoyne of Saratoga* (New York: Times Books, 1979), 63–64; and Paul Lewis, *The Man Who Lost America: A Biography of Gentleman Johnny Burgoyne* (New York: Dial Press, 1973), 49, for historical treatments of the celebration.

8. See Howson, *Burgoyne of Saratoga*, 59–61, and Hargrove, *General John Burgoyne*, 59–68, for succinct accounts of his parliamentary activities during this period. Into the list of "things to be temporarily forgotten," one could add the attack on Burgoyne's character by Solicitor General Alexander Wedderburn. The attack was part of the fallout from Burgoyne's own attack on Clive, and—through the caustic eye of Junius—it put Burgoyne's gambling and his suspect electioneering directly under public scrutiny.

9. See Sybil Rosenfeld, *Temples of Thespis: Some Private Theatres and Theatricals in England and Wales, 1700–1820* (London: Society for Theatre Research, 1978); and Gillian Russell, *Women, Sociability and Theatre in Georgian London* (Cambridge: Cambridge Univ. Press, 2007). Burgoyne's entertainment is itself an attack on the style of domiciliary entertainment associated with Teresa Cornelys that Russell tracks so carefully in her argument (17–38).

10. The relative neglect of pantomime as a cultural phenomenon in eighteenth-century culture has been recently addressed by John O'Brien in *Harlequin Britain: Pantomime and Entertainment, 1690–1760* (Baltimore: Johns Hopkins Univ. Press, 2004), and David Worrall, *Harlequin Empire: Race, Ethnicity and the Drama of the Popular Enlightenment* (London: Pickering & Chatto, 2007).

11. The singer and actor Joseph Vernon (1738–82) debuted at Drury in 1750 and was a regular performer in operatic entertainments in both London and Dublin. Although Mary Barthélemon (nee Young 1749–99) started her career at Covent Garden in 1762, she was most widely known from the late 1760s onward for singing Italian repertoire at the King's Theatre, in Marylebone Gardens and in Dublin.

12. *Morning Chronicle*, 12 June 1774, and *St. James Chronicle*, 11 June 1774.

13. *St. James Chronicle*, 11 June 1774.

14. See Eileen Harris, *The Genius of Robert Adam: His Interiors* (New Haven: Yale Univ. Press, 2001), 279.

15. *Morning Chronicle*, 12 June 1774.

16. Alistair Rowan, "Lord Derby's Reconstruction of The Oaks," *Burlington Magazine* 127.991 (October 1985): 678–87.

17. See Robert Malcolm Smuts, *Court Culture and the Origins of a Royalist Tradition in Early Stuart England* (Philadelphia: Univ. of Pennsylvania Press, 1987), 265–69. In Thomas Carew's *Coelum Britannicum* (1634), the Druidic past is situated in the antimasque, and the viewer witnesses a progress from pagan instability toward a more harmonious civilized governance under the care of Charles I and Henrietta. If Burgoyne's entertainment was in dialogue with this prior entertainment, then he generated an inversion of its progress toward peace. The signs of loving harmony in the first masque give way to a second masque that thoroughly entwines signs of martial supremacy with Druidic motifs. See also Barbara Ravelhofer, *The Early Stuart Masque: Dance, Costume, and Music* (Oxford: Oxford Univ. Press, 2009), 207–29.

18. See Martin Eidelberg, "Watteau Paintings in Early Eighteenth-Century England," *Burlington Magazine* 117.870 (September 1975): 576–83. Watteau's paintings were extensively engraved throughout the early and midcentury. Jean de Jullienne, whose *Figures de différents charactères, de Paysages, et d'Etudes dessinées d'après nature par Antoine Watteau* of 1728, brought most of the famous *fête galantes* to consumers in Europe and England.

19. There is an extensive body of work on the relationship between theatre and Watteau's oeuvre. For general discussions, see Margaret Morgan Grasselli and Pierre Rosenberg, *Watteau, 1684–1721* (Paris: Editions de la Réunion des musées nationaux, 1984); Marianne Roland-Michel and Daniel Rabreau, *Les arts du théâtre de Watteau à Fragonard* (Bordeaux: Galerie des Beaux-Arts, 1980); Robert Tomlinson *La fête galante: Watteau et Marivaux* (Geneva: Droz, 1981). For more detailed analyses of performance practices and conventions and their place in Watteau's work, see Thomas Crow, *Painters and Public Life in Eighteenth-Century Paris* (New Haven: Yale Univ. Press, 1985), 45–74; Julie Anne Plax, *Watteau and the Cultural Politics of Eighteenth-Century France* (New York: Cambridge Univ. Press, 2000), 108–52; Sarah R. Cohen *Art, Dance, and the Body in French Culture of the Ancien Régime* (Cambridge: Cambridge Univ. Press, 2000); and Suzanne R. Pucci, "Watteau and Theater: Movable Fetes" in *Antoine Watteau: Perspectives on the Artist and the Culture of his Time*, ed. Mary D. Sheriff (Newark: Univ. of Delaware Press, 2006), 106–22.

20. *St. James Chronicle*, 11 June 1774.

21. Donald Posner, "The Swinging Women of Watteau and Fragonard," *Art Bulletin* 64.1 (March 1982): 75–88.

22. Crow, *Painters and Public Life*, 45–54.

23. Plax, *Watteau*, 111–12.

24. See R. Raines, "Watteau and 'Watteaus' in England before 1760," *Gazette des Beaux-Arts*, 6th series, 89 (1977): 51, for a discussion of the dissemination of Watteau in England and for Reynolds's remarks on his work.

25. For a powerful summary of these debates that is attentive to the theatrical and musical dynamics of the Cythera paintings, see Georgia Cowart, "Watteau's Pilgrimage to Cythera and the Subversive Utopia of the Opera-Ballet," *Art Bulletin* 83 (September 2001): 460–78.

26. Plax, *Watteau*, 135–36.

27. See Posner, "The Swinging Women of Watteau and Fragonard."

28. Apparently Burgoyne was plundering everywhere in London for orange trees.

29. Crow, *Painters and Public Life*, 59–63.

30. *St. James Chronicle*, 9–11 June 1774. The *Morning Chronicle* uses the precisely the same words to describe the pantomime.

31. Plax, *Watteau*, 146–48.

32. The irony here is almost too much to bear. By late 1777, Burgoyne surrendered at Saratoga, and British rule in the American colonies would look anything but providentially secure. In 1779 Lady Elizabeth Hamilton left Lord Stanley, now Lord Derby, for the notorious libertine John Frederick Sackville. Derby eventually took up with the actress Elizabeth Farren. In short, the conjoined fantasy of military supremacy and conjugal fidelity would be in tatters shortly after its articulation on this particular evening.

33. *Oxford English Dictionary*. Johnson defines "propitious" as "favourable, kind."

34. *St. James Chronicle*, 9–11 June 1774.

35. Peter Borsay has offered a historical account of the conjunction of leisure and freedom in his recent study, *A History of Leisure: The British Experience since 1500* (New York: Palgrave Macmillan, 2006).

36. See Paul Langford, *A Polite and Commercial People: England, 1727–1783* (Oxford: Oxford Univ. Press, 1992), 576, for an account of craze for the "idyll of the Oaks" that swept through England in 1774.

37. There is also a satirical play entitled the *New Maid of the Oaks* by James Murray, which was never performed but which circulated in print after Burgoyne's return from the disastrous campaign at Saratoga.

38. John Burgoyne, *Songs, Choruses, &c. In the Dramatic Entertainment of The Maid of the Oaks. As performed at the Theatre-Royal in Drury-Lane* (London: T. Becket, 1774).

39. This, despite Michael Burden's careful discussion of the relationship between the play and event in "Robert Adam, De Loutherbourg and the Sets for *The Maid of the Oaks*," in *Adam in Context*, ed. Giles Worsley (London: Georgian Group Symposium, 1992), 65–69. See Gerald Howson, *Burgoyne of Saratoga: A Biography* (New York: Times Books, 1979), 64; and Lauran Paine, *Gentleman Johnny: The Life of General John Burgoyne* (London: Hale, 1973).

40. See "Advertisement" to Burgoyne, *Songs, Choruses, &c.* All references to the play itself in text and notes are to John Burgoyne, *The Maid of the Oaks: A New Dramatic Entertainment. As it is performed at the Theatre-Royal, in Drury-Lane* (London: T. Becket, 1774). A similar statement both linking the play to the Fête Champêtre and emphasizing that no such play took place at The Oaks appears on the first page of the preface.

41. *London Evening Post*, 5–8 November 1774.

42. See John O'Brien, *Harlequin Britain* (Baltimore: Johns Hopkins Univ. Press, 2004); and Jane Moody, *Illegitimate Theatre in London, 1770–1840* (Cambridge: Cambridge Univ. Press, 2000), for discussions of the generic battle pitched against pantomime and its eventual legitimation in the patent houses.

43. See Gillian Russell, *Women, Sociability and Theatre in Georgian London* (Cambridge: Cambridge Univ. Press, 2007), 17–37, for a detailed analysis of Cornelys's relation to the *Public Advertiser* and of her self-promotion via the papers more generally.

44. For a full discussion of the activism that led to the reporting of parliamentary debates in the papers, see Robert Rea, *The English Press in Politics, 1760–1774* (Lincoln: University of Nebraska Press, 1963).

45. See William Cowper, *The Task*, 4.84–87, in *The Poems of William Cowper*, vol. 2, *1782–1785*, ed. John D. Baird and Charles Ryskamp (Oxford: Clarendon Press, 1995). For compelling readings of Cowper's representation of the newspaper, see Mary Favret, *War at a Distance: Romanticism and the Making of Modern Wartime* (Princeton: Princeton Univ. Press, 2010), 3–5, 59–81; Kevis Goodman, *Georgic Modernity and British Romanticism: Poetry and the Mediation of History* (Cambridge: Cambridge Univ. Press, 2004), 67–78; and Julie Ellison, "News, Blues, and Cowper's Busy World," *Modern Language Quarterly* 62 (2001): 219–37.

46. See Daniel O'Quinn, *Staging Governance: Theatrical Imperialism in London* (Baltimore: Johns Hopkins Univ. Press, 2005), 22–23.

47. See Matthew Kinservik, *Sex, Scandal, and Celebrity in Late Eighteenth-Century England* (London: Palgrave Macmillan, 2007); and Anna Clark, *Scandal: The Sexual Politics of the British Constitution* (Princeton: Princeton Univ. Press, 2004), for recent studies of the representation of scandal in eighteenth-century culture.

48. Burgoyne, *Maid*, 58, 60. The pagination of the text goes from 1 to 64 and then continues from a second page 57 to 68. The references here are to the second pages 58 and 60 in the text.

49. Ralph G. Allen, "Topical Scenes for Pantomime," *Educational Theatre Journal* 17.4 (1965): 289.

50. And this is complicated even further by the intimation in some of the papers that there was already an exclusive group cognizant of the play's topical referent well before the play's production. See *Morning Chronicle*, 7 November 1774.

51. Arjun Appadurai, *Modernity at Large: Cultural Dimensions of Globalization* (Minneapolis: Univ. of Minnesota Press, 1996), 33–37.

52. *The Craftsman; or Say's Weekly Journal*, 12 November 1774.

53. It is also important because O'Daub has a theatrical afterlife as De Loutherbourg's artistic minion in Sheridan's *The Camp*.

54. Russell's reading of Fanny Abington's performance of this role in *Women*, 147–52, places the character of Lady Bab within the entire set of fashionable roles played by Abington during this period.

55. See, for example, *London Magazine*, November 1774, 517.

56. Oldworth's name resonates with Mr. Oldham in Samuel Foote's *The Nabob*.

57. See my discussion of this accommodation in O'Quinn, *Staging Governance*, 43–73.

58. Burgoyne is himself a topic of endless concern in the play. There are references to his gambling, his elopement, and his struggle with Clive. Similarly, on page 59, there is an explicit allusion to Lord Stanley's election as a knight of the shire for the county of Lancaster during the recently contested election of 5 October–10 November 1774. Stanley held his seat in Parliament as such until his succession to the peerage when he became Lord Derby.

59. *Morning Chronicle*, 7 November 1774. Simon Slingsby was the first British dancer to perform in the Paris ballet. He had performed at the King's Theatre opera house and

for Garrick throughout the late 1760s and early 1770s. Slingsby and Signora Hidou were among Garrick's principal dancers for the 1774 season.

60. *Morning Chronicle*, 7 November 1774.

61. *London Evening Post*, 5–8 November 1774.

62. This would be tantamount to saying, with some degree of accuracy, that Burgoyne was imitating the highly suspect practices of Teresa Cornelys. In light of Gillian Russell's reading of Cornelys's career, this carries with it the implication not only that Burgoyne's attempts to regulate sociability are undermined by his impersonation of Cornelys but also that he and, by extension, Garrick are unaware of the gender insubordination at the heart of the project.

63. The pagination is in error. This is the second page 58 in the printed text.

64. See Russell, *Women*, 144–46, for a related discussion of the set design.

65. The latter opinion was held by the reviewer for the *Morning Chronicle*, 7 November 1774. Other venues tended to praise the dance as the finest of its kind.

66. This is the second page 62 in the printed text.

67. *London Magazine*, November 1774, 518.

68. John Barrell, *The Birth of Pandora and the Division of Knowledge* (Philadelphia: Univ. of Pennsylvania Press, 1992), 86–87.

69. This is the second page 64 in the printed text.

70. *The Craftsman; or Say's Weekly Journal*, 12 November 1774.

71. A general election had only just concluded before the opening the play.

72. This prologue with variations in punctuation was printed in virtually every daily paper that reviewed the play and was featured in monthlies such as the *Gentleman's Magazine* and the *London Magazine* as a particularly worthy "poetical essay." See the issues for November 1774, 535 and 557, respectively. Lines 1 to 23 cited here are from the published version of the play.

73. St. George's Fields was the site of antigovernment rioting following the arrest of John Wilkes in the spring of 1768. On 10 May 1768 troops fired on a crowd of roughly fifteen thousand supporters of Wilkes and killed seven people. The Dog and Duck spa in Lambeth was "frequented by all the riff-raff and scum of the town" (Russell, *Women*, 6). For a survey of these repetitions of Burgoyne's celebration, see Langford, *A Polite and Commercial People*, 576.

74. See Russell, *Women*, 135–41, for a discussion King's performance at the Stratford Jubilee and its implications for Garrick's engagement with fashionable sociability. See Michael Dobson, *The Making of the National Poet: Shakespeare, Adaptation, and Authorship, 1660–1769* (Oxford: Clarendon Press, 2001), 215–16, for further discussion of King's performance.

75. *Morning Chronicle*, 14 November 1774.

76. *Morning Chronicle*, 19 November 1774.

77. *Morning Chronicle*, 14 November 1774.

78. Ibid.

79. *St. James Chronicle*, 5–8 November 1774.

80. *London Magazine*, November 1774, 519.

81. See Harris, *The Genius of Robert Adam*, 283.

82. Ibid., 280.

83. Harris gives the dimensions of *The Supper Room* as 6 ft. × 5 ft. 4 in. and argues that the painting was produced in either 1775 or 1778. *The Ball Room* is dated 1777 and measures 4 ft. 5 in. × 5 ft. 4 in. (Harris, *The Genius of Robert Adam*, 280 n. 20). The paintings are described in G. Scharf, *A Descriptive and Historical Catalogue of the Collection of Pictures at Knowsley Hall* (London: Bradbury, Agnew, & Co., 1875). The paintings were also the subject of engravings made by James Caldwell and published as part of the 1780 volume of *The Works in Architecture of Robert and James Adam*, ed. Robert Oresko, 3 vols. (New York: St. Martin's Press, 1975).

84. See my reading of the minuet in *Staging Governance*, 281–87.

85. Burgoyne's loss at Saratoga not only was a crushing blow to the army's fortunes but also precipitated the entry of France and Spain into the war as allies of the colonists. This led to an overall change in strategy away from the army's attempt to conquer New England toward a new focus on campaigning in the South and on the naval battles in the Caribbean. The titles of two of the most prominent histories of Saratoga mark it as a watershed in the war: Richard M. Ketchum, *Saratoga: Turning Point of America's Revolutionary War* (New York: Henry Holt, 1997); and Brendan Morrissey, *Saratoga 1777: Turning Point of a Revolution* (Oxford: Osprey Publishing, 2000).

86. See Hargrove, *General John Burgoyne*, 221–37, 256–75, for detailed accounts of how Germain and the Ministry moved against Burgoyne after his return from America. See also Michael Glover, *General Burgoyne in Canada and America: Scapegoat for a System* (London: Gordon and Cremonesi, 1976), and James Lunt, *John Burgoyne of Saratoga* (London: MacDonald and Jane's, 1976), 269–326. The best account of Germain's career in the early phases of the war remains Piers Mackesy, *The War for America, 1775–1783* (London: Longmans, 1974), 46–161.

87. In spite of his internment, Burgoyne was famously sociable during this period. See Elisa Tamarkin's *Anglophilia: Deference, Devotion, and Antebellum America* (Chicago: Univ. of Chicago Press, 2008), 95–100, for a fascinating discussion of the significance of the entertainment of Burgoyne after Saratoga for antebellum American historiography.

CHAPTER TWO Out to America: *Performance and the Politics of Mediated Space*

1. Mary Favret discusses this to great effect in *War at a Distance: Romanticism and the Making of Modern Wartime* (Princeton: Princeton Univ. Press, 2010), 73–74.

2. For discussion of how the tactics employed by the Americans at Bunker Hill presaged the difficulties faced by the British as the war unfolded, see Piers Mackesy, *The War for America, 1775–1783* (London: Longmans, 1964), 30.

3. Signed the Bellman. *Morning Chronicle*, 3 July 1775.

4. Donna Andrew and Randall McGowan, *The Perreaus and Mrs. Rudd: Forgery and Betrayal in Eighteenth-Century London* (Berkeley: Univ. of California Press, 2001).

5. See Gillian Russell, *The Theatres of War: Performance, Politics, and Society 1793–1815* (Oxford: Clarendon Press, 1995), 33–51; and Robert W. Jones, "Sheridan and the The-

atre of Patriotism: Staging Dissent during the War for America," *Eighteenth-Century Life* 26.1 (Winter 2002): 24–44.

6. John Sainsbury, *Disaffected Patriots: London Supporters of Revolutionary America, 1769–1782* (Kingston and Montreal: McGill-Queen's Univ. Press, 1987), 84, 91.

7. John Cannon, "Lyttelton, Thomas, second Baron Lyttelton (1744–1779)," in *Oxford Dictionary of National Biography*, ed. H. C. G. Matthew and Brian Harrison (Oxford: Oxford Univ. Press, 2004); online ed., ed. Lawrence Goldman, January 2008.

8. *Gazetteer*, 7 July 1775.

9. See Gillian Russell, *Women, Sociability and Theatre in Georgian London* (Cambridge: Cambridge Univ. Press, 2007), 17–62.

10. See, for example, the *Morning Post*, 26 June 1778, or the *Public Advertiser*, 26 June 1775.

11. *Morning Chronicle*, 26 June 1775.

12. *Gazetteer*, 7 July 1775. The report is dated 30 June. This report appears verbatim in the *Morning Chronicle* for 4 July 1775.

13. *Gazetteer*, 7 July 1775.

14. *Morning Chronicle*, 26 June 1775.

15. *Gazetteer*, 7 July 1775.

16. Ibid.

17. Karl Wolfgang Schweizer, "Stuart, John, third earl of Bute (1713–1792)," in Matthew and Harrison, *Oxford Dictionary of National Biography*; online ed., ed. Lawrence Goldman, October 2009.

18. *Gazetteer*, 7 July 1775.

19. For the complex position of the City merchants in this period, see Sainsbury, *Disaffected Patriots*, 69–82.

20. Ibid., 84.

21. *Morning Chronicle*, 6 July 1775.

22. *Morning Post*, 26 June 1775.

23. *London Evening Post*, 29 June–1 July 1775.

24. See, for example, *Morning Post*, 27 June 1775.

25. *Public Advertiser*, 26 June 1775.

26. Susan Aspden, "'An Infinity of Factions': Opera in Eighteenth-Century Britain and the Undoing of Society," *Cambridge Opera Journal* 9.1 (March 1997): 3.

27. *St. James Chronicle*, 22–24 June 1775.

28. *London Chronicle*, 29 June–1 July 1775, 618.

29. For a full discussion of the sexual politics of these fop roles, and of Garrick's deployment of them, see Kristina Straub, *Sexual Suspects: Eighteenth-Century Players and Sexual Ideology* (Princeton: Princeton Univ. Press, 1992), 60–63.

30. *Morning Post*, 27 June 1775.

31. *Morning Post*, 28 June 1775.

32. Russell, *Women*, 88–118, and "The Peeresses and the Prostitutes: The Founding of the London Pantheon, 1772," *Nineteenth Century Contexts* 27.1 (March 2005): 11–30.

33. *Public Advertiser*, 24 June 1775.

34. See *Morning Chronicle*, 23 June 1775.

35. Charles Dibdin, *The Waterman, or the First of August* (London: Becket, 1774), i. All subsequent references to this edition will be included by act, scene, and page number in the body of the text. The play was first performed at the Haymarket Theatre on 8 August 1774 and as Foote's primary afterpiece for every remaining show that summer except one.

36. The Doggett Coat and Badge Race was historically aligned with Whiggery, so this is far from a neutral political sign.

37. For the classic discussion of this separation in eighteenth-century life, see E. P. Thompson, "The Patricians and the Plebs," in his *Customs in Common: Studies in Traditional Popular Culture* (New York: New Press, 1993), 16–96.

38. Sheridan's *The Rivals* was in almost constant production in the months before the staging of Dibdin's ballad opera. That said, Mrs. Bundle shares a great deal with Mrs. Termagant from Murphy's *The Upholsterer*, which was performed frequently during this period. Murphy's farce had two productions at Covent Garden in April and May of 1775.

39. Charles Beecher Hogan, *The London Stage, 1660–1800*, part 5, vol. 1 (Carbondale: Southern Illinois Univ. Press, 1968), 22.

40. *St. James Chronicle*, 22–24 June 1775.

41. *Morning Chronicle*, 28 June 1775.

42. Ibid.

43. Ibid.

44. Ibid.

45. Ibid.

46. Ibid.

47. *London Evening Post*, 22–24 June 1775. This same report appears in many of the papers and is featured in the *Gentleman's Magazine* for July 1775.

48. *Morning Chronicle*, 28 June, 1775.

49. William C. Lowe, "Lennox, Charles, third duke of Richmond, third duke of Lennox, and duke of Aubigny in the French nobility (1735–1806)," in Matthew and Harrison, *Oxford Dictionary of National Biography*; online ed., ed. Lawrence Goldman, October 2008.

50. John Cannon, "Montagu, George, fourth duke of Manchester (1737–1788)," in ibid.

51. Neither figure was held in much regard at this point. The Duke of Cumberland was the butt of endless jokes on his stupidity, and he was repeatedly satirized as a cuckold.

52. *Gazetteer*, 26 June 1775.

53. The *Public Advertiser* has an extended joke on the difficulty of replicating the Thames Regatta that turns on the widespread imitation of Burgoyne's Fête Champêtre:

> The Citizens in the Neighbourhood of London, who attempted so many aukward Imitations of the Celebrated Fete Champetre, will be much puzzled how to treat their Friends with a Regatta, especially as all the Ponds, Puddles and Ditches in their little Gardens are exhausted by the long Continuance of hot Weather. Mr. Scrub, however, who is rendered justly famous by a Fete which he gave to his Friends, about four Miles from Town, is said to have projected a DRY Regatta, in which the Race-boats are to be Butcher's Trays, and the River the Grass-plot behind his House. (26 June 1775)

54. *St. James Chronicle*, 22–24 June 1775.

55. *Gazetteer*, 7 July 1775.

56. *London Chronicle*, 24–27 June 1775, 604.

57. See, for example, the *St. James Chronicle*, 22–24 June 1775. This song occasioned an elaborate parody entitled "A Grand Burlesque Ode as it Should have been Performed in the Temple of Neptune," which not only explicitly attacks the silliness of the men and the characters of the women involved but also indicts "Britannia's policy" of nursing folly.

58. Ibid.

59. *Morning Chronicle*, 26 June 1775.

60. *St. James Chronicle*, 24–27 June 1775.

61. Linda V. Troost, "The Characterizing Power of Song in Sheridan's *The Duenna*," *Eighteenth-Century Studies* 20.2 (Winter 1986–87): 153–72. See also Roger Fiske, "A Score for *The Duenna*," *Music and Letters* 42 (1961): 132–41.

62. John Loftis, *Sheridan and the Drama of Georgian England* (Oxford: Blackwell, 1976), 72.

63. Jack Durant, *Richard Brinsley Sheridan* (Boston: Twayne, 1975), 85.

64. Richard Brinsley Sheridan, *The Duenna*, in *The Dramatic Works of Richard Brinsley Sheridan*, ed. Cecil Price, 2 vols. (Oxford: Clarendon Press, 1973), 1:195–283. See 231 and 237 for the gun references. All subsequent references will be integrated into the text by act and scene number and will followed by page reference.

65. Spatially *The Duenna* moves between the interior space of Don Jerome's house or palazzo and the piazza. As Timothy J. Lukes has recently argued in "Descending to the Particulars: The Palazzo, the Piazzo, and Machiavelli's Republican Modes and Orders," *Journal of Politics* 71.2 (April 2009): 520–32, these two spaces have important symbolic valences for republican theories of government. Machiavelli opposes the considered response of the palazzo to the enthusiastic realm of the piazza in order to make an argument regarding the containment of political excess. It is not certain by any means that Sheridan had this connection in mind, but it is intriguing that the piazza in *The Duenna* is the scene of rational calculation among the sons and daughters, and the palazzo of Don Jerome is a scene of arbitrary expressions of parental authority and of Isaac Mendoza's most egregious prophecies. In other words, the play inverts the hierarchy that lies at the heart of Florentine political thought and which, according to J. G. A. Pocock, plays such a vital role in the theorization of republican government in the Atlantic world.

66. See Ruth Smith, *Handel's Oratorios and Eighteenth-Century Thought* (Cambridge: Cambridge Univ. Press, 1995), 327–33, for a detailed discussion of this allegory.

67. Jack D. Durant, "Sheridan's Grotesques," *Theatre Annual: A Journal of Performance Studies* 38 (1983): 13–30.

68. *Morning Chronicle*, 27 November 1775.

69. *London Packet*, 20–22 November 1775.

70. *Morning Chronicle*, 22 November 1775.

71. *Morning Chronicle*, 16 December 1775.

72. *Morning Chronicle*, 22 and 27 November 1775.

73. Michael Leoni was the stage name of the Jewish tenor Myer Lyon. A full account of *The Duenna*'s place in eighteenth-century anti-Semitism would have to encompass

both the fact of his employment in the production and the remarkable response to his performances.

74. *Morning Chronicle*, 22 November 1775.

75. Ibid.; *London Magazine*, November 1776, 47–48; *London Packet*, 20–22 November 1775.

76. *Morning Post*, 22 November 1775.

77. For a discussion of the opera's composition, see Cecil Price's introduction to *The Duenna*, in Price, *Dramatic Works of Sheridan*, 1:195–206.

78. See ibid., for an account of Sheridan and Linley's collaboration.

79. See John Loftis, *Sheridan and the Drama of England* (Oxford: Basil Blackwell, 1976), 85–102.

80. Russell, *Women*, 178–222.

81. See my "Theatre and Empire," in *The Cambridge Companion to British Theatre, 1730–1830*, ed. Jane Moody and Daniel O'Quinn (Cambridge: Cambridge Univ. Press, 2007), 238–39; and Mita Choudhury, *Interculturalism and Resistance in the London Theatre, 1660–1800: Identity, Performance, Empire* (Lewisburg, Pa.: Bucknell Univ. Press, 2000), 87–108.

82. Richard Brinsley Sheridan, *The School for Scandal*, in Price, *The Dramatic Works of Sheridan*, 1:4.1.

83. Patricia Meyer Spack's reading of the staging of gossip in the play in *Gossip* (New York: Knopf, 1985), 137–46, emphasizes how information impinges on social capital.

84. See James Thompson, "*The School for Scandal*, and Aggression," *Comparative Drama* 42.1 (Winter 2008): 89–98; and John M. Picker, "Disturbing Surfaces: Representations of the Fragment in *The School for Scandal*," *ELH* 65.3 (Fall 1998): 637–52, for recent readings of the play which stress its formal hybridity.

85. See Thompson, "*The School for Scandal*, and Aggression."

86. Or *Pizarro* for that matter.

87. *Morning Chronicle*, 19 November 1777. The *St. James Chronicle* for 18 November 1777 reported that the play only barely avoided damnation. All of the reviews indicate that the excision of some particularly poor colloquy allowed the play to remain on stage for a few more performances. One can gather from the reports that whatever success the play had was largely due to the music.

88. See *London Chronicle*, 18 November 1777, and *General Advertiser*, 20 November 1777.

89. Praise for More's tragedy was almost universal in spite of the fact that it was written by a woman. Some papers such as the *Morning Chronicle* for 11 December 1777 pointed to certain infelicities in the plot but also pointed to how effective the play was at eliciting emotion from the audience. For explicit statements of More's genius, of Mrs. Barry's effectiveness in the role of Elwina, and of the overall merit of the play, see the *Gazetteer*, the *Morning Post*, and the *Public Advertiser* for 11 December 1777.

90. *Gazetteer*, 11 December 1777, and *Morning Chronicle*, 11 December 1777.

91. Hannah More, *Percy* (London, 1778), 29–30.

92. See Friedrich Nietzsche, "On the Uses and Disadvantages of History for Life," in *Untimely Meditations*, ed. David Breazeale, trans. R. J. Hollingdale (Cambridge: Cambridge Univ. Press, 1997), 57–124.

93. Dror Wahrman, "*Percy*'s Prologue: From Gender Play to Gender Panic in Eighteenth-Century England," *Past and Present* 159.1 (1998): 113–60.

94. David Garrick, epilogue to Hannah More, *Percy, A Tragedy* (London: Cadell, 1778), 12–18.

95. Michael Dobson, *The Making of the National Poet: Shakespeare, Adaptation, and Authorship, 1660–1769* (Oxford: Clarendon Press, 2001), 215–16; and Christian Deelman, *The Great Shakespeare Jubilee* (London: M. Joseph, 1964), 228–31.

96. Garrick, epilogue to Hannah More, *Percy*, 44–47.

97. It is important to note that *Percy* was never presented without this frame and that the performers of the prologue and epilogue were always the ones called upon to enact the differential relation between the present and the past coded into these paratexts.

98. *Alfred* opened 21 January 1778 at Drury Lane, but was quickly superseded by *The Battle of Hastings* on 24 January 1778. *Alfred* survived only two performances. After initial success, *The Battle of Hastings* quickly lost its appeal, and after 2 March 1778 it received only two further productions. We could also place George Colman's adaptation of Beaumont and Fletcher's *Bonduca* in this company. The play was revived after 150 years of neglect on 30 July 1778 and had a brief run. See Wendy C. Nielsen's excellent reading of the revival of Bonduca in this period in "Boadicea Onstage before 1800, a Theatrical and Colonial History," *Studies in English Literature* 49.3 (Summer 2009): 595–614.

99. *London Magazine*, January 1778, 37.

CHAPTER THREE To Rise in Greater Splendor: *John André's Errant Knights*

1. For succinct discussions of the political fallout surrounding Howe's resignation and Burgoyne's return to Britain, see Piers Mackesy, *The War for America, 1775–1783* (London: Longmans, 1964), 148–54, 237–38.

2. Ira D. Gruber, "Howe, William, fifth Viscount Howe (1729–1814)," in *Oxford Dictionary of National Biography*, ed. H. C. G. Matthew and Brian Harrison (Oxford: Oxford Univ. Press, 2004); online ed., ed. Lawrence Goldman, January 2008. See also Troyer Steele Anderson, *The Command of the Howe Brothers during the American Revolution* (New York: Oxford Univ. Press, 1936); and Ira D. Gruber, *The Howe Brothers and the American Revolution* (Chapel Hill: Univ. of North Carolina Press, 1972).

3. See Gruber, *Howe Brothers*, 351–65, for a careful account of the critiques of Howe and the Ministry and a summation of his argument regarding Howe's divided purpose.

4. Fred Lewis Pattee, "The British Theatre in Philadelphia in 1778," *American Literature* 6.4 (1935): 385.

5. Jared Brown, *The Theatre in America during the Revolution* (Cambridge: Cambridge Univ. Press), 46.

6. *The Narrative of Lieut. Gen. Sir William Howe, in a Committee of the House of Commons on the 29th of April, 1779, relative to his Conduct, during his late command of the King's Troops in North America: to which are added, some observations upon a pamphlet, entitled, Letters to a Nobleman* (London: Baldwin, [14 September] 1780), 9.

7. Gruber, "Howe, William, fifth Viscount Howe (1729–1814)."

8. *A view of the evidence relative to the conduct of the American War under Sir William Howe, Lord Viscount Howe, and General Burgoyne; as given before a committee of the House of Commons last Session of Parliament. To which is added a collection of the celebrated Fugitive Pieces that are said to have given rise to that Important Enquiry*, 2nd ed. (London: Richardson and Urquhart, 1779), 135.

9. *Gentleman's Magazine*, August 1778, 353. This is the most extensive account of the Mischianza, and it is cited at length in Winthrop Sargent, *The Life and Career of Major John André, Adjutant General of the British Army in North America* (Boston: Ticknor and Fields, 1861), 64–77. Despite its anonymous publication, it was written by André. All subsequent descriptions of the celebration are drawn from this account.

10. The coverage of the Mischianza starts in early July 1778 and continues intermittently throughout the summer and fall. See *Gazetteer*, 6 July 1778; *General Advertiser*, 4 July 1778; *General Evening Post*, 2–4 July 1778; *London Chronicle*, 4–7 July 1778; *London Evening Post*, 2–4 July 1778; and *Morning Chronicle*, 6 July 1778. By the time the *Gentleman's Magazine* prints André's account in August 1778, the story had fully permeated the media. The ministerial *Morning Post* would be still fulminating about specific elements of the Mischianza as late as 3 March 1780.

11. See Mackesy, *War for America*, 124–26, 154, for discussions of Howe's disappointing campaigns in Pennsylvania.

12. Linda Colley, *Britons: Forging the Nation, 1707–1837* (New Haven: Yale Univ. Press, 1992), 148.

13. James Watt, *Contesting the Gothic: Fiction, Genre, and Cultural Conflict, 1764–1832* (Cambridge: Cambridge Univ. Press, 1999), 12–41.

14. Brown, *Theatre in America*, 51.

15. Watt, *Contesting the Gothic*, 32–33.

16. Simon During, "Mimic Toil: Eighteenth-Century Preconditions for the Modern Historical Reenactment," *Rethinking History* 11.3 (September 2007): 313–33.

17. Watt, *Contesting the Gothic*, 44.

18. Ibid., 42–69.

19. André's execution for espionage in 1780 and his subsequent lionization in Britain has been the subject of important scholarship on British patriotism in the postwar period. See especially Harriet Guest, *Small Change: Women, Learning, Patriotism, 1750–1810* (Chicago: Univ. of Chicago Press, 2000), 260–67. Martin Myrone writes of a similar reversal in the reception of Robert Adam's funerary monument for Major André that was installed in Westminster Abbey. See *Bodybuilding: Reforming Masculinities in British Art, 1750–1810* (New Haven: Yale Univ. Press, 2005), 201–8. The discussions of André's execution and of Benedict Arnold's treason among scholars of American history are numerous. The most compelling recent analyses of André's trial are Robert A. Ferguson, *Reading the Early Republic* (Cambridge, Mass.: Harvard Univ. Press, 2004), 12–150, and Sarah Knott, *Sensibility and the American Revolution* (Chapel Hill: Univ. of North Carolina Press, 2009), 154–93. For Alexander Hamilton's remarks on André, see Alexander Hamilton, *The Papers of Alexander Hamilton*, vol. 2, *1779–1781*, ed. Harold C. Syrett (New York: Columbia Univ. Press, 1961), 467–68. See also Andy Trees, "Benedict Arnold, John André, and His Three Yeoman Captors: A Sentimental Journey of American Virtue

Defined," *Early American Literature* 35 (2000): 246–73; Robert E. Cray, "Major André and the Three Captors: Class Dynamics and Revolutionary Memory Wars in the Early Republic, 1780–1831," *Journal of the Early Republic* 17 (1997): 31–39; Larry J. Reynolds, "Patriot and Criminals, Criminal and Patriots: Representations of the Case of Major André," *South Central Review* 9.1 (Spring 1992): 57–84; Robert D. Arner, "The Death of Major André: Some Eighteenth-Century Views," *Early American Literature* 11(1976): 52–67; and James Tomas Flexner, *The Traitor and the Spy: Benedict Arnold and John André* (Boston: Little Brown, 1975).

20. Gillian Russell, *Women, Sociability and Theatre in Georgian London* (Cambridge: Cambridge Univ. Press, 2007), 17–62.

21. As we have already noted in chapter 2, this event was an imitation of the grand canal festivals in Venice and it was reported to be the "first of its kind ever attempted in England." It received extensive reporting in the newspapers, and a long account was published in the *Gentleman's Magazine.*

22. André's first biographer explicitly cites these two events as precursors to the Mischianza. See Winthrop Sargent, *The Life and Career of Major John André,* ed. William Abbatt (New York: William Abbatt, 1902), 183. Gillian Russell also recognizes the elements Burgoyne's Fête-Champêtre in André's entertainment. See *The Theatres of War: Performance, Politics, and Society 1793–1815* (Oxford: Clarendon Press, 1995), 31.

23. See *Gazetteer,* 6 July 1778; *General Advertiser,* 4 July 1778; *General Evening Post,* 2–4 July 1778; *London Chronicle,* 4–7 July 1778; *London Evening Post,* 2–4 July 1778; and *Morning Chronicle,* 6 July 1778.

24. *Gentleman's Magazine,* August 1778, 353.

25. *London Evening Post,* 22–24 June 1775. This same report appears in many of the papers and is featured in the *Gentleman's Magazine* for July 1775.

26. *Gentleman's Magazine,* August 1778, 356.

27. *Gentleman's Magazine,* August 1778, 354.

28. *Gentleman's Magazine,* August 1778, 356.

29. *Gentleman's Magazine,* August 1778, 357, lines 1–12.

30. In the third line, "Whites and Blacks" distinguishes the knights.

31. See John Barrell, *The Birth of Pandora and the Division of Knowledge* (Philadelphia: Univ. of Pennsylvania Press, 1992), 63–87, for a detailed discussion of the deployment of Venus in the rhetoric surrounding civic virtue and aesthetic consumption.

32. Sargent, *Life and Career of Major John André* (1902), 178.

33. *Gentleman's Magazine,* August 1778, 357, 13–30.

34. Watt, *Contesting the Gothic,* 59. Watt is quoting Clara Reeve's *Memoirs of Sir Roger De Clarendon* (1793), which is essentially a celebration of Edward III as a model for reform. As Watt states, "Reeve's preface takes a staple ingredient of reformist discourse, the notion of *constitutional* degeneration, and translates it into military and heroic terms."

35. Richard Hurd, *Letters on Chivalry and Romance* (London: A. Millar, 1757), 9.

36. Ibid.

37. Hudson's banks is explained in an original footnote as "the North-river expedition from New York, last autumn."

38. *Gentleman's Magazine,* August 1778, 357, lines 31–48.

39. *Gentleman's Magazine,* August 1778, 354.

40. See Brown, *Theatre in America,* 51, for André's letter to Peggy Shippen, which claims that "the Mesquianza made me a complete milliner."

41. For a detailed discussions of the politics of women's clothing and hairstyle in Philadelphia, see Kate Haulman, "Fashion and the Culture Wars of Revolutionary Philadelphia," *William and Mary Quarterly* 62.4 (October 2005): 625–62.

42. See Watt, *Contesting the Gothic,* 50–51, and John Brewer, *Party Ideology and Popular Politics at the Accession of George III* (Cambridge: Cambridge Univ. Press, 1976), 216–17.

43. Ibid., 23.

44. *Gentleman's Magazine,* August 1778, 355.

45. *Gentleman's Magazine,* August 1778, 355–56.

46. *Strictures on the Philadelphia Mischianza or Triumph upon leaving America Unconquered from The Detail and Conduct of the American War, under Generals Gage, Howe, Burgoyne, and Vice Admiral Howe,* 3rd ed. (London, 1780), 6–7. The bracketed material is a note in the original text.

47. *A view of the evidence relative to the conduct of the American War under Sir William Howe, Lord Viscount Howe, and General Burgoyne,* 135–37.

48. Ibid., 138.

49. Sargent, *Life and Career of Major John André* (1902), 185.

50. The remediation of the Mischianza in antebellum American histories of the Revolution turns the deployment of chivalry to different ends. André's letter was incorporated into the most important nineteenth-century American histories of the period, such as John Fanning Watson's *Annals of Philadelphia and Pennsylvania in the Olden Time: Being a Collection of Memoirs, Anecdotes, and Incidents of the City and Its Inhabitants and of the Earliest Settlements of the Inland Part of Pennsylvania from the Days of the Founders,* 2 vols. (Philadelphia: Elijah Thomas, 1857), 1:292; Benson J. Lossing, *Pictorial Field-Book of the Revolution; or, Illustrations, by Pen and Pencil, of the History, Biography, Scenery Relics, and Traditions of the War for Independence,* 2 vols. (1850; repr., New Rochelle, N.Y.: Caratzas Brothers, 1976), 2:97–101; and Thomas Jones, *History of New York during the Revolutionary War, and the Leading Events of Other Colonies in that Period,* ed. Edward Floyd De Lancey (New York: New-York Historical Society, 1879), 241–51. The Mischianza was also fictionalized by James M'Henry in *Meredith; or, The Mystery of the Meschianza: A Tale of the American Revolution* (Philadelphia, 1831) and by John H. Mancur in "La Meschianza," in *Tales of the Revolution* (New York: Colyer, 1844). For a superb reading of the place of the Mischianza in the imperial nostalgia of antebellum historiography and fiction, see Elisa Tamarkin, *Anglophilia: Deference, Devotion, and Antebellum America* (Chicago: Univ. of Chicago Press, 2008), 127–32.

51. David Wheeler, "The Pathetic and the Sublime: The Tragic Formula of John Home's *Douglas,*" in *Man, God, and Nature in the Enlightenment,* ed. Donald C. Mell, Theodore E. D. Braun, and Lucia M. Parker (East Lansing, Mich.: Colleagues Press, 1988), 174.

52. This deployment of political allegory, of course, was also true of its initial production where Home was using the story from the ballad "Gil Morice" to allegorize both the Jacobite Rebellion and a series of internal debates within the Kirk of Scotland. For a

succinct account of these issues, see Barbara M. Benedict, "John Home," in *Restoration and Eighteenth-Century Dramatists: Second Series*, ed. Paula R. Backscheider (Detroit: Gale Research, 1989), 219–26. Lisa Freeman's "The Cultural Politics of Antitheatricality: The Case of John Home's *Douglas*," *Eighteenth Century: Theory and Interpretation* 43.3 (2001–2): 210–35, is the most thorough discussion of the political and religious controversy that enveloped the play in its early productions.

53. Brown, *Theatre in America*, 175–79.

54. Ibid.

55. Gruber, "Howe, William, fifth Viscount Howe (1729–1814)."

56. Ibid.

57. Sandro Jung, "Lady Randolph, The 'Monument of Woe': Love and Loss in John Home's *Douglas*," *Restoration and Eighteenth-Century Theatre Research* 20.1–2 (Summer 2005): 16.

58. John Home, *Douglas: A Tragedy* (London: A. Millar, 1757), 1.1.4. All subsequent citations present act and scene number followed by the page.

59. Home fought on the government side during the Jacobite Rebellion, but his pro-Hanoverian *The History of the Rebellion in the Year 1745* was not published until 1802 and thus would not have factored into how André and his associates thought about *Douglas*. Significantly, the play's nationalist prologue operates in distinct tension with Lady Randolph's pro-union speech (1.129–39). K. G. Simpson points to this contradiction and to other aspects of Home's career in order to argue that his relation to "the 45" was far more ambivalent than it would first appear.

60. See Yoon Sun Lee, "Giants in the North: Douglas, the Scottish Enlightenment, and Scott's *Redgauntlet*," *Studies in Romanticism* 40.1 (Spring 2001): 116–17, for a powerful discussion of how the confusion of generations and the hypostatization of the name Douglas impinge on the play's representation of national culture.

61. See Yoon Sun Lee's analysis of the play's relation to Adam Ferguson's thoughts on civic virtue (ibid., 111–14).

62. Paula R. Backscheider, "John Home's *Douglas* and the Theme of the Unfulfilled Life," in *Studies in Scottish Literature*, vol. 14, ed. G. Ross Roy (Columbia, S.C.: Univ. of South Carolina Press, 1979), 90. Backscheider is particularly good on how this fascination is coded into the gothic sets and the gloomy verse.

63. See Jung's survey of these objections in "Lady Randolph," 24.

64. J. G. A Pocock, *The Machiavellian Moment: Florentine Political Thought and the Atlantic Republican Tradition* (Princeton: Princeton Univ. Press, 1975).

65. Joseph Addison, *Cato: A Tragedy and Selected Essays*, ed. Christine Dunn Henderson and Mark E. Yellin (Indianapolis: Liberty Fund, 2004), 4.4.83.

66. See Randall Fuller, "Theaters of the American Revolution," *Early American Literature* 34.2 (September 1999): 126–46; and Jason Shaffer, *Performing Patriotism: National Identity in the Colonial and Revolutionary American Theater* (Philadelphia: Univ. of Pennsylvania Press, 2007), 59–65. See also Albert Furtwangler, "Cato at Valley Forge," *Modern Language Quarterly* 41 (1980): 38–53. The literature on the importance of *Cato* to emergent American identity is extensive. See Fuller, 132–33, for a succinct survey of this scholarship and Shaffer, 30–58, for a thorough genealogy of the play's colonial history.

67. See Fuller, "Theaters of the American Revolution," for a comparison of the Mischianza and the staging of Cato at Valley Forge.

68. Shaffer, *Performing Patriotism*, 61.

69. Ibid.

70. Wheeler, "The Pathetic and the Sublime," 180.

CHAPTER FOUR "THE BODY" of David Garrick: *Richard Brinsley Sheridan, America, and the Ends of Theatre*

1. *Morning Chronicle*, 4 August 1778 (emphasis added).

2. Ibid.

3. See *Morning Chronicle*, 7 and 10 August 1778.

4. Anonymous, "The Engagement between D'Orvilliers and Keppel," etching (1780), BM 5626, Department of Prints and Drawings, British Museum.

5. *Morning Post*, 28 August 1778.

6. The history of the trial and its mediation in the press have been superbly discussed by N. A. M. Roger in two separate works. See *Crowds, Culture, and Politics in Georgian Britain* (Oxford: Clarendon Press, 1998), 122–51, and "The Dynamic of News in Britain during the American War: The Case of Admiral Keppel," *Parliamentary History* 25.1 (2006): 49–67. See also J. H. Broomfield, "The Keppel-Palliser Affair, 1778–79," *Mariner's Mirror: The Journal of the Society for Nautical Research* 46 (1961): 195–207.

7. The identity of the letter's author, Lieutenant Berkeley, was revealed in the *Public Advertiser*, 5 January 1779. See Roger, *Crowds, Culture, and Politics*, 126–27, for a discussion of these allegations.

8. Palliser's exculpatory letter appears first in the *Morning Post*, 5 November 1778. It also appeared in the *London Chronicle, London Evening Post, Gazetteer, General Evening Post*, and *Morning Intelligencer*.

9. *Morning Chronicle*, 7 November 1778.

10. Roger, *Crowds, Culture, and Politics*, 122.

11. Anonymous, "Who's in Fault? (No Body) A View off Ushant," etching (1779), BM 5570, Department of Prints and Drawings, British Museum.

12. Roger, "The Dynamic of News in Britain," 122–51, offers a careful accounting of the column space devoted to the trial in a range of venues both metropolitan and provincial. For a related discussion of the Keppel celebrations, see Kathleen Wilson, *The Sense of the People: Politics, Culture and Imperialism in England, 1715–1785* (Cambridge: Cambridge Univ. Press, 1995), 254–61.

13. *Morning Post*, 14 December 1778.

14. See *Morning Post*, 10 August 1778.

15. See Ian McIntyre, *Garrick* (London: Penguin, 1999), 607–23, for a discussion of the funeral and its reception among Garrick's family and friends.

16. *Morning Chronicle*, 3 February 1779.

17. *Morning Post*, 1 February 1779.

18. *Morning Chronicle*, 3 February 1779. Other papers report that it was the largest assembled crowd in memory. For example, the *St. James Chronicle*, 30 January–2 February

1779, states, "A greater Concourse of People attended than was ever known on a similar occasion."

19. *Gazetteer and New Daily Advertiser*, 2 February 1779.

20. See Jean Benedetti, *David Garrick and the Birth of Modern Theatre* (London: Methuen, 2001), 110–12.

21. Joseph Roach, *Cities of the Dead: Circum-Atlantic Performance* (New York: Columbia Univ. Press, 1996), 36.

22. Ibid., 98.

23. See *The Tatler*, ed. Donald F. Bond, 3 vols. (Oxford: Clarendon Press, 1987), 2:424; and Roach, *Cities of the Dead*, 84.

24. Georg Christoph Lichtenberg, *Lichtenberg's visits to England as described in his Letters and Diaries*, trans. Margaret L. Mare and W. H. Quarrell (New York: B. Blom, 1969), 9–11.

25. Ibid., 9–11.

26. This could be extended to enfold Diderot's championing of Garrick as the poster child for new bourgeois theatre. See Michael Dobson, *The Making of the National Poet: Shakespeare, Adaptation and Authorship, 1660–1769* (Oxford: Clarendon Press, 1990); and Todd Andrew Borlik, "Visual Culture and the Performance of Stasis in David Garrick's *Hamlet*," *Shakespeare Bulletin* 25.1 (2007): 3–31.

27. See Dobson, *Making of the National Poet*, 140, 165–71, for a discussion of the identification of Shakespeare with Hamlet's Ghost.

28. A similar argument could be made with regard to the Stratford Jubilee itself. Its miserable failure called forth a compensatory mediation in the form of Garrick's enormously successful playlet *The Jubilee*. What I would suggest is that the failure of the famous procession in Stratford established the desire for the procession of Shakespeare's characters in *The Jubilee*, and thus the engine for canonization was activated by its failure and abetted by the commercial theatre's capacity to overwrite again and again the initial celebratory event.

29. The March 1779 issue of the *Town and Country Magazine* also published "Strictures on Garrick's Funeral," 146–77.

30. *Morning Chronicle*, 3 February 1779.

31. Marie Peters, "Pitt, William, first earl of Chatham [Pitt the elder] (1708–1778)," in *Oxford Dictionary of National Biography*, ed. H. C. G. Matthew and Brian Harrison (Oxford: Oxford Univ. Press, 2004); online ed., ed. Lawrence Goldman, May 2009.

32. Ibid.

33. *Morning Chronicle*, 3 February 1779.

34. "Victory: An Ode" was still being performed at the Haymarket as late as 17 March 1779. See *Morning Post*, 11 March 1779.

35. Anna Seward, "Prize Monody on the Death of Mr. Garrick, For the Vase at Bath Easton, February 11, 1779," *Universal Magazine* 64 (March 1779): 159, lines 1–4. All further references to this poem are to this edition, and line numbers are cited directly in text.

36. For a detailed discussion of how Garrick embodied Shakespeare during this period, see Dobson, *Making of the National Poet*, 164–84. Garrick's pursuit of this identification was carried out in myriad ways. The Stratford Jubilee is the most obvious site of

affiliation, but Dobson's reading demonstrates that Garrick also commissioned a statue of himself that imitated the statue of Shakespeare installed in Westminster Abbey. Garrick was buried facing the statue of Shakespeare, and thus this complex affiliation remained an issue until the actual installment of a Garrick monument in the Abbey in 1797. As Dobson states, "It is undeniably appropriate, however, that for nearly twenty years, Shakespeare's statue . . . should have served as the actor's headstone" (184).

37. See ibid., 140, 165–71, for a discussion of the identification of Shakespeare with Hamlet's Ghost.

38. See, for example, the *Universal Magazine* 64 (March 1779), 159–60, and the *Town and Country Magazine*, March 1779, 158–59. Both discuss the nature of the Sheridan fragment in order to emphasize the distinction between performance and printed text.

39. *Morning Post*, 12 March 1779. The printed versions of the poem do not mark which sections were sung or even where the musical interludes were placed.

40. Richard Brinsley Sheridan, *Verses to the Memory of Garrick. Spoken as a Monody at the Theatre Royal in Drury Lane* (London: T. Evans, J. Wilkie, E. and C. Dilly, A. Portal and J. Almon, 1779), 1–8. All subsequent references to his poem are to this edition, and line numbers are cited directly in the text.

41. "Throughout the composition, the soul and spirit of true poetry exist manifestly: all the thoughts are good; that of Shakespeare's monument, pointing out the grave of Garrick is admirable, and that of architectural ruins giving the architects fame additional grace from their decay, truly excellent." *Morning Chronicle*, 12 March 1779.

42. *Oxford English Dictionary*.

43. *Morning Chronicle*, 12 March 1779.

44. John Lodge, "Mr. Garrick delivering his Ode, at Drury Lane Theatre, on Dedicating a Building & erecting a Statue, to Shakespeare," etching (1769), BM Ee,3.163, Department of Prints and Drawings, British Museum.

45. See Dobson, *Making of the National Poet*, 214–22, for a discussion of the Ode's supplementary qualities. The most exhaustive account of the Stratford Jubilee remains Christian Deelman, *The Great Shakespeare Jubilee* (London: Michael Joseph, 1964).

46. It is difficult to identify the painting in question. It may be one of the inferior copies of the Prologue portrait discussed by David Mannings in *Sir Joshua Reynolds: A Complete Catalogue of His Paintings* (New Haven: Yale Univ. Press, 2000), 211. The possibility that the painting is a copy adds a further wrinkle to the argument.

47. Frontispiece to Sheridan, *Verses to the Memory of Garrick. Spoken as a Monody.*

48. *Morning Chronicle*, 12 March 1779.

49. Ibid.

50. Henry Webber's relief sculpture, the *Monument to the Memory of David Garrick*, would not be installed in the Abbey until the late 1790s.

51. See Gillian Russell, *The Theatres of War: Performance, Politics, and Society, 1793–1815* (Oxford: Clarendon Press, 1995), 33–51.

52. See Lisa Freeman's powerful analysis of the play in *Character's Theatre: Genre and Identity on the Eighteenth-Century English Stage* (Philadelphia: Univ. of Pennsylvania Press, 2002), 228–33.

53. The play was performed on 5 February 1777 and 12 May 1777 by Royal Command. A further production was mounted on 23 May with *The Padlock* as an afterpiece. For production details, see Charles Beecher Hogan, *The London Stage, 1660–1800*, part 5, vol. 1 (Carbondale: Southern Illinois Univ. Press, 1968), 56, 82, and 85. *The Padlock*'s famous representation of African servility tallied nicely with Cumberland's representation of a virtuous plantocracy. This latter night at the theatre would have amounted to a particularly thorough exercise in the fantasy of metropolitan control of the Atlantic colonies.

54. See Jared Brown, *The Theatre in America during the Revolution* (Cambridge: Cambridge Univ. Press, 1995), 88–90, for a detailed discussion of these performances of *The West Indian* in New York.

55. The play was offered six times in both seasons.

56. John Loftis, *Sheridan and the Drama of Georgian England* (Oxford: Blackwell, 1976), 120, n. 34.

57. Robert W. Jones, "Sheridan and the Theatre of Patriotism: Staging Dissent during the War for America," *Eighteenth-Century Life* 26.1 (Winter 2002): 25.

58. For the distinction between monumental and critical history, see Friedrich Nietzsche, "On the Uses and Disadvantages of History for Life," in *Untimely Meditations*, ed. David Braezeale and trans. R. J. Hollingdale (Cambridge: Cambridge Univ. Press, 1997), 67–77, 87–100.

59. See Russell, *Theatres of War*, 26–51, and Jones, "Sheridan and the Theatre of Patriotism," 24–45, for powerful readings of Sheridan's political dissent in *The Camp* and *The Critic*. James Morwood also handles the political implications of *The Critic* in *The Life and Works of Richard Brinsley Sheridan* (Edinburgh: Scottish Academic Press, 1985).

60. See Russell on camp culture in *Theatres of War*, 26–51.

61. William Tasker, *An Elegy on the Death of David Garrick, Esq.* (London: Dodsley, Bew and Beckett, 1779), 103–8. Subsequent references to the poem cite line references within the text.

62. See David Garrick, *An ode upon dedicating a building, and erecting a statue, to Shakespeare, at Stratford upon Avon* (London, 1769), 66–67: "But when our *Shakespeare's* matchless pen, / Like *Alexander's* sword, had done with men." All subsequent references are to "Ode" with line references.

63. "Ode," 245–51.

64. See David Crane, "Satire and Celebration in *The Critic*," in *Sheridan Studies*, ed. James Morwood and D. E. L. Crane (Cambridge: Cambridge Univ. Press, 1995), 87–96, for a bracing analysis of the metatheatrical ramifications of the staging of acts 2 and 3.

65. As Morwood, *Life and Works of Sheridan*, 92, argues, Sheridan also adapts elements of George Colman's *New Brooms!* and Garrick's *A Peep behind the Curtain*. In *Plays about the Theatre in England, 1737–1800; or, The Self-Conscious Stage* (Cranbury, N.J.: Associated Univ. Press, 1979), 91–94, Dane Farnsworth Smith and M. L. Lawhon make a case for further adaptations from even lesser known materials. To this list one could also add *The Meeting of the Company*, Garrick's adaptation of *The Rehearsal*.

66. See the *Morning Post* and the *Morning Chronicle* for 5 November 1779.

67. Richard Brinsley Sheridan, *The Critic*, ed. David Crane (New York: Norton, 1989), 1.1.1–8. All references to *The Critic* are to this edition and are marked in the text by act, scene, and line number.

68. Morwood, *Life and Works of Sheridan*, 98.

69. See ibid., 98–99, for a careful explication of how Sheridan rehearses Cumberland's diction.

70. See Benedetti, *David Garrick*, 111. See George Winchester Stone Jr., "Garrick's Long Lost Alteration of *Hamlet*," *PMLA* 38 (September 1934): 890–921, and the extended commentary on the 1773 adaptation in Harry William Pedicord and Frederick Louis Bergmann, *Garrick's Adaptations of Shakespeare, 1759–1773*, vol. 4 of *The Plays of David Garrick* (Carbondale: Southern Illinois University Press, 1980), 433–36.

71. *Gazetteer and New Daily Advertiser*, 11 August 1779. The same text appears in the *Public Advertiser*, 11 August 1779, and in the *Morning Chronicle*, 10 August 1779. The *Morning Chronicle*'s review is supplemented with a brief paragraph not only extolling the virtues of the music and the decoration but also predicting immense success.

72. *Morning Chronicle*, 10 August 1779; *Gazetteer and New Daily Advertiser*, 11 August 1779; and *Public Advertiser*, 11 August 1779.

73. *Morning Chronicle*, 12 August 1779.

74. Morwood, *Life and Works of Sheridan*, 90.

75. *London Evening Post*, 30 October–2 November 1779.

76. See Christopher Baugh, "Philippe James de Loutherbourg and the Early Pictorial Theatre: Some Aspects of Its Cultural Context," *Themes in Drama* 9 (1987): 99–128.

77. *Morning Post*, 5 November 1779. The procession of rivers is also reminiscent of the Thames Regatta.

78. See Eric S. Rump, "Sheridan, Politics, the Navy, and the Musical Allusions in the Final Scene of *The Critic*," *Restoration and Eighteenth-Century Theatre Research* 6 (1991): 30–34.

79. Michel Foucault, "Nietzsche, Genealogy, History," in *Language, Counter-Memory, Practice* (Ithaca, N.Y.: Cornell Univ. Press, 1977), 160.

80. *Morning Chronicle*, 17 August 1779.

81. See James Shapiro, *A Year in the Life of William Shakespeare: 1599* (New York: Harper, 2006), for a recent discussion of this epochal year in Shakespeare's career.

82. *Morning Post*, 28 August 1778.

83. *The Critic* was most frequently staged with Garrick's adaptation of *A Winter's Tale*. It was also performed, in descending order of frequency, with *Hamlet, Othello, Julius Caesar, The Tempest, Henry VI Part 1*, and *As You Like It*. The pairings are all documented in Hogan, *The London Stage, 1660–1800*, part 5, vol. 1. Three of these Shakespearean plays are the product of the year 1599, and *Othello* has frequently been interpreted in relation to the English victory over the Spanish Armada. The remaining performances of *The Critic* were paired with standard plays, such as *The Way of the World* or *The Provok'd Husband*, and never with a new production.

84. Morwood, *Life and Works of Sheridan*, 101.

85. Ibid., 100.

86. *Morning Chronicle*, 1 November 1779.

87. Richard Fitzpatrick, prologue, *The Critic*, 25.

88. *Gazetteer*, 29 October 1779.

89. *Morning Chronicle*, 5 November 1779.

90. *Morning Post*, 5 November 1779.

91. See Pedicord and Bergmann, *Garrick's Adaptations of Shakespeare*, 433–36.

92. A similar argument could be built around the allusions to *Othello* and *The Critic*'s second performance with *Othello* as the corresponding mainpiece.

93. *Morning Chronicle*, 1 November 1779.

94. This is also why Sheridan attacks newspapers while he was both writing his own paper, *The Englishman*, and contributing to other papers. It is only through an imminent critique of the papers that commercial print culture's value for the social and cultural life of the nation can be realized.

95. Garrick's alteration was last performed on 21 April 1780 with *The Critic* as its afterpiece. For observers such as John Genest, this final performance could not come soon enough. See Genest, *Some Account of the English Stage, from the Restoration in 1600 to 1830*, vol. 6 (Bath: H. E. Carrington, 1832), 133.

CHAPTER FIVE Which Is the Man? *Remediation, Interruption, and the Celebration of Martial Masculinity*

1. *Morning Post*, 12 February 1779.

2. Keppel's defense was basically a reprise of his defense in the House of Commons in early December 1778; see *Morning Chronicle*, 3 December 1778, and *Morning Post*, 3 December 1778. The conflict between Keppel and Palliser in the House of Commons raged for much of early December. On the 12 December both the *Morning Chronicle* and the *Morning Post* traded conflicting accounts of conspiracy on the part of the Ministry and the opposition respectively.

3. Nicholas Roger offers a careful accounting of the column space devoted to the trial in a range of venues both metropolitan and provincial in "The Dynamic of News in Britain during the American War: The Case of Admiral Keppel," *Parliamentary History* 25.1 (2006): 54–57. See also his authoritative analysis of the acquittal celebrations in *Crowds, Culture, and Politics in Georgian Britain* (Oxford: Oxford Univ. Press, 1998), 122–51. For a related discussion of the Keppel celebrations, see Kathleen Wilson, *The Sense of the People: Politics, Culture and Imperialism in England, 1715–1785* (Cambridge: Cambridge Univ. Press, 1995), 254–61. See also J. H. Broomfield, "The Keppel-Palliser Affair, 1778–79," *Mariner's Mirror: The Journal of the Society for Nautical Research* 46 (1961): 195–207.

4. *General Advertiser*, 10 February 1779.

5. In London, because of preexisting radical constituencies, the celebrations were far more volatile.

6. *Morning Chronicle*, 13 February 1779.

7. Anonymous, "The Fate of Palliser and Sandwich," etching (1779), BM 5537, Department of Prints and Drawings, British Museum.

8. *Morning Post*, 15 February 1779.

9. Ibid.

10. Ibid.

11. *Morning Chronicle*, 13 February 1779. The *Morning Chronicle* went so far as to name William Parker in this regard.

12. *Morning Chronicle*, 12 February 1779.

13. See Roger, *Crowds, Culture, and Politics*, 122–51.

14. Ruth Smith, *Handel's Oratorios and Eighteenth-Century Thought* (Cambridge: Cambridge Univ. Press, 1995), 50–57.

15. But there are also ways in which the allegory signifies too much. For observers cognizant of the song's comparison to the events of 1745, the very question of internal division is far more complex. After all, the Rockingham faction, although not in league with the French, was sympathetic to the American cause, so it does not sit comfortably in the position of the Maccabees as represented by Morrell and Handel. But it does bear comparison with the rebellious Maccabees of the Bible, and thus the careful political alignments of the original oratorio are fundamentally destabilized. This is a direct result of the palpable difference between the political threat of Scottish insurgents in the 1745 and the more complex threat posed by the American rebels.

16. *Morning Post*, 2 March 1780.

17. Rodney was en route to the West Indies but had orders to relieve Gibraltar. He defeated the Spanish first at Cape Finisterre on 8 January and then decisively at Cape St. Vincent.

18. For detailed account of the strategic importance of the battle, see David Spinney, *Rodney* (London: George Allen and Unwin, 1969), 296–316; and Peter Trew, *Rodney and the Breaking of the Line* (London: Peter Trew, 2006), 45–56.

19. *Morning Post*, 1 March 1780.

20. The extraordinary shelf life of the phrase "handsomely" in Keppel's letter is borne out in the satirical prints as well. For example, in an anonymous print entitled "Count de Grasse delivering his sword to the gallant Admiral Rodney" printed after Rodney's victory at Les Saintes, the French admiral states yet again that Rodney has "fought him handsomely." See BM 5991, Department of Prints and Drawings, British Museum.

21. *Morning Post*, 2 March 1780.

22. *Morning Post*, 3 March 1780.

23. Roger, *Crowds, Culture, and Politics*, 122–51.

24. Gillian Russell, *Women, Sociability and Theatre in Georgian London* (Cambridge: Cambridge Univ. Press, 2007), 222. Russell's argument that Mrs. Racket remediates Lady Bab Lardoon indicates that, in this struggle between the theatres, it was the very performance of fashionable sociability both on stage and in the house that was at stake. See especially p. 224.

25. Charles Beecher Hogan, *The London Stage, 1660–1800*, part 5, vol. 1 (Carbondale: Southern Illinois Univ. Press, 1968), 319.

26. Ibid., 321.

27. *Gazetteer*, 1 March 1780, and *General Evening Post*, 29 February 1780.

28. *Gazetteer*, 26 February 1780.

29. Hannah Cowley, *The Belle's Stratagem* (London: T. Cadell, 1782), 1.1.3. All further citations are incorporated into the text and provide act, scene, and page number.

30. *Gazetteer,* 26 February 1780.

31. See Russell, *Women, Sociability and Theatre,* 217–18, for further discussion of the importance of the replication of the Pantheon's space and lighting to the ideology of the play.

32. See Lisa Freeman, *Character's Theater: Genre and Identity on the Eighteenth-Century English Stage* (Philadelphia: Univ. of Pennsylvania Press, 2002), 170–83, for a detailed discussion of the relationship between Farquhar's *The Beaux's Stratagem* and Cowley's play.

33. Erin Isikoff, "Masquerade, Modesty and Comedy in Hannah Cowley's *The Belle's Stratagem,*" in *Look Who's Laughing: Gender and Comedy,* ed. Gail Finney (Langhorne: Gordon and Breach, 1994), 99–117.

34. Russell, *Women, Sociability and Theatre,* 214.

35. Mrs. Racket's agency is crucial to all of these arguments. See Elizabeth Kowaleski-Wallace, "Theatricality and Cosmopolitanism in Hannah Cowley's *The Belle's Stratagem,*" *Comparative Drama* 35.3–4 (2001): 415–33; Misty Anderson, *Female Playwrights and Eighteenth-Century Comedy: Negotiating Marriage on the London Stage* (New York: Palgrave-St. Martin's Global, 2002), 139–70; and Russell, *Women, Sociability and Theatre,* 212–27.

36. J. G. A. Pocock, "Political Thought in the English-Speaking Atlantic, 1760–1790, Part 1: The Imperial Crisis," in *The Varieties of British Political Thought, 1500–1800,* ed. J. G. A. Pocock, Gordon J. Schochet, and Lois G. Schwoerer (Cambridge: Cambridge Univ. Press, 1993), 256–67.

37. Russell, *Women, Sociability and Theatre,* 229.

38. This assertion is, of course, speculative, but there are no other moments in act 4, scene 1, which seem likely.

39. *Gazetteer,* 1 March 1780.

40. *Gazetteer,* 23 March 1780.

41. G. Wilson Knight, *The Golden Labyrinth: A Study of British Drama* (London: Phoenix House, 1962), 185.

42. Charles Dibdin, *The Musical Tour of Mr. Dibdin* (Sheffield: J. Gales, 1788), 260, quoted in Richard Brinsley Sheridan, *The Dramatic Works of Richard Brinsley Sheridan,* ed. Cecil Price, vol. 1 (Oxford: Clarendon Press, 1973), 213.

43. *Gazetteer,* 1 March 1780.

44. Ibid.

45. Russell, *Women, Sociability and Theatre,* 229.

46. *Gazetteer,* 1 March 1780.

47. Arthur Murphy, *The Upholsterer, or What News?* (London: Vaillant, 1758), 1.3.13.

48. *London Courant,* 11 February 1782.

49. Anderson, *Female Playwrights and Eighteenth-Century Comedy,* 161.

50. *London Courant,* 11 February 1782.

51. As Kristina Straub argues in *Sexual Suspects: Eighteenth-Century Players and Sexual Ideology* (Princeton: Princeton Univ. Press, 1992), 47–61, fop roles code predatory heterosexuality as a form of effeminacy.

52. This move on Cowley's part goes some way beyond the representation of fops in Cibber and Garrick and that has been examined by Straub, *Sexual Suspects,* 47–68, and

Susan Staves, "A Few Kind Words for the Fop," *Studied in English Literature* 22 (1982): 413–28.

53. Anderson, *Female Playwrights and Eighteenth-Century Comedy*, 162.

54. The *London Courant Westminster Chronicle and Daily Advertiser*, 11 February 1782, states "Mr. Lee Lewis, who was habited in the same manner as the Prince of Wales on her Majesty's birth-day, played Lord Sparkle with great ease and spirit."

55. Hannah Cowley, *Which is the Man?* (London: C. Dilly, 1783), 2.1.10. All subsequent citations are given in the text by act, scene, and page number.

56. Anderson, *Female Playwrights and Eighteenth-Century Comedy*, 167.

57. Timothy Jenks, *Naval Engagements: Patriotism, Cultural Politics, and the Royal Navy, 1793–1815* (Oxford: Oxford Univ. Press, 2006), 144–48.

58. Christopher Leslie Brown, *Moral Capital: Foundations of British Abolitionism* (Chapel Hill: Univ. of North Carolina Press, 2006).

59. See Spinney, *Rodney*, 356–87, for an account of Rodney's actions at St. Eustatius and the ensuing recriminations.

60. Kenneth Breen, "Rodney, George Bridges, first Baron Rodney (bap. 1718, d. 1792)," in *Oxford Dictionary of National Biography*, ed. H. C. G. Matthew and Brian Harrison (Oxford: Oxford Univ. Press, 2004); online ed., ed. Lawrence Goldman, January 2008.

61. Ibid.

62. Ibid.

63. Spinney, *Rodney*, 385–87.

64. See ibid., 389–412, and Trew, *Rodney and the Breaking of the Line*, 151–72, for detailed accounts of how Rodney broke De Grasse's line. The victory was tactically innovative and in many ways allowed the Ministry to enter into peace negotiations on better terms.

65. *Public Adverstiser*, 24 September 1781.

66. Anonymous, "Count de Grasse delivering his sword to the gallant Admiral Rodney," etching (1782), BM 5991, Department of Prints and Drawings, British Museum.

67. See Stephen Conway, "'A Joy Unknown for Years Past': The American War, Britishness and the Celebration of Rodney's Victory at the Saints," *History* 86 (2001): 180–99, for a detailed account of the political valences of the celebration of Rodney's victory. Gilray produced a series of prints attacking Fox in June 1782.

68. In addition to Conway, see Spinney, *Rodney*, 413–16, and Trew, *Rodney and the Breaking of the Line*, 173–75, for discussions of the celebrations.

69. Breen, "Rodney, George Bridges."

70. See P. J. Marshall, *The Making and Unmaking of Empires: Britain, India, and America, c. 1750–1783* (Oxford: Oxford Univ. Press, 2007), 364.

71. *St. James Chronicle*, 28 May 1782.

72. Ibid.

73. See Peter Hulme, *Colonial Encounters: Europe and the Native Caribbean, 1492–1797* (London: Routledge, 1986), 225–63; and Frank Felsenstein, *English Trader, Indian Maid: Representing Gender, Race, and Slavery in the New World* (Baltimore: Johns Hopkins Univ. Press, 1999), for the most sustained discussions of the story's cultural centrality.

Both of these accounts of the Inkle and Yarico phenomenon are indebted to Lawrence Marsden Price, *Inkle and Yarico Album* (Berkeley: Univ. of California Press, 1937).

74. The Steele version is from the 13 March 1711 number of the *Spectator*, and there is no question as to the centrality of his account to all subsequent versions.

75. Felsenstein, *English Trader, Indian Maid*, 19.

76. Elizabeth Inchbald, *The British Theatre; or, A Collection of Plays which are acted at the Theatres Royal Drury Lane, Covent Garden and Haymarket*, vol. 20 (London: Longman, Hurst, Rees, and Orme, 1808), 3.

77. Ibid., 4. See Felsenstein, *English Trader, Indian Maid*, 18–19, for copious examples in the play that confuse the conventional visual and discursive distinctions between Africans and Native Americans.

78. Christopher Leslie Brown, *Moral Capital: Foundations of British Abolitionism* (Chapel Hill: Univ. of North Carolina Press, 2006), 333–89.

79. There is a second and far more violent discourse network operative in the archive that has its roots in Jean Mocquet's *Travels and Voyages into Africa, Asia, America, the East and West-Indies* (1645). The text is collected in Felsenstein, and the early phases of the narrative are roughly the same, but the conclusion of the tale makes it far less susceptible to co-optation by the dominant discourse:

> At last they arrived at the New foundland, guiding himself by his Compass: They had a Child together; and found there an English Ship a Fishing: He was very glad to see himself escaped from so many Dangers, and gave these English an account of all his Adventures: They took him on Board their Vessel to make good cheer; but being ashamed to take along with him this Indian-Woman thus Naked, he left her on Land, without regarding her cry more: But she seeing herself thus forsaken by him, whom she had so dearly Loved, and for whose sake she had abandoned her Country and Friends. . . . After having made some Lamentation, full of Rage and Anger, she took her Child, and tearing it into two pieces, she cast the one half towards him into the Sea, as if she would say, that belonged to him, and was his part of it; and the other she carried away with her, returning back to the Mercy of Fortune, and full of Mourning and Discontent. (294–95)

If one reads the tearing of the mixed-race child in half as that which must remain unspoken in all subsequent versions of the tale, then the act becomes a figure for the anxieties of cross-cultural sexual practice. What is so important about Mocquet's text is that the native woman exhibits deadly agency. The extremity of her action is condemned, but Mocquet emphasizes that the witnesses see the Inkle figure as not only responsible for this death but also monstrous: "The Seaman who took this Pilot into their Boat, seeing this horrible and cruel Spectacle, asked him, why he had left this woman; but he pretended she was a Savage, and that he did not now heed her; which was an extreme Ingratitude and Wickedness in him: Hearing this, I could not look upon him, but always with Horrour and great Detestation" (295). This monstrosity is also invoked in Ligon and Steele, but its subsequent reconfiguration in Colman is, I believe, symptomatic of emergent notions of race, sexuality, and class identity in the late eighteenth century.

80. Felsenstein, *English Trader, Indian Maid*, 2.

81. Quoted in Barry Sutcliffe, ed., *Plays by George Colman the Younger and Thomas Morton* (Cambridge: Cambridge Univ. Press, 1983), 21. Colman's play opened on 4 August 1787 at the Haymarket, so it is one of the latest manifestations of the Inkle and Yarico tale. It was extraordinarily successful, not only in its opening runs at the Haymarket and at Covent Garden but also in subsequent runs over the next twenty-five years.

82. Jeremy F. Bagster-Collins, *George Colman the Younger, 1762–1836* (Morningside Heights: King's Crown Press, 1946), 33.

83. It is important to recognize the shifting role of pregnancy as the story moves from Mocquet to Ligon to Steele and finally to Colman. As already noted, the mixed-race child is crucial to the attribution of monstrosity to the Inkle figure in Mocquet. In Steele, the problem of mixed-race offspring is vestigial because Yarico has not yet given birth to Inkle's child. This subtle repositioning of the narrative replaces the torn body of the child as a sign of violent colonial betrayal with what, in the logic of the narrative, amounts to an unborn future commodity. In other words, the living embodiment of interracial sexual practice shifts from the child to the pregnant Yarico, now understood as a doubly valuable object of exchange in the economy of plantation slavery. The narrative is still repulsed by Inkle, but Yarico's agency has been both textually suppressed and politically redirected. For Yarico to repeat the scene in Mocquet now requires violence directed at herself either through abortion or through suicide. Neither possibility can enter representation because it is crucial that the reader identify or empathize with Yarico's romantic suffering. Following Steele's version, Yarico is no longer a figure for racial otherness but rather a prototype for normative femininity. As we will see, this fetishization of gender reaches its culmination in Coleman where Yarico is desexualized by a series of gestures including the erasure of her pregnancy.

84. Felsenstein, *English Trader, Indian Maid*, 21.

85. The deployment of Jekyll in Felsenstein's argument in *English Trader, Indian Maid* is symptomatically cautious. Jekyll's prefatory memoir to the *Letters of the Late Ignatius Sancho, an African* (1782) is accurately described as "a conscious effort to exonerate black people at large from the accusations of those who had endeavored to degrade them 'as a deterioration of the human'" (23). However, Felsenstein stops short of declaring a similar consciousness to Colman's play: "In turn, Colman does not tell us exactly how he profited from Jekyll's advice, though it seems reasonable to assume that the bias of the play could only have been positively influenced by one who had written eloquently in favor of the nobility and mental abilities of the black man at liberty in his native Africa" (23–24).

86. Felsenstein, *English Trader, Indian Maid*, 27.

87. Bagster-Collins, *George Colman the Younger*, 33.

88. Drury Lane staged Cumberland's play three times in the 1787–88 season, seven times during the 1788–89 season, and four times during the 1789–90 season. During this same period, *Inkle and Yarico* moved from an almost nightly run at the Haymarket to having three performances a month at Covent Garden.

89. See Julie Carlson, "Race and Profit in English Theatre," in *The Cambridge Companion to British Theatre, 1730–1830*, ed. Jane Moody and Daniel O'Quinn (Cambridge: Cambridge Univ. Press, 2007), 175–88, for a powerful discussion of how race generated profits in the London theatres.

90. National Portrait Gallery, London, NPG D12322.

91. Thomas Gainsborough, *Lord Rodney* (1788), Dalmeny House, Edinburgh. Admiral Rodney sat for Gainsborough on 2, 5, 9, and 14 May 1788 and 2 March 1789. The image reproduced here is a mezzotint by Richard Josey from 1874 that is based on Gainsborough's painting.

92. Sir Joshua Reynolds, *Lord Rodney* (1788), Royal Collection, 2010, Her Majesty Queen Elizabeth II. See David Mannings, *Sir Joshua Reynolds: A Complete Catalogue of His Paintings*, vol. 2 (New Haven: Yale Univ. Press, 2000), 397. There is also a copy of the painting in the collection of the National Maritime Museum in Greenwich.

93. George Colman, *Inkle and Yarico,* in Sutcliffe, *Plays by George Colman,* 3.3.108. All references to *Inkle and Yarico* are to this edition and are henceforth included parenthetically by act, scene, and page number in the text.

94. Sutcliffe, *Plays by George Colman,* 93, marks this rhetorical gesture in his gloss to act 2, scene 2.

95. See Moira Ferguson, *Subject to Others: British Women Writers and Colonial Slavery, 1670–1838* (New York: Routledge, 1992), for an extensive discussion of this frequent correlation.

96. See Nandini Bhattacharya, "Family Jewels: George Colman's *Inkle and Yarico* and Connoisseurship," *Eighteenth-Century Studies* 34:2 (2001): 207–26, for a fascinating discussion of how this scene fits not only into the cultural discourse of connoisseurship in the period but also into Colman's personal history of collecting.

97. Laura Brown, *Alexander Pope* (London: Basil Blackwell, 1985), 28–42.

98. *Aeneid* 1:539–40.

99. Helen Deutsche and Felicity Nussbaum, *"Defects": Engendering the Modern Body* (Ann Arbor: Univ. of Michigan Press, 2000), 1.

100. Sutcliffe, *Plays by George Colman,* 25, is quoting from *General Magazine and Impartial Review,* August 1787. He goes on to speculate whether Colman wrote the play as a vehicle for Kemble.

101. James Boaden, *Memoirs of Mrs. Siddons* (London, 1827), 1:214–15, quoted in Sutcliffe, *Plays by George Colman,* 26.

102. John Adolphus, *Memoirs of John Bannister,* 2 vols. (London, 1839), 166. Adolphus's description of Miss Elizabeth Harper, who married Bannister on 26 January 1783, gives some sense of her physical presence on stage:

> Miss Elizabeth Harper was principal singer at the Haymarket theatre. . . . She had improved a voice of the first quality by an excellent musical education. It is a feeble tribute to say, that her character was without blemish; there was, in her appearance and conduct, an unpretending innocence, a candid simplicity, which every one hailed as the sure guarantee of a spotless mind. Yet she wanted not a proper spirit and dignity: the true scope of character might be gathered from her performance of the Lady, in "Comus," a part which she adorned, not only by her musical talents, but by a demeanour which expressed confiding gentleness, supported by immovable principle, with all the charm of reality. (1:82)

103. See my "Mercantile Deformities: George Colman's Inkle and Yarico and the Racialization of Class Relations," *Theatre Journal* 54.3 (October 2002): 389–409.

104. Ann Laura Stoler, *Race and the Education of Desire: Foucault's History of Sexuality and the Colonial Order of Things* (Durham: Duke Univ. Press, 1995), 101–36.

105. Adolphus, *Memoirs of John Bannister,* 1:168.

CHAPTER SIX Days and Nights of the Living Dead: *Handelmania*

1. Claudia Johnson, "'Giant HANDEL' and the Musical Sublime," *Eighteenth-Century Studies* 19.4 (Summer 1986): 516.

2. See Johnson (ibid.) for a detailed discussion of how the criticism of Handel's music partook of the literary rhetoric of the sublime.

3. Charles Burney, *An Account of the Musical Performances in Westminster-Abbey, and the Pantheon, May 26th, 27th, 29th; and June the 3d, and 5th, 1784 in Commemoration of Handel* (London: T. Payne and G. Robinson, 1785).

4. William Weber, "The 1784 Handel Commemoration as Political Ritual," *Journal of British Studies* 28.1 (1989): 43–69.

5. Gillen D'Arcy Wood, *Romanticism and Music Culture in Britain, 1770–1840: Virtue and Virtuosity* (Cambridge: Cambridge Univ. Press, 2010), 23.

6. *London Magazine,* May 1784, 421. Also printed in the *European Magazine,* June 1784 supplement.

7. The best account of the Shakespeare Jubilee remains Christian Deelman, *The Great Shakespeare Jubilee* (London: Michael Joseph, 1964). For extended discussions of the trial of the Duchess of Kingston, see Matthew Kinservik, *Sex, Scandal, and Celebrity in Late Eighteenth-Century England* (London: Palgrave Macmillan, 2007); and Gillian Russell, *Women, Sociability and Theatre in Georgian London* (Cambridge: Cambridge Univ. Press, 2007), 153–77.

8. See James Thomson, "Autumn," in *The Seasons, and Other Poems* (London: J. Millan, 1735), lines 211–13; and *Spectator* 265 (3 January 1712): 323, dedicated to the Duke of Marlborough.

9. Gillian Russell's analysis of the significance of "big hair" during the late phases of the American war helps to situate the critique of excessive female ornament in this passage (*Women, Sociability and Theatre,* 179–204).

10. Weber, "The 1784 Handel Commemoration as Political Ritual," 43–44.

11. For cogent accounts of the constitutional crisis, see John Cannon, *The Fox-North Coalition* (Cambridge: Cambridge Univ. Press, 1969); Leslie G. Mitchell, *Charles James Fox* (London: Oxford Univ. Press, 1992), 60–65; and my *Staging Governance: Theatrical Imperialism in London* (Baltimore: Johns Hopkins Univ. Press, 2005), 127–44.

12. By far the most biting criticism involved remarks on the gambling debts of Fox and other prominent Whigs. As Phyllis Deutsch has argued in "Moral Trespass in Georgian London: Gaming, Gender and Electoral Politics in the Age of George III," *Historical Journal* 39.3 (1996): 637–56, this association between Whigs and gaming was one of the most divisive aspects of the 1784 election and arguably did more to damage the Whig's reputation than any particular instance of policy or ideology.

13. *Morning Herald*, 27 May 1784.

14. See Anne Stott, "'Female Patriotism': Georgiana, Duchess of Devonshire, and the Westminster Election of 1784," *Eighteenth-Century Life* 17 (1993): 60–84.

15. *Public Advertiser*, 30 May 1784.

16. *Morning Herald*, 28 May 1784; *London Magazine*, May 1784, 423. Other papers reported that the Prince of Wales attended as a "Private Gentleman" and thus was not in the Royal Gallery. See *Gazetteer*, 28 May 1784, and *General Evening Post*, 27–29 May 1784.

17. *Public Advertiser*, 28 May 1784.

18. *Morning Post*, 25 May 1784.

19. *Gazetteer*, 26 May 1784.

20. *Public Advertiser*, 27 May 1784.

21. William Cowper, *The Letters and Prose Writings of William Cowper*, ed. James King and Charles Ryskamp, vol. 2 (Oxford: Clarendon 1981), 254.

22. H. Diack Johnstone, "A Ringside Seat at the Handel Commemoration," *Musical Times* 125.1701 (November 1984): 632.

23. *St. James Chronicle*, 29 May–1 June 1784.

24. *London Magazine*, May 1784, Postscript, 422.

25. For sake of clarity, I refer to the each day's program as the first, second, or third performance.

26. Ruth Smith, *Handel's Oratorios and Eighteenth-Century Thought* (Cambridge: Cambridge Univ. Press, 1995), 305.

27. Burney, *Account of the Musical Performances in Westminster-Abbey*, 28–29.

28. *Morning Post*, 22 May 1784.

29. *Morning Post*, 4 June 1784.

30. Donald Burrows, *Handel and the English Chapel Royal* (New York: Oxford Univ. Press, 2005), 392.

31. Burney, *Account of the Musical Performances in Westminster-Abbey*, 29 (emphasis in original).

32. Burrows, *Handel and the English Chapel Royal*, 392.

33. The program was printed in all the papers and is reproduced in Burney.

34. Winton Dean, *Handel's Dramatic Oratorios and Masques* (London: Oxford Univ. Press, 1959), 300.

35. Burrows, *Handel and the English Chapel Royal*, 97–99.

36. Dean, *Handel's Dramatic Oratorios and Masques*, 279–80.

37. Ruth Smith's detailed analysis of the oratorio's political allegory is helpful here, for *Saul* is fundamentally about the king's relation to the law. However, its complexity is manifold because the Saul narrative had multiple allegorical possibilities for its original audiences in the early 1740s. The first set has to do with the question of royal succession and the second has to do with the opposition's attempt to remove Robert Walpole and the Whigs from power:

> The story of Saul's downfall was widely used in contemporary rhetoric justifying the Glorious Revolution drawing a parallel between Saul and James II. However it was also used in sermons for the Feast of King Charles the Martyr drawing a paral-

> lel between Saul and Charles I to condemn the execution of the king (and, for those who wished to make the connection, the deposition of his son James II). The biblical narrative is admirably convenient to both purposes, because on the one hand (Hanoverian) God Himself has willed the succession away from Saul's family to David, who, no less than Saul, is God's anointed; on the other hand (Stuart) the killing of Saul is regarded as an appalling crime. (*Handel's Oratorios*, 328)

In the 1740s, when the question of succession remained very much at the center of British politics, the question of David's response to the killing of Saul was freighted with political significance. His immediate expression of horror and the killing of an Amalekite messenger conveys an outrage over the regicide and would seem to suggest a Stuart reading of the allegory. But the entire third act emphasizes not only Saul's religious apostasy but also his disobedience to God's commands. As Smith states,

> Jennens also stresses the enormity of Saul's attempt to seek guidance through the false practices of apostate religion. In contemporary terms, James II's Catholicism and lawbreaking autocracy justified his removal: the king must govern within the law of the land and support its religion. The audience of Jennens' unsigned libretto would not necessarily have deduced his political leanings from it, for David is faultless and God is clearly on his side, endorsing the (in contemporary terms) the Hanoverian succession. (ibid., 332)

The emergence of David—and, by extension, the Hanoverian line—as the new faultless leader capable of restoring the Israelites had obvious political import, but what interests me is how this all transfers to the historical moment of 1784. I would suggest that it is the potential for the narrative to bear radically opposed political interpretations that makes it so useful following the setbacks of the early 1780s.

38. For the significance of this trope to debates surrounding the American war, see Jay Fliegelman, *Prodigals and Pilgrims: The American Revolution against Patriarchal Authority, 1750–1800* (Cambridge: Cambridge Univ. Press, 1982).

39. Smith, *Handel's Oratorios*, 331.

40. Ibid., 332–33.

41. Ibid., 103.

42. See ibid., 104–7, for a detailed table that compares the source texts and Handel's adaptation.

43. Ibid., 104–5.

44. Burrows, *Handel and the English Chapel Royal*, 373.

45. Ibid., 376.

46. Burney, *Account of the Musical Performances in Westminster-Abbey*, 34–35.

47. See Christopher Hogwood, *Handel* (London: Thames and Hudson, 1984), 240, for a discussion of the constrictions placed on Burney's text.

48. Psalm 93:5.

49. Burney, *Account of the Musical Performances in Westminster-Abbey*, 37.

50. Ibid., 38.

51. Ibid., 38. Burney is referring to a passage from Addison's *Remarks on Several Parts of Italy, in the year 1701, 1702 and 1703*. See Joseph Addison, *The Works of Right Honourable Joseph Addison*, ed. R. Hurd, vol. 1 (London: Henry G. Bohn, 1854), 478.

52. John Dryden, *The Aeneid*, 9.878–83, from *The Works of Virgil in English, 1697*, in *The Works of John Dryden*, ed. William Frost, vol. 6 (Berkeley: Univ. of California Press, 1987), 669.

53. Ibid., 9.899–913.

54. Ibid., 9.846.

55. Smith, *Handel's Oratorios*, 200.

56. *London Magazine*, May 1784, 422.

57. This is in part because this program was performed only once, whereas both the first performance and the performance of *Messiah* were given repeat royal command performances, and thus were the occasion for further acclamation.

58. Gillian Russell, "The Peeresses and the Prostitutes: The Founding of the London Pantheon, 1772," *Nineteenth-Century Contexts* 27.1 (March 2005): 11–30.

59. Russell, *Women, Sociability and Theatre*, 88–116.

60. Ibid., 117.

61. *London Magazine*, May 1784, 422.

62. *European Magazine and London Review*, May 1784, 324–25.

63. See ibid., 325.

64. *Morning Chronicle*, 7 June 1784.

65. There are no performances of Handel's operas from 1775 to 1800 with the exception of Arnold's pasticcio of the *Giulio Cesare*. This cannot be attributed simply to a lack of interest in Italian opera among elite audiences: there are plenty of Italian operas being staged in this period. What is clear is that a handful of Handel's oratorios completely overwhelm the performance history of his music in this period. In addition to the repeated performance of a program based explicitly on the Commemoration entitled *Redemption, Judas Maccabaeus, Messiah, Acis and Galatea*, and *Alexander's Feast* dominate the production history.

66. Anthony Hicks, "Orlando," in *The New Grove Dictionary of Opera*, ed. Stanley Sadie (London: Oxford, Univ. Press, 1992).

67. Ibid.

68. Burney, *Account of the Musical Performances in Westminster-Abbey*, 49.

69. Ibid., 63.

70. Winton Dean and John Merrill Knapp, *Handel's Operas, 1704–1726* (Oxford: Clarendon Press, 1987), 495.

71. Burney, *Account of the Musical Performances in Westminster-Abbey*, 61–62.

72. Ibid, 62.

73. Ibid., 61.

74. Ibid., 68.

75. Jeremy Summerly, "Liner Notes" to Handel, *Coronation Anthems and Silete Venti* (Naxos, 2002), 3.

76. *Morning Herald*, 28 May 1784; *London Magazine*, May 1784, 422.

77. Burney, *Account of the Musical Performances in Westminster-Abbey*, 70.

78. Weber, "The 1784 Handel Commemoration as Political Ritual," 63.

79. Ibid., 45.

80. See Johnson, "'Giant HANDEL' and the Musical Sublime," for commentary regarding the sublimity of the third performance.

81. Weber, "The 1784 Handel Commemoration as Political Ritual," 63–64.

82. Nicola Fracesco Haym, *Giulio Cesare in Egitto. A Serious Opera, in two acts, as performed at the King's Theatre in the Hay-Market. The music entirely by Handel, and selected from the various operas set by that Incomparable composer, Under the Direction of Dr. Arnold* (London: D. Stuart, 1787), 1.

83. The canonical treatment of this misadventure remains Ranajit Guha, *A Rule of Property for Bengal: An Essay on the Idea of Permanent Settlement* (Durham: Duke Univ. Press, 1996).

84. What I am describing here is not that distant from the notion of "traumatic nationalism" recently articulated by Lauren Berlant in *The Queen of America Goes to Washington City: Essays on Sex and Citizenship* (Durham: Duke Univ. Press, 1997), 1–4. I have also explored this issue in "The State of Things: Olaudah Equiano and the Volatile Politics of Heterocosmic Desire," in a special issue of *Romantic Praxis* entitled *Historicizing Romantic Sexuality*, ed. Richard C. Sha (January 2006). For my discussion of the Tipu plays at Astley's and Sadler's Wells, see my *Staging Governance*, 312–48.

85. Cornwallis became governor-general of Bengal in 1786.

86. Linda Colley, *Captives: Britain, Empire and the World, 1600–1850* (New York: Pantheon, 2002), 269–77.

87. Kate Teltscher, *India Inscribed: European and British Writing on India, 1600–1800* (New Delhi: Oxford Univ. Press, 1995), 240.

88. Colley, *Captives*, 243.

89. See Franklin Wickwire and Mary Wickwire, *Cornwallis: The Imperial Years* (Chapel Hill: Univ. of North Carolina Press, 1980), for a detailed account of the place of prior American experience in Cornwallis's correspondence on Medows's failures in Mysore in 1790.

90. *Gentleman's Magazine* 72 (August 1792): 760. For thorough accounts of the discursive construction of this event and its significance for popular acceptance of British policy in India, see P. J. Marshall, "'Cornwallis Triumphant': War in India and the British Public in the Late Eighteenth Century," in *War, Strategy and International Politics*, ed. Lawrence Freedman, Paul Hayes, and Robert O'Neill (Oxford: Oxford Univ. Press, 1992), 71–72; and Teltscher, *India Inscribed*, 248–51.

91. See Denys Forrest, *Tiger of Mysore: The Life and Death of Tipu Sultan* (London: Chatto and Windus, 1970), 347–50, for a discussion of the pictorial representations of Cornwallis's victory.

92. See Jill H. Casid, "'His Master's Obi': Machine Magic, Colonial Violence, and Transculturation," in *Visual Culture Reader*, ed. Nicholas Mirzoeff (New York: Routledge, 2002), 533–45.

93. *World* (Calcutta), 28 April 1792.

94. Ibid.

95. *Madras Courier*, 17 May 1792.

96. This word cannot be determined with certainty.

97. *World* (Calcutta), 28 April 1792.

98. Ibid.

99. See John Barrell's reading of the Lyttleton prospect in Thomson's "Spring" in *English Literature in History: An Equal Wide Survey* (New York: St. Martin's Press, 1983), 56–61.

100. Beth Fowkes Tobin, *Picturing Imperial Power: Colonial Subjects in Eighteenth-Century British Painting* (Durham: Duke Univ. Press, 1999), 117–43.

101. John Barrell, *The Dark Side of the Landscape: The Rural Poor in English Painting, 1730–1840* (Cambridge: Cambridge Univ. Press, 1980), 1–33.

102. *Madras Courier*, 17 May 1792.

103. See Joseph Addison, *The Campaign, A Poem, To His Grace the Duke of Marlborough* (London: Jacob Tonson, 1705), lines 145–48.

104. See ibid., lines 131–40.

105. Ruth Smith, "The Meaning of Morrell's Libretto of 'Judas Maccabaeus,'" *Music and Letters* 79.1 (February 1998): 50–57.

106. Ibid., 59.

107. Ibid., 61–62.

108. Sudipta Sen, *Distant Sovereignty: National Imperialism and the Origins of British India* (New York: Routledge, 2002), 13.

109. For evidence of Cornwallis's fear of interracial relations, see Wickwire and Wickwire, *Cornwallis*, 110. As C. A. Bayly argues in *Imperial Meridian: The British Empire and the World, 1780–1830* (London: Longman, 1989), 149, "Cornwallis moved heavily against European revenue officers involved in Indian trade and tried to create a wall of regulations to separate the Indian and European worlds." See Bayly (133–62) for wide-ranging account of the consolidation of racial and social hierarchies from the governor-generalship of Cornwallis. Tobin, *Picturing Imperial Power*, 117–18, also argues that Cornwallis's reforms were designed not only to minimize the amount of intermingling between British and Indian subjects in the realms of commerce and civil administration but also to avert miscegenation. See E. M. Collingham, *Imperial Bodies: The Physical Experience of the Raj, c. 1800–1947* (Cambridge: Polity Press, 2001), 51–89, for a detailed account of the segregation policies that eventually infused nineteenth-century Anglo-Indian relations. See also Sen, *Distant Sovereignty*, 119–49, for a discussion of "the decline of intimacy" promulgated during the Raj.

110. See Theodor Reik, *Masochism in Sex and Society*, trans. Margaret H. Beigel and Gertrud M. Kurth (New York: Grove Press, 1962), 304, for a discussion of the manipulation of "adverse incidents" in masochistic fantasy.

111. Smith, *Handel's Oratorios*, 251–52.

112. As P. J. Marshall notes in "Barlow, Sir George Hilario, first baronet (1763–1846)," *Oxford Dictionary of National Biography* (London: Oxford Univ. Press, 2004), Sir George Hilario Barlow "was very closely concerned with the devising and implementing of the permanent settlement of Bengal revenue enacted by Cornwallis in 1793. He was given responsibility for drafting the judicial regulations, known as the Cornwallis code. Barlow's correspondence with Cornwallis shows his total commitment to the principles em-

bodied in the permanent settlement: security of property and government accountable to law. Cornwallis was generous enough to say that his 'system' had been based on 'adopting and patronizing your suggestions.' "

113. Bayly, *Imperial Meridian*, 186.

114. *World* (Calcutta), 28 April 1792, and *Madras Courier*, 17 May 1792.

115. For an extended discussion of this biopolitical turn in imperial performance, see O'Quinn, *Staging Governance*, 260–68.

116. See Sen, *Distant Sovereignty*, 85–149, and Collingham, *Imperial Bodies*, 51–89. for a similar set of arguments regarding coloniality, biopolitics, and governmentality.

117. Smith, *Handel's Oratorios*, 299.

118. See Dror Wahrman, "The English Problem of Identity in the American Revolution," *American Historical Review* 106.4 (October 2001): 1236–62; James E. Bradley, *Popular Politics and the American Revolution in England: Petitions, the Crown, and Public Opinion* (Macon: Univ. of Georgia Press, 1986); Linda Colley, *Britons: Forging the Nation, 1707–1837* (New Haven: Yale Univ. Press, 1992); Jonathan C. D. Clark, *The Language of Liberty, 1660–1832: Political Discourse and Social Dynamics in the Anglo-American World* (Cambridge: Cambridge Univ. Press, 1994); Peter N. Miller, *Defining the Common Good: Empire, Religion and Philosophy in Eighteenth-Century Britain* (Cambridge: Cambridge Univ. Press, 1994); Kathleen Wilson, *The Sense of the People: Politics, Culture and Imperialism in England, 1715–1785* (Cambridge: Cambridge Univ. Press, 1995); Eliga H. Gould, *The Persistence of Empire: British Political Culture in the Age of the American Revolution* (Chapel Hill: Univ. of North Carolina Press, 2000); J. G. A. Pocock, "Political Thought in the English-Speaking Atlantic, 1760–1790: (i) The Imperial Crisis," in *The Varieties of British Political Thought, 1500–1800*, ed. J. G. A. Pocock, Gordon J. Schochet, and Lois G. Schwoerer (Cambridge: Cambridge Univ. Press, 1993), 246–82.

119. See Jean-François Lyotard, *The Differend: Phrases in Dispute*, trans. Georges Van Den Abbeele (Minneapolis: Univ. of Minnesota Press, 1988), 161–71.

120. Kaja Silverman, *Male Subjectivity at the Margins* (New York: Routledge, 1992), 196.

Coda: *"In praise of the oak, its advantage and prosperity"*

1. See Laura Brown's reading of "Windsor Forest," in her *Alexander Pope* (London: Wiley-Blackwell, 1985), 28–42.

2. William Whitehead, "Ode XXIX For his Majesty's Birth-Day, June 4, 1775," in *The Works of the English Poets*, ed. Samuel Johnson, vol. 73 (London: John Nichols, 1790), 7–18.

3. Edmund Burke, *Reflections on the Revolution in France*, ed. Conor Cruise O'Brien (London: Penguin, 1986), 180.

4. Ibid., 120.

5. I am using Foucault's notion of the "symbolics of blood" advisedly because, as both Foucault and Ann Laura Stoler have argued, the transformation of this symbolics plays a crucial role in the emergence of biological state racism in the nineteenth century. I am arguing that Burke's text can be folded into the prehistory of biopower. See Ann

Laura Stoler, *Race and the Education of Desire: Foucault's History of Sexuality and the Colonial Order of Things* (Durham: Duke Univ. Press, 1995), 19–54, 60–61.

6. For a pair of stimulating essays addressing the afterlife of Cowper's poem in Wordsworth and Clare, see Tim Fulford, "Wordsworth's 'The Haunted Tree' and the Sexual Politics of Landscape," *Romantic Praxis*, November 2001, and "Cowper, Wordsworth, Clare: The Politics of Trees," *John Clare Society Journal* 14 (1995): 47–59.

7. William Cowper, *The Letters and Prose Writings of William Cowper*, ed. James King and Charles Ryskamp, 5 vols. (Oxford: Clarendon, 1984), 1:555. All subsequent references will be presented in the text by volume and page number.

8. William Cowper, "Yardley Oak," in *The Poems of William Cowper*, vol. 3, *1785–1800*, ed. John D. Baird and Charles Ryskamp (Oxford: Clarendon, 1995), 1–6. All subsequent references are given by line number in the text.

9. Balachandra Rajan, *Under Western Eyes: India from Milton to Macaulay* (Duke: Duke Univ. Press, 1999), 60–61.

10. William Cowper, *The Task*, 4.88, in *The Poems of William Cowper*, vol. 2, *1782–1785*, ed. John D. Baird and Charles Ryskamp (Oxford: Clarendon Press, 1995). See Kevis Goodman, *Georgic Modernity and British Romanticism: Poetry and the Mediation of History* (Cambridge: Cambridge Univ. Press, 2004), 67–105, for the most thorough reading of the "loop-hole of retreat" figure. If I am correct about the Miltonic overtone here, then Cowper's complex engagement with the mediating effects of the newspapers in *The Task* is being scrutinized yet again in this late poem.

Index

Page references followed by "*fig*" indicate illustrations